Exam Ref 70-487: Developing Windows Azure and Web Services

William Ryan
Wouter de Kort
Shane Milton

ISBN: 978-0-7356-7724-1

Third Printing: May 2014

Printed and bound in the United States of America.

Microsoft Press books are available through booksellers and distributors worldwide. If you need support related to this book, email Microsoft Press Book Support at *mspinput@microsoft.com*. Please tell us what you think of this book at *http://www.microsoft.com/learning/booksurvey*.

Microsoft and the trademarks listed at *http://www.microsoft.com/about/legal/ en/us/IntellectualProperty/Trademarks/EN-US.aspx* are trademarks of the Microsoft group of companies. All other marks are property of their respective owners.

The example companies, organizations, products, domain names, email addresses, logos, people, places, and events depicted herein are fictitious. No association with any real company, organization, product, domain name, email address, logo, person, place, or event is intended or should be inferred.

This book expresses the author's views and opinions. The information contained in this book is provided without any express, statutory, or implied warranties. Neither the authors, Microsoft Corporation, nor its resellers, or distributors will be held liable for any damages caused or alleged to be caused either directly or indirectly by this book.

Acquisitions Editor: Jeff Riley
Developmental Editor: Ginny Bess Munroe
Production Editor: Kara Ebrahim
Editorial Production: Box Twelve Communications
Technical Reviewer: Shane Milton
Copyeditor: Nancy Sixsmith
Indexer: Angie Martin
Cover Design: Twist Creative • Seattle
Cover Composition: Ellie Volckhausen
Illustrator: Rebecca Demarest

Contents at a glance

Contents

What do you think of this book? We want to hear from you!

Microsoft is interested in hearing your feedback so we can continually improve our
books and learning resources for you. To participate in a brief online survey, please visit:

www.microsoft.com/learning/booksurvey/

What do you think of this book? We want to hear from you!

Microsoft is interested in hearing your feedback so we can continually improve our
books and learning resources for you. To participate in a brief online survey, please visit:

www.microsoft.com/learning/booksurvey/

Introduction

Most books take a low-level approach, teaching you how to use individual classes and how to accomplish granular tasks. Like other Microsoft certification exams, this book takes a high-level approach, building on your knowledge of lower-level Microsoft Windows application development and extending it into application design. Both the exam and the book are so high level that there is little coding involved. In fact, most of the code samples in this book illustrate higher-level concepts.

The exam is written for developers who have three to five years of experience developing Web Services and at least one year of experience developing Web API and Azure solutions. Developers should also have at least three years of experience working with Relational Database Management systems and ADO.NET and at least one year of experience with the Entity Framework.

This book covers every exam objective, but it does not cover every exam question. Only the Microsoft exam team has access to the exam questions themselves, and Microsoft regularly adds new questions to the exam, making it impossible to cover specific questions. You should consider this book a supplement to your relevant real-world experience and other study materials. If you encounter a topic in this book that you do not feel completely comfortable with, use the links you'll find in the text to find more information and take the time to research and study the topic. Valuable information is available on MSDN, TechNet, and in blogs and forums.

Microsoft certifications

Microsoft certifications distinguish you by proving your command of a broad set of skills and experience with current Microsoft products and technologies. The exams and corresponding certifications are developed to validate your mastery of critical competencies as you design and develop, or implement and support, solutions with Microsoft products and technologies both on-premise and in the cloud. Certification brings a variety of benefits to the individual and to employers and organizations.

> **MORE INFO** **ALL MICROSOFT CERTIFICATIONS**
>
> For information about Microsoft certifications, including a full list of available certifications, go to *http://www.microsoft.com/learning/en/us/certification/cert-default.aspx*.

Acknowledgments

I'd like to thank Ginny Munroe and Shane Milton for the immense help they provided in preparing this book. My wife and daughter were extremely supportive throughout this stressful and difficult time. I'd also like to thank Walter Bellhaven and Herb Sewell for always keeping things uplifting.

Errata & book support

We've made every effort to ensure the accuracy of this book and its companion content. Any errors that have been reported since this book was published are listed on our Microsoft Press site:

http://aka.ms/ER70-487/errata

If you find an error that is not already listed, you can report it to us through the same page.

If you need additional support, email Microsoft Press Book Support at *mspinput@ microsoft.com.*

Please note that product support for Microsoft software is not offered through the addresses above.

We want to hear from you

At Microsoft Press, your satisfaction is our top priority, and your feedback our most valuable asset. Please tell us what you think of this book at:

http://www.microsoft.com/learning/booksurvey

The survey is short, and we read every one of your comments and ideas. Thanks in advance for your input!

Stay in touch

Let's keep the conversation going! We're on Twitter: *http://twitter.com/MicrosoftPress.*

Preparing for the exam

Microsoft certification exams are a great way to build your resume and let the world know about your level of expertise. Certification exams validate your on-the-job experience and product knowledge. While there is no substitution for on-the-job experience, preparation through study and hands-on practice can help you prepare for the exam. We recommend that you round out your exam preparation plan by using a combination of available study materials and courses. For example, you might use the Exam Ref and another study guide for your "at home" preparation, and take a Microsoft Official Curriculum course for the classroom experience. Choose the combination that you think works best for you.

Note that this Exam Ref is based on publically available information about the exam and the author's experience. To safeguard the integrity of the exam, authors do not have access to the live exam.

CHAPTER 1

Accessing data

It's hard to find a modern software application that doesn't make extensive use of data access. Some exist, but particularly in the business realm, most have a heavy data access component. There are many ways to build data-centric applications and many technologies that can be used. Microsoft provides several, including ADO.NET, Entity Framework, and SQL Server. This objective covers about 24 percent of the exam's questions.

> **_important_**
> ### **_Have you read page xvii?_**
> It contains valuable information regarding the skills you need to pass the exam.

Objectives in this chapter:

- Objective 1.1: Choose data access technologies
- Objective 1.2: Implement caching
- Objective 1.3: Implement transactions
- Objective 1.4: Implement data storage in Windows Azure
- Objective 1.5: Create and implement a WCF Data Services service
- Objective 1.6: Manipulate XML data structures

Objective 1.1: Choose data access technologies

There's no law that states that only one data access technology must be used per application. However, unless you have a specific need, it's generally advisable to pick a data access technology and stick with it throughout the application. Three obvious choices covered by this exam are *ADO.NET, Entity Framework (EF)*, and *WCF Data Services*.

> **This objective covers how to:**
>
> - Choose a technology (ADO.NET, Entity Framework, WCF Data Services) based on application requirements

Choosing a technology (ADO.NET, Entity Framework, WCF Data Services) based on application requirements

Choosing a data access technology is something that requires thought. For the majority of cases, anything you can do with one technology can be accomplished with the other technologies. However, the upfront effort can vary considerably. The downstream benefits and costs are generally more profound. WCF Data Services might be overkill for a simple one-user scenario. A console application that uses ADO.NET might prove much too limiting for any multiuser scenario. In any case, the decision of which technology to use should not be undertaken lightly.

Choosing ADO.NET as the data access technology

If tasked to do so, you could write a lengthy paper on the benefits of using ADO.NET as a primary data access technology. You could write an equally long paper on the downsides of using ADO.NET. Although it's the oldest of the technologies on the current stack, it still warrants serious consideration, and there's a lot to discuss because there's a tremendous amount of ADO.NET code in production, and people are still using it to build new applications.

ADO.NET was designed from the ground up with the understanding that it needs to be able to support large loads and to excel at security, scalability, flexibility, and dependability. These performance-oriented areas (security, scalability, and so on) are mostly taken care of by the fact that ADO.NET has a bias toward a *disconnected model* (as opposed to ADO's commonly used *connected model*). For example, when using individual commands such as INSERT, UPDATE, or DELETE statements, you simply open a connection to the database, execute the command, and then close the connection as quickly as possible. On the query side, you create a SELECT query, pull down the data that you need to work with, and immediately close the connection to the database after the query execution. From there, you'd work with a localized version of the database or subsection of data you were concerned about, make any changes to it that were needed, and then submit those changes back to the database (again by opening a connection, executing the command, and immediately closing the connection).

There are two primary reasons why a connected model versus disconnected model is important. First of all, connections are expensive for a relational database management system (RDBMS) to maintain. They consume processing and networking resources, and database systems can maintain only a finite number of active connections at once. Second, connections can hold locks on data, which can cause concurrency problems. Although it doesn't solve all your problems, keeping connections closed as much as possible and opening them only for short periods of time (the absolute least amount of time possible) will go a long way to mitigating many of your database-focused performance problems (at least the problems caused by the consuming application; database administrator (DBA) performance problems are an entirely different matter).

To improve efficiency, ADO.NET took it one step farther and added the concept of *connection pooling*. Because ADO.NET opens and closes connections at such a high rate, the minor overheads in establishing a connection and cleaning up a connection begin to affect performance. Connection pooling offers a solution to help combat this problem. Consider the scenario in which you have a web service that 10,000 people want to pull data from over the course of 1 minute. You might consider immediately creating 10,000 connections to the database server the moment the data was requested and pulling everybody's data all at the same time. This will likely cause the server to have a meltdown! The opposite end of the spectrum is to create one connection to the database and to make all 10,000 requests use that same connection, one at a time.

Connection pooling takes an in-between approach that works much better. It creates a few connections (let's say 50). It opens them up, negotiates with the RDBMS about how it will communicate with it, and then enables the requests to share these active connections, 50 at a time. So instead of taking up valuable resources performing the same nontrivial task 10,000 times, it does it only 50 times and then efficiently funnels all 10,000 requests through these 50 channels. This means each of these 50 connections would have to handle 200 requests in order to process all 10,000 requests within that minute. Following this math, this means that, if the requests can be processed on average in under ~300ms, you can meet this requirement. It can take ~100ms to open a new connection to a database. If you included that within that 300ms window, 33 percent of the work you have to perform in this time window is dedicated simply to opening and closing connections, and that will never do!

Finally, one more thing that connection pooling does is manage the number of active connections for you. You can specify the maximum number of connections in a connection string. With an ADO.NET 4.5 application accessing SQL Server 2012, this limit defaults to 100 simultaneous connections and can scale anywhere between that and 0 without you as a developer having to think about it.

ADO.NET compatibility

Another strength of ADO.NET is its cross-platform compatibility. It is compatible with much more than just SQL Server. At the heart of ADO.NET is the System.Data namespace. It contains many base classes that are used, irrespective of the RDBMS system. There are several vendor-specific libraries available (System.Data.SqlClient or System.Data.OracleClient, for instance) as well as more generic ones (System.Data.OleDb or System.Data.Odbc) that enable access to OleDb and Odbc-compliant systems without providing much vendor-specific feature access.

ADO.NET architecture

The following sections provide a quick overview of the ADO.NET architecture and then discuss the strengths and benefits of using it as a technology. A few things have always been and probably always will be true regarding database interaction. In order to do anything, you need to connect to the database. Once connected, you need to execute commands against the database. If you're manipulating the data in any way, you need something to hold the data that you just retrieved from the database. Other than those three constants, everything else can have substantial variability.

.NET Framework data providers

According to MSDN, .NET Framework *data providers* are described as "components that have been explicitly designed for data manipulation and fast, forward-only, read-only access to data." Table 1-1 lists the foundational objects of the data providers, the base class they derive from, some example implementations, and discussions about any relevant nuances.

TABLE 1-1 .NET Framework data provider overview

Provider object	Interface	Example items	Discussion
DbConnection	IDbConnection	SqlConnection, OracleConnection, EntityConnection, OdbcConnection, OleDbConnection	Necessary for any database interaction. Care should be taken to close connections as soon as possible after using them.
DbCommand	IDbCommand	SqlCommand, OracleCommand, EntityCommand, OdbcCommand, OleDbCommand	Necessary for all database interactions in addition to Connection. Parameterization should be done only through the Parameters collection. Concatenated strings should never be used for the body of the query or as alternatives to parameters.
DbDataReader	IDataReader	SqlDataReader, OracleDataReader, EntityDataReader, OdbcDataReader, OleDbDataReader	Ideally suited to scenarios in which speed is the most critical aspect because of its forward-only nature, similar to a Stream. This provides read-only access to the data.
DbDataAdapter	IDbDataAdapter	SqlDataAdapter, OracleDataAdapter, OdbcDataAdapter, OleDbDataAdapter	Used in conjunction with a Connection and Command object to populate a DataSet or an individual DataTable, and can also be used to make modifications back to the database. Changes can be batched so that updates avoid unnecessary roundtrips to the database.

Provider object	Interface	Example items	Discussion
DataSet	N/A	No provider-specific implementation	In-memory copy of the RDBMS or portion of RDBMS relevant to the application. This is a collection of DataTable objects, their relationships to one another, and other metadata about the database and commands to interact with it.
DataTable	N/A	No provider-specific implementation	Corresponds to a specific view of data, hether from a SELECT query or generated from .NET code. This is often analogous to a table in the RDBMS, although only partially populated. It tracks the state of data stored in it so, when data is modified, you can tell which records need to be saved back into the database.

The list in Table 1-1 is not a comprehensive list of the all the items in the System.Data (and provider-specific) namespace, but these items do represent the core foundation of ADO.NET. A visual representation is provided in Figure 1-1.

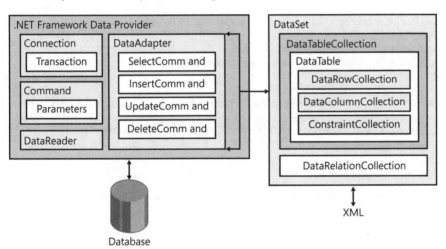

FIGURE 1-1 .NET Framework data provider relationships

DataSet or DataReader?

When querying data, there are two mechanisms you can use: a *DataReader* or a *DataAdapter*. These two options are more alike than you might think. This discussion focuses on the differences between using a DataReader and a DataAdapter, but if you said, "Every SELECT query operation you employ in ADO.NET uses a DataReader," you'd be correct. In fact, when you use a DataAdapter and something goes wrong that results in an exception being thrown, you'll typically see something like the following in the StackTrace of the exception: "System. InvalidOperationException: ExecuteReader requires an open and available Connection." This exception is thrown after calling the Fill method of a SqlDataAdapter. Underneath the abstractions, a DataAdapter uses a DataReader to populate the returned DataSet or DataTable.

Using a DataReader produces faster results than using a DataAdapter to return the same data. Because the DataAdapter actually uses a DataReader to retrieve data, this should not surprise you. But there are many other reasons as well. Look, for example, at a typical piece of code that calls both:

```
[TestCase(3)]
public static void GetCustomersWithDataAdapter(int customerId)
{
    // ARRANGE
    DataSet customerData = new DataSet("CustomerData");
    DataTable customerTable = new DataTable("Customer");
    customerData.Tables.Add(customerTable);

    StringBuilder sql = new StringBuilder();
    sql.Append("SELECT FirstName, LastName, CustomerId, AccountId");
    sql.Append("  FROM [dbo].[Customer] WHERE CustomerId = @CustomerId ");

    // ACT
    // Assumes an app.config file has connectionString added to <connectionStrings>
    section named "TestDB"
    using (SqlConnection mainConnection =
        new SqlConnection(ConfigurationManager.ConnectionStrings["TestDB"].
ConnectionString))
    {
        using (SqlCommand customerQuery = new SqlCommand(sql.ToString(), mainConnection))
        {
            customerQuery.Parameters.AddWithValue("@CustomerId", customerId);
            using (SqlDataAdapter customerAdapter = new SqlDataAdapter(customerQuery))
            {
                try
                {
                    customerAdapter.Fill(customerData, "Customer");
                }
                finally
                {
                    // This should already be closed even if we encounter an exception
                    // but making it explicit in code.
                    if (mainConnection.State != ConnectionState.Closed)
                    {
                        mainConnection.Close();
                    }
                }
            }
        }
    }

    // ASSERT
    Assert.That(customerTable.Rows.Count, Is.EqualTo(1), "We expected exactly 1 record
to be returned.");
    Assert.That(customerTable.Rows[0].ItemArray[customerTable.Columns["customerId"].
Ordinal],
        Is.EqualTo(customerId), "The record returned has an ID different than
```

```
        expected.");
    }
```

Query of Customer Table using SqlDataReader

```csharp
[TestCase(3)]
public static void GetCustomersWithDataReader(int customerId)
{
    // ARRANGE
    // You should probably use a better data structure than a Tuple for managing your
data.
    List<Tuple<string, string, int, int>> results = new List<Tuple<string, string, int,
int>>();

    StringBuilder sql = new StringBuilder();
    sql.Append("SELECT FirstName, LastName, CustomerId, AccountId");
    sql.Append("  FROM [dbo].[Customer] WHERE CustomerId = @CustomerId ");

    // ACT
    // Assumes an app.config file has connectionString added to <connectionStrings>
    section named "TestDB"
    using (SqlConnection mainConnection =
        new SqlConnection(ConfigurationManager.ConnectionStrings["TestDB"].
ConnectionString))
    {
        using (SqlCommand customerQuery = new SqlCommand(sql.ToString(),
mainConnection))
        {
            customerQuery.Parameters.AddWithValue("@CustomerId", customerId);
            mainConnection.Open();
            using (SqlDataReader reader = customerQuery.ExecuteReader(CommandBehavior.
CloseConnection))
            {
                try
                {
                    int firstNameIndex = reader.GetOrdinal("FirstName");
                    int lastNameIndex = reader.GetOrdinal("LastName");
                    int customerIdIndex = reader.GetOrdinal("CustomerId");
                    int accountIdIndex = reader.GetOrdinal("AccountId");

                    while (reader.Read())
                    {
                        results.Add(new Tuple<string, string, int, int>(
                          (string)reader[firstNameIndex], (string)reader[lastNameIndex],
                            (int)reader[customerIdIndex], (int)reader[accountIdIndex]));
                    }
                }
                finally
                {
                    // This will soon be closed even if we encounter an exception
                    // but making it explicit in code.
                    if (mainConnection.State != ConnectionState.Closed)
                    {
                        mainConnection.Close();
                    }
                }
            }
```

```
        }
    }

    // ASSERT
    Assert.That(results.Count, Is.EqualTo(1), "We expected exactly 1 record to be
returned.");
    Assert.That(results[0].Item3, Is.EqualTo(customerId),
        "The record returned has an ID different than expected.");
}
```

Test the code and note the minimal differences. They aren't identical functionally, but they are close. The DataAdapter approach takes approximately 3 milliseconds (ms) to run; the DataReader approach takes approximately 2 ms to run. The point here isn't that the DataAdapter approach is 50 percent slower; it is approximately 1 ms slower. Any data access times measured in single-digit milliseconds is about as ideal as you can hope for in most circumstances. Something else you can do is use a profiling tool to monitor SQL Server (such as SQL Server Profiler) and you will notice that both approaches result in an identical query to the database.

> *IMPORTANT* **MAKE SURE THAT YOU CLOSE EVERY CONNECTION YOU OPEN**
>
> To take advantage of the benefits of ADO.NET, unnecessary connections to the database must be minimized. Countless hours, headaches, and much misery result when a developer takes a shortcut and doesn't close the connections. This should be treated as a Golden Rule: If you open it, close it. Any command you use in ADO.NET outside of a DataAdapter requires you to specifically open your connection. You must take explicit measures to make sure that it is closed. This can be done via a try/catch/finally or try/finally structure, in which the call to close the connection is included in the finally statement. You can also use the Using statement (which originally was available only in C#, but is now available in VB.NET), which ensures that the Dispose method is called on IDisposable objects. Even if you use a Using statement, an explicit call to Close is a good habit to get into. Also keep in mind that the call to Close should be put in the finally block, not the catch block, because the Finally block is the only one guaranteed to be executed according to Microsoft.

The following cases distinguish when you might choose a DataAdapter versus a DataReader:

- Although coding styles and technique can change the equation dramatically, as a general rule, using a DataReader results in faster access times than a DataAdapter does. (This point can't be emphasized enough: The actual code written can and will have a pronounced effect on overall performance.) Benefits in speed from a DataReader can easily be lost by inefficient or ineffective code used in the block.

- DataReaders provide multiple asynchronous methods that can be employed (BeginExecuteNonQuery, BeginExecuteReader, BeginExecuteXmlReader). DataAdapters on the other hand, essentially have only synchronous methods. With small-sized record sets, the differences in performance or advantages of using asynchronous methods are trivial. On large queries that take time, a DataReader, in conjunction with asynchronous methods, can greatly enhance the user experience.

- The Fill method of DataAdapter objects enables you to populate only DataSets and DataTables. If you're planning to use a custom business object, you have to first retrieve the DataSet or DataTables; then you need to write code to hydrate your business object collection. This can have an impact on application responsiveness as well as the memory your application uses.

- Although both types enable you to execute multiple queries and retrieve multiple return sets, only the DataSet lets you closely mimic the behavior of a relational database (for instance, add Relationships between tables using the Relations property or ensure that certain data integrity rules are adhered to via the EnforceConstraints property).

- The Fill method of the DataAdapter completes only when all the data has been retrieved and added to the DataSet or DataTable. This enables you to immediately determine the number of records in any given table. By contrast, a DataReader can indicate whether data was returned (via the HasRows property), but the only way to know the exact record count returned from a DataReader is to iterate through it and count it out specifically.

- You can iterate through a DataReader only once and can iterate through it only in a forward-only fashion. You can iterate through a DataTable any number of times in any manner you see fit.

- DataSets can be loaded directly from XML documents and can be persisted to XML natively. They are consequently inherently serializable, which affords many features not natively available to DataReaders (for instance, you can easily store a DataSet or a DataTable in Session or View State, but you can't do the same with a DataReader). You can also easily pass a DataSet or DataTable in between tiers because it is already serializable, but you can't do the same with a DataReader. However, a DataSet is also an expensive object with a large memory footprint. Despite the ease in doing so, it is generally ill-advised to store it in Session or Viewstate variables, or pass it across multiple application tiers because of the expensive nature of the object. If you serialize a DataSet, proceed with caution!

- After a DataSet or DataTable is populated and returned to the consuming code, no other interaction with the database is necessary unless or until you decide to send the localized changes back to the database. As previously mentioned, you can think of the dataset as an in-memory copy of the relevant portion of the database.

Why choose ADO.NET?

So what are the reasons that would influence one to use traditional ADO.NET as a data access technology? What does the exam expect you to know about this choice? You need to be able to identify what makes one technology more appropriate than another in a given setting. You also need to understand how each technology works.

The first reason to choose ADO.NET is consistency. ADO.NET has been around much longer than other options available. Unless it's a relatively new application or an older application that has been updated to use one of the newer alternatives, ADO.NET is already being used to interact with the database.

The next reason is related to the first: stability both in terms of the evolution and quality of the technology. ADO.NET is firmly established and is unlikely to change in any way other than feature additions. Although there have been many enhancements and feature improvements, if you know how to use ADO.NET in version 1.0 of the .NET Framework, you will know how to use ADO.NET in each version up through version 4.5. Because it's been around so long, most bugs and kinks have been fixed.

ADO.NET, although powerful, is an easy library to learn and understand. Once you understand it conceptually, there's not much left that's unknown or not addressed. Because it has been around so long, there are providers for almost every well-known database, and many lesser-known database vendors have providers available for ADO.NET. There are examples showing how to handle just about any challenge, problem, or issue you would ever run into with ADO.NET.

One last thing to mention is that, even though Windows Azure and cloud storage were not on the list of considerations back when ADO.NET was first designed, you can use ADO.NET against Windows Azure's SQL databases with essentially no difference in coding. In fact, you are encouraged to make the earlier SqlDataAdapter or SqlDataReader tests work against a Windows Azure SQL database by modifying only the connection string and nothing else!

Choosing EF as the data access technology

EF provides the means for a developer to focus on application code, not the underlying "plumbing" code necessary to communicate with a database efficiently and securely.

The origins of EF

Several years ago, Microsoft introduced *Language Integrated Query (LINQ)* into the .NET Framework. LINQ has many benefits, one of which is that it created a new way for .NET developers to interact with data. Several flavors of LINQ were introduced. *LINQ-to-SQL* was one of them. At that time (and it's still largely the case), RDBMS systems and *object oriented programming (OOP)* were the predominant metaphors in the programming community. They were both popular and the primary techniques taught in most computer science curriculums. They had many advantages. OOP provided an intuitive and straightforward way to model real-world problems.

The relational approach for data storage had similar benefits. It has been used since at least the 1970s, and many major vendors provided implementations of this methodology. Most all the popular implementations used an ANSI standard language known as *Structured Query Language (SQL)* that was easy to learn. If you learned it for one database, you could use that knowledge with almost every other well-known implementation out there. SQL was quite powerful, but it lacked many useful constructs (such as loops), so the major vendors typically provided their own flavor in addition to basic support for ANSI SQL. In the case of Microsoft, it was named *Transact SQL* or, as it's commonly known, *T-SQL*.

Although the relational model was powerful and geared for many tasks, there were some areas that it didn't handle well. In most nontrivial applications, developers would find there was a significant gap between the object models they came up with via OOP and the ideal structures they came up with for data storage. This problem is commonly referred to as impedance mismatch, and it initially resulted in a significant amount of required code to deal with it. To help solve this problem, a technique known as *object-relational mapping (ORM, O/RM, or O/R Mapping)* was created. LINQ-to-SQL was one of the first major Microsoft initiatives to build an ORM tool. By that time, there were several other popular ORM tools, some open source and some from private vendors. They all centered on solving the same essential problem.

Compared to the ORM tools of the time, many developers felt LINQ-to-SQL was not powerful and didn't provide the functionality they truly desired. At the same time that LINQ-to-SQL was introduced, Microsoft embarked upon the EF initiative. EF received significant criticism early in its life, but it has matured tremendously over the past few years. Right now, it is powerful and easy to use. At this point, it's also widely accepted as fact that the future of data access with Microsoft is the EF and its approach to solving problems.

The primary benefit of using EF is that it enables developers to manipulate data as domain-specific objects without regard to the underlying structure of the data store. Microsoft has made (and continues to make) a significant investment in the EF, and it's hard to imagine any scenario in the future that doesn't take significant advantage of it.

From a developer's point of view, EF enables developers to work with entities (such as Customers, Accounts, Widgets, or whatever else they are modeling). In EF parlance, this is known as the conceptual model. EF is responsible for mapping these entities and their corresponding properties to the underlying data source.

To understand EF (and what's needed for the exam), you need to know that there are three parts to the EF modeling. Your .NET code works with the conceptual model. You also need to have some notion of the underlying storage mechanism (which, by the way, can change without necessarily affecting the conceptual model). Finally, you should understand how EF handles the mapping between the two.

EF modeling

For the exam and for practical use, it's critical that you understand the three parts of the EF model and what role they play. Because there are only three of them, that's not difficult to accomplish.

The conceptual model is handled via what's known as the *conceptual schema definition language (CSDL)*. In older versions of EF, it existed in a file with a .csdl extension. The data storage aspect is handled through the *store schema definition language (SSDL)*. In older versions of EF, it existed in a file with an .ssdl file extension. The mapping between the CSDL and SSDL is handled via the *mapping specification language (MSL)*. In older versions of EF, it existed in a file with an .msl file extension. In modern versions of EF, the CSDL, MSL, and SSDL all exist in a file with an .edmx file extension. However, even though all three are in a single file, it is important to understand the differences between the three.

Developers should be most concerned with the conceptual model (as they should be); database folk are more concerned with the storage model. It's hard enough to build solid object models without having to know the details and nuances of a given database implementation, which is what DBAs are paid to do. One last thing to mention is that the back-end components can be completely changed without affecting the conceptual model by allowing the changes to be absorbed by the MSL's mapping logic.

Compare this with ADO.NET, discussed in the previous section. If you took any of the samples provided and had to change them to use an Oracle database, there would be major changes necessary to all the code written. In the EF, you'd simply focus on the business objects and let the storage model and mappings handle the change to how the data came from and got back to the database.

Building EF models

The early days of EF were not friendly to the technology. Many people were critical of the lack of tooling provided and the inability to use industry-standard architectural patterns because they were impossible to use with EF. Beginning with version 4.0 (oddly, 4.0 was the second version of EF), Microsoft took these problems seriously. By now, those complaints have been addressed.

There are two basic ways you can use the set of *Entity Data Model (EDM)* tools to create your conceptual model. The first way, called *Database First*, is to build a database (or use an existing one) and then create the conceptual model from it. You can then use these tools to manipulate your conceptual model. You can also work in the opposite direction in a process called *Model First*, building your conceptual model first and then letting the tools build out a database for you. In either case, if you have to make changes to the source or you want to change the source all together, the tools enable you to do this easily.

> **NOTE   CODE FIRST**
>
> An alternative way to use EF is via a *Code First* technique. This technique enables a developer to create simple classes that represent entities and, when pointing EF to these classes, enables the developer to create a simple data tier that just works. Although you are encouraged to further investigate this technique that uses no .edmx file, the exam does not require that you know how to work with this technique much beyond the fact that it exists. As such, anywhere in this book that discusses EF, you can assume a Model First or Database First approach.

When you create a new EF project, you create an .edmx file. It's possible to create a project solely from XML files you write yourself, but that would take forever, defeat the purpose for using the EF, and generally be a bad idea. The current toolset includes four primary items that you need to understand:

- The *Entity Model Designer* is the item that creates the .edmx file and enables you to manipulate almost every aspect of the model (create, update, or delete entities), manipulate associations, manipulate and update mappings, and add or modify inheritance relationships.

- The *Entity Data Model Wizard* is the true starting point of building your conceptual model. It enables you to use an existing data store instance.

- The *Create Database Wizard* enables you to do the exact opposite of the previous item. Instead of starting with a database, it enables you to fully build and manipulate your conceptual model, and it takes care of building the actual database based on the conceptual model.

- The *Update Model Wizard* is the last of the tools, and it does exactly what you'd expect it to. After your model is built, it enables you to fully modify every aspect of the conceptual model. It can let you do the same for both the storage model and the mappings that are defined between them.

There's one other tool that's worth mentioning, although it's generally not what developers use to interact with the EF. It's known as the *EDM Generator* and is a command-line utility that was one of the first items built when the EF was being developed. Like the combination of the wizard-based tools, it enables you to generate a conceptual model, validate a model after it is built, generate the actual C# or VB.NET classes that are based off of the conceptual model, and also create the code file that contains model views. Although it can't hurt to know the details of how this tool works, the important aspects for the exam focus on each of the primary components that go into an EDM, so it is important to understand what each of those are and what they do.

Building an EF Model using the Entity Data Model Wizard

This section shows you how to use the tools to build a simple model against the TestDB created in the beginning of Chapter 1. You can alternatively manually create your models and use those models to generate your database if you alter step 3 and choose Empty Model instead.

However, before you begin, make sure that your TestDB is ready to go, and you're familiar with how to connect to it. One way is to ensure that the tests back in the ADO.NET section pass. Another way is to ensure that you can successfully connect via *SQL Server Management Studio (SSMS)*. For the included screen shots, the EF model is added to the existing MySimpleTests project.

1. First, right-click on your Project in Solution Explorer and add a New Item.

2. In the Add New Item dialog box, select Visual C# Items → Data on the left and ADO.NET Entity Data Model in the middle (don't let the name of this file type throw you off because it does include "ADO.NET" in the name). Name this **MyModel.edmx** and click Add (see Figure 1-2).

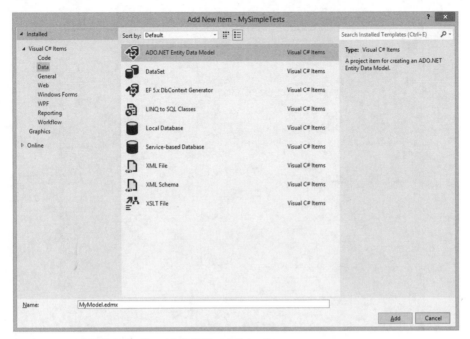

FIGURE 1-2 ADO.NET Entity Data Model Wizard dialog box

3. In the Entity Data Model Wizard dialog box, select Generate From Database and click Next.

4. Next, the Entity Data Model Wizard requires that you connect to your database. Use the New Connection button to connect and test your connection. After you're back to the Entity Data Model Wizard dialog box, ensure that the check box to save your connection settings is selected and name it **TestEntities** (see Figure 1-3).

FIGURE 1-3 Choose Your Data Connection dialog box

5. In the next screen of the Entity Data Model Wizard, select all the tables and select both check boxes under the database objects. Finally, for the namespace, call it **TestModel** and click Finish (see Figure 1-4).

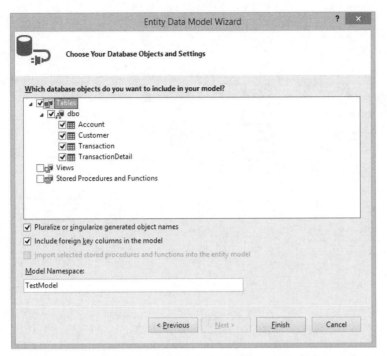

FIGURE 1-4 Choose Your Database Objects And Settings dialog box

6. You should now see the Entity Model Designer in a view that looks similar to an entity relationship diagram shown in Figure 1-5.

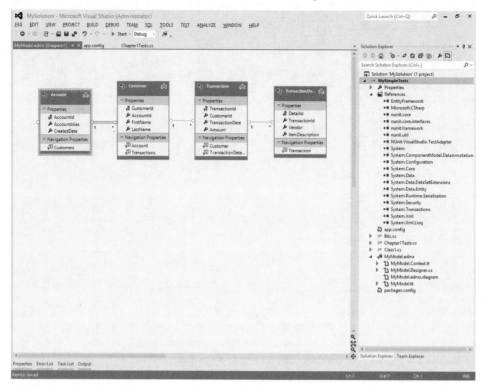

FIGURE 1-5 Entity Model view

After generating your EF models, you now have a fully functioning data tier for simple consumption! Quickly test this to investigate everything you just created. See the code for a quick test of your new EF data tier:

Entity Framework test

```
[TestCase(3)]
public static void GetCustomerById(int customerId)
{
    // ARRANGE
    TestEntities database = new TestEntities();

    // ACT
    Customer result = database.Customers.SingleOrDefault(cust => cust.CustomerId ==
customerId);

    // ASSERT
    Assert.That(result, Is.Not.Null, "Expected a value. Null here indicates no record
with this ID.");
    Assert.That(result.CustomerId, Is.EqualTo(customerId), "Uh oh!");
}
```

There are a few things to note about what happens in this test. First, the complexity of the code to consume EF is completely different compared with the prior ADO.NET tests! Second, this test runs in approximately 4 ms compared with the 2–3 ms for ADO.NET. The difference here isn't so much 50–100 percent, but rather 1–2 ms for such a simple query. Finally, the query that runs against SQL Server in this case is substantially different from what was run with the ADO.NET queries for two reasons: EF does some ugly (although optimized) aliasing of columns, tables, and parameters; and this performs a SELECT TOP (2) to enforce the constraint from the use of the Linq SingleOrDefault command.

> **MORE INFO**   **SINGLE VERSUS FIRST IN LINQ**
>
> When using LINQ, if you have a collection and you want to return a single item from it, you have two obvious options if you ignore nulls (four if you want to handle nulls). The First function effectively says, "Give me the first one of the collection." The Single function, however, says, "Give me the single item that is in the collection and throw an exception if there are more or fewer than one item." In both cases, the xxxOrDefault handles the case when the collection is empty by returning a null value. A bad programming habit that many developers have is to overuse the First function when the Single function is the appropriate choice. In the previous test, Single is the appropriate function to use because you don't want to allow for the possibility of more than one Customer with the same ID; if that happens, something bad is going on!

As shown in Figure 1-6, there's a lot behind this .edmx file you created. There are two things of critical importance and two things that are mostly ignorable. For now, ignore the MyModel.Designer.cs file, which is not currently used, and ignore the MyModel.edmx.diagram file, which is used only for saving the layout of tables in the visual designer.

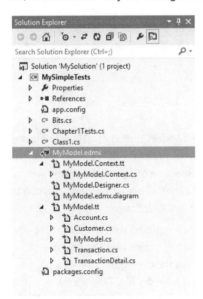

FIGURE 1-6 EF-generated files

First, look at the MyModel.tt file and then its Customer.cs file. Double-click the MyModel.
tt file and you'll see the contents of this T4 text template. This template generates simple
classes that represent the records in your tables in your database. Now open the Customer.cs
file. The only two pieces of this file that might be new to you are the ICollection and Hash-
Set types. These are simple collection types that are unrelated to EF, databases, or anything
else. ICollection<T> is a simple interface that represents a collection; nothing special here. A
HashSet<T> is similar to a generic List<T>, but is optimized for fast lookups (via hashtables, as
the name implies) at the cost of losing order.

T4-Generated Customer.cs

```
public partial class Customer
{
    public Customer()
    {
        this.Transactions = new HashSet<Transaction>();
    }

    public int CustomerId { get; set; }
    public int AccountId { get; set; }
    public string FirstName { get; set; }
    public string LastName { get; set; }

    public virtual Account Account { get; set; }
    public virtual ICollection<Transaction> Transactions { get; set; }
}
```

Next, look at the file MyModel.Context.tt generated: MyModel.Context.cs. There are three
important things to see in this file. First, the TestEntities class inherits the DbContext class. This
class can be thought of as the EF runtime that does all the magic work. The DbContext API
was introduced with EF 4.1, and Microsoft has an excellent series of documentation on how to
work with this API at *http://msdn.microsoft.com/en-us/data/gg192989.aspx*.

Inheriting DbContext enables it to talk to a database when coupled with the .edmx file and
the connection string in the config file. Looking at this example, notice that the parameter
passes to the base constructor. This means that it depends on the config file having a properly configured EF connection string named TestEntities in the config file. Take a look at it and
notice how this connection string differs from the one you used for the ADO.NET tests. Also

notice the DbSet collections. These collections are what enable us to easily work with each table in the database as if it were simply a .NET collection. Chapter 2, "Querying and manipulating data by using the Entity Framework," investigates this in more detail.

T4-Generated MyModel.Context.cs

```
public partial class TestEntities : DbContext
{
    public TestEntities()
        : base("name=TestEntities")
    {
    }

    protected override void OnModelCreating(DbModelBuilder modelBuilder)
    {
        throw new UnintentionalCodeFirstException();
    }

    public DbSet<Account> Accounts { get; set; }
    public DbSet<Customer> Customers { get; set; }
    public DbSet<Transaction> Transactions { get; set; }
    public DbSet<TransactionDetail> TransactionDetails { get; set; }
}
```

Entity Data Model Designer

When you double-click the .edmx file and are given the ERD-like view, you invoke the *EDM Designer*. This is the primary tool for manipulating your models, whether you're manually creating a new one, updating your existing models based on changes in the schema of your data, or choosing to manually tweak your conceptual model without changes to your storage model.

When you have the Designer open, there is a window that is useful to have at times that can be opened by clicking View → Other Windows → Entity Data Model Browser. This is especially useful as your .edmx begins to cover a large number of tables and you have difficulty locating a particular one.

If you want to manage your models in the Designer, typically you'd just right-click anywhere inside the design canvas of the .edmx model file you're working with or on a specific entity or property that you want to manage. If you want to update your models based on data schema changes, it can be done with the Update Model Wizard by right-clicking in the design canvas and selecting Update Model From Database. In the Update Model Wizard, you can choose to add new tables or simply click Finish for it to pull in schema changes to existing tables.

The options that might raise some questions are likely to be the Inheritance and Complex Type options. Otherwise, editing the conceptual model is straightforward. Inheritance is a way to create entities with OOP class hierarchies that is primarily used in Code First and Model First (but not Database First) scenarios. With Inheritance, you can have both an Employee and

Customer type that inherits a Person type. Although an Employee might have a Salary field, a Customer certainly wouldn't. Behind-the-scenes in your data store, this can be represented in a couple different ways.

The default mapping strategy, called *Table per Hierarchy (TPH)*, is the most straightforward way to do this. It creates a single table for all objects in an inheritance hierarchy, and it simply has nullable columns for fields that aren't common across all types. It also adds a Discriminator column so EF can keep track of the type of each individual record. This strategy is often the best balance of tradeoffs available because it provides the best performance. The primary disadvantage is that your data is slightly denormalized.

The prevailing alternative strategy, called *Table per Type (TPT)*, creates a table for your base type that has all common fields in it, a table for each child type that stores the additional fields, as well as an ID to the base type's record that stores the common fields. The multiple inheriting types' tables are linked to one another via a foreign key that has a shared primary key value. In this case, to get all the data for a single entity, EF must perform a join across multiple tables. The primary advantage is that your data is properly normalized. The primary disadvantage is that your performance suffers.

Your other mapping options include *Table per Concrete Type (TPC)* and *Mixed Inheritance*. These two options are not currently supported in the EDM Designer, although the EF runtime does support them. The exam will likely not cover these mapping options, nor are they usually your most practical choice to use because of the limited tooling support for them.

A *Complex Type* is a logical designation for a common group of fields on multiple entities. When you have a Complex Type, your conceptual model has an object to work with for easier usability of these repeated groups of fields (an example is a date range). Many tables in many databases have a StartDate field and a StopDate field. You could take these two fields, identify them as being parts of a Complex Type called a DateRange, and then your conceptual model could specify when an entity has a Date Range instead of arbitrary date fields.

The only other major item is the actual editing of the conceptual entity items. If you select any given entity on the conceptual model canvas, right-click it, and select Add New, you'll see a menu with the following items:

- Scalar Property
- Navigation Property
- Complex Property
- Association
- Inheritance
- Function Import

From there, the remaining features are self-explanatory. Following is a brief description of each:

- **Table Mapping** enables you to change the relationship to the underlying table. For instance, you can add fields, remove fields, or change fields from the specific property originally mapped to.

- **Stored Procedure Mapping** is based on the Stored Procedures defined in the database. It enables you specify an Insert, Update, and Delete function. Select queries are already handled by the language semantics of LINQ.

- **Update Model from Database** is the same behavior described previously in the canvas-based designer.

- **Generate Database from Model** is the same behavior described previously in the canvas-based designer.

- **Validate** is the same behavior described previously in the canvas-based designer that ensures the validity of the .edmx file.

Using the generated items

So far, everything has involved the .edmx files and their respective components. It's critical to understand each of the pieces and why they matter when designing an application, but understanding how to generate a model is only one part of the equation. A tremendous amount of time is spent developing and maintaining business objects and their interaction with the database, so having this handled for you is beneficial. But just as important is to understand what you do with everything after it is generated.

In the simplest scenario, the conceptual model provides you with classes that map directly to the underlying tables in your RDBMS structure (unless, of course, you specify otherwise). These classes are actual C# or VB.NET code, and you can work with them just like any other class you create. To understand things and prepare for the exam, I highly recommend that you generate a few different .edmx files (try both Database First and Model First) and examine them closely.

At the top level, the primary object you'll work with is an ObjectContext or DbContext object. Choose a name for the context early on in the wizard. It can be changed just like everything else, but the important takeaway for the exam is that this is the primary item from which everything else flows. If you do want to change the name, however, you simply have focus in the Designer for the .edmx file and set the Entity Container Name value in the Properties window.

ObjectContext versus DbContext

Older versions of EF did not have DbContext. Instead, ObjectContext was the equivalent class that funneled most of the functionality to the developer. Modern versions of EF still support the ObjectContext object, and you can even consume modern EF in much the same way as the older versions. Suffice it to say, if you're beginning a new project, DbContext is where you should look to for your EF needs. However, both flavors of the API are important from a real-world legacy code perspective as well as a testing perspective for this exam. In other words, be prepared to answer questions about both ways of using EF. Fortunately, many of the concepts from the one flavor are directly applicable to the other flavor.

The steps for creating an .edmx are intended for creating a DbContext usage scenario. If you want to work in an ObjectContext scenario, you have three primary options. The intimate details of these approaches are beyond this book; you are encouraged to investigate these approaches:

- **Legacy approach**   Follow similar steps using Visual Studio 2008 or 2010 to create an .edmx file and its corresponding ObjectContext and entities.

- **Downgrading your entities**   Take the .edmx file that was generated, open the Properties window, and set focus in the Designer's canvas. From here, change the Code Generation Strategy from None to Default in the Properties window. Finally, delete the two .tt files listed as children to your .edmx file in the Solution Explorer window.

- **Hybrid approach**   Get the ObjectContext (via a nonobvious approach) from the DbContext and work with the ObjectContext directly. Note that even with modern versions of EF, in some rare and advanced scenarios this is still required:

Hybrid approach

```
public static ObjectContext ConvertContext(DbContext db)
{
    return ((IObjectContextAdapter)db).ObjectContext;
}


[TestCase(3)]
public static void GetCustomerByIdOnObjectContext(int customerId)
{
    // ARRANGE
    TestEntities database = new TestEntities();
    ObjectContext context = ConvertContext(database);

    // ACT
    ObjectSet<Customer> customers = context.CreateObjectSet<Customer>("Customers");
    Customer result = customers.SingleOrDefault(cust => cust.CustomerId == customerId);
    //Customer result = database.Customers.SingleOrDefault(cust => cust.CustomerId ==
customerId);

    // ASSERT
    Assert.That(result, Is.Not.Null, "Expected a value. Null here indicates no record
with this ID.");
    Assert.That(result.CustomerId, Is.EqualTo(customerId), "Uh oh!");
}
```

As you can tell from this test with the commented line of code, basic consumption of a DbContext is quite similar to that of an ObjectContext. In fact, most T4 templated instances of ObjectContexts already have properties pregenerated for you, so you can simply access the equivalent ObjectSet<Customer> collection directly off of the generated class that derives ObjectContext. This simple consumption truly is identical to that of a the generated DbContext-derived class and its DbSet collection.

ObjectContext management

Two important things happen when an ObjectContext constructor is called. The generated context inherits several items from the ObjectContext base class, including a property known as ContextOptions and an event named OnContextCreated. The ContextOptions class has five primary properties you can manipulate:

- LazyLoadingEnabled
- ProxyCreationEnabled
- UseConsistentNullReferenceBehavior
- UseCSharpNullComparisonBehavior
- UseLegacyPreserveChangesBehavior

The LazyLoadingEnabled property is set when any instance of the context is instantiated and is used to enable lazy loading. If left unspecified, the default setting is true. Lazy loading enables entities to be loaded on-demand without thought by the developer. Although this can be handy in some scenarios, this behavior can have very serious performance implications depending on how relationships are set up. A good deal of thought should be taken into consideration regarding this enabling or disabling lazy loading. Feature development and even application architecture might change one way or another based on the use of this feature. And some architectures make it necessary to disable this feature.

In EF, lazy loading is triggered based on a Navigation Property being accessed. By simply referencing a navigation property, that entity is then loaded. As an example, let's take the Customer class and the related Transaction class. If LazyLoadingEnabled is set to true, and you load one customer, you'll just get back data just for that customer record. But if you later access a Navigation Property within the same ObjectContext, another roundtrip to the database will be made to fetch that data. If you loop through a collection of entities (in this case, the Transactions), an individual roundtrip is made to the database for each entity. If you have LazyLoadingEnabled set to false, you have two options. You can either use explicit lazy loading with the ObjectContext's LoadProperty() method or you can use eager loading with the ObjectSet's Include() method. With explicit lazy loading, you must write code to explicitly perform this additional roundtrip to the database to conditionally load the data. With eager loading, you must specify up front what related data you want loaded. Although explicit lazy loading, like regular lazy loading, can reduce the amount of data flowing back and forth, it's a chatty pattern, whereas eager loading is a chunky pattern.

Of the five ContextOption properties, LazyLoadingEnabled is by far the most important one with the most serious implications for your application. Although it is inappropriate to refer to the other properties as unimportant, lazy loading can very quickly make or break your application.

The ProxyCreationEnabled property is one of the other properties of the ObjectContextOptions class that simply determines whether proxy objects should be created for custom data classes that are persistence-ignorant, such as *plain old common object (POCO)* entities (POCO entities are covered more in Chapter 2). It defaults to true and, unless you have some specific reason to set it to false, it generally isn't something you need to be overly concerned about.

This property is available only in newer versions of EF. A very common problem with this property occurs if you initially target .NET Framework 4.5 with your application code, reference this property, and then later drop down to .NET 4.0 where this property does not exist.

This functionality that this property controls is a little confusing if you disable lazy loading and load a Customer object from the TestDB database. If you inspect the AccountId, you can see a value of the parent record. But if you inspect the Account navigation property, it is null because it has not yet been loaded. Now with the UseConsistentNullReferenceBehavior property set to false, you can then attempt to set the Account navigation property to null, and nothing will happen when you try to save it. However, if this setting is set to true, the act of setting the Account navigation property to null attempts to sever the relationship between the two records upon saving (which results in an error because the AccountId is not a nullable field). If, on the other hand, you had the Customer object loaded and its Account property was also loaded (either by eager loading or lazy loading), the UseConsistentNullReferenceBehavior setting has no effect on setting the Account property to null.

As the name implies, C# NullComparison behavior is enabled when set to true; otherwise, it is not enabled. The main implication of this property is that it changes queries that require null comparisons. For example, take a look at a test and see what happens. To set the data up for this test, ensure that your Account table has three records in it: one with an AccountAlias set to Home, one with an AccountAlias set to Work, and one with AccountAlias set to null. You can tweak the second parameter of the test to other numbers if you want to work with a different number of records:

Null comparison behavior

```
[TestCase(true, 2)]
[TestCase(false, 1)]
public static void GetAccountsByAliasName(bool useCSharpNullBehavior, int recordsToFind)
{
    // ARRANGE
    TestEntities database = new TestEntities();
    ObjectContext context = ConvertContext(database);
    ObjectSet<Account> accounts = context.CreateObjectSet<Account>("Accounts");

    // ACT
    context.ContextOptions.UseCSharpNullComparisonBehavior = useCSharpNullBehavior;
    int result = accounts.Count(acc => acc.AccountAlias != "Home");

    // ASSERT
    Assert.That(result, Is.EqualTo(recordsToFind), "Uh oh!");
}
```

Behind the scenes, when this setting is enabled, EF automatically tweaks your query to also include cases in which AccountAlias is set to null. In other words, depending on whether it is enabled or disabled, you might see the two following queries hitting your database:

```
SELECT COUNT(*) FROM Account WHERE AccountAlias <> 'Home' - Disabled
SELECT COUNT(*) FROM Account WHERE AccountAlias <> 'Home' OR AccountAlias IS NULL --
Enabled
```

This property can be set to true or false and is quite confusing. This setting causes EF to use either the .NET Framework 4.0 (and newer) functionality for MergeOption.PreserveChanges or use the .NET Framework 3.5 SP1 version when merging two entities on a single context. Setting this to true gives you some control over how to resolve Optimistic Concurrency Exceptions while attaching an entity to the ObjectContext when another copy of that same entity already exists on the context. Starting with.NET Framework version 4.0, when you attach an entity to the context, the EF compares the current local values of unmodified properties against those already loaded in the context. If they are the same, nothing happens. If they are different, the state of the property is set to Modified. The legacy option changes this behavior. When the entity is attached, the values of unmodified properties are not copied over; instead, the context's version of those properties is kept. This might be desirable, depending on how you want to handle concurrency issues in your application. Dealing with concurrency issues and all the implications that come with it is well beyond the scope of both the exam and this book.

ObjectContext entities

Understanding the structure of ObjectContext is critical for the exam. In addition, you need to understand the structure of the Entity classes that are generated for it. Thanks to the appropriate T4 templates, each entity that you define in the conceptual model gets a class generated to accompany it. There are a few options for the types of entities that can be generated. In EF 4.0, the default base class for entities was EntityObject. Two other types of entities could also be created: POCO entities (no required base class for these) and Self-Tracking entities (STEs) (no base class, but they implemented IObjectWithChangeTracker and INotifyProperty-Changed). Chapter 2 covers POCO entities and STE in more detail, but very little knowledge of them is required for the exam.

The ObjectContext entities of significant interest inherit from the EntityObject class. The class declaration for any given entity resembles the following:

```
public partial class Customer : EntityObject
{
    /* ... */
}
```

EXAM TIP

As noted earlier, you need to pay attention to the derived class that the given context is derived from because it is likely to be included in the exam. The same is the case with entities that derive from the EntityObject base class. These entities have several attributes decorating the class definition that you should be familiar with. There are also several similar distinctions surrounding properties of each entity class (or *attributes*, as they are called in the conceptual model).

Next, each entity will be decorated with three specific attributes:

- EdmEntityTypeAttribute
- SerializableAttribute
- DataContractAttribute

So the full declaration looks something like the following:

```
[EdmEntityTypeAttribute(NamespaceName = "MyNameSpace", Name = "Customer")]
[Serializable()]
[DataContractAttribute(IsReference = true)]
public partial class Customer : EntityObject
{
    /* ... */
}
```

The Entity class needs to be serializable. If you want to persist the object locally, pass it between tiers, or do much else with it, it has to be serializable. Because ObjectContext's incarnations of the EF were created to work in conjunction with WCF and WCF Data Services, the

DataContractAttribute must decorate the class (more on this later in the chapter, but for now, just understand that this is required for WCF's default serialization).

The last attribute is the EdmEntityTypeAttribute, which contains the item's namespace and the Name. Remember that the power of the EF comes from the fact that it gives you such tremendous designer support. In order to do that, you'd need either a lot of code or a lot of metadata, and in most cases, a decent amount of both. This EdmEntityTypeAttribute does little more than tell the world that the class is an EDM type and then provides a basic amount of supporting information about it.

Look at the definition of each class that's generated corresponding to each entity and as much as possible in the .edmx. Each property needs to be marked with the DataMember attribute (more about this in Objective 1.5). In addition to the DataMember attribute, the EdmScalarProperty Attribute decorates each property definition. The two main properties that it defines are EntityKeyProperty and IsNullable. The EntityKeyProperty simply indicates whether it is an EntityKey or not. IsNullable simply indicates whether this value allows Nulls.

C# 3.0 introduced a new kind of property: *auto-properties*. An example of an auto-property might look like this:

```
public int CustomerID { get; set; }
```

No matching private variables were declared, and the backing variables were just inferred. They were still there, but it was essentially syntactical sugar to save a few lines of code. The one big "gotcha" was that it was usable only when the get and set accessors did nothing but return or accept a value. If any logic happened inside of the accessor, you still needed to define a backing variable. An example of an EntityKey property on an entity follows:

```
[EdmScalarPropertyAttribute(EntityKeyProperty=true, IsNullable=false)]
[DataMemberAttribute()]
public global::System.Int32 CustomerId
{
    get
    {
        return _CustomerId;
    }
    set
    {
        if (_CustomerId != value)
        {
            OnCustomerIdChanging(value);
            ReportPropertyChanging("CustomerId");
            _CustomerId = StructuralObject.SetValidValue(value, "CustomerId");
            ReportPropertyChanged("CustomerId");
            OnCustomerIdChanged();
        }
    }
}
private global::System.Int32 _CustomerId;
partial void OnCustomerIdChanging(global::System.Int32 value);
partial void OnCustomerIdChanged();
```

The get accessor does nothing but return the private backing variable. The set accessor verifies that the value you're attempting to set is different from the value it currently holds. This makes sense, if you're only going to set something back to itself; why waste the effort? Once it verifies that the value has in fact changed, the OnChanged event is raised passing in the new value. Next, the ReportPropertyChanging event is raised, passing in a string corresponding to the entity name. The ReportPropertyChanging and ReportPropertyChanged events (the latter of which is called shortly afterward) are both members of the EntityObject base class and are used for fundamentally different purposes than the entity-specific events are.

So after the ReportPropertyChanging event is raised, the backing variable is updated with the new value. After that's been successfully completed, the ReportPropertyChanged event is raised, indicating that the operation has completed as far as the UI or host is concerned. Finally, the OnXChangedEvent specific to that entity is raised and processing is finished.

> **NOTE THOSE WEREN'T EVENTS**
>
> Even though these last few paragraphs just called some things "events," what you see in the generated code aren't events. Technically, they're nothing more than partial methods that are invoked. Even if some other portion of this partial class implements them, doing so doesn't make them events. However, the underlying implementation of these partial functions does, in fact, raise the events we're discussing. So although you might not actually see any generated code working with events here, this generated code does result in the discussed events being raised.

Why choose the EF?

The EF is just one of many choices you have available for data access. Compared with ADO.NET data services, you could argue that it's more similar than different; however, the opposite is true. Microsoft has made a tremendous investment in the EF and continues to, which is indicative of its future plans and where it intends data access to go. The EF provides many benefits over previous data access technologies, and now that the toolset has matured, there's not much downside. Following are the benefits:

- There is tremendous tooling support that enables you to build and maintain the data access elements of your application in a much shorter time than ADO.NET would.
- You can focus on dealing with business objects of your application and don't have to spend your time overly concerned about the underlying data store.
- It allows for a clear separation of concerns between the conceptual model and the underlying data store.

- The data store can be changed (quite dramatically) without having to rewrite core application logic. Microsoft has made a tremendous investment into the EF, and all indications point to the fact it has made a firm commitment to the success of the EF.

- The EF is built to fit right in with WCF, which makes them very complementary technologies.

Choosing WCF Data Services as the data access technology

The development landscape has changed over the past few years, even faster and more dynamically than it has in other equivalent periods. Three of the highly notable changes are these:

- *Open Data Protocol (OData)*
- *Representational State Transfer (REST)*
- *JavaScript Object Notation (JSON)*

WCF Data Services, originally called ADO.NET Data Services, is the main mechanism of Microsoft to deal with exposing these features to developers. WCF Data Services are particularly well-suited to applications that are exposed via *Service-Oriented Architecture (SOA)* and enable you to build applications that outsiders (and insiders for that matter) can easily consume and work with. *Web Services and Windows Communication Foundation (WCF)* were certainly big steps forward in this regard, but WCF Data Services takes it all one step farther in making the whole process a much easier endeavor.

Changing the nature of data access

If you think of how you typically approach getting a set of data, the first thing that probably comes to mind is writing a SQL query. If you've been a user of EF, you might think of an Entity Model. If you want to make the application accessible to outsiders, you will likely consider building and publishing a web service.

Consumers of that web service would have to go through several steps to build an application that consumed your service. This typically involves using the *Web Service Definition Language (WSDL)* to let the consumer know what methods were available. From there, they'd query it and likely use a tool to automate referencing the service. In the .NET world, the toolset would look at the metadata and build a proxy class that handled all the network communication. The proxy class would typically be written in C# or VB.NET and, once generated, the developer would use it just like any other class.

OData

OData is an abbreviated form of the name Open Data Protocol. OData.org describes OData in the following way:

> The Open Data Protocol (OData) is a Web protocol for querying and updating data that provides a way to unlock your data and free it from silos that exist in applications today. OData does that by applying and building upon Web Technologies such as HTTP, Atom Publishing Protocol (AtomPub) and JSON to provide access to information from a variety of applications, services and stores. The protocol emerged from experiences implementing AtomPub clients and servers in a variety of products over the past several years. OData is being used to expose and access information from a variety of sources including, but not limited to, relational database, file systems, content management systems and traditional websites.
>
> OData is consistent with the way the Web works—it makes a deep commitment to URIs for resource identification and commits to an HTTP-based, uniform interface for interacting with those resources (just like the Web). This commitment to core Web principles allows OData to enable a new level of data integration and interoperability across a broad range of clients, servers, services, and tools.

JSON

According to json.org, *JSON* is described as follows:

> JSON (JavaScript Object Notation) is a lightweight data-interchange format. It is easy for humans to read and write. It is easy for machines to parse and generate... These properties make JSON an ideal data-interchange language.

JSON is easy to use and consume. It is built on two fundamental mechanisms:

- **A name/value pair of data**   You have a name that you reference it by and a value that corresponds to that name.
- **An ordered list of values**   The list can take just about any form and serves as a container or collection to hold the name/value pairs.

Because JSON is little more than text, there are no proprietary file formats to deal with, it is straightforward, and it lends itself well to the mechanisms that comprise WCF Data Services.

WCF Data Services as data access mechanisms

Because Microsoft moved its original Web Services implementation (*.asmx*) to WCF, service names now end in the .svc extension. WCF is powerful and provides features well beyond what will be discussed here, but for the time being, it is worth it to understand that, underlying it all, the name was originally ADO.NET Data Services and has since been changed to WCF Data Services. Despite this change in name, the underlying technology is still much the same in that it intends to be a data access mechanism.

In a typical scenario, you build a WCF Data Service by performing the following steps:

1. Create an ASP.NET Web Application.

2. Use the EF to define an EDM.

3. Add a Data Service to the Web Application (which is there just to host the application and expose it over the web).

4. Enable access to the service.

Why choose WCF Data Services?

WCF Data Services has advantages and disadvantages. Because it uses the EF as a foundation, most (but not all) scenarios that were appropriate for one would be appropriate for the other. WCF Data Services would be overkill for simple one-user scenarios. On the other hand, it provides several out-of-the-box benefits that ADO.NET and the EF do not. These include the following:

- Because data is exposed, when using OData, resources are addressable via URIs. That alone makes it very nonproprietary and opens the service up to be consumed by everyone from Microsoft developers, to folks writing apps for iPhones, and everyone in between.

- WCF Data Services are accessed over HTTP, and almost everyone is familiar with HTTP these days and has access to it. Someone can literally query your application and get data back without having to write a single line of code.

- OData feeds can take several different forms, including Atom, JSON, or XML. All those formats can be represented as text, so many problems with firewalls, security, installing applications, and so forth immediately disappear.

- Very powerful queries can be constructed with very simple semantics. Without knowing SQL, someone would have a hard time returning all the Customers from your in-house database, let alone returning a customer with the last name of Doe.

In SQL, they'd have to have a specific toolset, know the connection information to your database, and then write something like "SELECT * FROM Customers WHERE LastName = 'Doe' (and yes, in a production app the = 'Doe' should be parameterized, but this is just for the sake of illustration). To do the same with WCF Data Services, all they'd need to do is enter *http://my company uri/MyApplication/MyService.svc/Customers* in the address bar of Internet Explorer to get a list of all the customers. To return the exact equivalent of what was shown before, they'd simply need to make one small change: *http://my company uri/MyApplication/MyService.svc/Customers('Doe')*.

To take full advantage of WCF Data Services, the EF is meant to be used. But the EF can get its data from just about anywhere, and the tooling support makes it very easy to swap out or modify underlying data sources.

WCF Data Services provide a feature known as *Interceptors*. Interceptors enable you to build in quite sophisticated business logic, as you'll see when you build a WCF Data Service.

Thought experiment
Dealing with legacy issues

In the following thought experiment, apply what you learned about the "Choosing a data access technology" objective to determine the data access strategy for new application development at your company. You can find answers to these questions in the "Answers" section at the end of this chapter.

Contoso has several applications that currently use ADO.NET to interact with the database. Each application used to run locally inside the corporate network. Now, there's tremendous pressure to expose many of them to the outside world. You're tasked with deciding whether ADO.NET should continue to be used or whether a move should be made to another technology. If a move away from ADO.NET is made, you need to decide which other technology should be used.

With this in mind, answer the following questions:

1. Should you continue building applications with ADO.NET?

2. Does using the EF provide any benefit toward the stated goal that ADO.NET doesn't?

3. Would WCF Data Services provide any benefit toward the stated goal that ADO.NET doesn't?

Objective summary

1. ADO.NET has been around the longest and has several advantages. It does not require persistent connections to the underlying data store, enables you to access virtually all major database implementations, and enables you to access data through custom objects or through objects specifically suited to the tasks at hand (DataSet and DataTable).

2. By using the EF, developers can focus on the conceptual model (solving business logic and dealing with business issues) without being overly concerned with the underlying data store. EF is specifically focused on working with an entity, but not quite as much as working with bulk data all at once.

3. With EF, the underlying data stores can be easily modified and changed without requiring changes of the client code. The EF enables you to generate models based on an existing database schema, or it can work in reverse and build a database schema based on a conceptual model. Both are supported and quite easy to learn and use.

4. WCF Data Services let your applications provide universal data access. The consumption of WCF Data Services is not tied to any proprietary technology, so can be consumed by both Microsoft and non-Microsoft technologies. WCF Data Services are meant to be used in conjunction with the EF on the back end. They provide a very fast and easy way to build applications and make the data easily accessible to any consumer.

Objective review

Answer the following questions to test your knowledge of the information in this objective. You can find the answers to these questions and explanations of why each answer choice is correct or incorrect in the "Answers" section at the end of this chapter

1. You are building an ADO.NET EF application. You need to add a property of type NVARCHAR(50) named Notes to the underlying database table named Customer and have it reflected in the Customer entity. What should you do?

    A. Drop the Customer table and re-create it with the new field; then choose the Generate Database From Model option.

    B. Add the field to the underlying table, add a Scalar property of type String to the Customer entity, and update the mapping.

    C. Run the Update Model Wizard.

    D. Run the EDM Generator.

2. You have been asked to choose a data access technology to retrieve data from a SQL Server database and have it exposed over the web. The application will be consumed exclusively by external parties that have no access to the internal database. Which data access technologies should you recommend? (Choose all that apply.)

   A. LINQ-to-SQL

   B. ADO.NET Entity Framework

   C. WCF Data Services

   D. ADO.NET Data Services

3. You are working with an EDM and suspect there's a problem with the mappings. Which file should you look at to see the underlying code?

   A. CSDL file

   B. SSDL file

   C. MSL file

   D. EDMX file

Objective 1.2: Implement caching

The way applications are used and the corresponding demands have changed in just the last few years. Users are much more demanding, less tolerant of inconveniences, and much more concerned about performance. It is commonly mentioned that if users have to wait more than five seconds for a page to load, they will typically leave the page.

Just try to imagine how many users an application like Bing has, and imagine what would happen if Bing kept open connections to the underlying databases for each user. There are several techniques that have been developed to deal with such issues, but one of the most effective ones is caching. Some data (for instance, stock quotes) needs to be the absolute latest every time it is accessed in some applications. Other data, such as a list of states that populates a combo box control, seldom changes and needs to be accessed rarely after initially retrieved.

If used effectively, data caching can greatly enhance responsiveness and provide a much better user experience. However, it must be used carefully. To see why, simply imagine a hospital's patient management system. During intake, the patient is unconscious, but the staff can get much of what it needs from information in the patient's wallet. They enter the data and assume that it is immediately cached and updated only every 12 hours. Imagine then that a member of the patient's family arrives and informs the staff that the patient is a Type 1 diabetic and has several medical allergies. If this information isn't immediately reflected in the application, the patient could end up facing severe consequences because doctors made decisions based on stale information.

Understanding caching options

There are several caching mechanisms you need to be familiar with for the exam. The first is the ObjectCache class. Although there are several different ways to cache data via the .NET Framework, not to mention your own or custom approaches, for the exam you should focus on the ObjectCache and the HttpContext.Cache items in particular. ASP.NET (which is not the specific target of this exam, but has aspects that might be covered) has Application State, Session State, and View State, all of which can be considered caching mechanisms. Outside of specific mechanisms, items such as DataSets, DataTables, or serializable business objects can all be serialized and therefore be considered cached in such a state. Finally, classes and properties (and methods, for that matter) can all be defined as static, which can have the effective result of providing cache functionality. For this portion of the exam, you should focus on the ObjectCache and its features, as well as HttpContext.Cache. Although many different items and technologies might qualify semantically as a cache, this chapter looks at those features built specifically to address caching needs.

> *NOTE* **WINDOWS AZURE–PROVIDED CACHING OPTIONS**
>
> Although this version of the exam does not require you know the caching options available specifically in Windows Azure, you certainly should be aware of them. These options will certainly be on future versions of the exam! You currently have two primary options: *Shared or Co-Located Caching* and *Dedicated Caching*.
>
> With Co-Located Caching, Windows Azure takes a sliver of your Web Role or Worker Role instance's resources (memory being one of the most important resources) and uses that to store the cached data. The value here is that you don't have to pay for anything extra in terms of price; it is just a slight performance hit. If your cache needs to store only a few MB of data, this is a very good option.
>
> With Dedicated Caching, you add a new role type to your project, a Cache Worker Role, which results in an instance whose entire purpose in life is to manage and host the cache. The benefits are that you can easily manage the number of these instances independent of other instances, and hosting very large amounts of cached data doesn't directly affect performance on your other servers or your application.

Using the ObjectCache

To put data into the ObjectCache, it first needs to be created. The current constructor is protected, so it isn't instantiated using the new keyword. Instead, you use the MemoryCache. Default property to get an instance.

Conveniently, the ObjectCache class alone provides nearly all the functionality for caching. Outside of the Extension methods, it is simple to memorize all its properties (there are four). Depending on the version of the .NET Framework being used, there are about 10 methods, and most of them have names used extensively throughout the Framework, so they are dead giveaways as to what they do. When you exclude methods that have unquestionably clear features (for example, GetEnumerator and GetCount), you're left with Add, AddOrGetExisting, Get, and Set. Some classes, particularly those that inherit from powerful base classes, have large numbers of extension methods, or implement multiple interfaces, and won't be so easy to memorize by just looking at a few code snippets, but many classes will. So when preparing for this exam, look at the following code samples to get a visual understanding of how things work and what the most commonly used major features are.

Very simple ObjectCache example

```
[TestCase("Cache1", 1)]
[TestCase("Cache1", 2)]
[TestCase("Cache1", 3)]
public void CanCache(string key, int value)
{
    // ARRANGE
    ObjectCache cache = MemoryCache.Default;
    var policy = new CacheItemPolicy
    {
        AbsoluteExpiration = new DateTimeOffset(DateTime.Now.AddMinutes(1))
    };

    // ACT
    cache.Remove(key);
    cache.Add(key, value, policy);
    int fetchedValue = (int)cache.Get(key);

    // ASSERT
    Assert.That(fetchedValue, Is.EqualTo(value), "Uh oh!");
}
```

This code example has various numbers in the cache for up to one minute. Notice that it first removes the item from cache. If the item isn't in cache, this gracefully fails and continues; you can never be guaranteed that an item is in a cache at any moment in time, even if you just checked for it 3 ms ago. You remove it because the second time this test runs, the item from the first run will still be in there. The way the Add method works in this case is that it calls the underlying AddOrGetExisting method (more on this later), so it doesn't actually replace an existing value when used this way. Try the tests again, but delete the line calling Remove and see what happens.

After you create an instance of the cache and put items in it, you can verify the existence of those items by using the default indexer on the ObjectCache and the string value you chose as a key whenever you added the item. Assume, for instance, that you added a string value that was the PublicKeyValue of an encryption key. The following code tells you whether the item was in the ObjectCache (using the as keyword enables you to attempt the reference without throwing an exception if the item is not present). You don't have to use this technique specifically, but you will want to verify that something exists in the cache before trying to reference it just like as would with any other collection.

Safely checking cached items

```
String encryptionPublicKey = CacheInstance["encryptionpublickey"] as String;
if (String.IsNullOrWhiteSpace(encryptionPublicKey))
{
    // Build encryption policy here and cache it.
}
```

There are several mechanisms for adding items into the CacheInstance:

- Add(CacheItem, CacheItemPolicy)
- Add(String key, Object value, DateTimeOffset absoluteExpiration)
- Add(String key, Object value, CacheItemPolicy policy, String regionName)
- AddOrGetExisting(CacheItem, CacheItemPolicy)
- AddOrGetExisting(String key, Object value, DateTimeOffset absoluteExpiration)
- AddOrGetExisting(String key, Object value, CacheItemPolicy policy, String regionName)
- Set(CacheItem, CacheItemPolicy)
- Set(String key, Object value, CacheItemPolicy policy, String regionName)

As noted, the items in the cache are stored as key/value pairs. When examining the overloads for the Add and AddOrGetExisting methods, overloads support both entering in a key/value pair or a CacheItem. The three primary properties in the CacheItem base class are, unsurprisingly, Key, Value, and RegionName. If you examine each of the overloads for Add or AddOrGetExisting, you'll note that they're functionally equivalent in the sense that you can use a Key to reference the item, or you can use a CacheItem to reference it, which in turn, provides the Key, and, if desired, the Value and RegionName. The cache implementation is allowed to store the cached data in any internal format it wants. The only restrictions are that the APIs provide that the data is represented in CacheItem objects, not that those CacheItem objects are actually stored internally.

It's worth noting that many of these are functional equivalents. For instance, according to the MSDN documentation, the Add method that uses a CacheItem and CacheItemPolicy as parameters does the following: When overridden in a derived class, it tries to insert a cache entry into the cache as a CacheItem instance and adds details about how the entry should be evicted. It describes the equivalent Set method as follows: When overridden in a derived class, it inserts the cache entry into the cache as a CacheItem instance, specifying information about how the entry will be evicted.

The main differences between the two reside in the return types. With the Add method, a value of True is returned if no item with that key was present and the insertion was successful. When a value of False is returned, there is no need to add it because it already exists, so insertion of the value actually failed. Internally, the Add method actually calls the AddOrGet Existing method.

The Set method has no return value, and if the key is not present, it inserts the value. If the key is present, it is updated with the value from the CacheItem parameter. In the previous test case, Set would have been a more appropriate method to use, but would have missed showing this very important point. You should review these on MSDN if they aren't immediately intuitive, but they each work the same way. The only real nuance is setting the CacheItem-Policy, which is also quite straightforward.

CacheItemPolicy

Using a CacheItemPolicy is simple. Once you instantiate an instance of it, you'll then want to set an expiration policy by using either an AbsoluteExpiration or a SlidingExpiration. The difference between the two is apparent to most. With the AbsoluteExpiration, the CacheItem is purged after a specified amount of time. With the SlidingExpiration, it is purged only if it has not been accessed after a specified amount of time. Using either mechanism is simply a matter of determining which one you want to use and picking an interval to use in conjunction with it.

The previous test used an AbsoluteExpiration; the following test shows a SlidingExpiration in action:

SlidingExpiration

```
[TestCase("Sliding1", 1)]
[TestCase("Sliding2", 2)]
[TestCase("Sliding3", 3)]
public void TestSlidingExpiration(string key, int value)
{
    // ARRANGE
    ObjectCache cache = MemoryCache.Default;
    CacheItemPolicy policy = new CacheItemPolicy
    {
        SlidingExpiration = new TimeSpan(0, 0, 2)
    };
    cache.Set(key, value, policy);

    // ACT
    for (var i = 0; i < 22; i++)
    {
        System.Threading.Thread.Sleep(100);
        Assume.That(cache.Get(key), Is.EqualTo(value));
    }
    System.Threading.Thread.Sleep(2001);

    // ASSERT
    Assert.That(cache.Get(key), Is.Null, "Uh oh!");
}
```

CacheItemPriority

Both the System.Web.Caching and System.Runtime.Caching namespaces have a CacheItem-Priority Enumeration that dictates the order of item removal from the cache. Both of these will be discussed because they might appear on the exam, but it's important to know the difference between them and that they are not the same enumeration even if they share the same name, same function, and many other characteristics. For now, the focus is on the System.Runtime.Caching namespace.

If no value is specified for the CacheItemPriority, the default value of Default is used. A value of Default means that there is No Priority. Although trying to memorize every member and every property of everything covered on the exam would be a challenging undertaking, memorizing each of the possible values of this version of the CacheItemPriority and the resulting behavior is so simple that I highly recommend doing so. See Table 1-2 to see each of the available values and what happens as a result of using the value.

TABLE 1-2 System.Runtime.Caching.CacheItemPriority enumeration value

Item name	Description
Default	There is no priority for removing this entry. As noted previously, this is the default value for the enumeration, so unless your intent is to make your code's intention clear, there's no value in setting this property and using this value.
Not Removable	Specifies that this entry should never be removed from the cache.

If you're thinking that the only two options seem to be to set no priority at all or set the priority in a way that ensures it's never automatically removed, you're correct.

One common source of confusion regarding CacheItemPriority (both the System.Runtime. Caching and the System.Web.Caching version) is that, by setting it, you could somehow create a situation in which the item can never be removed after it is inserted into the cache. That is not the case. Each version of the cache has methods specifically created for the removal of items from the cache. These values simply dictate the order of importance of the Cache Items when resources are low and the runtime needs to clean things up in order to continue processing.

Setting the value to NotRemovable can have very serious consequences, and you should clearly understand what they are before using this value. Setting the value to Default simply specifies that all CacheItems should be treated equally when a decision needs to be made to purge them because the system is getting low on resources. Striking the correct balance here is important because it is much better to take a painful database hit that causes an operation to be slow or even time out when the alternative is that the application crashes due to insufficient memory.

It is easy to overuse caching. There are many items that are clear candidates for caching and others that should almost never be placed into a cache. This determination is not always an easy one to make before an application goes to production with respect to each item you might choose to place in cache. Although this can be debated, it is often best to err on the side of not caching a particular set of data until you have the metrics necessary to prove that the data should be cached for performance reasons and can be done so without negatively affecting functionality.

If you choose the NotRemovable option, it is critical that you effectively monitor the object you're dealing with and take steps to ensure its removal from the cache explicitly. As previously mentioned, CacheItemPriority has no bearing on whether something can be removed manually; it simply prevents system optimization operations for purging it when trying to free up resources. If it stopped such removals from happening, anything put into cache with a CacheItemPriority would exist in cache for the life of the session, no matter what else happened. If you do not watch the items you marked as NotRemovable, you could easily find yourself in a situation in which the application's resources are completely consumed and it has no means by which to free up enough of them to keep functioning correctly.

The ChangeMonitor class

In addition to understanding the expiration policy, you need to be aware of the ChangeMonitor class, which the CacheItemPolicy has a collection of. If you refer to my example about the hospital intake application, it's quite obvious that, if the underlying data source changes, the cache needs to know about it. If it doesn't, there will be latency and a potential for very serious problems in many applications.

Although you don't use the ChangeMonitor class directly, it's a base class that has several derivations (and other ones can certainly be added):

- CacheEntryChangeMonitor
- FileChangeMonitor
- HostFileChangeMonitor
- SqlChangeMonitor

The CacheEntryChangeMonitor serves as a base class to build derived classes from that simply monitor the CacheItems for changes.

The FileChangeMonitor does exactly what its name implies: It monitors a specific file to see whether any changes are made to it, and, if so, the changes will be reflected in the cache, provided the CacheItemPolicy dictates it.

The HostFileChangeMonitor monitors directories and file paths for changes to them. If it detects changes, it responds accordingly. Because files and directories are fundamentally different from the other items, there are several specific items this class handles that you don't necessarily need to memorize for the exam, but should at least be familiar with. Each of the following triggers a change notification if a HostFileChangeMonitor is being used:

- The name of the monitored file or directory changed.
- The specified file or directory did not exist at the time the monitor was created, but was created later. In other words, a file or directory was created in the scope of the monitored items.
- The size of a monitored file changed.
- The contents of a monitored file changed, or the contents of a monitored directory changed.
- The *access control list (ACL)* of the file or directory changed.
- The monitored file or directory was deleted.

Using the HttpContext.Cache

ASP.NET applications (which are frequently used to host WCF Data Services) natively provide several different caching mechanisms. Because HTTP is a stateless protocol, state management is more of a challenge than it would be for a technology that used a different underlying protocol. In ASP.NET, you can use Application State, Session State, and View State to store values and thereby minimize roundtrips to the database. Each has strengths and weaknesses, and decisions about which to use should be undertaken carefully. Additionally, there are several options with regard to those features on what backing store can be used to host the data.

Because ASP.NET and applications hosted in Internet Information Server, for example, communicate using the HTTP protocol, it should come as no surprise that such applications are built in a way to include an HttpContext. The Cache class resides in the System.Web library and the System.Web.Caching namespace specifically. In a typical ASP.NET web application or service that's hosted in ASP.NET, the cache is accessed through the HttpContext.Current object. (The Page object also has a Page.Cache property and a Page.Context.Cache property; there are multiple ways to get to the Cache object.)

One of the most important things to understand about the Cache class is that it was built specifically for use with ASP.NET applications. If you need caching functionality in another type of application (for instance, a Windows Forms application), you should specifically use the ObjectCache class instead. (This might seem obvious, but more than a few developers have tried to add the System.Web.dll reference to Winforms apps or similar application types just so they could use the Cache feature.)

The following code snippet could certainly be added to a Console or Winforms application (provided that a reference to System.Web were added), but if you tried to execute it, it would result in a Null Reference Exception (and should be used only as an example of what *not* to do):

```
[Test]
public void BadCaching()
{
    // ARRANGE
    System.Web.Caching.Cache myCache = new System.Web.Caching.Cache();

    // ACT
    // ASSERT
    Assert.Throws<NullReferenceException>(() => myCache.Insert("asdf", 1));
}
```

If you want to pursue things that won't work and that you shouldn't do, you can try to add an HttpContext instance to a Winforms or Console app and then try to get the caching to work using it. The System.Web.Caching.Cache is meant to be used only with ASP.NET applications, not with other types of applications.

EXAM TIP

When taking the exam, you might see questions that specifically reference the HttpContext.Cache (or Page.Cache or some other similar form) directly. Such a question might be: "Datum Corporation has an application that's currently caching several collections of data in the HttpContext.Cache object. You need to _____. How should you do it?" In such cases, you can and should make the assumption that the application is an ASP.NET application or a WCF Data Service hosted inside of ASP.NET. Everything else that makes reference to caches (from determining what mechanism should be used the whole way to specific implementations) should be assumed to be referencing the ObjectCache unless specifically stated otherwise.

Another noteworthy item is that this class is created only once per AppDomain. Once created, it remains alive (even if it's empty) as long as the AppDomain is still active. There are several ways to add data to it, retrieve data from it, and control other aspects of its behavior, so let's go through them one at a time.

Cache items are implemented as name/value pairs where the name is implemented as System.String and the value is implemented as System.Object. You can put any serializable object in the cache (whether you should is a different decision altogether).

Abbreviated System.Web.Caching.Cache usage

The actual cache discussed is a property of HttpContext. You can refer to it directly as Cache["Key"] instead of HttpContext.Cache["Key"], which is done for the sake of readability.

In its simplest form, you reference the cache, provide a key name, and give it a value:

```
Cache["FullNameKey"] = "John Q. Public";
```

This works in a manner reminiscent of View State or Session State. If there is already a key defined in the collection with the same name, the value you specify overwrites it. If no such key/value pair exists already, it simply adds it. Because the value part of the equation is typed as System.Object, you can set the value to just about anything.

In addition to the Add method, you can use the Insert method, which has several overloads; the simplest needs only a Key and a Value:

```
HttpContext.Current.Cache.Insert("AccountIdKey", new Account());
```

Table 1-3 shows each of the Cache.Insert overloads.

TABLE 1-3 Cache.insert overloads

Name	Description
Insert(String Key, Object Value)	Inserts an item into the cache with the corresponding key name and Object Value. The CacheItemPriority enumeration value is set to its default value, Normal.
Insert(String Key, Object Value, CacheDependency dependencyItem)	Inserts an item into the cache with the corresponding key name and Object Value that has file dependencies, key dependencies, or both.
Insert(String Key, Object Value, CacheDependency dependencyItem, DateTime absoluteExpiration, TimeSpan slidingExpiration)	Inserts an item into the cache with the corresponding key name and Object Value. This overload also includes file or key dependencies and expiration policies. When setting expiration policies, either the NoAbsoluteExpiration or NoSlidingExpiration predetermined value must be passed for the expiration policy not being used.

Name	Description
Insert(String Key, Object Value, CacheDependency dependency-Item, DateTime absoluteExpira-tion, TimeSpan slidingExpiration, CacheItemUpdateCallback updateCall-back).	Inserts an item into the cache with the corresponding key name and Object Value. This overload includes key or file dependencies as well as expiration policies. It also includes a delegate object that can provide notification before an item is removed from the Cache collection.
Insert(String Key, Object Value, CacheDependency dependencyItem, DateTime absoluteExpiration, TimeSpan slidingExpiration, CacheItemPriority pri-ority, CacheItemRemovedCallback rem-oveCallback).	Inserts an item into the cache with the corresponding key name and Object Value. This overload includes key or file dependencies as well as expiration policies. It also includes a delegate object that can provide notification that the inserted item is removed from the Cache collection.

The initial example showed how to use the simplest method to add an item to the cache. The second showed an example of using the Insert method and provided a list of overloads and their corresponding signatures. Figure 1-7 shows the signature of the Add method of the cache.

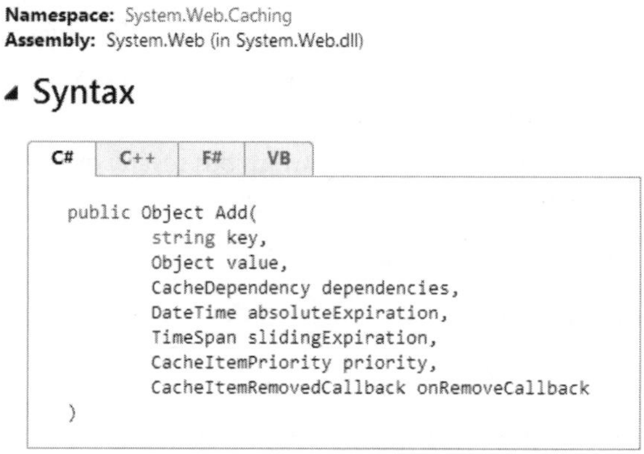

Namespace: System.Web.Caching
Assembly: System.Web (in System.Web.dll)

◢ Syntax

```
C#    C++    F#    VB

public Object Add(
        string key,
        Object value,
        CacheDependency dependencies,
        DateTime absoluteExpiration,
        TimeSpan slidingExpiration,
        CacheItemPriority priority,
        CacheItemRemovedCallback onRemoveCallback
    )
```

FIGURE 1-7 System.Web.Caching.Cache Add signature

If you compare Add to the last version of the Insert method, you should notice quite a few similarities. In fact, they are virtually identical in just about every regard. For something to be added to the cache, you need a Key and a Value at a minimum.

If there are either file dependencies or dependencies to other cache keys, they are handled via the CacheDependency parameter. It's worth a quick digression to mention this. Although there are several overloaded constructors for a CacheDependency, it is safe to describe them collectively as definitions for dependencies related to both cache keys and files (well, files or directories).

So the Insert method, just like the most comprehensive version of the Add method, ac-cepts a string name for the Key, an object for the Value, CacheDependencies if they are to be included, a DateTime value that indicates an AbsoluteExpiration DateTime, a TimeSpan pa-rameter to indicate how much time should elapse without an object being accessed before it is removed from the cache, a CacheItemPriority value to indicate where the given object falls on the removal hierarchy, and finally a delegate that can be used to notify the application if/when the corresponding CacheItem was removed.

In the final analysis, the only real difference between the two methods involves Update-Callback in the Insert method as opposed to CacheItemRemovedCallback employed in the Add method. They seem to be the same, so what's the noteworthy differentiator?

RemoveCallback (whose type is System.Web.Caching.CacheItemRemovedCallback) is called when an object is removed from the cache. UpdateCallback (whose type is System.Web.Caching.CacheItemUpdateCallback) executes a notification right before an object is removed from the cache. The behavioral difference can be exploited so that the cached item is updated and can be used to prevent the item from being removed from the cache. It's a subtle difference and one that you don't typically find necessary in many applications. Much of the time, when an item is removed from the cache, it is done so intentionally. However, expiration policy can cause objects to be removed from a cache without someone intentionally trying to remove it. Coupled with CacheItemPriority, scenarios can definitely be presented in which an item might be removed from cache contrary to the initial intention. When an item is different from others in terms of being automatically removed from the cache or when you need to be careful that it isn't removed (perhaps because retrieval of the object is quite expensive or resource-intensive), you might want to fine-tune behavior using the CacheItemUpdateCallback as opposed to the CacheItemRemovedCallback.

As mentioned earlier, both the System.Web.Caching and System.Runtime.Caching namespaces have a CacheItemPriority Enumeration that dictates the order of item removal from the cache. Although the one in the System.Runtime.Caching namespace is limited in what it provides, the one in the System.Web.Caching namespace affords a granular level of behavioral control.

The values of the enumeration are mostly self-explanatory because they do exactly what you expect, but Table 1-4 provides each available value and a description of the corresponding behavior. Just note that, although CacheItemPriority.Default was the behavior in System.Runtime.Caching version, a value of CacheItemPriority.Normal is the default value of the System.Web.Caching CacheItemPriority. Oddly enough, CacheItemPriority.Default here actually sets it to a Normal priority.

TABLE 1-4 System.Web.Caching.CachItemPriority enumeration values

Member	Description
Low	The lowest priority and therefore the first to be removed if the system starts removing items to free resources.
BelowNormal	The second least critical indicator of the enumeration. Only items marked as Low have lower priority.
Normal	The midpoint of what the system will remove. Lower in priority than High and AboveNormal, and more important than Low and BelowNormal.

Member	Description
AboveNormal	These items are considered less important than those specified as High, but more important than those specified as Normal.
High	These items are considered the most important and are the last to be removed when the system attempts to free memory by removing cached items.
NotRemoveable	Although this value stops something from being removed when resources are needed, it does not interfere with either the Absolute or Sliding expiration defined in the policy.
Default	Sets the value to Normal.

Using the CacheDependency class enables you to monitor and respond to a wide variety of changes to underlying objects. In most cases, you'll find that the CacheDependency can handle your needs quite well. If you are caching data that is sourced from a SQL Server database (versions 7.0, 2000, 2005, and later are supported), you can use the SqlCacheDependency class. SqlCacheDependency monitors the underlying table that the data originally came from. If any changes are made to the table, the items added to the Cache are removed, and a new version of the item is added to the cache.

To create a SqlCacheDependency, you can use either of two overloads:

1. You provide a SqlCommand instance. This initializes a new instance of the SqlCacheDependency class and, coupled with the command, creates a cache-key dependency.

2. You provide two strings. The first string is the name of the database defined in the databases element of the application's web.config file. The second string is the name of the table that the SqlCacheDependency will be associated with.

As you can imagine, creating such a dependency carries overhead and is laden with nuances that you need to be aware of. It is rare that you'll run into a situation in which some item outside of your application dictates what constructor must be used, but there are several "gotchas" related to the SqlCacheDependency in general. For instance, the version of SQL Server that's being used can dictate which constructor must be used.

It's worth noting that the baggage that comes with using the SqlCacheDependency is so significant that many consider it too substantial to justify the benefits. If you read through the MSDN documentation combined with what I call out in the following list, you'll find that there are many requirements that come with using the SqlCacheDependency, and a tremendous number of things need to be in place in order for it to be used correctly. If you know all of them, you know that there are several things that can result in not being able to use SqlCacheDependency for an application. Knowing these can certainly help you eliminate possible choices when it comes to answering test questions:

- The constructor that takes SqlCommand as a parameter is the one that should be used if you are using SQL Server 2005 or later. The fact that different constructors are supposed to be used based on the underlying database version is quite inconvenient in theory, but in practice most companies have at least migrated to SQL Server 2005 by now.

- With the SqlCommand-based constructor, two exceptions can be encountered: the ArgumentNullException and the HttpException. The first arises if you pass in a Sql-Command value that's null. This should come as no surprise because, without a valid command, it is impossible to determine what source the data came from. The second exception, however, is a little strange. It happens only when the SqlCommand passed to the constructor has the NotificationAutoEnlist value set to true *and* the @Output-Cache directive is set on the page and it has a SqlDependency attribute value set to CommandNotification.

- Table names that are used in the CommandText property of SqlCommand must include the name of the table owner. So if your initial query's command text were "SELECT FirstName, LastName FROM Customer," the association would not work. If you use the same query but change the last portion to "... FROM dbo.Customer," the association should work if everything else is in place.

- Although using "SELECT *" is generally considered a poor practice from a performance perspective, using it actually breaks the functionality provided by the SqlCacheDependency. Using the previous query as an example, "SELECT * FROM dbo. Customer" would result in a failure.

- If page-level output caching is enabled on the page, this first constructor does not perform the association.

Although it might seem like this constructor carries with it a rather large number of requirements, those pale in comparison to the requirements and issues that surround the use of the second constructor:

- When using the second constructor, six different exceptions can be encountered (as opposed to just two when using the first one). These include HttpException, Argument Exception, ConfiguationErrorsException, DatabaseNotEnabledForNotificationsException, TableNotEnabledForNotificationsException, and ArgumentNullException. Table 1-5 provides a list of each of the exceptions and all the conditions that can trigger them.

- The connectionString that contains the table that the SqlCacheDependency is enabled for must be specifically included in the <connectionStrings> section of the web.config file of the ASP.NET application.

- The SQL Server database specified in the databaseEntryName parameter must have notifications enabled.

- The table specified in the tableName parameter must have notifications enabled as well.

- You cannot set monitoring up on multiple tables with one SqlCacheDependency. DataSets and most EF models make frequent use of related tables, and it seldom makes sense to cache a parent table and not any of the related tables. If you need this functionality, set up separate dependencies for each of the tables you are querying against and write application logic to deal the changes at each level in many cases. Suppose you have an Accounts table and a related AccountDetails table. If you wanted to implement a caching strategy, you'd probably want to cache both the Account information and the corresponding AcccountDetails information as well. At some point, however, any benefit realized by caching is offset by the overhead associated with the additional code required for cache monitoring. Finding that point is not always obvious and is often difficult.

TABLE 1-5 Exceptions related to second SqlCacheDependency constructor

Name	Description
HttpException	SqlClientPermission was not present or did not allow the operation access required. The DatabaseEntryName was not found in the list of databases. SqlCacheDependency could not make a connection to the configured database when the instance was initialized. The configured account lacked the permissions (either on the database or the stored procedures used internally to support SqlCacheDependency).
ArgumentException	The TableName parameter used to create the dependency association has a value of String.Empty.
ArgumentNullException	DatabaseEntryName passed in to the constructor was null. The TableName parameter used to create the dependency association was null. (Yes, this is different than if the parameter were an empty string.)
ConfigurationErrorsException	SqlCacheDependency does not have Polling enabled. Polling is enabled, but the interval is not correctly configured. There was no connectionString matching the parameter name in the <connectionStrings> section of the configuration file. The connectionString specified in the configuration file could not be found. The connectionString specified in the configuration file contained an empty string. Although the MSDN documentation doesn't mention it specifically, if the connectionString is configured in an invalid format or can't be parsed, a ConfigurationErrorsException is thrown as well.
DatabaseNotEnabledForNotificationException	The configured database entry indicated by the databaseEntryName parameter does not have change notifications enabled.
TableNotEnabledForNotifications	The name of the table specified in the tableName parameter does not have change notifications enabled.

Using a SqlCacheDependency can be a daunting task. Spend the time to configure everything necessary to actually see SqlCacheDependency in action; doing so will certainly be educational.

Thought experiment

Develop a caching strategy

In the following thought experiment, apply what you've learned about the "Implement caching" objective to predict what steps you need to develop an effective caching strategy. You can find answers to these questions in the "Answers" section at the end of this chapter.

Contoso has determined that its primary database is experiencing tremendous traffic volumes. Upon analysis, it determines that much of the traffic is around identical requests.

With this in mind, answer the following questions:

1. What type of data would you consider as a candidate for caching?
2. What factors would you consider when determining a caching strategy?
3. What would you contemplate regarding data changes?

Objective summary

- Although caching data isn't a magic wand to fix performance problems, most applications have very obvious aspects that lend themselves well to data caching.
- ObjectCache is the primary mechanism you can use to cache data.
- The Cache property of HttpContext can be used to provide caching functionality in ASP.NET applications.
- When using ObjectCache, the two most high profile elements are ExpirationPolicy and ChangeMonitoring.
- A specific date and time can trigger cache expiration, which is known as AbsoluteExpiration. For instance, by using AbsoluteExpiration, you can wipe out the cache or remove an item from it at midnight every day, once an hour, or at whatever time makes sense.
- Expiration can be handled so that an object is removed from the cache only if it has not been accessed for a certain specified interval using SlidingExpiration. For instance, you can remove an item from the cache if it has not been accessed for two hours.

Objective review

Answer the following questions to test your knowledge of the information discussed in this objective. You can find the answers to these questions and their corresponding explanations in the "Answers" section at the end of this chapter.

1. Which of the following are provided for use by the .NET Framework as ChangeMonitors when defining a CacheItemPolicy? (Choose all that apply.)

   A. CacheEntryChangeMonitor

   B. FileChangeMonitor

   C. MsmqChangeMonitor

   D. SqlChangeMonitor

2. Which values are valid choices when defining the Priority property of the CacheItemPolicy using the System.Runtime.Caching version of the Cache? (Choose all that apply.)

   A. Normal

   B. High

   C. NotRemovable

   D. Low

3. You have set up an ObjectCache instance using the following code:

```
List<String> fileList = new List<String>();
fileList.Add(@"C:\SomeDirectory\SampleFile.txt");
ObjectCache cacheInstance = MemoryCache.Default;
CacheItemPolicy accountPolicy = new CacheItemPolicy();
accountPolicy.Priority = CacheItemPriority.Default;
accountPolicy.AbsoluteExpiration = DateTime.Now.AddMinutes(60);
accountPolicy.ChangeMonitors.Add(new HostFileChangeMonitor(fileList));
CacheItem exampleItem1 = new CacheItem("ExampleItemId", "Example Item Value",
"AccountObjects");
```

   Which of the following items add an item to the cache with a key named "ExampleItemId," a value of "Example Item Value," a region named "AccountObjects," and a CacheItemPolicy with a Default CacheItemPriority? (Choose all that apply.)

   A. cacheInstance.Add(exampleItem1, accountPolicy);

   B. cacheInstance.Add(exampleItem1, accountPolicy.Priority.Default);

   C. cacheInstance.Add("ExampleItemId", "Example Item Value", accountPolicy);

   D. cacheInstance.Add("ExampleItemId", "Example Item Value", accountPolicy, "AccountObjects");

Objective 1.3: Implement transactions

Once upon a time, flat *indexed sequential access method (ISAM)* databases ruled the world, and transactions weren't a big deal and were seldom even a concern on most developers' minds. Today, with e-commerce booming and even traditional commerce being largely computerized, the need for transactions shows itself frequently in applications (and this should in no way imply that transactions are only relevant to commerce).

Transactions are powerful and, when used correctly, provide tremendous functionality commensurate to the effort it takes to use them. At the same time, transactions are not free in terms of resource utilization, and incorrect implementations have been the source of countless headaches for database administrators, developers, salespeople, and end users alike.

For this exam, you should be familiar with how to effectively implement a transaction with ADO.NET, the EF, and general characteristics of transactions. System.Transactions is the core namespace that facilitates generic transaction functionality. You also need at least a basic understanding of EntityTransaction (located in the System.Data.EntityClient namespace) and the SqlTransaction class.

> **This objective covers how to:**
> - Understand the characteristics of transactions
> - Implement distributed transactions
> - Specify a transaction isolation level
> - Use the TransactionScope
> - Use the EntityTransaction
> - Use the SqlTransaction

Understanding characteristics of transactions

To meet the technical criteria for a database transaction, it must be what's known as *ACID*, which is an acronym for atomic, consistent, isolated, and durable. Entire books and research papers have been written on the subject, so being an expert in transaction theory is not necessary (or even necessarily helpful) for this exam, but it will help you understand why the specific implementations that are covered on the exam operate as they do.

Although referencing Wikipedia is something that must be done with extreme caution, the content in one Wikipedia article is good. It states that transactions have two primary purposes:

> *To provide reliable units of work that allow correct recovery from failures and keep a database consistent even in cases of system failure, when execution*

stops (completely or partially) and many operations upon a database remain uncompleted, with unclear status.

To provide isolation between programs accessing a database concurrently. If this isolation is not provided, the program's outcome, are possibly erroneous.

Transactions serve to make database interactions all-or-nothing propositions. Once executed, they need to complete successfully, or they need to be completely undone and leave things exactly as they were had the change attempt not been made if they failed. If you understand that, you understand the fundamental concept of transactions.

One aspect of transactions that you probably need to know for the exam is the concept of *isolation levels*. To be of much value, one transaction needs to be kept from, or isolated from, all other transactions. SQL Server has extensive support for both transactions and isolation levels, so they are likely to appear on the exam.

The other concept that you will likely encounter is that of *simple transactions* versus *distributed transactions*. A simple transaction is the most common-use case you've probably heard of. An application attempts to insert a record into an Account table and then an Account Details table. If either fails, both should be undone, so there aren't any orphaned records or incorrectly recorded items. Simple transactions affect one database, although multiple tables might be involved. Other cases, and this is particularly relevant in today's world of large distributed networks, are distributed transactions that span multiple systems.

Implementing distributed transactions

It's not uncommon for one company to purchase software products for specific functionality that's written by different vendors. They often write an application that consolidates critical information from each system into one place or that tries to get the applications to work together. Proprietary software that wasn't designed to work with external systems was once the norm, but that time has passed, and customers increasingly find such self-serving functionality unacceptable. In these cases, transactions become important.

Imagine a system that handles front-end cash register purchases, and imagine another one that records the purchases and returns in the accounting system. If a purchase is made and successfully recorded in the register system but it fails to record the transaction in the ledger system, a problem results. If the reverse is true, it is also a serious problem.

Now imagine that you also incorporate an inventory system in the equation that automatically handles ordering things when certain thresholds are set. If this system goes down for 30 minutes, if the purchases are made and recorded correctly, and the items are accounted for in the accounting system correctly, but the inventory system has no idea any of these sales just happened, it would think that many things still existed in inventory that didn't. So it wouldn't order more of them to replenish inventory just yet. You can see how this can have serious consequences for the company.

The problem is that, in a case like this, you'd likely be dealing with three separate applications written by three separate companies, so the simple transaction model wouldn't work.

That's because in a simple transaction scenario, one database connection is used. In this case, you have three separate ones, and it's possible that those three databases aren't even of the same type. Although this in no way indicates a deficiency on the part of the developers of the System.Data.SqlClient.SqlTransaction class, it should come as little surprise that it does not provide support for an Oracle database, a Sybase database, or a CouchDB database. It doesn't mean that they aren't sufficient or couldn't be used individually on each machine, but that wouldn't do much to solve the problem at hand.

To address these scenarios, Microsoft made a significant investment in building solid tools to deal with them using distributed transactions. These tools will be discussed in depth and, outside of a limited number of questions on basic transactions, it's likely you'll see at least some questions on the exam related to distributed transactions. The core Transactions objects exist in in the System.Transactions namespace. The two other relevant ones are the System.Data.SqlClient and System.Data.EntityClient namespaces (the latter being from the System.Data.Entity assembly).

Specifying a transaction isolation level

The IsolationLevel enum is used to manage how multiple transactions interact with one another. Another way to describe it is that IsolationLevels control the locking behavior employed for the execution of a command. However, there's a problem that many developers stumble over, so let's first get this out of the way. There are actually two Isolation enums: one in System.Data.IsolationLevel and a second in System.Transaction.IsolationLevel. Just as there were two CacheItemPriority enums that generally served the same purpose, these two IsolationLevel enums generally serve the same purpose, but for two different sets of classes. Fortunately, both have the same values, so there isn't much to remember between the two other than the fact that the two exist; sometimes you need one, and other times you need the other.

EXAM TIP

The IsolationLevel enumeration values have not changed since the enumeration was introduced initially. Table 1-6 covers each of the values and what they do, but you would be well advised to learn each of these and understand them. The official documentation for each behavior is available on MSDN at the following URL: *http://msdn.microsoft.com/en-us/library/system.data.isolationlevel.aspx*. Because questions regarding IsolationLevel are very likely to appear on the exam, by understanding what each level does, you'll be able to distinguish the correct answer based on requirements mentioned in the question. You'll likely see something in a question stub indicating that you need to allow or prevent exclusive range locks or you need to ensure that users are prevented from reading data locked by other transactions. Such verbiage is a dead giveaway to which isolation level is correct.

Table 1-6 lists each value of the enumeration and describes the implications of using it according to MSDN:

TABLE 1-6 System.Data.IsolationLevel

Member	Description
Unspecified	The actual transaction level being used cannot be determined. According to MSDN, if you are using an OdbcConnection and do not set this value at all, or you do set it to Unspecified, the transaction executes according to the isolation level that is determined by the driver that is being used.
Chaos	The pending changes from more highly isolated transactions cannot be overwritten. This is not supported in SQL Server or Oracle, so it has very limited use.
ReadUncommitted	No shared locks are issued; exclusive locks are *not* honored. The important implication is that this isolation level can result in a dirty read, which is almost always undesirable.
ReadCommitted	Shared locks are held during reads. This has the result of avoiding dirty reads, unlike ReadUncommitted. However, the data can be changed before the end of the transaction, resulting in nonrepeatable reads or phantom data.
RepeatableRead	Locks are placed on all data used in the query, which completely prevents others from updating any data covered by the lock. It stops nonrepeatable reads, but the phantom data problem is still possible.
Serializable	A range lock is placed specifically on a DataSet. No one else can update the data or insert rows into the set until the transaction is completed. Although very powerful and robust, this state can cause major problems if it is not used quickly.
Snapshot	An effective copy of the data is made, so one version of the application can read the data while another is modifying the same data. You can't see data from one transaction in another one, even if you run the query again. The size of them can also cause problems if overused.

> *NOTE* **CHANGING THE ISOLATIONLEVEL DURING EXECUTION**
>
> As you look at the constructors of classes such as EntityCommand, SqlCommand, TransactionScope, and many other data classes, you'll notice they each have the ability to specify a transaction. Although there are not many use cases you'll typically run across, you might encounter a situation in which a different IsolationLevel is desired for different phases of the transaction's execution. The default IsolationLevel of one set initially remains in effect for the life of the transaction, unless it is explicitly changed. It can be changed at any time the transaction is alive. The new value takes effect at execution time, not parse time. So if the IsolationLevel is changed somewhere midstream in execution, it applies to all remaining statements.

Managing transactions by using the API from the System.Transactions namespace

The TransactionScope class was introduced in version 2.0 of the .NET Framework. It's easy to use and powerful. Other than the declaration and instantiation of it, the only thing you need to know about it is that it has a method named Complete() that you should call if you are satisfied it completed successfully. This is a key point. Calling Complete() tells the transaction manager that everything should be committed. If it isn't called, the transaction is automatically rolled back. Also, when called correctly in a using block, if an Exception is thrown during execution inside the TransactionScope, the transaction will be rolled back as well.

Here's a nonfunctional sample (connections and commands aren't what they should be) of how to use the TransactionScope in conjunction with a SqlConnection:

```
using (TransactionScope mainScope = new TransactionScope())
{
    using (SqlConnection firstConnection = new SqlConnection("First"))
    {
     firstConnection.Open();
     using (SqlCommand firstCommand = new SqlCommand("FirstQueryText", firstConnection))
        {
            Int32 recordsAffected = firstCommand.ExecuteNonQuery();
        }
        using (SqlConnection secondConnection = new SqlConnection("Second"))
        {
            secondConnection.Open();
            using (SqlCommand secondCommand = new SqlCommand("SecondQueryText",
secondConnection))
            {
                Int32 secondAffected = secondCommand.ExecuteNonQuery();
            }
        }
    }
    mainScope.Complete();
}
```

Besides its simplicity, it also has the benefit of being able to handle both simple and distributed connections and promote simple transactions to distributed ones automatically. In the previous example, a new TransactionScope was declared and instantiated. Then two SqlConnections were created inside of it and two corresponding SqlCommands. There are no exception handlers, so any exceptions result in the transaction being rolled back.

There are two important takeaways here. First, when the call to Open() is made on FirstConnection, it's created inside a simple transaction. When Open is called on SecondConnection, the transaction is escalated to a full distributed transaction. This happens automatically with no intervention on the developer's part. The second takeaway is that, in order for everything to happen correctly, the last statement, the call to Complete(), must happen before the transaction commits.

Distributed transactions are not simple in just about any regard, even if the Transaction-Scope makes it look easy. A lot has to happen in order for them to work correctly. People frequently assume that they can do anything inside a TransactionScope (such as copy files or call Web Services), and if Complete isn't called, it's all rolled back. Although Web Services can be created to support transactions, it doesn't just happen automatically. In the same respect, not all databases support transactions, so if one is being used that doesn't, there's not much that can be done about it. Another obvious example is that, if you send an e-mail in the middle of a TransactionScope, you cannot undo sending that e-mail just because you don't call Complete on your TransactionScope later.

It's doubtful that much would be covered in the exam with respect to the Transaction-Scope outside of what has been covered already: know to call Complete(), know that promotion happens automatically, know that some additional requirements are there if you want to have distributed transactions, and know that exceptions result in a rollback if you use the TransactionScope inside a using block. Focusing on those aspects is much more fruitful than trying to memorize the complete list of items supported by the distributed transaction coordinator.

Using the EntityTransaction

The main purpose of this class is to specify a transaction for an EntityCommand or to use in conjunction with an EntityConnection. It inherits from the DBTransaction base class. The EntityTransaction class has two main properties to be concerned with: the Connection property and the IsolationLevel property. It has two methods of primary concern as well: Commit() and Rollback(). There are a few other methods, such as Dispose(), CreateObjReference(), ToString(), and some others, but they are unlikely to appear on the exam.

One important note is that, when trying to implement a transaction within the EF, it isn't necessary to explicitly use the EntityTransaction class (or TransactionScope, for that matter). Look at the following code:

```
 using (TestEntities database = new TestEntities())
{
    Customer cust = new Customer();
    cust.FirstName = "Ronald";
    cust.LastName = "McDonald";
    cust.AccountId = 3;
    database.Customers.Add(cust);
    database.SaveChanges();
}
```

Although it might not be obvious (especially because this is a section on the EntityTransaction class), the SaveChanges method of the DbContext automatically operates within the context of a transaction. When the SaveChanges() method is called, each item in the current context instance is examined for its EntityState. For each record that has a status of Added, Deleted, or Modified, an attempt is made to update the underlying store corresponding to the EntityState. If any of the items can't be saved back to the source, an exception is thrown, and the transaction that the changes were executing in is rolled back.

Of course, there are times when you are using a different approach or need to explicitly manage the transactions yourself. If you are in a situation in which you are using an EntityCommand instead of the ObjectContext, you can use the EntityTransaction almost identically to the way you use the SqlTransaction: You simply create a new EntityConnection, declare a new EntityTransaction by calling BeginTransaction, and then perform your logic. Based on the results, you can choose to call the Commit method or the Rollback method.

```
using (EntityConnection connection = new EntityConnection("TestEntities"))
{
    using (EntityTransaction trans = connection.BeginTransaction(System.Data.
IsolationLevel.Serializable))
    {
        EntityCommand CurrentCommand = new EntityCommand("SOME UPDATE STATEMENT",
connection, trans);
        connection.Open();
        Int32 RecordsAffected = CurrentCommand.ExecuteNonQuery();
        trans.Commit();
    }
}
```

Using the ObjectContext and SaveChanges is usually more than sufficient for most application needs, and the TransactionScope can equally handle most cases when transactional functionality is needed. If you need to use the EntityCommand specifically, however, you can use the EntityTransaction, as shown previously.

Using the SqlTransaction

If you look at the last few paragraphs, the discussion there is virtually identical to what's covered here. The behavior of the SqlTransaction is identical; to perform the same scenario, the only things that changed were the names of the objects and their types.

You create a SqlConnection, call the BeginTransaction() method specifying an IsolationLevel, create a SqlCommand setting the CommandText Property (or Stored Procedure name and changing the CommandType property), add a SqlConnection to it, and pass in a SqlTransaction as the last parameter. Then you perform whatever action you want on the SqlCommand instance, and call Rollback or Commit when you're done, depending on the outcome of the execution.

Thought experiment
Working with transactions

In the following thought experiment, apply what you've learned about the "Implement transactions" objective to predict what steps you should take to effectively manage transactions. You can find answers to these questions in the "Answers" section at the end of this chapter.

Contoso has several mission-critical processes that are starting to cause problems. Users are reporting increasingly frequent processing errors. Additionally, there are several problems with partial or incomplete records being created. For instance, users are receiving Order Processing Failure messages and then getting tracking numbers for their order.

With this in mind, answer the following questions:

1. What would make an operation a good candidate for a transaction?

2. Why not make every operation transactional?

3. What considerations would guide the choice of transaction implementation?

Objective summary

- There are several ways to implement database transactions in the current .NET Framework, including using the EF SaveChanges method, the EntityTransaction, the SqlTransaction, and the TransactionScope.
- TransactionScope is often the quickest and easiest way to work with transactions in .NET.
- IsolationLevel is common to every form of transaction and is the one thing that has the biggest effect on transaction behavior. Its importance is often taken for granted, but it is probably the most important aspect of any transaction besides committing and rolling back.
- Transactions can take two forms: simple and distributed. You can often identify distributed transactions by seeing multiple or different types of connection objects.

Objective review

Answer the following question to test your knowledge of the information discussed in this objective. You can find the answers to this question and its corresponding explanation in the "Answers" section at the end of this chapter.

1. You are developing an ASP.NET application that reads data from and writes data to a SQL Server database. You should avoid nonrepeatable reads and not concern yourself with phantom data. Which isolation level should you use?

   A. ReadUncommitted

   B. RepeatableRead

   C. Chaos

   D. Snapshot

2. Which items would benefit from being made transactional?

   A. Long-running queries that span multiple tables

   B. Quick-running queries that involve only one table

   C. Queries that make use of the file system on a Windows operating system.

   D. Queries that make use of the file system of a non-Windows operating system.

Objective 1.4: Implement data storage in Windows Azure

You wouldn't be taking this test if you weren't at least nominally familiar with Web Services and the cloud. Windows Azure is a big area, and there are several books on it. This objective specifically relates to data storage in Windows Azure. Although learning all about other aspects of Windows Azure is great, keep focused on the fact that you are just dealing with data storage for this particular objective.

> **This objective covers how to:**
>
> - Access data storage in Windows Azure
> - Choose a data storage mechanism in Windows Azure (blobs, tables, queues and SQL Database)
> - Distribute data by using the Windows Azure Content Delivery Network (CDN)
> - Manage Windows Azure Caching
> - Handle exceptions by using retries (SQL Database)

Accessing data storage in Windows Azure

Data storage can mean a lot of things and cover a lot of areas, so let's be specific. You should make sure that you fully understand the storage options that are available and their respective strengths and weaknesses. You should understand how to read and write data using these methods. There are several other objectives in other chapters that relate to multiple other aspects of Windows Azure, but for this portion, keep focused on data storage.

Whether you're pondering it in the real world or just for the exam, when deciding about data storage in Windows Azure, it needs to be compared against something. What is that something? You can come up with all sorts of options: a USB flash drive, an SD card, a USB or SATA drive, a traditional hard drive, or all of these in a storage area network. But that's the wrong context. No one is running a production SQL Server and storing the data on a USB card. Because this is a Microsoft-specific exam, you can also rule out non-Microsoft solutions. So data storage with Windows Azure versus data storage in a Windows Server environment is what you need.

You can deduce that, if Windows Azure data storage options didn't work closely to existing mechanisms, it would greatly impede adoption. Few people have gotten fired for playing it safe and doing what always worked (although they often sit by and watch companies slowly die of attrition). Countless numbers of people have been fired for pushing some new technology that results in failure. You can be sure that a company such as Microsoft is quite aware of such dynamics. It is also aware of the fact that people focus on total cost of ownership. So any benefits from Windows Azure will be weighed against costs and compared against the existing storage solution. There's nothing Windows Azure could offer that would convince many companies to adopt it if doing so meant porting all their existing apps to a brand new storage mechanism that was totally different from what they have now. So things, for the most part, map to existing technologies quite well, and in many cases can be migrated transparently.

But everyone who has ever written software and lived through a few versions is aware of how challenging issues such as breaking changes and legacy anchors can be. It's impossible to make any substantive improvements without some risk. And sometimes you have no choice but to introduce breaking changes and end support for items. Similarly, cloud-based storage, for instance, has to have some other benefits and features other than "someone else can worry about our data." That's a verbose way of saying that, although much of what you'll encounter in Windows Azure data storage is identical to that of Windows Server storage, there are a few things that are notably different or completely new.

Finally, following are some significant concerns to be aware of when implementing data storage in Windows Azure:

- Applications ported to the Windows Azure platform are dependent on network access. Lose your Internet connection and you have problems. This is a lot different from the typical in-house application scenario, in which you can take consistent access to resources such as the database or a message queue for granted.

- If you use local storage with Windows Azure, existing code and methodologies are almost identical. It's only when you are dealing with Table and Blob storage (introduced shortly) that you see access methods different from what you're familiar with.

You are dealing with a large layer between your application and the data store. The whole reason to use cloud-based options is so you no longer have to worry about data storage or uptime of the apps; someone else does. But that doesn't magically make things always work. A *Service Level Agreement (SLA)* or Uptime Agreement might promise the mythical 5-9s, but that doesn't mean it is so. It just means you have recourse if the expectations aren't met. Just as you don't have unlimited processor utilization, you also can't take always-available Internet for granted.

Depending on how you want to count things, there are either five or three storage offerings in Windows Azure. Table 1-7 shows these offerings. You can consider Windows Azure storage as an offering, or you can consider each individual component as an offering. At the highest level, you have Local Storage, Windows Azure Storage, and SQL Database as options (three). If you count the components of each, you have Local Storage, Blob, Table, and Queue (all of which are part of Windows Azure storage), and SQL Database.

TABLE 1-7 Windows Azure platform storage options

Offering	Purpose	Capacity
Local Storage	Per-instance temporary storage	<20 GB–2 TB
Blob	Durable storage for large binary objects (audio, video, image files)	200 GB–1 TB (1 TB per page Blob, 100 TB per account)
Table	Tabular or structured data	100 TB
Queue	Items that you normally store in a Message Queue (MSMQ)	100 TB
SQL Database	Exactly what you expect: an online version of SQL Server	150 GB

Please make sure that you understand the differences between these options. There's also additional detail available at *http://social.technet.microsoft.com/wiki/contents/articles/1674. data-storage-offerings-on-the-windows-azure-platform.aspx*, which you will likely find helpful.

For the exam, it is likely that you will run into a situation in which you are given a scenario and then asked what items fit each piece of it. When you read Video, Audio, Image, it's almost certain to be a candidate for Blob storage. When it's structured data of any format, it will be Table storage or SQL Database storage if the structured data is also relational. Queue storage is typically hinted at by something along the lines of needing a guarantee of message delivery. SQL Database items should be clear enough to denote in and of themselves. That leaves Local storage. The clue to it is that it is temporary storage, it mimics your typical file system, and it is per-instance.

Choosing a data storage mechanism in Windows Azure (blobs, tables, queues and SQL Database)

At the most basic level, blobs, queues, and tables differ in the following ways:

- **Blobs** are ideally suited for unstructured binary and text data. There's nothing stopping you from breaking apart an Excel file and storing it as binary in Blob storage. There's nothing even stopping you from taking a SQL Server or Oracle data file, reading the bytes and storing it as a blob. But it makes little sense to do so because there are much better ways to store structured data (just in case you missed it, each of the aforementioned items is considered a traditional "structured" data store). In the same respect, though, storing backups or copies of these files is something you might typically consider doing. You can store structured data in Blob storage, but the cases in which you'll need or want to do it are few if any.

- **Tables** are ideally suited for storing structured but nonrelational data. If you're familiar with them, think NoSQL databases such as CouchDB or MongoDB. Suppose that you were developing a YouTube-like service that enabled users to upload videos, and you wanted to store the metadata of the video, the user, and so on. You'd typically want to store the videos in Blob storage and store the other metadata in Table storage (which might entail multiple tables or just one).

- **Queues** are essentially the Windows Azure equivalents of an MSMQ. If you're unfamiliar with Queues or MSMQ, do a quick search and become familiar with them. A queue is a First In, First Out (FIFO) data structure that can store almost anything that can be serialized. Queues are ideally suited for situations in which delivery of a message or processing of information absolutely must happen. It's similarly well suited to operations characterized by long-running processes and asynchronous jobs. There is a specific WCF Binding to use for queues that is the primary way reliable messaging is facilitated with Windows Azure.

Bindings and reliable messaging haven't been introduced yet, but if you're unfamiliar with them, an overview is provided in the following coverage.

Blob storage

Blob storage enables you to retrieve and store large amounts of unstructured data. One of the main benefits is that, once stored, the corresponding information can be accessed from anywhere using the HTTP or HTTPS protocols. If you have Internet access, you can retrieve and manipulate these items. The items you store in Blob storage can range in size up to 100 TB, although the more likely scenario is that you will deal with several smaller items.

Recall that you can store SQL Server data files or Oracle data files in Blob storage, but it makes little sense to do so because you have the option to use SQL, Windows Azure, and Table storage. At the same time, it makes perfect sense to store your backups for them in Blob storage. Why one and not the other? Because Blob storage is ideally suited to large sizes and unstructured data. The data file for a production database needs to be written to and read from constantly, whereas the backup just needs to be uploaded and accessed if and when needed. Blob storage is ideally suited for the following:

- Images that can be directly viewed in a browser
- Document storage
- Secure backups as part of a disaster recovery plan
- Streaming video and audio

The structural makeup of Blob storage needs to be discussed at this point. At the highest level, you have the storage account. Storage accounts hold containers. Containers in turn contain blobs.

At the top of the entire storage structure is the storage account. Without it, you have nothing. You'll notice that in Table 1-8, there is a 1 terabyte (TB) limit on Page Blob size, but there's a 100 TB limit on a storage account. If your data storage exceeds 100 TB, you have to handle everything notably differently than you would otherwise. If you are dealing with that much data, however, there will be some complexities and difficulties irrespective of storage mechanism. A storage account's main purpose with respect to blobs is to be a holding mechanism for containers. In practical terms, there's no limit on the number of containers that a storage account can hold (as long as they don't exceed the size limit).

Although hardly a perfect metaphor, think of a container as a subdirectory used to organize your blobs within a storage account. Although containers cannot be nested within one another, they can be used in many different ways for organizational purposes. A storage account can contain any number of containers, provided that the sum of each container's size doesn't exceed 100 TB. Containers have one essential task: to provide a logical and physical grouping for blobs.

A blob is merely a file. There are no type restrictions, so they can hold almost anything. Windows Azure has two distinct categories of blobs:

- Blocks
- Pages

Block blobs have a 200 gigabyte (GB) size limit. Page blobs, on the other hand, can store anything up to 1 TB.

You have two choices for accessing blob data. The first is that you can just reference it by URL. The structure of the URL uses the following format:

```
http://<storage account name>.blob.core.windows.net/<container>/<blob>
```

The next method involves using the API. To reference these namespaces, you have to add a project reference to the Microsoft.WindowsAzure.Storage.dll assembly. The API for Blob storage includes the following namespaces:

- Microsoft.WindowsAzure.Storage
- Microsoft.WindowsAzure.Storage.Auth
- Microsoft.WindowsAzure.Storage.Blob

Ensure that you have a storage account created within your Windows Azure subscription. The storage account is represented by the CloudStorageAccount class. It's instantiated in a few ways. First, you can use the two constructors, which work in one of two ways. The first overload takes an instance of StorageCredentials as the first argument and then a *uniform resource identifier (URI)* representing the blob endpoint, Queue endpoint, or Table endpoint, in that order. If you're using the Blob, as in this case, just leave the other values null. You do the same sort of thing if you are using just a queue or just a table. The second one works similarly: Specify an instance of the StorageCredentials and whether to use HTTPS. You need to set the values for the URIs in your code afterward or manually configure them through the Windows Azure UI:

First Blob storage upload

```
[TestCase("1234", "count.txt", "file", "INSERT YOUR ACCOUNT NAME", "INSERT YOUR KEY")]
public void UploadBlob(string fileContents, string filename, string containerName,
string accountName, string accountKey)
{
    // ARRANGE
    StorageCredentials creds = new StorageCredentials(accountName, accountKey);
    CloudStorageAccount acct = new CloudStorageAccount(creds, true);
    CloudBlobClient client = acct.CreateCloudBlobClient();
    CloudBlobContainer container = client.GetContainerReference(containerName);

    // ACT
    container.CreateIfNotExists();
    ICloudBlob blob = container.GetBlockBlobReference(filename);
    using (MemoryStream stream = new MemoryStream(Encoding.UTF8.GetBytes(fileContents)))
    {
        blob.UploadFromStream(stream);
    }

    // ASSERT
    Assert.That(blob.Properties.Length, Is.EqualTo(fileContents.Length));
}
```

A much better way to do this is using the static Parse or TryParse methods of the CloudStorageAccount. You have two choices with either approach. You can use the specific CloudConfigurationManager and call the GetSetting method, which pulls the setting from the .CSCFG file associated with your compiled Windows Azure Cloud project. Or you can use the ConfigurationManager from the System.Configuration assembly; reference the name key as a parameter; and use the ConnectionStrings property, which will pull the setting from the application's web.config or app.config file.

Following is an example that pulls the connection info from the test project's app.config file:

```
[TestCase("1234", "count.txt", "file")]
public void UploadBlobFromConfig(string fileContents, string filename, string
containerName)
{
```

```
    // ARRANGE
    CloudStorageAccount acct = CloudStorageAccount.Parse(ConfigurationManager.Connection
Strings["StorageConnection"].ConnectionString);
    CloudBlobClient client = acct.CreateCloudBlobClient();
    CloudBlobContainer container = client.GetContainerReference(containerName);

    // ACT
    container.CreateIfNotExists();
    ICloudBlob blob = container.GetBlockBlobReference(filename);
    using (MemoryStream stream = new MemoryStream(Encoding.UTF8.GetBytes(fileContents)))
    {
        blob.UploadFromStream(stream);
    }

    // ASSERT
    Assert.That(blob.Properties.Length, Is.EqualTo(fileContents.Length));
}
```

To get this to work, you need the following line in your app.config file, slightly tweaked with your settings:

```
<add name="StorageConnection" connectionString="DefaultEndpointsProtocol=https;Account
Name=ACCOUNT_NAME_GOES_HERE;AccountKey=ACCOUNT_KEY_GOES_HERE" />
```

You can, and probably should, use the TryParse method in a similar fashion. The debate between using Parse versus TryParse is out of the scope of this book.

After you build up a storage account reference, you need to create a client using the CloudBlobClient class. Next, get a container reference, ensure that it's been created, get your blob reference, and save it. Downloading blobs is just as easy when using the DownloadToStream method from the ICloudBlob object.

Remember that blobs come in two forms: Block blobs and Page blobs. As such, there's a CloudBlockBlob class and a CloudPageBlob class to represent either of them. You retrieve either of them by using the CloudBlobContainer class and calling the GetBlockBlobReference method or the GetPageBlobReference method passing in the name of the item, respectively. They both work the exact same way as the prior tests.

The next thing is how to write to a blob. Once you have a reference to a CloudBlockBlob or CloudPageBlob, you need to call the UploadFromStream method, passing in a FileStream or some other Stream reference. There are several overloads and asynchronous methods to accompany it, and it's a good idea to do a quick review of them when preparing for the exam. Uploading huge amounts of data isn't usually the fastest process in the world, so you typically should make sure that you use asynchronous methodology so you don't block the primary thread of your application.

You should wrap the call to the UploadFromStream in an exception handler and respond to any problems that you might encounter. Keep in mind that UploadFromStream overwrites data if it is already there, so that's the mechanism for updating existing blobs, too. Deleting blobs is just a matter of calling the Delete or DeleteIfExists methods of the respective items:

```
[TestCase("count.txt", "file")]
public void DeleteBlobFromConfig(string filename, string containerName)
{
    // ARRANGE
    CloudStorageAccount acct = CloudStorageAccount.Parse(ConfigurationManager.Connection
Strings["StorageConnection"].ConnectionString);
    CloudBlobClient client = acct.CreateCloudBlobClient();
    CloudBlobContainer container = client.GetContainerReference(containerName);

    // ACT
    container.CreateIfNotExists();
    ICloudBlob blob = container.GetBlockBlobReference(filename);
    bool wasDeleted = blob.DeleteIfExists();

    // ASSERT
    Assert.That(wasDeleted, Is.EqualTo(true));
}
```

All the default functionality with blobs and containers creates them in a secure manner. All the previous tests that created containers actually created private containers. However, with different settings, you can also create public containers. Likewise, you can take a private container and modify it to be publicly available.

If you want to create a public container, it can be done with the container's SetPermissions method, in which you pass in a BlobContainerPermissions object preconfigured with PublicAccess enabled. You can also distribute storage access signatures to users to give temporary access to private containers or blobs via the GetSharedAccessSignature method on either the blob or container object. If you do this, be careful about the policy you set on the shared access signature.

Table and Queue storage

Table and Queue storage APIs are similar to Blob storage APIs at a high level. To work with tables and queues, you again start with the CloudStorageAccount object to access the obvious CreateCloudTableClient and CreateCloudQueueClient methods. Unlike blobs, queues and tables are always private and have no public access capabilities, so this simplifies the API a bit.

Queues are the simpler of the two in that there is no real searching functionality. Aside from the capability to get an approximate count of items in the queue, it's mostly just a push-and-pop mechanism to get messages into or off of the queue. The only interesting aspect of working with the queue API is what happens when you get a message. The act of getting a message does not actually perform the pop for that message. In fact, it causes that message to become invisible for a period of time (it defaults to one minute, but you can also specify it). During this period of time, you're guaranteed that nobody else will retrieve this message. If it takes you longer than this time period to process the message, you should periodically update the message to keep it hidden while you continue to process it. After you finish processing the message, you should then delete the message from the queue.

Tables are a little more interesting in that you can search the data and interact with it. The main way to fetch a single record is to execute a TableOperation. However, if you want to fetch many records, use a TableQuery. Following is a test showing the lifecycle of creating a table, adding a record, fetching that record, and then deleting that record. Notice the Record class it references and how it derives the TableEntity class. This enables you to quickly and easily manage the schema of the table as well as having .NET objects that can represent the data in the tables.

```
public class Record : TableEntity
{
    public Record() : this(DateTime.UtcNow.ToShortDateString(), Guid.NewGuid().
ToString())
    { }
    public Record(string partitionKey, string rowKey)
    {
        this.PartitionKey = partitionKey;
        this.RowKey = rowKey;
    }

    public string FirstName { get; set; }
    public string LastName { get; set; }
}


[TestCase("file")]
public void UploadTableFromConfig(string tableName)
{
    // ARRANGE
    CloudStorageAccount acct = CloudStorageAccount.Parse(ConfigurationManager.Connection
Strings["StorageConnection"].ConnectionString);
    CloudTableClient client = acct.CreateCloudTableClient();
    var table = client.GetTableReference(tableName);
    Record entity = new Record("1", "asdf"){FirstName = "Fred", LastName =
"Flintstone"};

    // ACT
    table.CreateIfNotExists(); // create table
    TableOperation insert = TableOperation.Insert(entity);
    table.Execute(insert); // insert record
    TableOperation fetch = TableOperation.Retrieve<Record>("1", "asdf");
    TableResult result = table.Execute(fetch); // fetch record
    TableOperation del = TableOperation.Delete(result.Result as Record);
    table.Execute(del); // delete record

    // ASSERT
    Assert.That((((Record)result.Result).FirstName, Is.EqualTo("Fred"));
}
```

Distribute data by using the Windows Azure Content Delivery Network (CDN)

The *Windows Azure Content Delivery Network (CDN)* is a way to cache Windows Azure blobs and static content. The idea is that you can use specific strategically placed nodes to maximize performance and bandwidth. Currently, you can specify node locations in the United

States, Europe, Asia, Australia, and South America. (When the number of missing nodes is greater than the number of nodes shown, it is probably a good sign that things are out of date and not worth going into.) In any case, the important takeaway is that you use CDN when performance is absolutely critical or when there are times you need to distribute the load placed on your resources (think Amazon on Cyber-Monday).

So the two primary benefits, according to MSDN, are these:

- Better performance and user experience for end users who are far from a content source, and are using applications in which many Internet trips are required to load content.

- Large distributed scale to better handle instantaneous high load, say at the start of an event such as a product launch.

This section is intentionally short because CDN-specific questions are rare in the exam because it's changed substantively (this is not an official statement from Microsoft). The UI, for instance, has changed regularly over the course of its existence, and screen shots I took from some previous writing on the subject were completely obsolete by the time I started writing this book.

CDN is an advanced feature, and although useful and necessary, it is something that's unquestionably going to evolve over the next few months and years. Focus on understanding what CDN is used for, the use cases, and a basic overview of it, and you should be prepared for the exam.

To use CDN, you must enable it on your storage account in the Windows Azure Management Portal. (At the time of the writing of this book, the CDN management tools are available only in the legacy version of the Windows Azure Management Portal.)

Next, understand how a request processed through CDN differs from a traditional request. Remember that a big selling point of the cloud is that you don't have to worry about many of the specifics about where things are stored (other than a URI). So when you make a request, the request is processed through the blob service or hosted service where your data is located. When the same thing is done with CDN enabled and configured, the request is transparently redirected to the closest endpoint to the location where the request was made. This minimizes the Internet trips mentioned previously. But there's a little more to it than this. All your data is not stored at the closest node, and you can't know in advance where the request will be made. So the only way to make sure that any given blob was at the closest node would be to have it on all nodes that were accessible. This is problematic because ,the first time a request is made, the item won't be at the closest node in many circumstances. In those cases, it is retrieved from the service and cached, actually causing a one-time performance hit prior to the performance gains. Subsequent requests to that node will use the cached item.

The only real nuance is staleness of the cached files. Anyone making any request after the first user gets a cached copy, so if the item changes frequently, it needs to be updated frequently. If it needs to be updated constantly (imagine a spreadsheet with stock quotes), the expiration needs to happen so frequently that it would offset any benefit from the caching.

Expiration is handled specifically by setting the *Time To Live (TTL)* value, which controls cache expiration.

How exactly do you make content available on CDN? First, it must exist in a public container. Second, the public container must be available for anonymous access. Again, only items that are publically available can be cached using CDN. This can be done through the Windows Azure Management Portal, but can also be facilitated through the API and the Cloud-BlobContainer class, for instance, in conjunction with the BlobContainerPermissions class. The CloubBlobContainer's Permissions property has a PublicAccess property of type BlobContainerPublicAccessType. The three values are Container, Off, and Blob. In this case, the container must be public, so BlobContainerPublicAccessType.Container should be used.

So after a container is set up, it's simply a matter of setting up the expiration policy and accessing the data. To access the content directly from the blob service, the URI is identical to what it was originally:

```
http://<storage account name>.blob.core.windows.net/<container>/<blob>
```

To access it directly through the Windows Azure CDN URL, use the following syntax, which is almost identical:

```
http://<storage account name>.vo.msecnd.net/<container>/<blob>
```

For the purposes of this exam, the hosted services component of CDN is pretty much identical other than the URIs. There are some other general things to keep in mind, though, when using CDN. Remember that you're using cached objects, so the more dynamic the object, the less likely it is a good candidate for caching. In fact, if it's too dynamic or the policy is too frequent in terms of expiration, it adversely affects performance. And that's part of the problem. What is too frequent? Every case will be different.

Manage Windows Azure Caching

Keep in mind that caching in Windows Azure is a completely different creature from the other types of caching discussed in this chapter. They are completely different. In a nutshell, it provides a caching layer to your Windows Azure applications. There are times when you benefit from caching with self-hosted applications after all, so why wouldn't the same hold true for Windows Azure-hosted applications? Moreover, CDN does cache data, but it's hardly the comprehensive caching solution needed for many much simpler scenarios.

Caching in the Windows Azure context has one additional advantage over traditional caching. In the Windows Azure context, it can greatly reduce costs associated with database transactions when using SQL databases. If you cache an item that is accessed 10,000 times, for instance, that's 10,000 fewer requests to the SQL database that are being made. Depending on the item, this could be quite substantial. I also point out that, if ignored or taken for granted, it could end up being a very costly mistake.

Caching in Windows Azure is known as *role-based caching*. That's because, as you might infer, it enables you to host caching within any Windows Azure role. Any given cache can be used by any of the other roles within the same cloud service deployment.

To facilitate this, there are two main mechanisms or topologies: dedicated topology and co-located topology. The names are the dead giveaway here, but in a dedicated topology, you define a role that is specifically designated to handle the caching. The Worker Role's available memory (all of it, if necessary) is dedicated to caching items in it and the necessary overhead to manage access to and from it.

In a co-located topology scenario, you assign specific thresholds, and only those thresholds or amounts under them can be used to facilitate the caching. If you had four Web Role instances, you could assign 25 percent to each of them.

Outside of these two mechanisms is an optional service known as *Windows Azure shared caching*. It's optional, and each separate service that employs caching is consumed as a managed service. These caches, unlike the role-based counterparts, do not exist in your own roles. They exist instead in a group of servers in a multitenant environment.

Handling exceptions by using retries (SQL Database)

Using a SQL Database in the cloud can be useful. You get a completely managed database without any prior configuration. It scales well and can be used from within your cloud or on-premise applications.

However, there is one thing different in the cloud than running a SQL database on-premise: latency. Because the physical distance between your database and application server is determined by the infrastructure in the datacenter, you get a higher latency than you would in an on-premise environment. Because of this, you will be more likely to experience timeouts when connecting to a database.

These types of errors are transient, meaning those errors will often go away after some time. For these types of errors, it makes sense to implement retry logic. This basically means that you inspect the error code that's returned from SQL Server, determine whether it's transient, wait for a set amount of time, and then try again to access the database.

The amount of time you wait before trying the action can be flexible. Maybe you want to retry three times, such as after one second, then two seconds, and then five seconds. Windows Azure offers the transient fault handling framework to help you with creating retry logic in your own applications. The following code shows an example of a retry strategy that retries on deadlocks and timeouts:

```
class MyRetryStrategy : ITransientErrorDetectionStrategy
{
    public bool IsTransient(Exception ex)
    {
        if (ex != null && ex is SqlException)
        {
            foreach (SqlError error in (ex as SqlException).Errors)
            {
```

```
                switch (error.Number)
                {
                    case 1205:
                        System.Diagnostics.Debug.WriteLine("SQL Error: Deadlock
condition. Retrying...");
                        return true;

                    case -2:
                        System.Diagnostics.Debug.WriteLine("SQL Error: Timeout expired.
Retrying...");
                        return true;
                }
            }
        }

        // For all others, do not retry.
        return false;
    }
}
```

You can use the retry strategy when executing a query from ADO.NET:

```
RetryPolicy retry = new RetryPolicy<MyRetryStrategy>(5, new TimeSpan(0, 0, 5));

using (SqlConnection connection = new SqlConnection(<connectionstring>))
{
    connection.OpenWithRetry(retry);

    SqlCommand command = new SqlCommand("<sql query>");
    command.Connection = connection;
    command.CommandTimeout = CommandTimeout;

    SqlDataReader reader = command..ExecuteReaderWithRetry(retry);

    while (reader.Read())
    {
        // process data
    }
}
```

When working on your application or service in Visual Studio you work with a lot of files. Some of those files contain code; others contain markup or configuration settings.

> **MORE INFO**   **TRANSIENT FAULT HANDLING FRAMEWORK**
>
> For more information on the transient fault handling framework, see *http://social.technet. microsoft.com/wiki/contents/articles/4235.retry-logic-for-transient-failures-in-windows- azure-sql-database.aspx.*

Thought experiment

Choosing a Windows Azure strategy

In the following thought experiment, apply what you've learned about the "Implement data storage in Windows Azure" objective to design an appropriate Windows Azure strategy. You can find answers to these questions in the "Answers" section at the end of this chapter.

Your company is looking to move its core applications to the cloud. You have two primary applications: one that hosts video training files and another that provides advanced statistics about user interaction patterns. All the consumers of the application are currently clustered around three major metropolitan U.S. cities.

With these items in mind, answer the following questions:

1. What storage options would you consider for each of the two scenarios?

2. Would one storage option suffice or would you want more than one?

3. Would this be a good candidate for the CDN? Why or why not?

Objective summary

- Windows Azure offers a variety of storage options. Some of these are very similar to what on-premises servers utilize; others are very different.

- Local storage is available on most Windows Azure hosting offerings, including all cloud services and VMs.

- Blob storage is available for storing files in a durable file store. Blob storage can be empowered by the CDN to provide faster downloads and lower latencies for end users downloading files during heavy loads.

- Queue storage is similar to MSMQ and is the storage mechanism of choice for messages that need guaranteed delivery, even when the receiving system is down for hours at a time.

- Table storage is Windows Azure's NoSQL implementation. It allows for some very high-volume and high-speed inserts and accesses, much higher than what SQL databases allow if architected properly.

- Windows Azure offers you an additional caching framework that is very easy to use and can grow as your number of servers grows or can remain stable with dedicated instances.

Objective review

Answer the following question to test your knowledge of the information discussed in this objective. You can find the answer to this question and its corresponding explanation in the "Answers" section at the end of this chapter.

1. You are developing an ASP.NET application that hosts an online chat room. What Windows Azure Storage options should you consider for storing the contents of these chat rooms?

    A. Table storage

    B. Queue storage

    C. Blob storage

    D. CDN storage

2. Benefits of using Windows Azure Content Delivery Network include (choose all that apply)?

    A. Increased performance for users geographically close to the content source.

    B. Increased performance for users geographically far from a content source.

    C. Large distributed scale to better handle instanteously increased loads.

    D. Improved security.

3. Which of the following queries take advantage of the Content Delivery network?

    A. *http://atlanta.vo.mysite.net/documents*

    B. *http://myaccount.blob.core.windows.net/documents*

    C. *http://myaccount.atlanta.blob.core.windows.net/documents*

    D. *http://atlanta.mysite.net/documents*

Objective 1.5: Create and implement a WCF Data Services service

The discussion of WCF Data Services was short compared with the other technologies in Objective 1.1's coverage because it is discussed in depth in this objective. This section walks through creating and implementing a service and shows a few examples of how to work with it. Just keep in mind that, throughout the coverage, you specifically deal with WCF Data Services, WCF, the EF, and SQL Server. (Yes, there could be other data stores, but there aren't a lot of questions about MySql on the exam.)

Addressing resources

Visual Studio gives you ample tools for building and implementing WCF Data Services, but a basic walkthrough of how to do it is of little value for preparation of the exam. The approach in this section is to show you how to create the WCF Data Service and focus on generated content and what you need to know for the exam.

MSDN provides the following link, which has a start-to-finish walkthrough of creating a WCF Data Service (*http://msdn.microsoft.com/en-us/library/vstudio/cc668184.aspx*). Generally, you'll need to do the following:

1. Create an ASP.NET application (this serves as the host for the Data Service).

2. Use the EF tools to build an EntityModel.

3. Add a WCF Data Service to the ASP.NET application.

4. Specify a type for the Service's definition (which is the name of the model container created in your EF project).

5. Enable access to the Data Service. This is accomplished by explicitly setting specific properties of the DataServiceConfiguration (SetEntitySetAccessRule, SetServiceOperationAccessRule and DataServiceBehavior).

When you add a WCF Data Service to an ASP.NET application (and you can certainly use other hosting mechanisms and hand-code all this if you're so inclined; it's just a lot more cumbersome and error-prone), you get a class definition that looks something like the following:

```
public class ExamSampleService : DataService<FILL IN MODEL NAME NERE>
{}
```

First, make sure that you understand that WCF Data Services inherit from the System.Data.Services.DataService base class. The constructor takes in a generic type that is indicated by the template class and is absolutely instrumental to the way everything operates.

The next thing you can see in the generated code is the InitializeService method, which takes in a parameter of type DataServiceConfiguration. The generated code is marked with a TODO comment and some commented-out code that is used as a visual tool to help you get started. It looks like this:

```
// This method is called only once to initialize service-wide policies.
public static void InitializeService(DataServiceConfiguration config)
{
```

```
 // TODO: set rules to indicate which entity sets and service operations are visible,
updatable, etc.
 // Examples:
 // config.SetEntitySetAccessRule("MyEntityset", EntitySetRights.AllRead);
 // config.SetServiceOperationAccessRule("MyServiceOperation", ServiceOperationRights.
All);
 config.DataServiceBehavior.MaxProtocolVersion = DataServiceProtocolVersion.V2;
}
```

There are several properties and methods defined in the DataServiceConfiguration class, but the important ones to be familiar with are the SetEntitySetAccessRule method, the SetServiceOperationAccessRule method, and the DataServiceBehavior.MaxProtocolVersion property.

SetEntityAccessRule

This method takes two parameters and is very easy to understand and use. The first parameter is a string that names the entity set that the next parameter applies to. The next parameter is the Rights parameter, which is part of the EntitySetRights enumeration. The one noteworthy thing about this enumeration is that it is decorated with the Flags attribute and intended to be used that way. So, for example, when the access rules for the Courses entity set and give it AllRead and WriteMerge permissions, the following definition is used:

```
config.SetEntitySetAccessRule("Courses", EntitySetRights.AllRead | EntitySetRights.
WriteMerge);
```

Because it's likely to come up in one form or another, walk through the EntitySetRights enumeration's possible values. The names are intuitive, but it's likely that you'll see something in a question stub that might tip you off to the necessity of one or more of them. Table 1-8 shows each member and behavior of the EntitySetRights enumeration.

TABLE 1-8 EntitySetRights

Member name	Behavior
None	All rights to the data are explicitly revoked.
ReadSingle	Single data items can be read.
ReadMultiple	Entire sets of data can be read.
WriteAppend	New items of this type can be added to data sets.
WriteReplace	Data can be updated or replaced.
WriteDelete	Data can be deleted.
WriteMerge	Data can be merged.
AllRead	Across-the-board access to read data of this type.
AllWrite	Across-the-board access to write data of this type.
All	All Creation, Read, Update and Delete operations can be performed.

It should go without saying, but just for the sake of being clear, none of these override permissions are set by the DBA or defined at the database level. You can have the All permission, for instance, but if the DBA revokes your access to the database or that object, you won't be able to access it just because it's specified here.

What might not seem quite as obvious, though, is that EntitySetRight values can be overruled by ServiceOperationRights. As you'll see, ServiceOperationRights are intended to be used as flags, so whatever other values are specified, the OverrideEntitySetRights value can be set, too. When there's a conflict, EntitySetRights lose to both the database's permission and the ServiceOperationRights.

SetServiceOperationAccessRule

This method is commented out, but it is part of the TODO section, as you saw with EntitySetRights. It pertains to any given operation name, and it too defines the permissions that should be applied to the operation through the ServiceOperationRights enumeration (which is also decorated with the flags attributed and is meant to be used as such).

```
config.SetServiceOperationAccessRule("OperationName", ServiceOperationRights.All);
```

Table 1-9 describes this enumeration in detail, and again it's worth a look so you can recognize values when you see them if they appear on the exam.

TABLE 1-9 ServiceOperationRights

Member name	Behavior
None	No authorization to access the operation is granted.
ReadSingle	One single data item can be read using this operation.
ReadMultiple	Multiple data items can be read using this operation.
AllRead	Single and multiple data item reads are allowed.
All	All rights are granted to the service operation.
OverrideEntitySetRights	Overrides EntitySetRights that are explicitly defined in the Data Service.

DataServiceBehavior.MaxProtocolVersion

This value affects the service only to the extent that it will be used with OData (this feeble attempt at humor is actually intentional; it's there to drive home how important this seemingly simple and mundane property is).

Table 1-10 shows the allowable values of this enumeration (which is *not* decorated with the Flags attribute, as you probably guessed).

TABLE 1-10 DataServiceProtocolVersion

Member name	Behavior
V1	Supports version 1.0 of the OData Protocol
V2	Supports version 2.0 of the OData Protocol

Obviously, I'm not saying you need to know nothing else, but for the exam, make sure that you understand fully what the constructor for a WCF Data Service looks like, what base class it inherits from, how to specify the generic type parameter in the base class' constructor, and the details discussed previously.

Creating a query

Sometimes it's a little awkward to discuss things in different sections. This is one of those cases. QueryInterceptors and ChangeInterceptors would probably fit pretty well in this discussion, but I will defer coverage until the end because they deserve their own section, that and the fact that you need to understand how to query data before some of the coverage for those features will make sense.

OData Support is one of the main reasons to use WCF Data Services, and it is URI addressable. You can query data and do quite a bit with it by changing and manipulating URIs. For each example, assume that you have a WCF Service defined and it is named the ExamPrepService. It is based on an Entity Model that contains topics, questions, and answers as entities.

If you want to get all the topics from the service, use the following query:

```
http://servicehost/ExamPrepService.svc/Topics
```

Use Service/EntitySetName to get all the entities. Assume that you want to do the same thing, but instead of wanting all Topic items returned, you want just the Topic named "First" returned:

```
http://servicehost/ExamPrepService.svc/Topics('First')
```

In this case, it is Service/EntitySetName to get the entity, ('KeyValue') to restrict results to the item that has a key matching items in the parentheses.

Assume that this time you want to do the same as the previous example, but you need only the Description property returned. Here's how to do it:

```
http://servicehost/ExamPrepService.svc/Topics('First')/Description
```

So to return just the specified property, add another slash to the previous query and add the Property name to it.

At any time, if you want just the primitive type, not the corresponding XML, you can accomplish it by appending $value at the end of your URI (query). Using the previous example, returning just the primitive value string, just use the same query, with /$value appended on the end:

```
http://servicehost/ExamPrepService.svc/Topics('First')/Description/$value
```

As long as there are relationships defined in the Entity Model, you can use a few different semantics to return related entities. Each of the following is supported:

- Parent entity—Specific child entity
- Parent entity—All child entities
- Set of related entities

Change things up and assume (just for review) that you want to return the Question entity with a key value of "1" and you want just the QuestionText property:

```
http://servicehost/ExamPrepService.svc/Questions('1')/QuestionText
```

That would give you the Question text, but what if you wanted the Answers to it? You would use:

```
http://servicehost/ExamPrepService.svc/Questions('1')/Answers
```

You can work it the other way around, too, of course. If you want the Question that corresponded to an Answer entity with a key of ('1:4'):

```
http://servicehost/ExamPrepService.svc/Answers('1:4')/Question
```

You can technically "filter" data using the previous semantics, but filtering can be applied using the filter keyword, and in many cases needs to be. In the previous example, you returned questions that had a key value of '1,' which had the effect of filtering it to a SQL statement that might look like the following:

```
SELECT Field1, Field2, Field3 etc from Questions WHERE KEY = '1'
```

All the previous semantics filter only according to key values. Sure, keys are good (and frequent) properties to run queries off of, but there are times when you need to use other values and combinations of values. If you need to restrict based off of anything other than key, you'll need to use the filter keyword.

If you want to return all the topics greater than Topic 1, though, using the previous semantics wouldn't work. What if you want to return just topic items that had the phrase "Data Service" in their text? Because their Text property isn't the key, you couldn't use what you have done so far. You don't have a way to append X number of additional keys into the one parenthesis, and at this point, you're not even sure whether that will work (it doesn't) or even necessarily know how many different topics there are. Who knows, that might be what you want to find out. So that's where filters come in. If you need a range of values, if you need to restrict data based on something that isn't a key field, or if you have multiple conditions, you need to start using the $filter value.

To tailor the behavior of queries, you need to take advantage of the various OData query options. $filter is one of the most common.

> **MORE INFO**   **ODATA FILTER OPERATORS**
>
> OData.org (*http://www.odata.org/documentation/odata-v2-documentation/uri-conventions/*) provides a full list of the OData URL conventions and how to use them. Refer to it if you have any questions about specific usage.

Table 1-11 shows a list of each of the query options available for OData through WCF Data Services.

TABLE 1-11 Query options

Member name	Behavior
$orderby	Defines a sort order to be used. You can use one or more properties that need to be separated by commas if more than one will be used: *http://servicehost/ExamPrepService.svc/Questions?$orderby=Id,Description*
$top	The number of entities to return in the feed. Corresponds to the TOP function in SQL: *http://servicehost/ExamPrepService.svc/Questions?$top=5*
$skip	Indicates how many records should be ignored before starting to return values. Assume that there are 30 topics in the previous data set, and you want to skip the first 10 and return the next 10 after that. The following would do it: *http://servicehost/ExamPrepService.svc/Questions?$skip=10&$top=5*
$filter	Specifies a condition or conditions to filter on: *http://servicehost/ExamPrepService.svc/Questions?$filter=Id gt 5*
$expand	Indicates which related entities are returned by the query. They will be included either as a feed or as an entry inline return with the query: *http://servicehost/ExamPrepService.svc/Questions?$expand=Answers*
$select	By default, all properties of an entity are returned in the feed. This is the equivalent of SELECT * in SQL. By using $select, you can indicate a comma separated list to just return the fields you want back: *http://servicehost/ExamPrepService.svc/Questions&$select=Id,Text,Description,Author*
$inlinecount	Returns the number of entries returned (in the <count> element). If the following collection had 30 total values, the feed would have a <count> element indicating 30: *http://servicehost/ExamPrepService.svc/Questions?$inlinecount=allpages*

In addition to making requests through a URI, you can execute queries through code imperatively. To facilitate this, the DataServiceQuery class is provided.

If you want to use the DataServiceQuery approach to get the same functionality, you build your service just as you already have, and you set up a DataServiceQuery instance and use the AddQueryOptions method. A quick sample should suffice:

```
String ServiceUri = "http://servicehost/ExamPrepService.svc";
ExamServiceContext ExamContext = new ExamServiceContext(new Uri(ServiceUri);
DataServiceQuery<Questions> = ExamContext.Question
                    .AddQueryOptions("$filter", "id gt 5")
                    .AddQueryOptions("$expand", "Answers");
```

You can, of course, accomplish the same thing using straight LINQ/EF syntax, but because that approach would have nothing specific to WCF Data Services to it, it might appear on some other exam or portion of the exam (but probably not appear here).

Accessing payload formats

There is support for both Atom and JSON formats. They are easy to use and are intuitive; you use the $format option with one of two values: $format=atom or $format=json. If you decide instead to access it via the WebClient or by specifying it through the request header, it works the same way, with just a small change: You need to append "application/" to the headers. To use JSON, you simply need to specify "application/json" or "application/atom+xml."

The issue of JSON and Atom as payload formats appears extensively in other portions of the exam, but in terms of the Data Service component, there's not much more to know than what was mentioned previously.

Working with interceptors and service operators

The WCF Data Services infrastructure enables you to intercept requests and provide custom logic to any given operation. Interceptors, as the name implies, are the mechanism you can use to accomplish this. When a request is made, it can be intercepted, and additional custom logic can be applied to the operation. Common use cases for interception include validation of inbound messages and changing the scope of a request.

To facilitate interception, you use the Interceptor type name, passing in the corresponding parameters, and decorate the method with it.

There are two basic types of interceptors you should be familiar with: ChangeInterceptors and QueryInterceptors. As the names imply, they have distinct usages depending on what you are looking for. ChangeInterceptors are used for NON-Query operations; QueryInterceptors are used for Query operations.

ChangeInterceptors are used for all nonquery operations and have no return type (void in C#, Nothing in VB.NET). They must accept two parameters:

- **Type**   A parameter of type that corresponds to the entity type associated with the entity set.
- **UpdateOperations**   When the operation is invoked, this value references the request that you want to perform.

The definition for the attribute on a method handling OnChangeTopics looks like the following:

```
[ChangeInterceptor("Topics")]

public void OnChangeTopics(Topic topic, UpdateOperations operations)
```

According to MSDN, QueryInterceptor items must meet the following conditions.

- Entity set authorization and validation is handled by methods decorated with the QueryInterceptor attribute.
- Entity set access control and validation is enabled through query operations by using composition. To accomplish this, the following conditions must be met:
  - The method must have public scope.
  - It must be decorated with the QueryInterceptor attribute.
  - The QueryInterceptor must take the name of an entity set as a parameter.
  - The method must not take any parameters.
  - The method must return an expression of type Expression<Func<T, Boolean>> that serves as the filter for the entity set.

So the signature for a method implementing a QueryInterceptor looks like the following:

```
[QueryInterceptor("Topics")]
public Expression<Func<Topic, bool>> FilterTopics(){}
```

The tipoff for which to use and when to use it is determined by what it is used for. It is denoted by the signature of the method. If you see <Func<SomeEntity, bool>> Whatever(), you can tell immediately that it's a QueryInterceptor. If you see anything else, it's a ChangeInterceptor.

Similarly, you can tell by the behavior which is which and which is being asked for. Delete-Topics would be a ChangeInterceptor question; a GetAdvancedTopics method asking about filtering Topics entity would be a QueryInterceptor question.

Thought experiment

Querying data services

In the following thought experiment, apply what you've learned about the "Create and implement WCF Data Services" objective to design a transport server infrastructure. You can find answers to these questions in the "Answers" section at the end of this chapter.

Your company has an application that currently is consumed by in-house applications. There is a need to make it accessible to outside parties that use this in-house application but extend it. As such, the capability to consume and manipulate the data is critical. Enabling users to accomplish this through URI-based semantics seems like the optimal solution.

With these facts in mind, answer the following questions:

1. Would it be possible to provide access through URI-based semantics using Data Services?

2. What operations are easily supported?

Objective summary

- WCF Data Services provide easily accessible data operations through OData.
- WCF Data Services can make use of both JSON and Atom.
- The SetEntitySetAccessRule controls the how an entity can be queried.
- The EntitySetRights enumeration is created with the Flags attribute and is intended to be used as such. In many or most cases, you'll specify more than one value for such access rules.
- Queries can be performed using URIs, and tremendous functional enhancements can be implemented by small changes.
- QueryOperations are denoted with the $ at the beginning of an operation and can control a wide variety of functions, including the number of items returned to specifying the TOP x of the resultset.

Objective review

Answer the following questions to test your knowledge of the information discussed in this objective. You can find the answers to these questions and their corresponding explanations in the "Answers" section at the end of this chapter.

1. You need to create an interceptor that runs each time you try to return Topic items. Which items should you use? (Choose all that apply.)

   A. ChangeInterceptor

   B. QueryInterceptor

   C. DataServiceProtocolVersion

   D. SetEntitySetAccessRule

2. You need to return all questions that have an Id greater than 5. Which query should you use?

   A. *http://servicehost/ExamPrepService.svc/Questions?$filter=Id gt 5*

   B. *http://servicehost/ExamPrepService.svc/Questions?$filter(ID> 5)*

   C. *http://servicehost/ExamPrepService.svc/Questions(>5)*

   D. *http://servicehost/ExamPrepService.svc/Questions?$select(Id) gt 5*

3. Assume you have the following C# code snippet.

   ```
   var selectedQuestions = from q in context.Questions
                   where q.QuestionNumber > 30
                   orderby q.QuestionId descending
                   select q;
   ```

   Which of the following URI queries is the equivalent?

   A. *http://Service/Question.svc/Questions?Orderby=QuestionId&?$QuestionNumber (gt 30)*

   B. *http://Service/Question.svc/Questions?Orderby=QuestionId&?$QuestionNumber gt 30*

   C. *http://Service/Question.svc/Questions?Orderby=QuestionId&?filter=(QuestionNumber > 30)*

   D. *http://Service/Question.svc/Questions?Orderby=QuestionId&?filter=QuestionNumber gt 30*

Objective 1.6: Manipulate XML data structures

Ever since it showed up on the scene, XML has made a huge impact. Today, virtually every application makes use of XML in some way or other. In some cases, it is used as a serialization format. In others, it is used to store configuration data in a way that doesn't necessitate registry access and the permissions such access requires. It is also used as a basis for Web Services and as a file format (as a matter of fact, it's the underlying file format for this document). These are just a few areas of what XML is used for. XML is the answer to so many problems that plagued the development world that it's one of the few technologies that not only lived up to the hype that surrounded it (and there was plenty) but it also completely exceeded the hype by a huge margin.

This objective covers how to:

- Read, filter, create, and modify XML structures
- Manipulate XML data by using XMLReader, XMLWriter, XMLDocument, XPath, and LINQ-to-XML
- Advanced XML manipulation

Reading, filtering, creating, and modifying XML structures

The first component of an XML Document is typically known as the *XML declaration*. The XML declaration isn't a required component, but you will typically see it in an XML Document. The two things it almost always includes are the XML version and the encoding. A typical declaration looks like the following:

```
<?xml version="1.0" encoding="utf-8" ?>
```

You need to understand the concept of "well-formedness" and validating XML. To be well-formed, the following conditions need to be met:

- There should be one and only one root element.
- Elements that are opened must be closed and must be closed in the order they were opened.
- Any element referenced in the document must also be well-formed.

The core structures of XML are *elements* and *attributes*. Elements are structures that represent a component of data. They are delineated by less-than and greater-than signs at the beginning and end of a string. So an element named FirstName looks like this:

```
<FirstName>
```

Each element must be closed, which is indicated by slash characters at the beginning of the element:

```
</FirstName>
```

To define an element named FirstName with the value "Fred" in it, this is what it would look like:

```
<FirstName>Fred</FirstName>
```

If an element has no data value, you can represent it in one of two ways:

- An opening element followed by a closing element with no value in between them:

  ```
  <FirstName></FirstName>
  ```

- An opening element with a slash at the end of string instead of the beginning:

  ```
  <FirstName/>
  ```

Attributes differ from elements in both syntax and nature. For instance, you might have the following structure that describes a "Name":

```
<?xml version="1.0" encoding="utf-8" ?>
<Name>
  <FirstName>John</FirstName>
  <MiddleInitial>Q</MiddleInitial>
  <LastName>Public</LastName>
</Name>
```

Name in this case is its own element, and FirstName, MiddleInitial, and LastName are their own elements, but have context and meaning only within a Name element. You could do the same thing with attributes, although they are necessarily part of the element to which they belong:

```
<Name FirstName="John" MiddleInitial="Q" LastName="Public"></Name>
```

If you tried to consume this data, the way you access it would differ, but the end result would be that you'd retrieve information about a Name, and the data would be identical. Which is better? Which one should you use? There's no correct answer to either question. It depends on style and personal preference. The Internet is full of passionate debate about this subject, which is testimony to the fact that there is not a definitive right or wrong answer for every case.

Manipulating elements and attributes are the crux of what you'll encounter on the exam, but for the sake of being thorough, there are two other items you should be familiar with: comments and namespaces. I can't say that you'll never need to concern yourself with retrieving comment information, but it's not something you come across very often, and I've never had to do it (and I've done a lot of XML parsing). The main thing you need to know is simply how to identify comments so you can distinguish them from other XML elements. You delineate a comment with the following character sequence:

```
<!-- Then you end it with the following:-->
```

So a full comment looks like this:

```
<!-- this is a comment about the Name element. Blah blah blah-->
```

Namespaces are a little more involved. Assume that you want to use an element name—something common. If namespaces didn't exist, it would mean that, after an element name was used, it couldn't be used for anything else. You can imagine how much difficulty this would cause when you're dealing with different vendors, all adding to an existing snippet of XML. This would be particularly problematic even if you didn't have different vendors but had a case in which different XML fragments were used. If you are familiar with DLL Hell, this is its evil cousin.

So namespaces were added to the spec. You can define namespaces in the root node or in the element node. In either case, they are delineated with the following syntax:

```
xmlns:Prefix="SomeValueUsuallyACompanyUrl"
```

The xmlns portion is what denotes a namespace declaration (*xml NameSpace* is abbreviated to xmlns). You then specify what prefix you want to use (Prefix in the previous example). Then you use an equal sign and give it a unique value. You could use any value you know to be unique, but using your own company URL is usually a good practice, coupled with something specific about the namespace. If you use namespaces only in the context of your company, you can use a slash and some other name that you know to be unique. If you don't, you'll have a collision that will make things confusing. So using this approach, here's what the document definition would look like along with an example of each being used in an element:

```
<DocumentCore xmlns:johnco="http://www.yourcompany.com/Companies" xmlns:billco="http://
www.mycompany.com/Customers">
  <johnco:Name>
    <johnco:Company>JohnCo</johnco:Company>
  </johnco:Name>
  <billco:Name>
    <billco:FirstName>John</billco:FirstName>
    <billco:MiddleInitial>Q</billco:MiddleInitial>
    <billco:LastName>Public</billco:LastName>
  </billco:Name>
</DocumentCore>
```

The previous example includes two different vendors, BillCo and JohnCo, that each happened to use an element named Name. Once you define a namespace, you simply prefix the element with the namespace and a colon, and then include the element name, as indicated previously.

You can also define namespaces at the element level instead. This is the same principle with just a slightly different definition. In general, it's more concise to define the namespaces globally if you have repeated instances of an element. Think of several Name instances of both the johnco: and the billco: Name element. Defining it inline each time would be repetitive, inefficient, and a lot harder to read. The following shows how to define a namespace inline:

```
<DocumentCore>
  <johnco:Name xmlns:johnco="http://www.yourcompany.com/Companies">
    <johnco:Company>JohnCo</johnco:Company>
  </johnco:Name>
  <billco:Name xmlns:billco="http://www.mycompany.com/Customers">
    <billco:FirstName>John</billco:FirstName>
    <billco:MiddleInitial>Q</billco:MiddleInitial>
    <billco:LastName>Public</billco:LastName>
  </billco:Name>
</DocumentCore>
```

The pros and cons of using each approach is beyond the scope of this discussion and not relevant for the test. You simply need to know that both forms of the syntax are valid and get you to the same place.

Manipulating XML data

The previous items are all the primary classes you can use to manipulate XML data outside of the LINQ namespace. They belong to the System.Xml namespace and all work essentially the same way. They have all been around for a while as far as the .NET Framework is concerned, and it's doubtful they'll comprise much of the exam as far as XML manipulation goes. They are important, but they have been around since version 1 of the Framework, and you're much more likely to encounter questions focused on LINQ. A basic familiarity with them, knowledge of their existence, and a basic understanding of how they work should more than suffice for the purposes of the exam.

XmlWriter class

The XmlWriter class can be used to write out XmlDocuments. It's intuitive to use and needs little explanation. The steps are as follows:

- Create a new instance of the XmlWriter Class. This is accomplished by calling the static Create method of the XmlWriter class (and for convenience, passing in a file name as a parameter).

- Call the WriteStartDocument method to create the initial document.

- Call the WriteStartElement, passing in a string name for the element name for the root element.

- Use the WriteStartElement again to create an instance of each child element of the root element you just created in the previous step.

- Use the WriteElementString method passing in the element name and value as parameters.

- Call the WriteEndElement method to close each element you created.

- Call the WriteEndElement method to close the root element.

- Call the WriteEndDocument method to close the document you created initially.

There are several other methods you can use, such as WriteComment, WriteAttributes, or WriteDocType. Additionally, if you opt to use Asynchronous methodology, you can call the corresponding Async methods that bear the same names, but have Async at the end of them.

> **NOTE** **SAMPLE CODE IS FOCUSED ON BEING READABLE**
>
> I intentionally left out items such as overloading base class methods and some other things I'd include in production code for the purposes of readability. So the class definition is hardly an example of an ideal sample of production code. In the same respect, the exam has to take readability into account, so it's likely to follow similar conventions.

Assume that you have the following class definition for Customer:

```
public class Customer
{
    public Customer() { }
    public Customer(String firstName, String middleInitial, String lastName)
    {
        FirstName = firstName;
        MiddleInitial = middleInitial;
        LastName = lastName;
    }
    public String FirstName { get; set; }
    public String MiddleInitial { get; set; }
    public String LastName { get; set; }
}
```

The following shows code based on the class definition and follows the steps outlined in the previous list:

```
public static class XmlWriterSample
{
    public static void WriteCustomers()
    {
        String fileName = "Customers.xml";
        List<Customer> customerList = new List<Customer>();
        Customer johnPublic = new Customer("John", "Q", "Public");
        Customer billRyan = new Customer("Bill", "G", "Ryan");
        Customer billGates = new Customer("William", "G", "Gates");
        customerList.Add(johnPublic);
        customerList.Add(billRyan);
        customerList.Add(billGates);

        using (XmlWriter writerInstance = XmlWriter.Create(fileName))
        {
            writerInstance.WriteStartDocument();
            writerInstance.WriteStartElement("Customers");

            foreach (Customer customerInstance in customerList)
            {
                writerInstance.WriteStartElement("Customer");
                writerInstance.WriteElementString("FirstName", customerInstance.
FirstName);
                writerInstance.WriteElementString("MiddleInitial", customerInstance.
MiddleInitial);
                writerInstance.WriteElementString("LastName", customerInstance.
LastName);
                writerInstance.WriteEndElement();
            }
            writerInstance.WriteEndElement();
            writerInstance.WriteEndDocument();
        }
    }
}
```

This code produces the following output:

```
<?xml version="1.0" encoding="UTF-8"?>
<Customers>
 <Customer>
  <FirstName>John</FirstName>
  <MiddleInitial>Q</MiddleInitial>
  <LastName>Public</LastName>
</Customer>-<Customer>
  <FirstName>Bill</FirstName>
  <MiddleInitial>G</MiddleInitial>
  <LastName>Ryan</LastName>
</Customer>-<Customer>
  <FirstName>William</FirstName>
  <MiddleInitial>G</MiddleInitial>
  <LastName>Gates</LastName>
 </Customer>
</Customers>
```

XmlReader class

The XmlReader is the counterpart to the XmlWriter, and it's equally simple to use. Although there are several different cases you can check for (attributes, comments, namespace declarations, and so on), in its simplest form, you simply do the following:

- Instantiate a new XmlReader instance passing in the file name of the XML file you want to read.

- Create a while loop using the Read method.

- While it iterates the elements, check for whatever you want to check looking at the XmlNodeType enumeration.

The following method iterates the document created in the previous section and outputs it to the console window:

```
public static void ReadCustomers()
{
    String fileName = "Customers.xml";
    XmlTextReader reader = new XmlTextReader(fileName);
    while (reader.Read())
    {
        switch (reader.NodeType)
        {
            case XmlNodeType.Element: // The node is an element.
                Console.Write("<" + reader.Name);
                Console.WriteLine(">");
                break;
            case XmlNodeType.Text: //Display the text in each element.
                Console.WriteLine(reader.Value);
                break;
            case XmlNodeType.EndElement: //Display the end of the element.
                Console.Write("</" + reader.Name);
                Console.WriteLine(">");
                break;
```

```
        }
    }
}
```

There's no need to go through each item available in the XmlNodeType enumeration, but you can become familiar with the available items on MSDN: *http://msdn.microsoft.com/en-us/library/system.xml.xmlnodetype.aspx.*

XmlDocument class

The XmlDocument class is the parent of the others in some ways, but it's even easier to use. You typically do the following:

- Instantiate a new XmlDocument class.
- Call the Load method pointing to a file or one of the many overloaded items.
- Extract the list of nodes.
- Iterate.

The following code shows how to walk through a Node collection and extracts the InnerText property (which is the value contained in the nodes). Although there are other properties you can take advantage of, this chapter is about data and working with it:

```
String fileName = "Customers.xml";
XmlDocument documentInstance = new XmlDocument();
documentInstance.Load(fileName);
XmlNodeList currentNodes = documentInstance.DocumentElement.ChildNodes;
foreach (XmlNode myNode in currentNodes)
{
    Console.WriteLine(myNode.InnerText);
}
```

Writing data using the XmlDocument class works intuitively. There's a CreateElement method that accepts a string as a parameter. This method can be called on the document itself (the first of which creates the root node) or any given element. So creating an initial document and then adding a root node named Customers that contains one element named Customer is created like this:

```
XmlDocument documentInstance = new XmlDocument();
XmlElement customers = documentInstance.CreateElement("Customers");
XmlElement customer = documentInstance.CreateElement("Customer");
```

In order to make this work right, you must remember the rules of well-formedness (and these in particular):

- Any tag that's opened must be closed (explicitly or with an close shortcut for an empty element, i.e., <FirstName/>.
- Any tag that's opened must be closed in a Last Opened First Closed manner. <Customers><Customer>SomeCustomer</Customer></Customers> is valid; <Customers><Customer>SomeCustomer</Customers></Customer> is not.

To that end, in the previous code, the XmlElement named Customers should be the last of the group to have a corresponding AppendChild method called on it, followed only by the AppendChild being called on the document itself.

One more thing needs to be mentioned here. The CreateElement method simply creates the element; it does nothing else. So if you want to create an element named FirstName and then add a value of John to it, use the following syntax:

```
XmlElement FirstNameJohn = DocumentInstance.CreateElement("FirstName");
FirstNameJohn.InnerText = "John";
```

The following segment shows the process, from start to finish, of creating the output specified after it:

Code

```
XmlDocument documentInstance = new XmlDocument();
XmlElement customers = documentInstance.CreateElement("Customers");
XmlElement customer = documentInstance.CreateElement("Customer");
XmlElement firstNameJohn = documentInstance.CreateElement("FirstName");
XmlElement middleInitialQ = documentInstance.CreateElement("MiddleInitial");
XmlElement lastNamePublic = documentInstance.CreateElement("LastName");
firstNameJohn.InnerText = "John";
middleInitialQ.InnerText = "Q";
lastNamePublic.InnerText = "Public";
customer.AppendChild(firstNameJohn);
customer.AppendChild(middleInitialQ);
customer.AppendChild(lastNamePublic);
customers.AppendChild(customer);
documentInstance.AppendChild(customers);
```

Output

```
<Customers>
    <Customer>
      <FirstName>John</FirstName>
      <MiddleInitial>Q</MiddleInitial>
      <LastName>Public</LastName>
    </Customer>
</Customers>
```

If you wanted to add additional Customer elements, you'd follow the same style, appending them to the corresponding parent element in the same manner as you did here.

For attributes, there's a SetAttribute method that accepts two strings as parameters and can be called on any given element. The first string is the attribute name; the second is the attribute value. Using the example, you can attain the same goal you accomplished earlier by using the XmlDocument class, as shown in the following:

Code

```
String fileName = "CustomersPartial2.xml";
XmlDocument documentInstance = new XmlDocument();
XmlElement customers = documentInstance.CreateElement("Customers");
XmlElement customer = documentInstance.CreateElement("Customer");
customer.SetAttribute("FirstNameJohn", "John");
customer.SetAttribute("MiddleInitialQ", "Q");
```

```
customer.SetAttribute("LastNamePublic", "Public");
customers.AppendChild(customer);
documentInstance.AppendChild(customers);
documentInstance.Save(fileName);
```

Output

```
<Customers>
<Customer LastNamePublic="Public" MiddleInitialQ="Q" FirstNameJohn="John"/>
</Customers>
```

XPath

One feature of navigating through a document is *XPath*, a kind of query language for XML documents. XPath stands for XML Path Language. It's a language that is specifically designed for addressing parts of an XML document.

XmlDocument implements *IXPathNavigable* so you can retrieve an XPathNavigator object from it. The XPathNavigator offers an easy way to navigate through an XML file. You can use methods similar to those on an XmlDocument to move from one node to another or you can use an XPath query. This allows you to select elements or attributes with certain values.

Let's say you are working with the following XML:

```
<?xml version="1.0" encoding="utf-8" ?>
<People>
  <Person firstName="John" lastName="Doe">
    <ContactDetals>
      <EmailAddress>john@unknown.com</EmailAddress>
    </ContactDetals>
  </Person>
  <Person firstName="Jane" lastName="Doe">
    <ContactDetals>
      <EmailAddress>jane@unknown.com</EmailAddress>
      <PhoneNunmber>001122334455</PhoneNunmber>
    </ContactDetals>
  </Person>
</People>
```

You can now use an XPath query to select a *Person* by name:

```
XmlDocument doc = new XmlDocument();
doc.LoadXml(xml);

XPathNavigator nav = doc.CreateNavigator();
string query = "//People/Person[@firstName='Jane']";
XPathNodeIterator iterator = nav.Select(query);

Console.WriteLine(iterator.Count); // Displays 1

while(iterator.MoveNext())
{
    string firstName = iterator.Current.GetAttribute("firstName","");
    string lastName = iterator.Current.GetAttribute("lastName","");
    Console.WriteLine("Name: {0} {1}", firstName, lastName);
}
```

This query retrieves all people with a first name of Jane. Because of the hierarchical structure of XML, an XPath query can help you when you're trying to retrieve data.

> **MORE INFO** **XPATH LANGUAGE**
>
> For a complete overview of the XPath language, see *http://www.w3.org/TR/xpath/.*

LINQ-to-XML

LINQ will likely be featured prominently in the exam. Entire books are written on LINQ and how to use it; this coverage is not intended to be a comprehensive discussion of LINQ (or anything even close to it). It does, however, cover the elements (no pun intended) that you're likely to encounter as you take the exam.

There's one point that can't be emphasized enough. The more you know about the technology, the more likely you are to be able to rule out incorrect answers. I have not only taken several certification exams and participated in every aspect of the process more times than I can count, but I have also been an item writer. Trust me; it's not an easy task. I won't go into all the details about it, but you almost always have to rely on subtle differences to come up with valid questions that adequately differentiate them from each other. The more you know about the technology, the more likely you are to pick up on something that just doesn't look right or that you know can't be the case. In most instances, that just increases the probability of guessing the right answer. On the visual drag-and-drop questions, having such knowledge can enable you to use the process of elimination, which can greatly increase your chances of getting the question right. LINQ semantics feature prominently in .NET Framework since it was introduced, and features have been added to the runtime just to support LINQ. Although this isn't a LINQ exam by any stretch, a good knowledge of LINQ and how it works is something I can all but promise you will be rewarding, both at work and on the exam.

The coverage of LINQ-to-XML is covered after the coverage of the primary System.Xml namespace classes. This is not an accident. Other than some tweaks and small improvements, the System.Xml namespace in version 4.0 or version 4.5 of the Framework is still very similar to what it was in earlier versions. There's not a lot of new material to cover there, so although it is certainly fair game for the exam, it's doubtful that you'll find a whole lot of emphasis on it. I can assure you, however, that LINQ-to-XML will be covered on the exam.

Coverage of System.Xml preceded LINQ-to-XML because the hope was to drive home how awkward XML parsing using traditional means is (and although the traditional means might be awkward or inelegant, they are much more elegant than the alternatives of the time) by juxtaposing it against the elegance and simplicity that LINQ-to-XML provides.

To take advantage of it, note that, to provide the features it does, it takes much advantage of the more modern aspects of each .NET language and the .NET Framework, such as each of these:

- Anonymous methods

- Generics
- Nullable types
- LINQ query semantics

To begin the discussion, let's start with where everything here lives. You'll find the classes for the LINQ-to-XML API in the System.Xml.Linq namespace.

The XElement class is one of the core classes of the LINQ-to-XML API and something you should be familiar with. It has five constructor overloads:

```
public XElement(XName someName);
public XElement(XElement someElement);
public XElement(XName someName, Object someValue);
public XElement(XName someName, params Object[] someValueset);
public XElement(XStreamingElement other);
```

Remember what you had to do before with the XDocument class to create a Customers element: a Customer element and then a FirstName, MiddleInitial, and LastName element corresponding to it. (To emphasize the difference, you might want to refer to the previous section if you can't immediately visualize it.)

Now let's look at the same process using just the XElement class:

```
XElement customers = new XElement("Customers", new XElement("Customer",
               new XElement("FirstName", "John"), new XElement("MiddleInitial", "Q"),
               new XElement("LastName", "Public")));
```

The code snippet produces the following output:

```
<Customers>
  <Customer>
    <FirstName>John</FirstName>
    <MiddleInitial>Q</MiddleInitial>
    <LastName>Public</LastName>
  </Customer>
</Customers>
```

That's just the beginning. You can easily reference items inside the node. Although these are all strings, you can easily cast them to different .NET types as needed if you query against a different object type or structure. Examine the following code:

```
XElement customers = new XElement("Customers", new XElement("Customer",
               new XElement("FirstName", "John"), new XElement("MiddleInitial", "Q"),
               new XElement("LastName", "Public")));
String fullName = customers.Element("Customer").Element("FirstName").ToString() +
               customers.Element("Customer").Element("MiddleInitial").ToString() +
               customers.Element("Customer").Element("LastName").ToString();
```

This code produces the corresponding output:

```
<FirstName>John</FirstName><MiddleInitial>Q</MiddleInitial><LastName>Public</LastName>
```

Like any language, XML has characters that define it. You might come across situations in which you need to use those characters (and many of them happen to be characters that are used quite often). Greater-than and less-than symbols are part of the language syntax; ampersands are as well. Normally, you have to manually escape these. > is used instead of a greater-than symbol; &lt needs to be used in place of a less-than symbol; &amp replaces an ampersand character. XElement automatically calls the XmlConvert class, which escapes these for you. As such, the following code snippet would work just fine:

```
XElement customers = new XElement("CustomerNote", "The customer
really likes to use < and  > in their correspondence. They love using &
and </div> as well");
```

The XDocument class almost seems redundant when compared with the XElement class. To quote MSDN:

> The XDocument class contains the information necessary for a valid XML document. This includes an XML declaration, processing instructions and comments. Note that you only have to create XDocument objects if you require the specific functionality provided by the XDocument class. In many cases you can work with the XElement. Working directly with XElement is a simpler programming mode.

The following list summarizes the basic components of an XDocument instance:

- **One XDeclaration object**   The declaration enables you to specify the version of XML being used, the encoding, and whether the document contains a document type definition.

- **One XElement object**   Because a valid document must contain one root node, there must be one XElement present. Note that, although you need to use an XElement to use an XDocument, the reverse is not the case.

- **XProcessingInstruction objects**   Represents an XML processing instruction.

- **XComment objects**   As with XProcessingInstruction, you can have one or more. According to MSDN, the only caveat is that this can't be the first argument in the constructor list. Valid documents can't start with a comment. The irony here is that there are no warnings generated if you use it as the first argument; the document parses correctly, and MSDN's own examples show example after example that specifically violate this rule. Answers to questions on the exam have to be 100 percent correct and provable. If you look around the Internet, there's a good bit of debate about this subject. It's doubtful you'll see questions on the exam that differentiates the correct versus incorrect answer. Suffice to say that, although MSDN says one thing, its own examples directly violate this rule, so if you did happen to fail the exam by this one question, you can certainly argue your case.

Because the issue is possibly confusing, the following example shows passing in an XComment as the first argument and the output:

Code:

```
XDocument sampleDoc = new XDocument(new XComment("This is a comment sample"),
    new XElement("Customers",
        new XElement("Customer",
            new XElement("FirstName", "John"))));
sampleDoc.Save("CommentFirst.xml");
```

Output:

```
<?xml version="1.0" encoding="utf-8"?>
<!--This is a comment sample-->
<Customers>
  <Customer>
    <FirstName>John</FirstName>
  </Customer>
</Customers>
```

The XAttribute class is so simple that it doesn't need much discussion. To declare one, you simply instantiate it, passing in the name of the attribute and the value:

```
XAttribute sampleAttribute = new XAttribute("FirstName", "John");
```

Attributes, by definition, have no meaning outside of the context of an element, so they are obviously used only in conjunction with an XElement.

XNamespace is easy to create and work with:

```
XNamespace billCo = "http://www.billco.com/Samples";
```

If you want to use an XNamespace in conjunction with an XElement, you simply append it to the Element Name. The following illustrates both the declaration and how to use it in conjunction with an XElement:

```
XNamespace billCo = "http://www.billco.com/Samples";
XElement firstNameBillCo = new XElement(billCo + "FirstName", "John");
```

This is a subject that has endless possibilities and permutations and is impossible to illustrate completely. The main thing to understand is how to create an XNamespace and how to use it.

Declaring and instantiating each of the X classes isn't complicated. However, things get tricky when it comes to queries. Let's look at the following code snippet:

```
String documentData = @"<Customers><Customer><FirstName>John</FirstName></Customer>
        <Customer><FirstName>Bill</FirstName></Customer>
        <Customer><FirstName>Joe</FirstName></Customer></Customers>";
XDocument docSample = XDocument.Parse(documentData);
var descendantsQuery = from desc in docSample.Root.Descendants("Customer")
                       select desc;
var elementsQuery = from elem in docSample.Root.Elements("Customer")
                    select elem;
Int32 descendantsCount = descendantsQuery.Count();
Int32 elementsCount = elementsQuery.Count();
```

```
Console.WriteLine(descendantsCount.ToString());
Console.WriteLine(elementsCount.ToString());
```

The output in both cases is 3. From a behavioral point of view, they look identical, don't they? Search on MSDN and see the way they are each defined and described in almost identical terms. The way to think of it is this: Descendants return whatever elements you choose from the entire subtree of each element. Elements, on the other hand, yield only the child elements. There are 1,000 different examples to illustrate this point, but they are more confusing than helpful. The only time it matters is when there are not child elements inside one of the ones you are searching for. It behaves differently only if there are child elements that also have the same name as the element you are looking for. The same queries run against this snippet yield the same results as they did originally, even though there are nested elements:

```
String documentData = @"<Root><CustomerName><FirstName>John</FirstName></CustomerName>
                        <CustomerName><FirstName>Bill</FirstName>
</CustomerName>
                        <CustomerName><Other><Another>Blah</Another>
</Other><FirstName>Joe</FirstName>
<MiddleInitial>Q</MiddleInitial>
                        <LastName>Public</LastName>
</CustomerName></Root>";
```

Make a slight modification, in which the search element name is used in a nested element, and you have totally different behavior:

```
String documentData = @"<Root><CustomerName><FirstName>John</FirstName></CustomerName>
                        <CustomerName><FirstName>Bill</FirstName></CustomerName>
                        <CustomerName><Other><CustomerName>Blah
</CustomerName></Other><FirstName>Joe</FirstName>
<MiddleInitial>Q</MiddleInitial>
                        <LastName>Public</LastName>
</CustomerName></Root>";
```

There are countless extension methods, but most are self-explanatory or used rarely enough so they shouldn't present much of a problem from an exam perspective. Just remember the difference in behaviors between these two because questions are likely to appear on the exam.

Advanced XML manipulation

If you know only LINQ, and you are an absolute expert, you'll probably do well on this portion of the exam (but don't take that as any sort of endorsement to not study the System.Xml. Linq namespace objects). Recall that you have to specifically escape several reserved characters and sequences unless you are using a class, method, or property that does it for you. So the first thing to know is that XmlConvert automatically escapes reserved items. It also does more than that. Think of the Convert class in the System namespace. It has several methods, such as ToInt32, ToDateTime, ToBoolean, and many more. Think of the XmlConvert class as its Xml obsessed sibling. XmlConvert.ToDateTime, XmlConvert.ToDecimal, XmlConvert.ToGuid, and any other method that contains "To," followed by a framework type, should be self-explanatory, but some aren't as intuitive (see Figure 1-8). Again, take a look at the class, run through it, and familiarize yourself with as much as possible; then determine whether things are valid or invalid. Table 1-12 covers several of these methods (this list is not comprehensive, but covers some of the less intuitive methods you might encounter).

TABLE 1-12 XmlConvert class methods

Name	Behavior
DecodeName	Decodes the name of an item that's been encoded already. The samples that follow this table illustrate it.
EncodeName	Encodes a string so that it can definitely be used as an XML node name.
EncodeLocalName	Behaves virtually identically to EncodeName, but with one major difference: It actually encodes the colon character, which ensures that Name can be used as the local name element of a namespace-qualified name. Again this method will be emphasized in the following code sample.
EncodeNmToken	Returns a valid name for a node according to the XML Language spec. It might sound identical to EncodeName, and they are very similar. The primary difference that EncodeNmToken encodes colons wherever they appear, which means that it could return a "valid" element according to syntax rules, but not according to the namespace specification.
IsStartNCNameChar	Determines whether the parameter is a valid non-colon-character type.
IsPublicIdChar	If the parameter is a valid public identifier, it returns it; otherwise, it returns null. If you're not familiar with XML public and system identifiers, try entering "XML Public Identifier" into Bing—there are plenty of links available on it. In reality, however, public identifiers are just magic strings and mainly exist because of legacy behavior more than any necessity.
ToDateTimeOffset	Represents a specific point in time with respect to *Coordinated Universal Time (UTC)*. There are three overloads for this method: one that just accepts a string, one that accepts a string and a second string that represents the format the date is represented in within the string, and the last that accepts a string and an array of strings containing the formats.

There are countless overloads for members, such as ToInt32 or ToDateTime, and they behave just as you expect and are easy to follow. The following code illustrates the encoding and decoding issues, which are the most relevant and what you're most likely to run into on the exam:

Code

```
String encodedFirstName = XmlConvert.EncodeName("First Name");
Console.WriteLine("Encoded FirstName: {0}", encodedFirstName);
String decodedFirstName = XmlConvert.DecodeName(encodedFirstName);
Console.WriteLine("Encoded FirstName: {0}", decodedFirstName);
String encodedFirstNameWithColon = XmlConvert.EncodeLocalName("First:Name");
Console.WriteLine("Encoded FirstName with Colon: {0}", encodedFirstNameWithColon);
decodedFirstName = XmlConvert.DecodeName(encodedFirstNameWithColon);
Console.WriteLine("Encoded FirstName with Colon: {0}", decodedFirstName);
```

The output is shown in Figure 1-8.

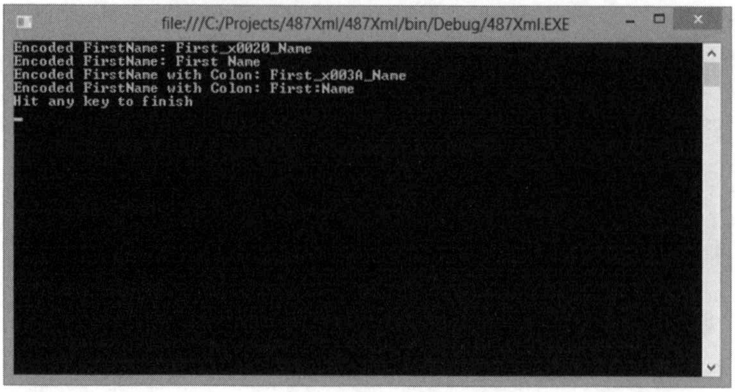

FIGURE 1-8 Encoding and decoding using the XmlConvert class

Thought experiment

Creating an XML manipulation strategy

In the following thought experiment, apply what you've learned about the "Manipulate XML data structures" objective to determine the data access strategy for new application development at your company. You can find answers to these questions in the "Answers" section at the end of this chapter.

You are building an application that makes extensive use of XML. The document structures follow very consistent patterns, and sometimes large applications to manipulate these structures are similar.

With this in mind, answer the following questions:

1. Would your application benefit from using LINQ-to-XML?

2. What could be done to simplify consumption of the documents?

Objective summary

- The XElement and XDocument classes are the primary or topmost objects you'll typically be working with, although XElement is frequently the better choice.

- Although very similar in most regards, the XDocument represents an entire XML document, whereas the XElement represents an XML fragment. The practical differences between those two are often trivial or nonexistent, but it's worth noting.

- Escaping reserved characters and dealing with namespaces are the two other nuances you'll probably encounter on the exam. You don't need to be an expert in either, but you should at least be familiar with the XmlConvert and XmlNamespace classes and what they are used for.

- Although there are different classes and methodologies in the .NET Framework regarding XML manipulation, don't think that you have to use either one approach (System.Xml) or the other (System.Xml.Linq). LINQ is built into the Framework, as its name indicates, and you can certainly use an XmlWriter class and then query a structure using LINQ-to-XML features. (The point is that you can mix and match as you see fit or as needed; using one methodology doesn't force your hand in dealing with the other.)
- Make sure that you understand the difference in behavior between the Elements and Descendants methods of the XContainer class.

Objective review

Answer the following questions to test your knowledge of the information in this objective. You can find the answers to these questions and explanations of why each answer choice is correct or incorrect in the "Answers" section at the end of this chapter.

1. You need to use an ampersand in the name of an element you create with an XElement item. Which of the following allows a correctly created element name?

   A. Just pass in the string to the XElement constructor; it handles it automatically by calling the XmlConvert class transparently.

   B. Manually escape the character sequence.

   C. Use the XmlConvert.Encode method to create the string to pass into the constructor.

   D. All of the above.

2. Which of the following are requirements for a valid and well-formed XML document?

   A. Every element must have a corresponding closing element.

   B. Every element must have at least one attribute.

   C. Every attribute must have a corresponding closing attribute.

   D. Elements and attributes can be used interchangeably as long as they have open and closing tags.

Chapter summary

- Microsoft provides developers with several different ways to access and manipulate data. These range from the older and more traditional to more cutting edge. ADO.NET, the EF, and ADO.NET Data Services are the three core areas that handle data access.
- Each of the data access methods provides many of the same features (with limited exceptions), but the ease with which they do it and tooling support varies greatly.

- Constantly querying the database for items that are relatively static just produces unnecessary overhead on the database, network resources, and server resources. By implementing a caching strategy, much of that overhead can be reduced.

- Caching, although very beneficial in many cases, must be carefully considered, and the costs and benefits must be weighed carefully. You can fix one type of problem (performance) while introducing very serious other types of problems (stale data) if you're not careful. This problem might be trivial or completely catastrophic, depending on the application's requirements.

- In complex distributed systems, transactions are more a necessity than a luxury. Transactions allow things to happen in an all-or-nothing fashion and enable you to walk back failures and mistakes without having to resort to costly and serious measures such as database restores.

- There are two types of transactions: simple and distributed. Simple transactions cover one connection to one data source; distributed transactions cover connections to one or more sources.

- You can implement transactions with the System.Transactions.TransactionScope class or the SqlTransaction class (or OracleTransaction and other implementations, as the case may be). TransactionScopes provide the benefit of being able to transparently handle both simple and distributed transactions by invisibly promoting them when needed without any developer involvement. Compared to how difficult performing distributed transactions were just a few years ago, the simplicity the TransactionScope provides is nothing short of amazing.

- Windows Azure provides several means for data storage when requirements dictate cloud-based storage. For structured data, you have TableStorage for nonrelational data and SQL databases for relational data. For large unstructured binary data, you have Blob storage. For less-complex scenarios, you have local storage that provides per-instance temporary storage.

- WCF Data Services are the latest incarnation of ADO.NET Data Services. Using the EF as a backdrop to manipulate entities in the form of .NET classes, Data Services enables you to build fully functioning data services that enable users to employ a full array of options in data manipulation. It has the elegance of allowing queries to be URL addressable and has a rich variety of formats that data can be transmitted with, including Atom and JSON.

- With the popularity of XML, even many tools and libraries meant to deal with XML parsing are still awkward and discomforting for many. There are existing well-established libraries for manipulating XML data, and there are many more-modern libraries, too. On the one hand, you have the System.Xml namespace items; on the other, you have System.Xml.Linq. The beauty is that they can almost always be used in conjunction with each other if you prefer, so you're never bound to just one or the other. Virtually everything you could ever need or want to do with XML can be done with these two libraries.

Answers

This section contains the solutions to the thought experiments and answers to the lesson review questions in this chapter.

Objective 1.1: Thought experiment

1. If you continue to build using ADO.NET, meeting application requirements will be increasingly difficult. It would provide consistency, but any functionality that needs to be exposed to the outside world will take more and more effort (arguably wasted effort to accomplish).

2. In and of itself, the EF doesn't get you closer to the goal, but it would enable easier interoperability with WCF Data Services, for instance. It would set the groundwork for moving to OData.

3. Moving legacy applications to WCF Data Services would not be trivial. They are already built and tested. However, moving them so they could be consumed externally will require changes, no matter how it is accomplished. WCF Data Services would allow for all the required features that don't currently exist.

Objective 1.1: Review

1. **Correct answers:** A, B, C, D

   A. **Correct:** This is technically correct, but dropping the table means that all the data goes with it. That could work in some development environments, but in production it is a terrible idea. Because the environment wasn't mentioned, this is still a correct answer.

   B. **Correct:** This would update the entity and the data source correctly.

   C. **Correct:** This would update the entity and the data source correctly.

   D. **Correct:** This would update the entity and the data source correctly.

2. **Correct answer:** C

   A. **Incorrect:** LINQ-to-SQL will facilitate data access, but does nothing to expose the data to the web.

   B. **Incorrect:** The EF will facilitate data access, but does nothing to expose the data to the web.

   C. **Correct:** This would enables you to meet all the data requirements as well as the transmission requirements.

   D. **Incorrect:** This technology no longer exists.

3. **Correct answer:** D

   A. Incorrect: This file technically no longer exists, so wouldn't be appropriate.

   B. Incorrect: This file technically no longer exists, so wouldn't be appropriate.

   C. Incorrect: This file technically no longer exists, so wouldn't be appropriate.

   D. Correct: Each of the preexisting files, including the mapping files, is included here.

Objective 1.2: Thought experiment

1. The more static and less volatile it is, the better the candidate is for caching.

2. How frequent repeat trips are to the source coupled with the size of it. At some point, reducing trips to the database can be offset by size of the data. Local storage or cache storage sizes can be burdensome, so caching isn't a magic bullet.

3. The more frequently data changes, the less likely it is to be a viable candidate for caching. Monitoring is not inexpensive, and although very helpful in some cases, it would offset the benefit of caching. In the same respect, if the expiration policy is very small, the benefit of caching is diminished. If monitoring needs to happen in most cases, any benefit from caching will be greatly reduced, and a scenario could arise in which things are much worse because of it. Such scenarios are atypical and usually arise from overuse, but they do happen.

Objective 1.2: Review

1. **Correct answers:** A, B, D

   A. Correct: CacheEntryChangeMonitor is a valid option.

   B. Correct: FileChangeMonitor is a valid option.

   C. Incorrect: There is no such thing as an MsmqChangeMonitor.

   D. Correct: SqlChangeMonitor is a valid option.

2. **Correct answer:** C

   A. Incorrect: The System.Runtime.Caching.CacheItemPriority enum does not have a Normal option. It does exist, however, in the System.Web.Caching.CacheItem Priority enum.

   B. Incorrect: The System.Runtime.Caching.CacheItemPriority enum does not have a High option. It does exist, however, in the System.Web.Caching. CacheItemPriority enum.

   C. Correct: There is a NotRemovable option.

   D. Incorrect: The System.Runtime.Caching.CacheItemPriority enum does not have a Low option. It does exist, however, in the System.Web.Caching. CacheItemPriority enum.

3. **Correct answers:** A, D

    A. **Correct:** This would accomplish the requirements.

    B. **Incorrect:** The second parameter cannot be a CacheItemPriority. It will not compile.

    C. **Incorrect:** This does not set the Region name.

    D. **Correct:** This would accomplish the requirements.

Objective 1.3: Thought experiment

1. Clearly defined boundaries are the main consideration. The more items affected in a transaction and the longer an operation takes, the more problems you'll see related to making it transactional.

2. There are several costs associated with implementing transactions, and these costs can add up quickly. If every operation were transactional, it would add tremendous cost without necessary benefit.

3. The importance of the data is one main consideration. How long-running the process is would be another consideration. The number of resources affected would be another one.

Objective 1.3: Review

1. **Correct answers:** B, D

    A. **Incorrect:** ReadUncommitted would result in nonrepeatable reads.

    B. **Correct:** RepeatableRead would be the loosest IsolationLevel that would meet these requirements.

    C. **Incorrect:** Chaos does not work with SQL Server.

    D. **Correct:** Snapshot would meet these requirements but might be overkill.

2. **Correct answer:** B

    A. **Incorrect:** Long running operations that span several tables may necessitate transactional support, but the duration and complexity would generally pose serious locking and contention issues.

    B. **Correct:** Small fast operations are generally the best candidates for transactions.

    C. **Incorrect:** Operations that involve the file system would generally be problematic and would not benefit from transactions.

    D. **Incorrect:** A non-Windows operating system would present many problems and would not be a good candidate for transactional support.

Objective 1.4: Thought experiment

1. Blog storage for the video and table storage for the statistical information would probably be best here.

2. It might be possible to use just one approach. However, although you could use Blob storage to store the statistical information, you couldn't use table storage for the media files in any practical sense.

3. If consumption is all clustered in well-defined areas, using CDN could be very beneficial.

Objective 1.4: Review

1. **Correct answer:** A

   A. **Correct:** Chatroom data is mostly nonrelational conversations that have structure to them. This is a perfect candidate for Table storage.

   B. **Incorrect:** Queues are not a good mechanism at all for this type of data because there is no way to query and fetch data based on those results.

   C. **Incorrect:** Blob storage is a terrible option for this type of data because it would lose any structure the data had and would be on a slow medium.

   D. **Incorrect:** The CDN would not work for this type of data.

2. **Correct answers:** B, C

   A. **Incorrect:** CDN allows manipulation of nodes to reduce intermediate traffic. The whole idea is to have nodes closer to the traffic source. Little or no benefit will be realized if the traffic source is already close.

   B. **Correct:** By specifying nodes closer to the traffic source, increased performance can be realized.

   C. **Correct:** CDN helps distributed scale issues and is particularly well suited to traffic spikes and surges (such as ones associated with product launches).

   D. **Incorrect:** CDN doesn't offer any security advantages that aren't already present in Azure offerings that do not take advantage of it.

3. **Correct answer:** A

   A. **Correct:** An Azure CDN URL is in the format *http://<identifier>.vo.mscend.net/*.

   B. **Incorrect:** This is a standard Azure storage URL.

   C. **Incorrect:** This is a standard Azure storage URI with a misplaced identifier.

   D. **Incorrect:** This is a completely malformed Azure storage URI.

Objective 1.5: Thought experiment

1. Yes, in fact, that's the primary benefit. Items can be accessed using traditional code or using URI-based semantics, but in this case, URI semantics would be particularly useful.

2. All Create, Retrieve, Update, and Delete (CRUD) operations.

Objective 1.5: Review

1. **Correct answer:** B

   A. **Incorrect:** This would be right only if the data were being changed. It's just being queried.

   B. **Correct:** This is the only one that can handle items when they are queried.

   C. **Incorrect:** This simply would not work for the task at hand or even come close to it.

   D. **Incorrect:** This simply would not work for the task at hand or even come close to it.

2. **Correct answer:** A

   A. **Correct:** The entity name, followed by a filter condition using gt for greater than 5 is what's required here.

   B. **Incorrect:** The query and filter syntax is incorrect.

   C. **Incorrect:** No mention is made of a filter here, and the syntax is incorrect.

   D. **Incorrect:** The id field and operator are correct, but the syntax is incorrect.

3. **Correct answer:** D

   A. **Incorrect:** The filter and query syntax are incorrect.

   B. **Incorrect:** The filter and query syntax are incorrect.

   C. **Incorrect:** The filter syntax is incorrect.

   D. **Correct:** The OrderBy field is specified correctly, as is the filter field.

Objective 1.6: Thought experiment

1. The more consistent the structures are, the more any approach will be simplified. LINQ semantics allow much simpler interaction with the documents, although any of the existing .NET XML libraries can work.

2. The more consistent the data, the more one approach can be reused. Because the documents are all similar, the hard part, so to speak, is largely addressed. You might consider doing an intermediate transform on the documents, though, to render them as one very consistent format that might make it even simpler.

Objective 1.6: Review

1. **Correct answer:** D

   A. **Incorrect:** Technically correct, but other answers are all correct, so choice D is the only one.

   B. **Incorrect:** Technically correct, but other answers are all correct, so choice D is the only one.

   C. **Incorrect:** Technically correct, but other answers are all correct, so choice D is the only one.

   D. **Correct:** Because each of the other answers is correct, this one is the right answer.

2. **Correct answer:** A

   A. **Correct:** An element can self-close, but each opening element must be closed.

   B. **Incorrect:** Elements might have attributes, but there is no requirement for an element to have an attribute.

   C. **Incorrect:** Attributes don't require matching closure tags.

   D. **Incorrect:** Elements can be nested and structured in a way that accomplishes the same goal as attributes, but attributes can't contain elements.

CHAPTER 2

Querying and manipulating data by using the Entity Framework

This chapter builds on what Chapter 1 covered, but it focuses specifically on LINQ and the *Entity Framework (EF)*. LINQ semantics feature prominently on any exam covering .NET technologies, including the 70-487 exam. You can expect this objective to cover about 20 percent of the questions on the exam.

Objectives in this chapter:

- Objective 2.1: Query and manipulate data using the Entity Framework
- Objective 2.2: Query and manipulate data by using Data Provider for Entity Framework
- Objective 2.3: Query data by using LINQ to Entities
- Objective 2.4: Query and manipulate data by using ADO.NET
- Objective 2.5: Create an Entity Framework data model

Objective 2.1: Query and manipulate data by using the Entity Framework

Although the Entity Framework (EF) was covered in Chapter 1 , "Accessing data," this chapter covers specifics about EF and the components that compose it. To help you with your exam preparation, the focus is on version 5.0 of the .NET Framework.

This objective covers how to:
- Query, update, and delete data by using DbContext
- Build a query that uses deferred execution
- Implement lazy loading and eager loading
- Create and run compiled queries
- Query data by using Entity SQL

Querying, updating, and deleting data by using DbContext

Earlier versions of the EF made use of the ObjectContext class as the interaction point between the code and the data. Starting with version 5.0 of the EF, ObjectContext was replaced with DbContext.

Querying data

Querying data is quite straightforward and can be done in several ways. The simplest approach lets you use LINQ semantics, which references the context.

```
var query = (from acct in context.Accounts
             where acct.AccountAlias == "Primary"
             select acct).FirstOrDefault();
```

In this instance, the *query* variable is used to hold the returning value. A DbContext instance named context contains an entity named Accounts. The restriction is performed by the where clause, and here the entire Account entity will be returned. The only thing truly different query-wise with using LINQ semantics (other than properties you can set to control the behavior of DbContext) versus using it with any other collection is that you reference the context.

You can do the same thing with a SQL statement, making a small change (calling the SqlQuery method and specifying a string that corresponds to the query you want to execute).

Updating data

After an entity is returned from a query, you can interact with it as you can with any other .NET class. You can make whatever changes you like to it; when you're done, call the SaveChanges() method of the context that will then persist all the object changes back to the database. When SaveChanges is called, it returns an integer value reflecting the total number of modifications that were made to the underlying database.

You can similarly update an item that you created (provided that it is a valid entity type defined in the context) by using the Add or Attach methods and then calling SaveChanges. Understanding the difference between the Add and Attach methods is critical. Including an entity in the context via the Add method results in the item having an EntityState value of Added. As a result, these items do not have original values in the ObjectStateEntry because there is no previous set of values for them. When SaveChanges is called, the context attempts to insert this entity into the data store. Attach, on the other hand, includes them in the context with an EntityState value of Unchanged. As such, it matters greatly when you decide to call Attach. If you call it after changes are made to the item that would differentiate it from those in the underlying store, nothing would happen. If you call Attach earlier in the process, before any of the attributes are changed, a call to SaveChanges would end up executing an update operation.

Suppose that you create an Account instance that you didn't get from the database using a variable named *microsoftAccount*. You can use the following to attach it to the context, which causes it to be persisted to the database when you attempt to call SaveChanges:

```
context.Accounts.Attach(microsoftAccount);
```

Deleting data

You can delete data by using the Remove method. Using the Set method, you need to specify the entity type you want to remove and then call the Remove method. Afterward, call SaveChanges, and the item should be deleted from the database unless an exception was raised (for instance, if there was a foreign key relationship):

```
context.Set<Account>().Remove(query);
```

Building a query that uses deferred execution

The EF was built to be the Microsoft solution for *object-relational mapping (ORM)*. ORM is a programming technique for converting data between incompatible type systems in object-oriented programming languages. This incompatibility is known as *impedance mismatch*.

The relational model for data storage is excellent for what it is intended for and has been in widespread use for more than 40 years. It is time-tested, proven, and refined. Although a 787 Dreamliner is well-suited to transporting people between continents, it is a terrible choice for getting to your office or the local gym. That doesn't mean it is deficient or bad; it just means that it is a tool that was created for a specific purpose, and the things that make it effective at what it is intended to do are precisely those that make it inadequate for some other tasks.

Object-oriented design is similar: It has been around for a long time, it has been heavily used in industry, it is time-tested, and it enables you to model real-world items in a manner that makes them intuitive and easy to work with. Object-oriented design is a design methodology, not a data storage one, however. What makes an effective object model doesn't necessarily make a good relational database schema; in many cases it almost seems that they're at odds with each other. These two paradigms are arguably the most prominent in their own development landscapes.

The most prominent solution to dealing with impedance mismatch is to use ORM; in fact, a good definition of ORM is "a programming technique for addressing impedance mismatch between an object model and a relational database schema."

The EF is designed specifically to provide a Microsoft-centric ORM for use in your applications. The elegance that the EF brings to the table is that it lets you deal with your data model and your object model as completely separate items, and it handles mapping the differences between them for you.

Think of an example in which you have an object that has properties that are collections of other objects. In this case, consider the metaphor of finances. Most people have one or more bank accounts. Accounts have transactions. Transactions have details. Now think about the last time you saw a spreadsheet on your computer or something that contained a grid in a webpage. How many items can you visually process at one time? It depends on a few factors (your vision, the size of your monitors, the size of the fonts, and so on), but usually there are between 10 and 30 items.

Now imagine the following application structure:

```
Bank class

    Customers

        Accounts

            Transactions

                Transaction details
```

Each bank has customers, a customer in turn has one or more accounts, an account has 0 or more transactions, and a transaction has 0 or more details. If you queried for a customer, would you want all the account information to come back with each customer request? Not usually, but perhaps. Would you want all the transactions? Even if you answer yes to each, you can imagine a situation in which you would have more data than you'd want to consume in a typical view. That's where the notion of *lazy loading* comes in. Deferred execution (slightly oversimplified here) means that just because you build a LINQ query, it doesn't mean that it has actually been executed against the database. Lazy loading means that you retrieve the data only when you actually need it. Look at the following code:

```
EntityFrameworkSamplesEntities context = new EntityFrameworkSamplesEntities();
var query = from acct in context.Accounts
            where acct.AccountAlias == "Primary"
            select acct;
```

If you're new to LINQ, the EF, and deferred execution, and were asked what the record count of query is for 20 accounts named Primary, what would you say? A typical answer is 20. At this point, nothing has happened in terms of data retrieval, however. This is the essence of deferred execution. It is only at the point at which you request the data by trying to reference it that you actually initiate a data retrieval. The following full block potentially triggers many database queries:

```
EntityFrameworkSamplesEntities Context = new EntityFrameworkSamplesEntities();
var query = from acct in Context.Accounts
            where acct.AccountAlias == "Primary"
            select acct;

foreach (var currentAccount in query)
{
    Console.WriteLine("Current Account Alias: {0}", currentAccount.AccountAlias);
}
```

The takeaway is that query expressions don't necessarily cause a data retrieval operation. Look at this query:

```
EntityFrameworkSamplesEntities context = new EntityFrameworkSamplesEntities();
var query = (from acct in context.Accounts
             where acct.AccountAlias == "Primary"
             select acct).Count();
```

The second method is virtually identical, but instead of returning a collection, it returns a scalar value, the count of the matching records. Is it possible to determine what the count value is without executing an actual query against the database? No. So the Aggregate function forces the execution.

Although both cases end up behaving markedly differently, they are the same with respect to deferred execution. Namely, data is retrieved when it is required, not beforehand.

Implementing lazy loading and eager loading

The previous examples were straightforward and neither involves querying data from multiple entities. There are cases that require you to pull down an entire data set (not necessarily the DataSet class, although it would apply here, too) and work with it. There are other times when you might deal with huge amounts of data that you might never need. Table 2-1 describes each of these items.

TABLE 2-1 Loading options

Type	Behavior
Lazy loading	When executed, the query returns the primary or target entity, but related data is not retrieved. For instance, If you performed a join on Account and Contact, account information would be retrieved initially, but contact information would be retrieved only when a NavigationProperty was accessed or the data was otherwise explicitly requested.
Eager loading	The target, or primary entity, is retrieved when the query is triggered and the related items come with it. In this example, the Account and all the corresponding Contact items would come with it. Essentially, this is the opposite of lazy loading. This behavior mimics the behavior you'd encounter with a DataAdapter and a DataSet (although there are some differences, the analogy is correct).
Explicit loading	Event when lazy loading is disabled; you can still make use of it to lazily load entities if you have the need to do so. The Load extension method enables you to execute queries individually, giving you *de facto* lazy loading if you want.

You might make the incorrect assumption that, if you're dealing with related entities, lazy loading is automatically the better choice. Why would this not be the case? If you know exactly what data you need, lazy loading can actually hurt performance, even when there are several related entities, because it requires multiple roundtrips to the database instead of just one. On the other hand, if you aren't sure of the number of roundtrips and have a high probability that you won't need all the data pulled back, lazy loading is generally a better option because you pull back only the data you need. If you're not making many roundtrips, the performance loss is likely going to be trivial.

You can enable or disable lazy loading visually or through code. To enable it through the designer, simply select your EF model and choose Properties. You'll see the Properties window (see Figure 2-1). Simply choose a value of either True or False for the Lazy Loading Enabled value.

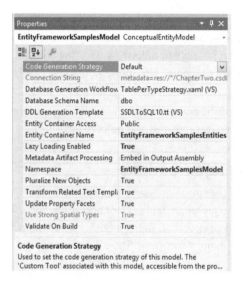

FIGURE 2-1 Entity Model Properties window

Setting this value through the designer causes the underlying .edmx file to be modified accordingly. Specifically, the LazyLoadingEnabled attribute of the EntityContainer gets set to the value you set in the designer:

```
<edmx:ConceptualModels>

 <Schema Namespace="EntityFrameworkSamplesModel" Alias="Self"
xmlns:annotation="http://schemas.microsoft.com/ado/2009/02/edm/annotation"
xmlns="http://schemas.microsoft.com/ado/2008/09/edm">
        <EntityContainer Name="EntityFrameworkSamplesEntities"
annotation:LazyLoadingEnabled="true">
```

The other option is to set it programmatically through code. To do that, you simply need a reference to the DataContext (if you generate a model, the generated model inherits from the DBContext class). The DataContext, in this example named EntityFrameworkSamplesEntities, has a Configuration property that has a LazyLoadingEnabled property. You can explicitly set the value to true or false to control the behavior at runtime. It is simple to set, as shown in the following:

```
private static void SetLoadingOptions(EntityFrameworkSamplesEntities context, Boolean
enableLazyLoading)
{
  context.Configuration.LazyLoadingEnabled = enableLazyLoading;
}
```

Run the included sample, build a similar model, or write a function similar to the following one. Call the function passing in a value of both true and false, and set a breakpoint on the first foreach loop. You can use the Visualizer in Visual Studio to see the contents of the result in each case. After running the code block under both scenarios, the difference in behavior should become readily evident if it isn't already:

```
private static void ShowLoadingOptions(EntityFrameworkSamplesEntities context, Boolean
enableLazyLoading)
{
    context.Configuration.LazyLoadingEnabled = enableLazyLoading;
    var query = (from acct in context.Accounts

            where acct.AccountAlias == "Primary"

            select acct).FirstOrDefault();
     // Set breakpoint below

    foreach (var cust in query.Customers)

{

      Console.WriteLine("Customer Id: {0}, FirstName: {1}, LastName: {2}", cust.
CustomerId
, cust.FirstName, cust.LastName);

      foreach (var trans in Cust.Transactions)

      {

        Console.WriteLine("Transaction Id: {0}", trans.TransactionId);

        foreach (var details in trans.TransactionDetails)

        {

            Console.WriteLine("Details Id: {0}, Item Id: {1}, Time: {2}", details.
DetailId,
 details.ItemId, details.TransactionTime);
          }

        }

      }
    }
```

Use the FirstOrDefault method to ensure that you bypass deferred execution because it requests a scalar value. If you call this function with a value of true, you'll see that Customers, Transactions, and TransactionDetails give you the inverse behavior (you'll get 0 on the subsequent records or the record count of each of the related entities, depending on the total record count you have).

In preparing for the exam, it's critical that you understand lazy loading and the implications using it entails. Even if lazy loading is enabled, there are several "greedy" operations. Each of the following fits that category:

- Calling the ToList, ToArray, or ToDictionary methods.

- Calling an aggregate function (Average, Count, Max) will cause the query to execute immediately but only if it's within the scope of the call. If, for instance, you called an aggregate, then proceeded to iterate through the item, two calls to the database would be made. The first would be necessary to determine the value of the aggregate. The second would happen because of the iteration. In such cases, calling one of the methods in the first bullet would be preferable, because you could use it to derive your aggregate and accomplish the iteration as well with only one trip to the database.

Creating and running compiled queries

When you execute a Linq-To-Entities query against the database, the Entity Framework takes care of translating your query to SQL. As you can understand, this process takes some time. Normally this happens each time you execute a query. However, the structure of a typical query doesn't change between executions. For example, when you have a query that filters a set of people on an email address, you have the same query, only the email parameter changes.

To speed up the processing of your queries, Entity Framework supports *compiled queries*. A compiled query is used to cache the resulting SQL and only the parameters are changed when you run the query.

Starting with .NET 4.5, queries are cached automatically. This is done by generating a hash of the query and comparing that hash against the in-memory cache of queries that have run previously.

If you need even more performance, you can start compiling the queries manually. For this, you use the CompiledQuery class:

```
static readonly Func<MyObjectContext, string, Person> compiledQuery =
    CompiledQuery.Compile<MyObjectContext, string, Person>(
    (ctx, email) => (from p in ctx.People
                    where p.EmailAddress == email
                    select p).FirstOrDefault());
```

You can use this query like this:

```
Person p = compiledQuery.Invoke(context, "foo@bar");
```

The compiled query needs to be static, so you avoid doing the compiling each time you run the query.

What's important to understand about compiled queries is that if you make a change to the query, EF needs to recompile it. So a generic query that you append with a Count or a ToList changes the semantics of the query and requires a recompilation. This means that your performance will improve when you have specific queries for specific actions.

When the EF caches queries by default, the need to cache them manually is not that important anymore. But knowing how it works can help you if you need to apply some final optimizations.

Querying data by using Entity SQL

Most of the time you will be querying your data by using LINQ to Entities. This is a nice syntax that allows you to express your queries in a readable way.

However, there is another option: Entity SQL. Entity SQL somewhat looks like SQL but has the extra knowledge of your conceptual model. This means that Entity SQL understands collections and inheritance.

Entity SQL is string based. This means that you have more control over composing your queries in a dynamic fashion at runtime.

The following code shows a simple example of executing a query with Entity SQL:

```
var queryString = "SELECT VALUE p " +
            "FROM MyEntities.People AS p " +
            "WHERE p.FirstName='John'";
ObjectQuery<Person> people = context.CreateQuery<Person>(queryString);
```

In this case you are using Entity Frameworks Object Services to run your query. It returns a strongly typed object that you can know use in your application.

Another scenario where you can use Entity SQL is when you don't need the returned data be materialized as objects. Maybe you want to stream the results of a query and you want to deal with only the raw data for performance. You can do this by using an EntityDataReader. A regular DataReader represents your query result as a collection of rows and columns. The EntityDataReader has a better understanding of your object model. The following code shows an example of how to use the EntityDataReader:

```
using (EntityConnection conn = new EntityConnection("name=MyEntities"))
{
    conn.Open();

    var queryString = "SELECT VALUE p " +
        "FROM MyEntities.People AS p " +
        "WHERE p.FirstName='Robert'";
```

```
EntityCommand cmd = conn.CreateCommand();
cmd.CommandText = queryString;
using (EntityDataReader rdr =
 cmd.ExecuteReader(CommandBehavior.SequentialAccess |
                    CommandBehavior.CloseConnection))
{
    while (rdr.Read())
    {
        string firstname = rdr.GetString(1);
        string lastname = rdr.GetString(2);
        Console.WriteLine("{0} {1}", firstname, lastname);
    }
}
}
```

The EntityConnection uses the connection string that you already know when working with EF and an EDMX file. This way, you tell the command where it can find the metadata required for mapping your queries to the database.

The EntityDataReader gives you a forward-only stream to your data. This is very fast and allows you to work with large amounts of data.

Remember however, normally you will use LINQ to Entities. If you discover a scenario where LINQ is not sufficient, you should first think about your design before switching to Entity SQL. But in some scenarios, having the ability to use Entity SQL is useful.

Thought experiment

Determining when to use lazy loading

In the following thought experiment, apply what you've learned about this objective to predict how to determine when to use lazy loading. You can find answers to these questions in the "Answers" section at the end of this chapter.

You have an object model that has a relational hierarchy three levels deep. In addition to one chain that nests three levels deep (parent, child, and grandchild), you have four other child relations. In total, you have a parent and five related children, and the first child has two children of its own.

With this in mind, answer the following questions:

1. Should you pull back the entire chain and all the data, or pull back only a portion and then make roundtrips for the additional data as needed?

2. If you pull back all the data, what problems might you face?

3. If you choose to lazy load, what problems might you face?

4. How should you go about determining which approach should be used?

Objective summary

- Deferred execution is a mechanism by which data queries are not fired until they are specifically asked for.

- Because deferred execution depends on being "requested," aggregates or other functions that necessitate a scalar value can cause execution to be immediate. Otherwise, it will be deferred until you reference the item or iterate the collection.

- Lazy loading is a mechanism by which the target entity is always returned with the initial request, but the related entities are retrieved only when a subsequent request is made or a NavigationProperty is referenced.

- Eager loading is the opposite of lazy loading. It causes execution of queries for related entities to happen at the same time the target is retrieved.

- Care should be taken when choosing a loading mechanism because the consequences can be extremely serious in terms of performance. This is particularly so when resources are limited or you are working against remote data stores.

Objective review

Answer the following questions to test your knowledge of the information in this objective. You can find the answers to these questions and explanations of why each answer choice is correct or incorrect in the "Answers" section at the end of this chapter.

1. You create a LINQ query as follows. Which of the statements is correct?

```
var query = (from acct in context.Accounts
            where acct.AccountAlias == "Primary"
            select Acct).FirstOrDefault();
```

   A. A foreach loop is needed before this query executes against the database.

   B. NavigationProperty needs to be referenced before this query executes against the database.

   C. The query returns results immediately.

   D. It depends on whether the LazyLoadingEnabled property is set.

2. Assume you call the Add method of a context on an entity that already exists in the database. Which of the following is true? (Choose all that apply.)

   A. A duplicate entry is created in the database if there is no key violation.

   B. If there is a key violation, an exception is thrown.

   C. The values are merged using a first-in wins approach.

   D. The values are merged using a last-in wins approach.

3. What happens if you attempt to Attach an entity to a context when it already exists in the context with an EntityState of unchanged?

A. A copy of the entity is added to the context with an EntityState of unchanged.

B. A copy of the entity is added to the context with an EntityState of Added.

C. Nothing happens and the call is ignored.

D. The original entity is updated with the values from the new entity, but a copy is not made. The entity has an EntityState of Unchanged.

Objective 2.2: Query and manipulate data by using Data Provider for Entity Framework

Now that the basics are covered, the focus moves to using the Data Provider for Entity Framework in order to manipulate data. It is not only easy to use but also easy to learn. While the majority of EF-related items focus on the model components of EF, using the Data Provider for Entity Framework will almost certainly be covered on the exam.

> **This objective covers how to:**
> - Query and manipulate data by using Connection, DataReader, Command from the System.Data.EntityClient namespace
> - Perform synchronous and asynchronous operations
> - Manage transactions (API)

Querying and manipulating data by using Connection, DataReader, Command from the System.Data.EntityClient namespace

The System.Data.EntityClient namespace is a subset of the System.Data namespace, and its components work similarly to the other System.Data subsets, but also have some augmented functionality.

To work with a database, you need a connection and a command; for retrieval operations, you need a variable or container to hold the resulting query information.

EntityConnection

In each code scenario that involves database interaction, some items need to be present. At a minimum, you need a connection of some sort. In the *SqlClient* namespace, the connection object used is the *SqlConnection* class. In the Oracle namespace, the connection object is the *OracleConnection* class. The same approach is used for every other provider, including the EF. The core connection object is the *EntityConnection* class.

The EntityConnection *class provides three constructors you can use to initialize a new instance of it.* The first of them uses the default constructor and accepts no parameters:

```
EntityConnection connection = new EntityConnection();
```

The second constructor accepts a connection string via a String parameter:

```
EntityConnection connection = new EntityConnection(ConnectionStringHere);
```

The first two work just as any other provider connection does, but the third one is fundamentally different. You need to specify information to the *Entity Data Model (EDM)*. Because you need to specify the metadata reference, you can't use the same ConnectionString formats you're used to, so it is best to use an EntityConnectionStringBuilder. It is common to use the EntityConnectionStringBuilder in conjunction with a SqlConnectionStringBuilder. The only noteworthy item is the specification of the metadata information that is specified through the EntityConnectionStringBuilder.Metadata property, as shown in the following:

```
String provider = "System.Data.SqlClient";
String serverName = "localhost";
String databaseName = "dbname";

SqlConnectionStringBuilder donnBuilder = new SqlConnectionStringBuilder();
ConnBuilder.DataSource = serverName;
ConnBuilder.InitialCatalog = databaseName;

EntityConnectionStringBuilder efBuilder = new EntityConnectionStringBuilder();
efBuilder.Provider = Provider;
efBuilder.ProviderConnectionString = ConnBuilder.ToString();
efBuilder.Metadata = @"*csdl, *ssdl, *msl";

EntityConnection Connection = new EntityConnection(EfBuilder.ToString());
```

As you expect, you have the Open and Close methods, the asynchronous counterparts, the BeginTransaction method, and a few others that aren't particularly noteworthy. The real differentiator is the specification of the Metadata model, as stated previously.

EntityCommand

EntityCommand works almost identically to its other provider-specific counterparts. Table 2-2 covers the primary methods, all of which are what you'd expect to see. This list isn't comprehensive, but it covers the methods you're likely to encounter on the exam or need to know to use the EntityCommand class, or both.

TABLE 2-2 EntityCommand methods

Method	Description
CreateParameter	Creates a new *EntityParameter* (used in conjunction with parameterized queries).
ExecuteNonQuery	Executes the Current command; used typically when you have an INSERT, UPDATE, or DELETE query. Also has an asynchronous counterpart named ExecuteNonQueryAsync.

Method	Description
ExecuteReader	Executes the query returning an EntityDataReader. Exhibits the same behavior that other provider DBDataReader implementations do. You can select the overloaded method, which enables you to specify a CommandBehavior that is usually desirable.
ExecuteScalar	Executes a query, returning only one value back. It is the equivalent of calling ExecuteReader and retrieving only the first value in the first row. If your query does not restrict results to one value, any other column values or any other rows are ignored. Also implemented with the ExecuteScalarAsync to provide asynchronous functionality.

EntityTransaction

Like its other siblings, EntityTransction can be used like the counterparts in other provider libraries. Other than setting the EntityConnection property and IsolationLevel, the only two members that you typically interact with are the Commit or Rollback methods. Remember that although you can use the EntityTransaction to provide transactional support, you can just as easily use a System.Transactions.TransactionScope, which is explained in Chapter 1.

Performing synchronous and asynchronous operations

Asynchronous operations are covered in depth in Chapter 1 (Objective 1.4). If you call the ExecuteScalar, ExecuteReader, or ExecuteNonQuery methods on an EntityCommand, they are blocking operations and nothing else can happen on that thread. The xxxAsync counterparts, on the other hand, don't block. Think about a typical operation to the database, particularly one that returns a large dataset or is on a constrained network. You have to connect to the database and execute the command, and the database then needs to process the command. If the command is a SELECT query or one that uses Output parameters or returns values, those values need to be buffered and returned. This can happen instantaneously in many cases or it can take a while. Even a few seconds can be enough to frustrate users tremendously, so implementing nonblocking methodology won't make the application run faster, but it will make it seem more responsive to end users.

The one notable difference between this implementation and previous versions is the existence of a CancellationToken property. The CancellationToken is of Type System.Threading. Tasks.Task<DBDataReader>.

Managing transactions (API)

Transactions are covered extensively in Chapter 1, but it is worth walking through the primary scenarios here that specifically pertain to the EF.

DbTransaction

The first choice you have is to use the *DbTransaction* directly. Note that this is an *IDbTransaction* instance, not *EntityTransaction* or something with EF-specific nomenclature.

How does it work? If you examine the DbContext class, you do not find a BeginTransaction method or anything nominally similar. The SaveChanges method initiates a Save on all the modified items and initiates a transaction on an item-by-item basis, but that's similar to what DataAdapters do when you call their Update method.

You have to get a hook to the underlying EntityConnection, which is exposed through the DbContext's Database property. From there, you call the BeginTransaction. Now note that there's no corresponding Commit or Rollback method on the EntityConnection. The Begin-Transaction returns an instance of a DBTransaction (if successful), so you need to provide an IDBTransaction variable to hold the reference to it. This reference is what you use to call either the Commit or Rollback methods:

```
EntityFrameworkSamplesEntities Context = new EntityFrameworkSamplesEntities();
IDbTransaction TransactionInstance = Context.Database.Connection.BeginTransaction();
try
{
  // Do Something
  Context.SaveChanges();
  TransactionInstance.Commit();
}
catch (EntityCommandExecutionException)
{
  TransactionInstance.Rollback();
}
```

You don't need to necessarily call the Rollback method in an Exception handler, but it is typically where you would do it. (Why roll back if things processed successfully?)

TransactionScope

The next approach that you're much more likely to encounter on the exam is the Transac-tionScope. The beauty of the TransactionScope is that you just need to call the Complete method after SaveChanges or whenever you're comfortable ending the transaction. If it fails, you don't need to do anything special; just handle processing as you normally would in case of a failure. For the Transaction, you need to concern yourself only with if/when it successfully completes. See the following example:

```
EntityFrameworkSamplesEntities Context = new EntityFrameworkSamplesEntities();
using (TransactionScope CurrentScope = new TransactionScope())
{
    try
    {
      Context.SaveChanges();
      CurrentScope.Complete();
    }
    catch (EntityCommandExecutionException)
    {
     //Handle the exception as you normally would
     //It won't be committed so transaction wise you're done
    }
}
```

The benefit of TransactionScope is that it handles everything from the simple to the complex in basically one method: Complete. Whether it is a WebService or any of the other providers, it never changes. This library, like its cousin System.Data.SqlClient (and OracleClient, OleDbClient, and so on), inherit, from the same set of classes or implement, the same interfaces. One library might have functionality that the others lack or do things more efficiently, but the behavior is virtually identical to other providers.

Thought experiment
When should you use Data Providers?

In the following thought experiment, apply what you've learned about this objective to predict what steps you need to take to build an application. You can find answers to these questions in the "Answers" section at the end of this chapter.

You have several applications that have been built using older versions of ADO.NET. Your development team is not very familiar with the EF and is still in the learning process. Your CTO has decided that everything should be ported to the newest version of the .NET Framework and all data access should use the EF.

With this in mind, answer the following questions:

1. Would using the Entity providers help facilitate the transition?

2. Is the decision to move all code to the EF a sound decision?

3. Should you employ any existing operations as asynchronous?

Objective summary

- Although the EF's purpose is to abstract as much as possible, you might need more advanced transaction support for operations that involve more than one record.

- A DBTransaction can be extracted from the DbContext.Database.Connection's BeginTransaction method. This method provides Commit and Rollback methods to handle both the success and failure of the operations.

- Although the DBTransaction class and BeingTransaction methods are available to implement transactional functionality, you can still use a TransactionScope to wrap database modification operations.

Objective review

Answer the following questions to test your knowledge of the information in this objective. You can find the answers to these questions and explanations of why each answer choice is correct or incorrect in the "Answers" section at the end of this chapter.

1. You need to execute a query against a SQL Server database and populate a set of objects. The retrieval operation is time-consuming, and users are complaining about sluggishness. You need to make sure the application doesn't seem to "hang" while the operation is taking place. Which of the following would accomplish that task? (Choose all that apply.)

   A. Use the ExecuteReader method of the EntityCommand class.

   B. Use the ExecuteScalarAsync method of the EntityCommand class.

   C. Use the ExecuteReaderAsync method of the SqlCommand class.

   D. Use the ExecuteReaderAsync method of the System.Data.OleDb.Command class.

2. The application you're working on uses the EF to generate a specific DbContext instance. The application enables users to edit several items in a grid and then submit the changes. Because the database is overloaded, you frequently experience situations that result in only partial updates. What should you do?

   A. Call the *SaveChanges* method of the *DbContext* instance, specifying the *UpdateBehavior.All* enumeration value for the *Update* behavior.

   B. Use a *TransactionScope* class to wrap the call to update on the *DbContext* instance.

   C. Create a Transaction instance by calling the *BeginTransaction* method of the *DbContext* Database property. Call the *SaveChanges* method; if it is successful, call the *Commit* method of the transaction; if not, call the Rollback method.

   D. Use a *TransactionScope* class to wrap the call to *SaveChanges* on the *DbContext*. Call *Complete* if *SaveChanges* completes without an exception.

3. The application you're working on uses the EF. You need to ensure that operations can be rolled back if there is a failure and you need to specify an isolation level. Which of the following would allow you to accomplish this? (Choose all that apply.)

   A. A EntityTransaction

   B. A TransactionScope

   C. A SqlTransaction

   D. A DatabaseTransaction

Objective 2.3: Query data by using LINQ to Entities

It should be clear by now that LINQ doesn't have to be used with the EF or vice versa, but each complements the other very well. Instead of using the ADO.NET libraries and traditional data structures to populate and manipulate objects, LINQ makes the job much easier. As you'll see, it is not an either/or situation; LINQ and EF work well with each other.

Querying data using LINQ operators

Unlike the current version of the EF, LINQ to Entities enables similar behavior, but items derive from the ObjectContext class.

Remember that a LINQ query consists of three distinct actions:

■ Obtain the data.

■ Create the query.

■ Execute the query.

For an item to be queryable through LINQ, it must implement either the IEnumerable or IQueryable interface. LINQ to Entities uses the ObjectQuery class, which happens to implement IQueryable.

A LINQ to Entities query does almost the same thing. To create a LINQ to Entities query, the following happens:

1. An *ObjectQuery* class instance is created from the *ObjectContext* class.

2. Compose a LINQ to Entities query using the *ObjectQuery* instance.

3. Convert to LINQ standard query operators or Expression Trees.

4. Execute the query.

5. Return the result to the client.

The semantics of an ObjectQuery are virtually identical to those of DbContext. You can use an ObjectQuery or derivative directly, or you can just use one of the interfaces passing in the object type you want to query. For instance, using the same model you have been using but instead using LINQ to Entities, you'd query the Account entities and return an Account with an AccountAlias property as follows:

```
IQueryable<Account> query = from acct in Context.Accounts
where acct.AccountAlias == "Primary"
select acct;
```

If you want to do the same by just retrieving one property (for instance, CreatedDate), simply make the following change, just as you would when using the EF and DbContext:

```
IQueryable<Account> query = from acct in Context.Accounts
where acct.AccountAlias == "Primary"
select acct.CreatedDate;
```

You can use the same features to populate your own objects (although usually that sort of defeats the purpose). Following is the first example creating a new Anonymous type:

```
IQueryable<Account> query = from acct in Context.Accounts
where acct.AccountAlias == "Primary"
select new{
            AccountAlias = acct.AccountAlias,
            CreatedDate = acct.CreatedDate
};
```

You could walk through hundreds of LINQ samples; for the purposes of this exam, just remember the difference. You use the ObjectContext class (or a derivative of it) when using LINQ to Entities; you use the DbContext (or derivatives) when using the current version of the EF.

EXAM TIP

You can use the var keyword, but an exam question might call it out with either IQueryable or IEnumerable. Note, however, that this doesn't mean one or the other is being used; both support either/both interface types.

The ObjectQuery class implements the IOrderedQueryable, IQueryable, IEnumerable, and IListSource interfaces. As indicated previously, the two return types you can use are IQueryable and IEnumerable, which are implemented in the previous examples. As such, an ObjectQuery is the most powerful of the bunch, but each is a valid option to use when querying LINQ to EDMs.

IEnumerable versus IQueryable

There are a few critical things you need to be able to distinguish on the exam. IEnumerable items are characterized by:

- Usage in LINQ to Objects or LINQ to XML
- Are performed in-memory
- Are performed on the heap

IQueryable items are notably different in most cases. They are characterized by:

- Run out of process
- Support several different datasources including remote ones
- Are used in LINQ to Entity Framework, LINQ to DataServices

Logging queries

Precisely because the Entity Framework or LINQ to SQL abstract queries from the developer, it's often important to be able to see what SQL Is being generated. There are several ways to accomplish this.

To log a query when using an ObjectQuery, you can simply use the ToTraceString method. Take a look at the following:

```
IQueryable<Account> Query = from Acct in Context.Accounts
where Acct.AccountAlias == "Primary"
select Acct;
```

You can cast this query explicitly to an ObjectQuery; upon doing so, you can trace the query information using the following addition:

```
String Tracer = (Query as ObjectQuery).ToTraceString();
```

The same can be accomplished using the DbContext in a similar manner:

```
String Output = (from Acct in ContextName.ContextSet
                        select Acct).ToString();
```

Thought experiment

What can you do to examine the SQL statements being generated to determine if they are the problem?

In the following thought experiment, apply what you've learned about this objective to predict what steps you need to take to build an application. You can find answers to these questions in the "Answers" section at the end of this chapter.

You're using LINQ to Entities and are experiencing serious performance problems. Your *database administrators (DBAs)* insist that your queries are the problem, but your developers tell you the opposite.

With this in mind, answer the following questions:

1. How can you determine the problem source?

2. What features should you implement?

Objective summary

- The primary difference between the current EF and LINQ to Entities is the class from which the context inherits. LINQ to Entities inherits from *ObjectContext*; EF inherits from *DbContext*.

- Return types for LINQ to Entities must implement either the *IQueryable* or *IEnumerable* interfaces. You can also use the generic form specifying the name of the class you want to query.

- You can retrieve the information about the query being constructed by calling the ToTraceString method of the ObjectQuery instance.

Objective review

Answer the following questions to test your knowledge of the information in this objective. You can find the answers to these questions and explanations of why each answer choice is correct or incorrect in the "Answers" section at the end of this chapter.

1. You are executing a query against a LINQ to EDM that contains an Account entity, among others. Which of the following are valid choices for storing the data?

   A. IListCollection<Account>

   B. ObjectQuery<Account>

   C. ObjectContext.Account

   D. IQueryable<Account>

2. Which interfaces must be implemented in order for something to be queried by LINQ? (Choose all that apply.)

   A. IEnumerable

   B. IQueryable

   C. IEntityItem

   D. IDbContextItem

Objective 2.4: Query and manipulate data by using ADO.NET

Although the EF is clearly the predominant data access path, Microsoft appears to have chosen, ADO.NET has been around for roughly 12 years and is a tried-and-true technology. There are countless books written on ADO.NET. Although each new ADO.NET version adds features, the basic workings and concepts remain the same.

> **This objective covers how to:**
> - Query data using Connection, DataReader, Command, DataAdapter, and DataSet
> - Perform synchronous and asynchronous operations
> - Manage transactions (API)

Querying data using Connection, DataReader, Command, DataAdapter, and DataSet

The Connection, DataReader, Command, DataAdapter, and Dataset/DataTable implementations are essential components of ADO.NET. Each implements a respective interface, as shown in Table 2-3.

TABLE 2-3 ADO.NET items

Type	Interface, implementation examples
Connection	IDbConnection is the interface that all Connection objects must implement. Examples include System.Data.SqlClient.SqlConnection and System.Data.OleDb.OleDbClient. OleDbConnection.
DataReader	DbDataReader is the base class that all provider-specific DataReader items inherit. Examples include System.Data.SqlClient.SqlDataReader, System.Data.OracleClient. OracleDataReader, and System.Data.OleDb.OleDbDataReader.
Command	IDbCommand is the interface that each Command object implements. Examples include System.Data.SqlClient.SqlCommand and System.Data.OleDb.OleDbCommand.
DataAdapter	IDbDataAdapter is the interface that DataAdapters implement. Examples include System. Data.SqlClient.SqlDataAdapter and System.Data.OleDb.OleDbDataAdapter.
DataTable	Part of the System.Data namespace. There are no provider-specific DataTable implementations.
DataSet	Part of the System.Data namespace. There are no provider-specific DataSet implementations.

Although there are provider-specific implementations of each of these, the exam focuses on the Microsoft-specific item if it is available. As such, those are the items that are covered.

SqlConnection

Any operation needs a connection to the database to do any processing. Information about the connection can be specified through the instance's properties directly; you can specify a name used in the <connectionStrings> section of the .config file or it can be specified inline. All you need to do is ensure that the connection that is opened is closed by explicitly calling the Close method in a try/finally block or a using block:

```
using (SqlConnection connection = new SqlConnection("ConnectionStringName"))
{
    connection.Open();
}
```

Several factors outside of your control can impede the creation and opening of a SqlConnection. As such, you should wrap any calls to the Open method in a try/catch or try/finally block.

SqlCommand

There are just a few major points to touch on with a SqlCommand, as follows:

- A SqlCommmand needs an open and available SqlConnection to operate.

- Other than the Connection property, CommandText is the only other item that you need to call. You can specify a stored procedure name instead of a SQL statement, but you need to specify CommandType.StoredProcedure if you are using a stored procedure.

- You should never concatenate values to build SQL strings. It leads to injection attack vulnerabilities, and even if you can protect the input sufficiently, it is wasted effort. If any dynamic values need to be added, use the SqlParameter class and include it in the SqlCommand's Parameters collection.

- There is much debate (and mythology) regarding the benefits of stored procedures versus "dynamic SQL." If SQL commands are built using parameterization, they can take advantage of cached execution plans that can lead to substantial performance increases. The argument of "Stored procedures versus dynamic SQL" has raged on for years (and probably will continue to do so), but as long as the dynamic SQL is parameterized, it will both perform better and be less vulnerable to attack.

- The *SqlCommand* has several execution options. You can use it as an input for a *SelectCommand* property in a *SqlDataAdapter*, you can call the *ExecuteScalar* method to retrieve an individual value, or you can call the *ExecuteReader* to retrieve a *SqlDataReader*.

- Each execution method features an asynchronous counterpart that is indicated by the prefix "Begin" at the beginning of it.

- Make sure that your SqlCommand is disposed of properly, so either call Dispose when you're done with it or wrap it in a using block.

The following code shows how to specify both a SqlConnection and SqlCommand using one SqlParameter named "@ID":

```
using (SqlConnection sqlConnection = new SqlConnection("ConnectionStringName"))
{
    connection.Open();
    using (SqlCommand sqlCommand = new SqlCommand("SELECT * FROM Transactions WHERE id =
@ID", Connection))
    {
        sqlCommand.Parameters.AddWithValue("@ID", "IDValue")
    }
}
```

SqlDataReader

SqlDataReader is a forward-only cursor that is the underpinning of all retrieval methods in ADO.NET. You invoke it by declaring an instance and calling the ExecuteReader or Begin ExecuteReader methods of the SqlCommand class. You need an open and available connection to use it, and you should always make sure that you explicitly close any SqlDataReader that you open.

Additionally, if you call ExecuteReader, the buffer is loaded, but it is not streamed back to the client until you actually iterate it by calling the Read method (typically, you'll wrap the Read method in a while loop to ensure that you iterate the complete set). You can tell if you have values by examining the HasRows property, but there's no way to tell how many records a SqlDataReader has without iterating it, which empties the buffer in the process.

```
using (SqlConnection Connection = new SqlConnection("ConnectionStringName"))
{
    Connection.Open();
    using (SqlCommand Command = new SqlCommand("SELECT * FROM Transactions WHERE id = @
ID", Connection))
    {
        Command.Parameters.AddWithValue("@ID", "IDValue");
        SqlDataReader Reader = Command.ExecuteReader(CommandBehavior.CloseConnection);
        while (Reader.Read())
        {
            // Do something.
        }
    }
}
```

SqlDataAdapter

SqlDataAdapter is the disconnected cousin of the *SqlDataReader*. After you iterate a *SqlDataReader*, you cannot iterate the same query again because it is empty. The *SqlData-Adapter*, on the other hand, populates a *DataSet* (with one *DataTable* per query specified in the *SelectCommand* property), and you can iterate the table as many times in as many directions as you see fit. You can even use LINQ semantics on it if you prefer. Additionally, if you insert rows in the underlying SQL Server table while a *SqlDataReader* is iterating (assume that you performed a query with no Restriction clause), the number of rows you end up with could be different than what it otherwise would have been if the INSERT had not happened. The adapter executes a query and builds the DataTable(s). You can immediately check the Count property of the DataTable Rows property to see the number of results, which is just one more thing differentiating the SqlDataAdapter from the SqlDataReader.

DataAdapters are designed to support the entirety of *Create, Retrieve, Update, Delete (CRUD)* operations. However, they can be used comprehensively or partially, meaning that you can use an adapter to simply perform retrieval operations, update operations, or insert operations. Adapters can also be used with either typed or untyped datasets, which should come as no surprise because typed datasets are simply descendants of untyped ones.

Data object lifecycle with a DataAdapter

When you call the Fill method of the DataAdapter (the most basic way to use the adapter), you can choose to have either a typed or an untyped dataset populated.

Untyped DataSets and DataTables

Assuming that you have a valid SqlCommand (with a correctly built connection and a valid SQL Statement) and you call Fill, the one line of code that executes actually causes a tremendous amount of work to happen. The adapter connects to the database, executes the command specified, and then handles the creation of the DataTable(s).

> **NOTE** **AUTOGENERATION OF DATACOLUMNS**
>
> By default, the DataAdapter uses the SELECT query's columns to generate DataColumns in the DataTable it is populating. If there are multiple columns defined in the query that have the same name (typically done by using an alias repeatedly), the adapter adds each of the columns, sequentially appending an integer value to the end of the column name. For the sake of illustration, assume that you had the following query:
>
> ```
> SELECT FirstName, FirstName, LastName as 'FirstName' FROM SampleTable
> ```
>
> The resulting DataTable would have three DataColumns added: FirstName1, FirstName2, and FirstName3, respectively.

If the CommandText contains only one SELECT statement, only one DataTable is created (if it does not exist already) and added to the DataSet. If a DataTable is used instead, it proceeds to create the schema and populate the rows. Each column specified in the SELECT query is examined, and a corresponding DataColumn value is added to the DataTable just created if the schema is not already specified. It interrogates the schema information and sets the corresponding DataColumn type. By default, DataColumns are the only items created by the adapter. However, the overloaded Fill method can be called, specifying a value of AddWith-Key to the MissingSchemeAction enumeration that will result in adding a primary key and integrity constraints (provided, of course, that they exist in the database table).

> **NOTE SETTING A PRIMARY KEY IN A DATATABLE**
>
> If a SELECT statement does not use a subquery or join, the adapter can be used to auto-matically generate a primary key or other constraints. If the results of the SELECT include an OUTER JOIN or subquery, however, there could easily be more than one key involved. There's no natural way for the adapter to know which key should take precedence, so it does not automatically generate one. In such cases, you need to manually create the primary key on the DataTable object. If you are using typed DataSets, each table can have a key designated at design time, and the integrity rules will be respected when the Fill method is called.

In addition to adding typed DataColumns based on the query statement, keys can also be generated by specifying the MissingSchemaAction property and setting it to Add. After the DataTable and DataColumn items are created, it takes the query values and builds a DataRow for each record returned. At this point, let's make a minor digression.

If you are just using a DataAdapter to execute SELECT queries, the state of the rows and the data they contain don't matter. Using this approach, it is your responsibility to track the changes to the data and decide whether it will be submitted to the database. If you plan instead to use the adapter to update the database, the DataTable in conjunction with the adapter will handle change tracking for you. The mechanism that's used to handle this change tracking is called DataRowState (which is accessed via the RowState property of a DataRow).

Although it depends on how InsertCommand, DeleteCommand, and UpdateCommand are generated, each value included in the SELECT command will map back to a column in the DataTable. A SqlParameter is created corresponding to each value, and when Update is called, each row is interrogated and the column in the DataRow is mapped to the respective parameter.

When the call to Fill is returned (unless you opt to set the AcceptChangesDuringFill property of the adapter to false, which is discussed in Table 2-5), each row that is returned from the database has a RowState value of Unchanged. So assume that you had the following code:

```
using (SqlConnection sqlConnection = new SqlConnection("ConnectionStringName"))
{
    using (SqlCommand sqlCommand = new SqlCommand("SELECT * FROM Transactions WHERE id =
@ID", sqlConnection))
    {
        sqlCommand.Parameters.AddWithValue("@ID", "IDValue");
        using (SqlDataAdapter sqlAdapter = new SqlDataAdapter(sqlCommand)
        {
            DataSet currentSet = new DataSet("CurrentSet");
            sqlAdapter.Fill(currentSet);
            sqlAdapter.Update(currentSet);
        }
    }
}
```

The call to Update would effectively do nothing because the RowState of each value in the DataSet would be Unchanged. If, on the other hand, you simply changed the AcceptChanges DuringFill property to false, as shown here, the call to Update would attempt to execute an Update statement for each row that was returned by calling the Fill method:

```
sqlAdapter.AcceptChangesDuringFill = false;
sqlAdapter.Fill(CurrentSet);
sqlAdapter.Update(CurrentSet);
```

If a typed DataSet or DataTable is used, the overall process is virtually identical, with the exception that the adapter isn't responsible for creating individual tables and columns.

Table 2-4 shows some interesting members you should be aware of.

TABLE 2-4 Refining Sqldata adapter behavior

Member	Comments
AcceptChangesDuringFill	Each DataRow in a DataTable has a RowState property that indicates the state of the row. By default, the RowState property is set to Unchanged when you call the Fill method. If you set AcceptChangesDuringFill to false, all the rows returned will have a RowState of Added. So if you had the adapter configured with an INSERT COMMAND, set AcceptChangesDuringFill to false, populated a DataTable, and then passed the same DataTable back to the adapter's Update method, you'd end up with attempted inserts for each of those rows (which would likely fail because of key constraints).

Member	Comments
AcceptChangesDuringUpdate	When the Update method is called, each row's RowState property is examined. If a RowState value is added, the adapter looks for an associated InsertCommand and attempts to insert the row in the underlying database table. If a RowState value of Modified is found, it looks for an Update command to use. If the RowState is deleted, a Delete command is fired against the row. After each row is updated successfully, the RowState is set back to Unchanged. Setting AcceptChangesDuringUpdate to false causes the RowState to remain. This can be desirable in transactional situations or if you want to reattempt to update the failed rows at a later time.
UpdateBatchSize	By default, rows are updated one at a time. This can lead to several roundtrips. By setting this property, modified rows are "batched" and sent back in groups. If you had 100 rows that were to be updated, and set this property to 100, calling Update would result in 1 round trip instead of 100.
OnRowUpdating/OnRowUpdated	Because rows can change and because you might want to provide end user feedback as updates progress, you can trap either or both of these events and use them to provide feedback about the update to the end user.
ContinueUpdateOnError	Assume you had an update that included 100 rows. Also assume that the 50th row caused a SqlException. Forty-nine rows would be updated and have a RowState of UnChanged and the rest would be left in the state they were in. If you set this to true, the SqlDataAdapter would try to continue to update the remaining rows 51-100.
FillSchema	FillSchema uses the SELECT command to build a corresponding DataTable object. This doesn't populate the table; it just builds it out according to the SELECT query.

To be fully functional, you can call both Fill and Update. The adapter needs each of the following properties set:

- SelectCommand
- InsertCommand
- UpdateCommand
- DeleteCommand

You do not have to have each of these in place to successfully call the Update method, but it is risky not to. Remember, on Update, the RowState of each row is examined, and depending on the RowState, the adapter makes a determination about which command to use. For a RowState of Added for instance, the InsertCommand property is used. For a RowState of modified, the UpdateCommand property is used.

DataAdapters are extremely powerful and, if used to their full potential, they provide an amazing amount of functionality. Although Adapters can perform some really complex functions, they can also be very easy to use.

```
using (SqlConnection sqlConnection = new SqlConnection("ConnectionStringName"))
{
    using (SqlCommand sqlCommand = new SqlCommand("SELECT * FROM Transactions WHERE id
= @ID", Connection))
    {
      //Note that there is no call to Open the adapter. When the Fill method
      // is called, the Adapter handles opening and closing the connection
      sqlCommand.Parameters.AddWithValue("@ID", "IDValue");
      using (SqlDataAdapter sqlAdapter = new SqlDataAdapter(Command))
      {
        DataSet CurrentSet = new DataSet("CurrentSet");
        sqlAdapter.Fill(CurrentSet);
      }
    }
}
```

Assume that you have a DataSet/DataTable that only has rows with RowState of Unchanged, but lacks a value for the InsertCommand, UpdateCommand, or DeleteCommand properties. As shown earlier, a call to Update will not cause a problem. If a single row has a RowState value of Added and there is no corresponding InsertCommand property set, an exception will be thrown. The same holds true for a missing UpdateCommand if a row with a RowState value of Modified is encountered or for a missing DeleteCommand if a row with a RowState value of Deleted is encountered.

Note that you have a choice in terms of handling the connection with the SqlDataAdapter. If you don't call the Open method of the underlying SqlConnection when you use a DataReader, you will encounter a SqlException. If you do not explicitly call the Open method of an adapter, it opens the connection and closes it as needed. If you do choose to manually open it, however, it defers responsibility back to you to close it. So if you open it, you must close it when it comes to SqlConnections. To illustrate how this works, here is one small modification to the previous example:

```
// Removing the using block on the SqlConnection instantiation to make sure the point
// isn't obscured

SqlConnection sqlConnection = new SqlConnection("ConnectionStringName");
using (SqlCommand sqlCommand = new SqlCommand("SELECT * FROM Transactions WHERE id = @
ID", Connection))
{
   sqlCommand.Parameters.AddWithValue("@ID", "IDValue");
   using (SqlDataAdapter sqlAdapter = new SqlDataAdapter(sqlCommand))
   {
     DataSet currentSet = new DataSet("CurrentSet");

     sqlConnection.Open();
   try{
     sqlAdapter.Fill(currentSet);
   }
  catch(SqlException){

 // Do something with the exception

}
finally{
    sqlCnnection.Close();
      }
   }
 }
```

Performing synchronous and asynchronous operations

The last section covered synchronous operations with each item. Asynchronous counterparts are simple to use and follow one basic pattern. Each asynchronous item is identified by the Begin modifier. So ExecuteReader is the SqlCommand method to create a SqlDataReader, and BeingExecuteReader is its asynchronous counterpart. Table 2-5 shows each asynchronous counterpart:

TABLE 2-5 Synchronous and asynchronous methods

Synchronous invocation	Asynchronous invocation
SqlCommand.ExecuteReader	SqlCommand.BeginExecuteReader
SqlCommand.ExecuteXmlReader	SqlCommand.BeginExecuteXmlReader
SqlCommand.ExecuteNonQuery	SqlCommand.BeginExecuteNonQuery

It is a straightforward process to use the asynchronous methods. First, you use an IAsyncResult and call the corresponding BeingXXX method. Next, you examine the IAsyncResult variable for the IsCompleted property to determine when completion has finished. Finally, call the EndXXX method passing in the IAsyncResult variable to it. At this point, you have a fully functional SqlDataReader, XmlReader, or completed result from an ExecuteNonQuery statement, as follows:

```
using (SqlConnection sqlConnection = new SqlConnection("ConnectionStringName"))
{
    sqlConnection.Open();
    using (SqlCommand sqlCommand = new SqlCommand("SELECT * FROM Transactions WHERE id
= @ID", Connection))
    {
        sqlCommand.Parameters.AddWithValue("@ID", "IDValue");
        IAsyncResult sqlResult sqlCommand.BeginExecuteReader(CommandBehavior.
CloseConnection);
        while (!sqlResult.IsCompleted)
        {
            //Wait or do something else
        }
        using (SqlDataReader sqlReader = sqlCommand.EndExecuteReader(Result))
        {
            // You have the reader, use it!
        }
    }
}
```

Managing transactions

Although the EF and ADO.NET provide a rich framework for data retrieval and state management, there's a distinct possibility that "something can go wrong" during both retrieval of data and updates. You have to make the determination about how you want to handle failures. Generally speaking, you can use an all-or-nothing approach (wrapping updates inside of a transaction and using Commit or Rollback functions) or a take-what-I-can-get approach (updating the items that worked and doing something else with the values that failed).

- A TransactionScope object supports DataAdapter.Update scenarios, DbContext or ObjectContext.SaveChanges operations, and just about any other traditional database– or MSM–based transaction scenario (including ones with transactional web services).

- You need to clearly understand the applications' goals and objectives before deciding how to handle transactions. In some cases, taking an all-or-nothing approach is desirable; after all, you know that all the data you have is the data you want. Conversely, if one single record is having a problem, a lot of time can be lost from the time the problem is first detected, the cause identified, and a resolution put in place. You can bypass this process altogether by accepting what you can and putting the rest on hold, but this can also have detrimental effects. It would depend largely on the organization, but imagine a scenario in which 100,000 records were written each day. Assume that they were all part of the end-of-day batch that attempted to update them all in an all-

or-nothing fashion. One failure would result in a day's delay (minimum) before things could continue. On the other hand, you might have a scenario in which 99 percent of the records complied, and only 1,000 records were left unattended. It might be much more difficult to get adequate attention and resources when only a small number of records is being stopped. These are all arbitrary and will vary from company to company, but it is worth noting that these concerns are quite common in development environments, and requirements can frequently change quite a bit over time.

Thought experiment
Performance problems

In the following thought experiment, apply what you've learned about this objective to predict what steps you need to take to build an application. You can find answers to these questions in the "Answers" section at the end of this chapter.

You've made extensive use of DataAdapters, and your application has been performing well. Lately, though, it has started to slow down dramatically, and users report that the longer they use the application, the more sluggish it becomes.

With this in mind, answer the following questions:

1. One manager is sure that it is a memory leak or something related to not closing connections, How can you determine the validity of such a statement?

2. What might you do to speed things up?

Objective summary

- The core objects in each provider-specific library are Connection, Command, Data-Adapter, and DataReader.

- Although you might not necessarily need a DataReader, chances are quite high that you will (remembering that, when you use a DataAdapter for retrieval operations, you are in turn using a DataReader under the hood). The same holds for less-obvious operations such as the ExecuteScalar method of the Command object or the Execute NonQuery method of the Command object.

- One can exert a great deal of control over an adapter's behavior by taking advantage of several of its properties, events, and methods. These include AcceptChangesDuringFill and AcceptChangesDuringUpdate, although there are quite a few more.

- For an adapter's Update operation to execute correctly, an appropriate SQL command is needed to match each operation that will be seen by virtue of the RowState of the contained rows. A DeleteCommand might not be necessary, for example, as long as there will never be rows that have a Rowstate of Deleted. If no rows will ever have a

RowState of Added, an InsertCommand property is not necessary. The same holds for Delete operations.

- Calling the AcceptChanges method on a DataRow ultimately sets the RowState value back to Unchanged. This happens, item by item, as an adapter runs an Update operation and finds changes. You can opt to ignore this behavior by setting AcceptChangesOnUpdate to false. Conversely, you can leave the rows with a uniform RowState of Added if the AcceptChangesDuringFill property is set to false.

- Although data column types can be ascertained from the columns used in a query, additional information can be identified and applied locally by using the MissingSchemaAction property. Even if you choose not to have the additions automatically generated, you can still define keys (through the primary key property of a DataColumn), constrain and type checks via the Constraints property, and even calculate fields by use of the Expression property.

- You can generate a data model from a database schema (or portions of it), or vice versa. And you can mix and match the methodologies.

Objective review

Answer the following questions to test your knowledge of the information in this objective. You can find the answers to these questions and explanations of why each answer choice is correct or incorrect in the "Answers" section at the end of this chapter.

1. You need to execute the following SELECT query using the COUNT aggregate to determine the total record count in a table:

   ```
   SELECT COUNT(*) FROM ExamQuestions;
   ```

   Which of the following enables you to do that? (Choose all that apply.)

   A. SqlDataAdapter in conjunction with a SqlDataReader

   B. SqlDataAdapter in conjunction with a DataTable

   C. SqlDataAdapter in conjunction with a DataSet

   D. The SqlDataReader ExecuteScalar method

2. Which of the following are true about SqlConnection objects? (Choose all that apply.)

   A. They should be opened at the last possible moment and closed at the earliest opportunity.

   B. They should be opened as early as possible and closed as early as possible.

   C. They should be opened as late as possible and closed as late as possible.

   D. As long as the Close statement is called in a catch block, the object will be closed and disposed of correctly.

3. What are the advantages of a compiled query?

    A. None. Every time you run the query you will hit the database.

    B. The results of the query are cached making the querying a lot faster.

    C. The translation of your query into SQL is cached.

    D. None. You can't change any of the parameters you use in a query, rendering the compiled query useless.

Objective 2.5: Create an Entity Framework data model

So the only thing that remains is building out a full Entity model. Although the important components needed for the exam are covered in Chapter 1, they are worth repeating because there will certainly be some coverage of the essential components of an EDM on the exam, as well as extensive coverage of what all features are provided by it.

> **This objective covers how to:**
>
> - Structure the data model using Table-per-Type and Table-per-Hierarchy inheritance
> - Choose and implement an approach to manage a data model (code first vs. model first vs. database first)
> - Implement POCO objects
> - Describe a data model by using conceptual schema definitions, storage schema definition, and mapping language (CSDL, SSDL, MSL)

Structuring the data model using Table-per-Type and Table-per-Hierarchy inheritance

For the exam, it's important to understand the inheritance mechanisms for an entity model. There are two primary mechanisms to be aware of:

- Table-per-Type
- Table-per-Heirarchy

The distinction between these is straightforward and easy to understand. Table-per-Type inheritance is accomplished by modifying the conceptual model (which should be no surprise). Architecturally, a separate database table is used to maintain data for non-inherited and key properties in the hierarchy.

Table-per-Type inheritance has several advantages and disadvantages over Table-per-Hierarchy inheritance. The benefits include:

- Data is not stored redundantly.

- Data is structured in third normal form so data integrity is improved.
- A much simpler implementation. Adding or removing an entity can be accomplished by simply adding or deleting the underlying table in the database.

There are downsides however and they include:

- There is a performance decrease, particularly around CRUD operations.
- Makes database administration more complicated because of all the additional tables in the system.

Table-per-Hierarchy inheritance, on the other hand, is characterized by the use of one database table for each item in the inheritance hierarchy. Table-per-Hierarchy has several advantages and disadvantages as well. The benefits include:

- Fewer database tables leading to a simplified database schema.
- Notably faster CRUD operations in most cases. (This is because all of the data is stored in one table.)

However with the benefits come costs and they are not inconsequential:

- There is necessary data redundancy, and because one of the main purposes of normalizing data is to remove redundancy, this is not a small issue.
- Data integrity issues are more likely because of data redundancy.
- Because of the data model, complexity is increased.

There's no one best answer or a one-size-fits-all solution. For the exam, pay close attention to the verbiage that will emphasize aspects that will lead you to choose one approach over the other.

Choosing and implementing an approach to manage a data model (code first vs. model first vs. database first)

Choosing a data model is an important concept but there's little to learn here. You have a specific set of options, and they aren't complex.

You can create an empty model and then add entities to it. As you add these entities, you can define relationships between them and control how they behave. After you define your EDM, you can elect to generate a database from the EDM; and the EF handles the database creation, the object/entity creation, and the mapping between them for you.

Or you can start with a database schema. From there, you can access any visible database object and generate an entity set from it. Again, the EF handles the creation of the Entity items and all the mapping that's needed between them.

You can take an existing model and change it as well. If the back end changes, you can re-generate the entities based on those changes, or you can visually edit the mappings between the new items and existing entity properties so that no breaking changes occur. (It is not always possible to fully avoid breaking changes, but they can be kept to a minimum through proper planning and design.)

The two approaches include starting with the database schema and using the designer as a starting point.

Take a look at how this works. First, you need to add an ADO.NET EDM to your project or open an existing one, as shown in Figure 2-2.

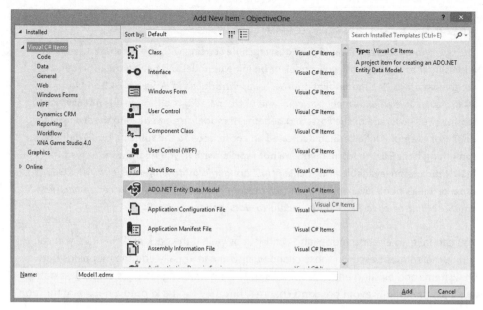

FIGURE 2-2 Adding an ADO.NET EDM

Next, you need to choose which approach you want to use. You can generate a model from a database or start with an empty model. Then build the entities and generate a database from it (or map it to an existing one). For this instance, opt for the Generate From Database option, as shown in Figure 2-3.

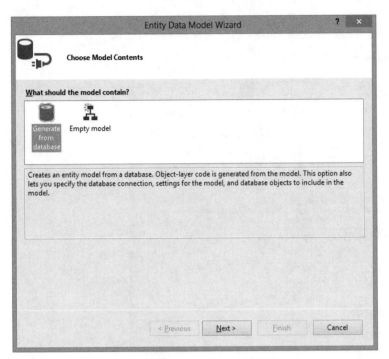

FIGURE 2-3 Generate from Database option

Next, specify connection information about the database. You have the option of including or excluding sensitive information, and you can optionally save it in the application's configuration file, as shown in Figure 2-4.

FIGURE 2-4 Choosing database connection information

Next is where the metaphorical rubber hits the road with the model. You are presented with all the database objects your connection permissions allow. Typically, you should choose Tables, but you also have views, functions, and stored procedures available if they are present. Select all of Tables, as shown in Figure 2-5.

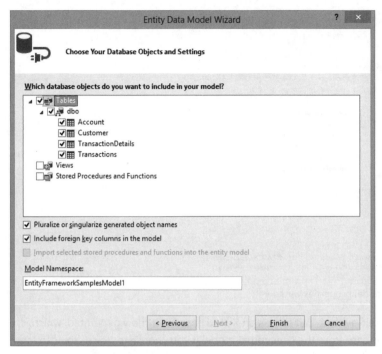

FIGURE 2-5 Choosing your database objects and settings

After you select the items, select Finish and you'll be presented with a canvas that shows each entity and the relationship it has to the other entities. If done correctly, you should see a designer surface that looks like Figure 2-6.

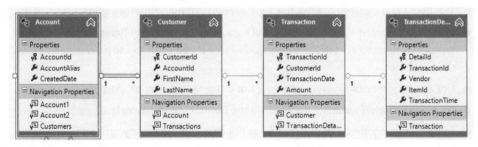

FIGURE 2-6 Entity diagram

The last thing you need to do is click inside the designer surface and then right-click and select Properties. You'll see the Properties grid, which has several options about the model you'll want to take note of (see Figure 2-7).

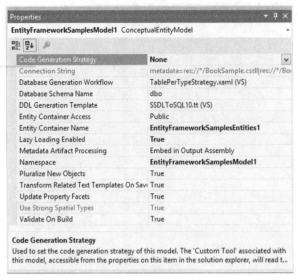

FIGURE 2-7 Conceptual model properties window

The properties are self-evident, but there's an XAML-based workflow generated, which is used to generate a database from the conceptual model if you choose to do so. You can indicate whether to use lazy loading; choose the namespaces you want to use; indicate the container access levels; and a few others, such as whether to pluralize the names of new objects.

If you click around on any of the entities or their properties, you can see clues that you're dealing with .NET classes. The following is a list of class properties that can be changed (via the Properties grid or by editing the underlying code file):

- The Base Class Library type, via the Type property in the Properties grid.

- Whether or not the type is Nullable. Because the class property types can be Value types, you need to set the Nullable value to true if you want to use nulls instead of default values.

- Get and set accessor visibility levels via the Getter and Setter properties.

- An autogenerated value for the field via the Default Value property.

- Ensuring that another user or process has not changed the value you're referencing prior to submitting a save with the Concurrency Mode property. To ensure that the value has not changed, you need to set the Concurrency Mode property to Fixed. There are two very noteworthy aspects of this property. First, there is currently no way to set this value at the entity level; you have to set it individually on each property. (This may be changed in a future update, but there's no hard documentation on it at the time of this writing.) The second is that setting this property to Fixed has performance implications. When set, prior to an attempt to save the record, the database must be queried to determine what the current value of the field is. Fortunately, if multiple fields are set to Fixed, they are consolidated into one query. So if you have 50 fields set to Fixed, one query determines that a value has changed, not 50 individual ones.

Click any one of the entities generated and examine the Properties window. Notice that you can select a Base type, and if you click in the grid to set a type, you will encounter a list of other types currently defined in the model. This means exactly what you would expect it would: One item can inherit from another, from another, from another (see Figure 2-8).

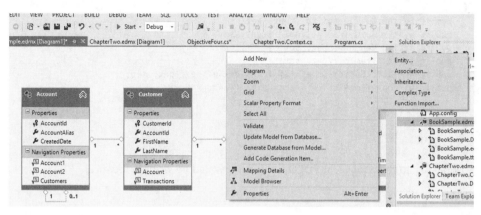

FIGURE 2-8 Designer canvas

As you can see, you can create new entity types, associations, inheritance definitions, and complex types. After you finish, you can select the Generate Database from Model option, and all the new items you added will appear there.

Implementing POCOs

You can (and frequently will) employ *plain old common objects (POCOs)* with your data model. To use a POCO, you simply need to abide by a few guidelines:

- The name of the entity type must match the POCO name.
- Each entity property must map to a public POCO property.
- The names of the types and the actual property types themselves must map and be equivalent (obviously there's no magic that can map the name "Microsoft" to a GUID).

When you define an entity in the EF, the default behavior is for EF to write .NET classes that match the definition you specify in the designer. Obviously, things can't work both ways; either your classes are generated for you, or you need to define them because the current incarnation of the EF won't build them for you. Because autogeneration is the default behavior, you need to disable it in order to build your POCOs. If you examine your model, you can see a value specified for the Custom Tool property in the Properties grid. Removing this value tells Visual Studio that it should not generate the corresponding classes. Examine the following code snippet, which is the autogenerated code that Visual Studio created for the TransactionDetails entity definition specified earlier:

```
namespace ObjectiveOne
{
    using System;
    using System.Collections.Generic;
    public partial class TransactionDetail
    {
        public System.Guid DetailId { get; set; }
        public System.Guid TransactionId { get; set; }
        public string Vendor { get; set; }
        public string ItemId { get; set; }
        public Nullable<System.DateTime> TransactionTime { get; set; }
        public virtual Transaction Transaction { get; set; }

    }

}
```

So what would the equivalent POCO look like? It would be virtually identical:

```
namespace ObjectiveOne
{
    using System;
    using System.Collections.Generic;
    public partial class TransactionDetail
    {
        public System.Guid DetailId { get; set; }
        public System.Guid TransactionId { get; set; }
        public string Vendor { get; set; }
        public string ItemId { get; set; }
        public Nullable<System.DateTime> TransactionTime { get; set; }

    }

}
```

As this example illustrates, other than the Transaction property, there is no real difference in the scalar values defined. Now, this definition is virtually identical, but what if you were building a POCO that contained a reference that was the "many" portion of a one-to-many relationship? It is quite simple, really. You build out the scalar properties as shown here, but add a property (defined as a generic type list using the "many" class definition).

You need to manually create each class that you want to employ as a POCO after instructing Visual Studio to refrain from autogenerating the items. The last step after doing this is to effectively wire up the POCO(s) to the context. If this step isn't done, then there's no way for the context (either the DbContext or ObjectContext, depending on the EF version you're using) to know these classes exist and therefore manipulate them. Fortunately, wiring these classes up to the context is quite easy; simply do the following:

1. Define a property in the context corresponding to each POCO you created.

2. Define the property using the ObjectSet (if you're using an ObjectContext) or DbSet (if you're using the DbContext) generic class, specifying your POCO as the target definition.

3. Add code to the context's constructor, initializing the property calling the CreateObjectSet base class method (again, passing in the POCO class definition to the method).

The approach to adding POCOs to a context is virtually identical whether you use the DbContext or ObjectContext, but both are covered in this section. For the sake of simplicity, assume that there is a POCO corresponding to each of the entity types shown in Figure 2-8.

DbContext

For each POCO, decorate the class definition with the Table attribute, specifying a name of the underlying table (pluralizing in most cases):

```
[Table("Account")]
public class Account{}

 [Table("Customers")]
public class Customers{}[Table("TransactionDetails")]
public class TransactionDetail{}Table("Transactions")]
public class Transaction{}
```

The previous examples assume that you have the ScalarProperty and NavigationProperty items created. After they are built, though, you simply need to define them in the DbContext and they are ready for use:

```
public partial class EntityFrameworkSamplesEntitiesDb : DbContext
{
      public EntityFrameworkSamplesEntitiesDb(): base("name=EntityFrameworkSamples
Entities1")
{}

public DbSet<Account> Accounts { get; set; }
      public DbSet<Customer> Customers { get; set; }
      public DbSet<TransactionDetail> TransactionDetails { get; set; }
      public DbSet<Transaction> Transactions { get; set; }
}
```

ObjectContext

If you use ObjectContext, the process is virtually identical, but has a few small differ-ences. First, your context inherits from the ObjectContext base class instead of the Db-Context class. Next, the properties inside the context are typed as DbSet types instead of ObjectSet types. Finally, you need to initialize the properties in the constructor using the new ObjectSet<TypeName>(); syntax:

```
public partial class EntityFrameworkSamplesEntitiesSample : ObjectContext
{
        public EntityFrameworkSamplesEntitiesSample(): base("name=EntityFramework
SamplesEntities1")
{
    Accounts = new ObjectSet<Account>();
    Customers = new ObjectSet<Customer>();
    TransactionDetails = new ObjectSet<TransactionDetail>();
    Transactions = new ObjectSet<Transaction>();
}
    public ObjectSet<Account> Accounts { get; set; }
    public ObjectSet<Customer> Customers { get; set; }
    public ObjectSet<TransactionDetail> TransactionDetails { get; set; }
    public ObjectSet<Transaction> Transactions { get; set; }
}
```

At this point, your POCOs are built and defined correctly, the properties in your context are defined, and the properties have been wired up and are ready to use.

Describing a data model using conceptual schema definitions, storage schema definitions, and mapping language (CSDL, SSDL, & MSL)

The current version of the EF wraps each of the component elements in the .edmx file, but this is more of a grouping difference than anything else. It is absolutely critical to understand-ing the role of each and why it matters. After you have that understanding, how they are stored becomes little more than a matter of elegance and convenience.

> **MORE INFO** .EDMX FILE
>
> In the original versions of the EF, an entity model comprised a CSDL file, an SSDL file, and an MSL file. The current incarnation uses an .edmx file instead. The .edmx file is an XML file that defines each of the elements that these previous three files contained (a conceptual model, a storage model, and a mapping model). In addition to containing the necessary information about each of these three components, it contains additional information that is used by Visual Studio and the Entity Designer to facilitate design time support of the model.

As a mnemonic cue, think of the following. The EF is an ORM. "Map" begins with "M," so it is easy to remember that the MSL (mapping specification language) is the last part of the equation; it maps the object model to the database model. The storage schema definition language (SSDL) has both "storage" and "schema" in the acronym, which is a sure giveaway that it deals with a data store component of the process. That leaves the conceptual schema definition language (CSDL): The letter "C" comes before the letter "S" in the alphabet, as does "O" (for "object"). This is not the most elegant way to memorize the differences, but it works. Thought of another way, the "S" represents "schema," which is indicative of a data store. The "C" represents the concept or the data abstraction. The "M" represents a map between the two.

Conceptual schema definition language (CSDL)

The CSDL aspect of the EDM is the "object" part of the object-relational mapper trinity. According to MSDN, it describes the entities, relationships, and functions that "comprise a conceptual model of a data-driven application." In short, the CSDL is the EF's implementation of the EDM.

Storage schema definition language (SSDL)

The SSDL is another XML syntax that represents the storage model of the underlying data-base. For the purposes of this exam, you don't need to memorize or learn the whole SSDL spec; just know that it holds the information about the data store, and, when built, that it is incorporated into the .edmx just like the other two files (.csdl, .msl).

Mapping specification language (MSL)

The MSL is the last portion of what builds the model. In the current EF version, there are several other files that are generated. An .edmx model contains each of the following items:

- An .edmx file that serves as the container for everything else.

- A ModelName.Context.tt file for template generation of the underlying .NET classes specified in the model.

- A ModelName.Context.cs class that contains the .NET code definition of the respective context. Each context instance built or generated for this context will appear in the source tree as a node of the ModelName.Context.cs node.

- A ModelName.Designer.cs class that provides design time support for the entity definitions.

- A ModelName.edmx.Diagram that includes an XML representation shown in the following:

```
<?xml version="1.0" encoding="utf-8"?>
    <edmx:Edmx Version="2.0" xmlns:edmx="http://schemas.microsoft.com/
ado/2008/10/edmx">
    <!-- EF Designer content (DO NOT EDIT MANUALLY BELOW HERE) -->
    <edmx:Designer xmlns="http://schemas.microsoft.com/ado/2008/10/edmx">
    <!-- Diagram content (shape and connector positions) -->
    <edmx:Diagrams>
<Diagram DiagramId="8576b1de6991436caba647ac89886831" Name="Diagram1">
<EntityTypeShape EntityType="EntityFrameworkSamplesModel1.Account" Width="1.5"
```

```
PointX="7.5" PointY="0.875" IsExpanded="true" />
<EntityTypeShape EntityType="EntityFrameworkSamplesModel1.Customer" Width="1.5"
PointX="9.75" PointY="0.875" IsExpanded="true" />
<EntityTypeShape EntityType="EntityFrameworkSamplesModel1.TransactionDetail"
Width="1.5" PointX="14.25" PointY="0.875" IsExpanded="true" />
<EntityTypeShape EntityType="EntityFrameworkSamplesModel1.Transaction" Width="1.5"
PointX="12" PointY="0.875" IsExpanded="true" />
<AssociationConnector Association="EntityFrameworkSamplesModel1.FK_Account_
Account" ManuallyRouted="false" />
<AssociationConnector Association="EntityFrameworkSamplesModel1.FK_Customer_
Account" ManuallyRouted="false" />
<AssociationConnector Association="EntityFrameworkSamplesModel1.FK_Transactions_
Customer" ManuallyRouted="false" />
<AssociationConnector Association="EntityFrameworkSamplesModel1.FK_
TransactionDetails_Transactions" ManuallyRouted="false" />

</Diagram>

</edmx:Diagrams>
</edmx:Designer>
</edmx:Edmx>
```

- A ModelName.tt file that contains template information needed to generate the data classes.

Looking at the .edmx definition in the Solution Explorer with each item expanded will show how it all fits together (see Figure 2-9).

FIGURE 2-9 .edxm file in depth

Each of these specs is supported and generated and happens to be incorporated into the .edmx file. All it does is perform as the map between the SSDL and CSDL. This is the component that tells them how to communicate, how the end-user objects end up in the database, and vice versa.

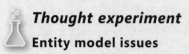

Thought experiment
Entity model issues

In the following thought experiment, apply what you've learned about this objective to predict what steps you need to take to build an application. You can find answers to these questions in the "Answers" section at the end of this chapter.

You have a huge set of legacy code that employs traditional ADO.NET. You have been charged with moving it to the EF.

With this in mind, answer the following questions:

1. Should you use POCOs or use entities exclusively?

2. Would it make sense to use EF to populate your existing business objects and leave everything else in place?

Objective summary

- The CSDL file holds the information about the EDM. It is a subset of the .edmx model.
- The SSDL file holds the information about the relational data store. It is also a subset of the .edmx model.
- The MSL is the final piece that defines the mappings between the entities and the underlying data store. It is also a subset of the .edmx model.
- You can generate a data model from a database schema (or portions of it), or vice versa. And you can mix and match the methodologies.
- You can use POCOs with the EF as long as you follow a few simple guidelines.

Objective review

Answer the following questions to test your knowledge of the information in this objective. You can find the answers to these questions and explanations of why each answer choice is correct or incorrect in the "Answers" section at the end of this chapter.

1. Which of the following are necessary components of an EDM? (Choose all that apply.)

   A. SSDL

   B. MSL

   C. CSDL

   D. .edmx

2. You have been tasked with completing a coworker's data model. You are told that there are some specific issues in the .ssdl file and the .msl file, but when you look at the project, you don't see either of them. What is the problem?

   A. The actual .csdl file no longer exists because it has been consolidated in the .edmx files. Its logical purpose is still contained and present, however.

   B. The actual .msl file no longer exists because it has been consolidated in the .edmx files. Its logical purpose is still contained and present, however.

   C. The actual .csdl file no longer exists because it has been consolidated in the .edmx files. Because it is no longer needed, there is no need to reference it or for anything to try to replace it.

   D. The actual .msl file no longer exists because it has been consolidated in the .edmx files. Because it is no longer needed, there is no need to reference it or for anything to try to replace it.

3. You are building an ADO.NET Entity Framework application. You need to validate each of the models. Which Entity Data Model tool can you use to accomplish this?

   A. The EDM Generator (EdmGen.exe)

   B. ADO.NET Entity Data Model Designer

   C. Entity Data Model Wizard

   D. Update Model Wizard

Chapter summary

- You can use the EF or ADO.NET with LINQ to perform very complex and intricate data manipulation.

- Deferred execution is a critical behavior of LINQ queries. Remember that you get the data back only when you "demand" it either through an aggregate or through referencing a *NavigationProperty*.

- You can use *lazy loading* to minimize bringing back data that you don't end up using, but it comes at the cost of more potential roundtrips.

- You can use *eager loading* to bring back all the data of related entities referenced in a LINQ query.

- There is substantial transaction support for each potential data access technology. Using the *System.Transactions.TransactionScope* is the most prominent and most flexible.

- The EF is the Microsoft ORM. The CSDL, SSDL, and MML files that comprised the previous versions are all wrapped in the .edmx file in the current version of the EF, but the underlying mechanisms and behaviors are exactly the same.

Answers

This section contains the solutions to the thought experiments and answers to the objective review questions in this chapter.

Objective 2.1: Thought experiment

1. The answer depends on how the data is used. Chances are that only a portion of the items in the chain will be referenced frequently. You might have an application that needs all the data or most of it for every typical use case, however. It depends on the nature of the application. It should be tested extensively, and logging and tracing should be used to see how frequently the nonparent data is referenced.

2. If you pull back all the data, you might have performance or responsiveness issues, especially if you have network constraints. If each of the children or grandchildren has only a few records and is small in size, this will be minimized. However, if there are substantially sized records or high record counts on any of the descendants, it might take a lot longer to query and update and could cause serious issues with application responsiveness.

3. If you chose to lazy load the data, and it is necessary for the majority of the use cases, you will cause several roundtrips to the server. Over a constrained network or a low-powered device, these frequent roundtrips could easily cause wait times that greatly exceed the overhead of pulling all the data back at once.

4. Several factors should go into your decision. First, the number of records should be considered. If you have only one or two records for each of the child relations, and the record sizes are small, pulling it all down at once will probably be beneficial. But even if the record count is small or the record size is small, if you don't need the data, there's no use of pulling it down. As such, the typical use cases should be tested extensively, and you should have logging in place to help build frequency distributions of usage. This necessitates a good bit more work up front, both in testing and analyzing, but will pay huge dividends down the road because getting it wrong is very expensive to correct.

Objective 2.1: Review

1. **Correct answer:** C

    A. **Incorrect:** Because of the *FirstOrDefault*, it is executed immediately.

    B. **Incorrect:** With the *FirstOrDefault*, it is executed immediately and does not need to be iterated.

C. **Correct:** Because the value is returned immediately, it works without any iteration.

D. **Incorrect:** Lazy loading is important, but not here.

2. **Correct answers:** A, B

A. **Correct:** If there is no key constraint violation, a second copy of the entity will be created in the database.

B. **Correct:** If there is a key constraint violation, an exception will be thrown.

C. **Incorrect:** The values will not be merged

D. **Incorrect:** The values will not be merged.

3. **Correct answer:** C

A. **Incorrect:** A copy is not added with an EntityState of Unchanged.

B. **Incorrect:** A copy is not added with an EntityState of Added.

C. **Correct:** There isn't an operation because it already exists.

D. **Incorrect:** The original entity is not updated or merged.

Objective 2.2: Thought experiment

1. The syntax is much closer to old ADO.NET, and it would make some sense to take an incremental approach. By using similar objects, testing is minimized and there is a higher likelihood that no new bugs will be introduced. You can make the converse argument that completely revamping everything saves some time and effort, but using an incremental approach is probably best in this case.

2. "Sound" is somewhat relative, and if existing applications are already in place, tested, and working, any changes introduce the possibility of new bugs. On the other hand, the EF is clearly the choice that Microsoft has made for data access, and if it is not done, two skill sets are ultimately needed. It really depends on how important consistency is and how much legacy code is in place.

3. Asynchronous operations have been available since the inception of .NET. If the operations should have been asynchronous initially and were implemented statically, this provides an opportunity to fix it. On the other hand, asynchronous programming is much more complicated, and bugs are often much harder to find and diagnose. Under the circumstances, it is prudent to replace the existing provider code with entity data provider code as closely as possible, unless big mistakes were made originally by overlooking asynchronous operations.

Objective 2.2: Review

1. **Correct answer:** C

   A. **Incorrect:** Using the ExecuteReader method, the EntityCommand would carry as much, and likely more, overhead than the ADO.NET equivalent. There is no benefit in processing or on the client side.

   B. **Incorrect:** Using the async call can keep the operation from blocking, but the type here is incorrect.

   C. **Correct:** Using the ExecuteReaderAsync in conjunction with the SqlCommand class would accomplish this goal. Overall processing wouldn't speed up, but the blocking on the client would be reduced, giving the impression of a much more responsive UI.

   D. **Incorrect:** Provider-specific libraries are always the fastest. Because this database is SQL Server, the SqlClient namespace can be used, and it would operate more quickly and with more features than the more generic OleDb equivalent.

2. **Correct answer:** D

   A. **Incorrect:** SaveChanges can help the scenario, but only if done in the context of another transaction. Without one, it is of no value in this case.

   B. **Incorrect:** A TransactionScope would be a good choice, but the DbContext doesn't have an Update method, so it is irrelevant.

   C. **Incorrect:** This approach could work, but the transaction would need to be established on the connection, not on the context.

   D. **Correct:** Calling SaveChanges inside of a TransactionScope and selecting the Complete property if things are successful accomplishes this goal perfectly.

3. **Correct answers:** A, B

   A. **Correct:** An EntityTransaction would accomplish each goal as it provides rollback functionality and setting of an isolation level.

   B. **Correct:** A TransactionScope would accomplish each goal as it provides rollback functionality and setting of an isolation level.

   C. **Incorrect:** A SqlTransaction would work, but not in this context.

   D. **Incorrect:** There is not a valid class called DatabaseTransaction.

Objective 2.3: Thought experiment

1. Obviously, logging is needed to determine what SQL is being sent back to the database. It is possible that the problem is the queries, the database, or both. The only way to know is to rule out one thing at a time—in this case, start with the entity logging.

2. Depending on the source, the LINQ queries might need restructuring. Lazy loading and caching might be in order. Moving the queries to stored procedures might help (not because stored procedures are inherently faster, but because they would yield the same queries each time, which in turn might help with cached execution plans).

Objective 2.3: Review

1. **Correct answers:** B, D

   A. **Incorrect:** IListCollection is not a valid interface and would not work.

   B. **Correct:** ObjectQuery implements IOrderedQueryable, IQueryable, IEnumerable, IListSource, and Account is a valid type.

   C. **Incorrect:** The ObjectContext base class does not have or use a custom Account entity.

   D. **Correct:** IQueryable passing in the Account type will definitely work.

2. **Correct answer:** D

   A. **Incorrect:** There is no UpdateBehavior enumeration.

   B. **Incorrect:** A SqlDataAdapter has an Update method, but there is no Update method on the DbContext.

   C. **Incorrect:** There is no Commit or Rollback method of the database's Connection property.

   D. **Correct:** Wrapping the operation in a TransactionScope and calling Complete will work outside of the current zone.

3. **Correct answers:** A, B

   A. **Correct:** The item must be either IEnumerable or IQueryable.

   B. **Correct:** The item must be IEnumerable or IQueryable.

   C. **Incorrect:** IEntityItem will not work and has no value here.

   D. **Incorrect:** IDbContextItem will not work and has no value here outside of the current zone.

Objective 2.4: Thought experiment

1. If you're opening the adapters, there's a possibility they aren't being closed and disposed of properly. However, if you're relying on the adapter to open and close the connection, it is unlikely that it is the problem. The more likely issue is that you are caching too much data locally, and it is being held on to well past its useful life. Less caching and more round trips to the database might actually help in this case, depending on the exact nature of the problem, but each area should be looked at.

2. Overuse of a DataAdapter could be a problem. Remember that an adapter always uses a DataReader. There might be times when individual values are being queried using an adapter that could be replaced with a DataReader. You might be able to determine counts and aggregates from the returned data instead of executing aggregate queries. You might be able to rely less on joins and use DataRelations locally to enforce constraints. You could also consider disabling and reenabling constraints before and after load operations.

Objective 2.4: Review

1. **Correct answers:** B, C, D

   A. **Incorrect:** A SqlDataAdapter cannot be used with a SqlDataReader together at all.

   B. **Correct:** A SqlDataAdapter and a DataSet will work for this (use the Rows property of the primary DataTable).

   C. **Correct:** A SqlDataAdapter and a DataTable will work for this (use the Rows property of the DataTable).

   D. **Correct:** ExecuteScalar would work assuming that the COUNT aggregate function was used, which it was.

2. **Correct answer:** A

   A. **Correct:** Leaving connections open when they aren't being used is wasteful and can cause serious performance problems. Accordingly, they should always be opened at the last possible moment before they are needed and closed immediately when they are no longer needed.

   B. **Incorrect:** Opening a connection before it is needed is wasteful and could have serious performance implications.

   C. **Incorrect:** Leaving a connection open when it is no longer needed is wasteful and could cause serious performance problems.

   D. **Incorrect:** Calling Close in a Finally block, or wrapping it in a using statement would ensure that it is closed properly. If Close is called inside a Catch block, it is entirely possible that another exception could be thrown there, leading to the connection dangling unclosed.

3. **Correct answer:** C

   A. **Incorrect:** It's true that you will hit the database each time you execute the query. But there is still a performance gain because a compiled query caches the steps required to convert your query to SQL.

   B. **Incorrect:** It's not the results of the query that are cached. Instead the generated SQL is cached. This can be parameterized to get specific data from the database.

   C. **Correct:** By caching the generated SQL a compiled query can execute faster.

D. Incorrect: The generated SQL is cached but it's also parameterized so you can specify new values for your parameters on each execution.

Objective 2.5: Thought experiment

1. POCOs might make sense; they might not. The more you're moving to Entities, the less relevant POCOs will generally be, although that's a general statement and there are plenty of exceptions. If you have the POCOs already, it would help make the case to continue their use. If not, and you're using DataSets and DataTables exclusively, moving to Entities completely would probably make more sense.

2. One could make the case that just changing the plumbing, so to speak, would be a good intermediate strategy. But generally it is not worth the effort. If there's a ton of code with a lot of complex UI behavior, it could provide some benefit because you wouldn't need to regression test as much. On the other hand, for smaller-sized projects, it is probably just a waste of extra effort with very little value proposition.

Objective 2.5: Review

1. **Correct answers:** A, B, C, D

    A. Correct: The SSDL file is necessary to define the database schema information.

    B. Correct: The MSL file is necessary to define the mappings between the other two files.

    C. Correct: The CSDL file is necessary to define the entity layer of the application.

    D. Correct: The MSL, CSDL, and SSDL files are all necessary and are rolled into the .edmx file.

2. **Correct answers:** A, B

    A. Correct: The CSDL file doesn't physically exist in later versions of EF. However, the core of what they do is still needed; they just take a different form and are consolidated inside the .edmx model.

    B. Correct: The MSL file doesn't physically exist in later versions of EF. However, the core of what they do is still needed; they just take a different form and are consolidated inside the .edmx model.

    C. Incorrect: The CSDL file contents might be incorporated into the .edmx file, but the service it provides is still necessary. Without an equivalent functionality, the model will not work.

    D. Incorrect: The MSL file contents might be incorporated into the .edmx file, but the service it provides is still necessary. Without an equivalent functionality, the model will not work.

3. **Correct answers:** A, B

- **A.** **Correct** The EdmGen.exe tool can be used with the ValidateArtifacts switch to validate a model.

- **B.** **Correct:** The ADO.NET entity model designer can be used to validate models.

- **C.** **Incorrect:** The entity data model wizard may validate a model during creation but will not perform the validation after the fact.

- **D.** **Incorrect:** The Update Model Wizard is intended to let you update an .edmx file after changes have been made to the underlying database. It is not intended to perform validation.

CHAPTER 3

Designing and implementing WCF Services

This chapter covers designing and implementing *Windows Communication Foundation (WCF)* Services. WCF is a major component on the exam. Several questions on the exam deal with WCF, as the exam outline clearly indicates (19 percent, according to Microsoft). There are also other areas of the exam that make sense only in the same context as WCF, such as Data Services.

You do not need to be an expert in WCF to do well on this exam, but you need a strong background in it. If you came to .NET after version 3.0 of the Framework, you likely started off using WCF. If you started on an earlier version, you likely would have done it either directly through client-server programming or by using one of the technologies that WCF wrapped up, namely .NET Remoting, .asmx web services, *Web Services Enhancements (WSE*—pronounced "wizzy"), .NET Enterprise Services, and *Microsoft Message Queue (MSMQ)*.

Again, keep in mind that although technically this objective is just 19 percent of the exam according to Microsoft, WCF features so prominently that the more familiar you are with it as a whole, the better prepared you'll be.

Objectives in this chapter:

- Objective 3.1: Create a WCF service
- Objective 3.2: Configure WCF services by using configuration settings
- Objective 3.3: Configure WCF services by using the API
- Objective 3.4: Secure a WCF service
- Objective 3.5: Consume WCF services
- Objective 3.6: Version a WCF service
- Objective 3.7: Implement messaging patterns
- Objective 3.8: Host and manage services

Objective 3.1: Create a WCF service

WCF is a runtime and a corresponding set of application programming interfaces (APIs) that facilitate building distributed applications. WCF Services can range from the absolutely trivial (little more than outputting "hello world" to a screen) to extremely sophisticated, which should come as no surprise because WCF is Microsoft's premier technology for building applications employing Service-Oriented Architecture (SOA).

> **This objective covers how to:**
> - Define SOA concepts
> - Create contracts
> - Implement message inspectors
> - Implement asynchronous operations in the service

Defining SOA concepts

Before going into a discussion on building or maintaining services, there are some definitions and principles that need to be defined:

- **Service**   A component that is capable of performing one or more tasks.
- **Service definition**   Precise term defining a feature of the service. The service definition takes the form of a contract. Use of contracts is a defining characteristic of SOA. It's also an absolute requirement for a WCF Service (and one of the main things that differentiate it from traditional web services). Service definition contracts are a requirement, although the requirement can be met a few different ways. In WCF, the requirement is most commonly (and as we'll explain shortly, most easily) met by the use of an interface definition.
- **Binding**   Item used to specify the transport, encoding, and protocol details required for a client and server to communicate with each other.
- **Serialization**   Because SOA (and WCF, for that matter) involves communication between different processes, data in one process needs to be represented in a manner that allows it to be transferred and consumed by another process. Serialization is the mechanism that allows this to happen.

Although there is no authoritative definition of SOA, there are several tenets that are generally regarded as its basis:

- **Boundaries are explicit**   To communicate across processes, you need to know something about them. Where is the service entry point? What operations does it support?

What communication mechanisms does it support? Without answering these questions, it would be impossible to consistently and reliably communicate with a service.

- **Services are autonomous**   The service and any items it contains must be independently deployed, versioned, and managed.

- **Services share schema and contract, not class**   To communicate with a service, a client needs to know the uniform resource identifier (URI), the protocol the communication will happen with, and what operations are supported. It should not need a copy of the class or library that provides the operations.

- **Service compatibility is based on policy**   Although *Web Service Definition Language (WSDL)* can provide a tremendous amount of information, it cannot communicate every possible requirement a service might have. MSDN put it most eloquently, "Policy expressions can be used to separate structural compatibility (what is communicated) from semantic compatibility (how or to whom a message is communicated)."

In its simplest form, a WCF Service is just another compiled class file (or group of files). You can create a simple class library and add some specific references, use some specific classes and attributes, and end up with a WCF Service. Or, you can use Visual Studio and built-in templates to create your services. The former approach isn't even worth discussing other than to point out that there's nothing magical about WCF Services; they're just like any other item you'll work with in Visual Studio.

If you're taking the test, I have to assume that you are at least familiar with some of the basic concepts of WCF such as hosting, bindings, and endpoints. If you are not familiar with these concepts, you should become familiar with an overview of WCF before proceeding.

Creating contracts

Remember from SOA tenet 3 that "Services share schema and contract, not class." As such, the critical elements of a service should be represented by a contract so that clients and services can communicate in a much more flexible manner. There are several types of contracts that can be used inside a WCF Service, including the following:

- **ServiceContract attribute**   What actually makes a given .NET type a WCF Service. Without a ServiceContract, you don't have a WCF Service unless other contract elements are defined; it does nothing more than identify something as a service.

- **OperationContract attribute**   Marks a function as an operation that is part of a given service.

- **DataContract attribute**   Informs the runtime that the contained type will be serializable.

- **FaultContract attribute**   Provides information on exceptions in a platform-agnostic manner.

As stated before, WCF Services are simply assemblies at their core. So you can build a WCF Service and consume it just like any other class in .NET. But doing so won't provide any benefits that creating it as any other class wouldn't, and it would add unnecessary overhead. In order to create it in a manner that it can be consumed in a different process in a distributed manner, or both, it needs to be hosted. Any .NET AppDomain can host a WCF Service, and like its sibling Workflow Foundation, WCF Services have the capability to be self-hosted.

When you're ready to create a WCF Service, you have a few choices:

- You can use the New Web Site option and then choose WCF Service. Visual Studio does not just create the core WCF project and add the needed assembly references for you. It also builds the host application. In so doing, the corresponding bindings are automatically added, and starting with version 4.0 of the .NET Framework, much of the configuration is handled by default. If you use this approach, however, the bindings you can use are limited. Figure 3-1 illustrates the dialog box in which you can create a new website using the WCF template.

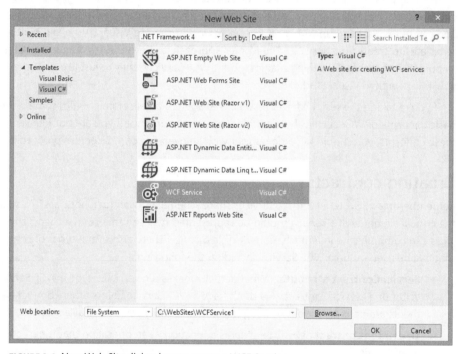

FIGURE 3-1 New Web Site dialog box to create a WCF Service

- You can create the WCF Service using one of the WCF-specific templates, including the WCF Service Library, WCF Application, WCF Workflow Service Application, and the Syndication Service Library template. Figure 3-2 shows the available options for using one of the default WCF templates.

Because versioning and hosting are covered among other topics, the sample code is done using a WCF Service Library project. You start with it and build on it.

If you examine the available options shown in Figure 3-2, the two most common options are WCF Service Library and WCF Service Application. If you think back to creating a Windows Form or console application, you usually want to avoid putting all your application logic in the executable program. Doing so greatly reduces your ability to reuse or distribute your code. The same principle applies here. You'll likely need to reuse your service or components of the service and you'll frequently need to create more than one service in an application. Creating a service library helps facilitate reuse and isolation. The distinction, however, is much simpler than it might sound. If you want to create a host independent service or set of services, use the WCF Service Library template. If you want to create a service or set of services that in-cludes a host—and that host will be Internet Information Services (IIS) or Windows Activation Service (WAS)—use the WCF Service Application template.

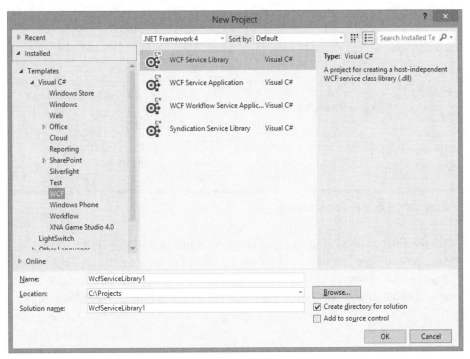

FIGURE 3-2 Creating a WCF Service using WCF Service templates

At this point, if you want to follow along with building the code, create an empty solution (this one is named Microsoft.FourEightySeven.ChapterThree). To do this, follow these steps:

1. Open Visual Studio, select File→New Project→Other Project Types→Empty Solution. Figure 3-3 illustrates the New Project dialog box in Visual Studio 2012.

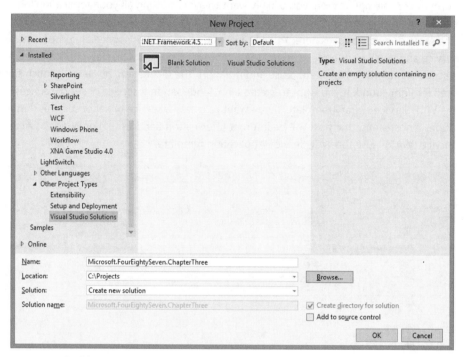

FIGURE 3-3 Creating an empty solution

2. Click the Solution node of the solution you just created in Step 1 (here, it is named Microsoft.FourEightySeven.ChapterThree). Go to the Project menu and select Add New Project→WCF→Service Library (here, it is named Samples.WCF.Services, but you can name it whatever you like). Figure 3-4 shows the Add New Project dialog box.

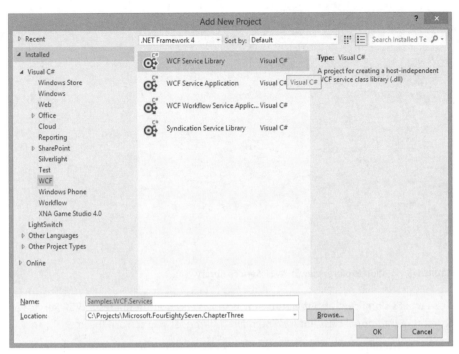

FIGURE 3-4 Adding a new WCF Service library

> **MORE INFO** WINDOWS ACTIVATION SERVICE (WAS): A SERVICE LIBRARY IS JUST A .DLL
>
> You don't have to use any of the installed templates. As you'll see shortly, the output is simply a traditional assembly (.dll). You can just create a standard class library project and add a few project references, but don't waste your time and effort using that approach unless you feel like doing it the challenging way.

At this point, you see a project (named Samples.WCF.Services, unless you named it otherwise). When you create the WCF Service Library project, Visual Studio adds several references for you: a default service class and an interface class. The interface and service class are both predecorated with the ServiceContract and OperationContract attributes. These classes along with attribute decorations form the basis of what's needed for a regular .NET Assembly to become a WCF Service (or Services). This sets the groundwork for this chapter. Figures 3-5 and 3-6 show images of the Solution Explorer window after the solution and project have been created. Become familiar with them.

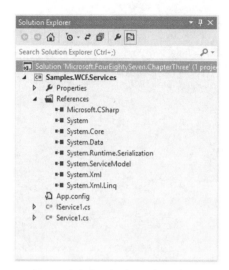

FIGURE 3-5 Solution Explorer view of WCF Service library

So what's significant about Figure 3-5? It shows what differentiates a WCF Service as opposed to a traditional class library. The main differences you see are these:

- An assembly reference is automatically added to the System.ServiceModel and the System.Runtime.Serialization assemblies.

- An Application Configuration file is added to the project. (The contents of this file are covered in-depth in the "Configure WCF Service settings by using configuration settings" and "Host and manage services" sections.)

A file representing the service (Service1.cs) was added, along with a matching file containing the interface definition for the service (IService.cs). By default, the name of the interface and the corresponding file name match the name of the service, differentiated only by the letter "I" at the beginning (which is the Microsoft-recommended naming convention for interface definitions). In practice, you might have one definition for different services because one service can implement several different interfaces, so the names don't necessarily match. Additionally, many developers find it beneficial to separate the service interfaces into their own assemblies, but the reasons for doing so are not something tested on this exam.

If you right-click the Project node and select the Properties option, you see the project options related to WCF Service libraries (see Figure 3-6) under the Application section.

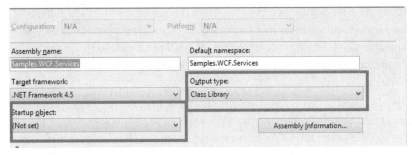

FIGURE 3-6 Project options related to WCF Service libraries

You'll see the Assembly Name and Default Namespace settings just as you would on any other project, but the two items of distinction are these:

- The Output Type is specified as a class library (again, this reinforces the statement that WCF Service libraries are just like any other class library with minor differences).

- The Startup Object is not set because there is no specific startup object needed here. In some cases, you might have one service definition in an assembly, but it's possible to have any number of services contained in a library, and none of them is inherently dependent on any other one.

For the sake of readability, change the name of the Service to TestService and the interface to ITestService, so the file names reflect those changes. If you change the file name using the Visual Studio rename feature, it'll prompt you to change the names of the contents, which in turn automatically makes the configuration contents match the new names. If you don't use the rename feature, you have to do this manually, which tends to be both tedious and error-prone.

Because each service must include a contract, Microsoft decided to use interfaces to implement this feature. Because interfaces are contracts by their nature, they're a natural and intuitive way to implement the requirement.

A service is denoted by the use of the ServiceContract attribute. You can decorate your class definition with the ServiceContract attribute, but it makes much more sense to add the definition to the interface instead. Because the Service has to implement the interface, applying the ServiceContract attribute to the interface definition has the effect of basically marking the class as a ServiceContract. Although it would be a bit of an oversimplification, if I state that the only difference between a WCF Service class and any other .NET class was that the WCF Service class had to implement a corresponding interface, and that either the class or the interface was decorated with the ServiceContract attribute, I am making a true statement.

Besides decorating the class or interface definition with the ServiceContract attribute, the only other necessary code requirement is that each method you want the service to provide has to have the OperationContract attribute decorating it. Again, you can do this in the interface definition or you can do it on the actual method, but for several reasons, it makes more sense to do so on the interface definition.

You will likely need to use custom types in your applications. In order for these types to be used in WCF, they need to be serializable. The most common way this is accomplished, particularly with respect to this exam, is by decorating the type with the DataContract attribute.

Assuming that you changed the names from IService1 and Service1 to ITestService and TestService, respectively, the default layout of each is shown in Listings 3-1 and 3-2.

LISTING 3-1 Contract definition

```
[ServiceContract]
public interface ITestService
{
  [OperationContract]
  string GetData(int value);
  [OperationContract]
  CompositeType GetDataUsingDataContract(CompositeType composite);
}
```

LISTING 3-2 Class definition

```
public class TestService : ITestService
{
    public string GetData(int value)
    {
      return string.Format("You entered: {0}", value);
    }
public CompositeType GetDataUsingDataContract(CompositeType composite)
{
    if (composite == null)
    {
      throw new ArgumentNullException("composite");
     }
     if (composite.BoolValue)
     {
       composite.StringValue += "Suffix";
     }
    return composite;
   }
}
```

You will modify this code sample next, but first review a few of the core components:

- Notice that the ServiceContract and OperationContract attributes decorate the interface members, not the service members. You can define those attributes on the service and service members instead, but that limits reuse, couples the contract with the implementation, and creates several other undesirable consequences.

- The interface defines each aspect of the service, and the service in turn implements the interface just as it would any other interface that you would typically work with.

- Although not illustrated in the code, you can certainly have methods that are defined in the service that are not defined in the interface, but they are not accessible from a client application. Similarly, you can have members defined in the interface that are not decorated with the OperationContract attribute, but if they are not decorated accordingly, they aren't part of the service as far as the rest of the world is concerned.

Other than the Interface definition, the most important key elements are the ServiceContract and the OperationContract. These attributes differentiate a WCF Service class from a standard .Net class. At the same time, saying they are the most important components is a bit misleading in the same way that saying the engine and transmission are the two key elements to a car. Much less important elements, such as the ignition, don't necessarily have to be there for something to be considered a car, but if you build a car, you want to have an ignition. Tires are another element you need; they aren't absolutely necessary for something to meet the definition of a car, but any discussion of car building (or a certification exam covering cars) will likely have some mention of them.

Two elements that don't technically have to be present for something to be a WCF Service, but that you'll frequently find yourself dealing with, are FaultContracts and a serialization format, which for the purposes of this exam, are likely be the DataContract. A small digression into a discussion of endpoints is necessary to bring these components all into the proper context.

EXAM TIP

On the exam, if you see a custom data type, remember that you must be able to serialize it. As such, the class definition should be decorated with a DataContract attribute or another serializer type. Custom exception types can also be presented. These should be decorated with a FaultContract attribute.

Endpoints

When dealing with a WCF Service, one item you must be aware of (even if you don't know it and have to use a discovery mechanism to find it out at runtime) is the service endpoint. If you're heading off on a trip, you need to know where you're going. The "where" is the endpoint. You'll frequently come across the expression "ABC" in WCF literature about endpoints, which stands for the following:

- **"A" stands for "address"**   Corresponds to the "where" component of the equation and typically takes the form of a URI.

- **"B" stands for "binding"**   Equates to the "how" of the transport process. If you plan a trip to Seattle (or any other city that's far away), part of the planning involves how you plan to get there. You can choose a commercial airline, a chartered plane, a helicopter, a car, a motorcycle, or even your own two feet. Each has clear benefits and costs associated with it. Bindings, which are critical components of endpoints, are the equivalent of the vehicle. The hosting mechanism you use can limit what bindings are available, but that's only a limitation of the hosting mechanism as opposed to a limitation of WCF. Finally, the bindings are defined at the service level, and one service can expose itself through several different bindings at one time. (This is one of the main reasons why WCF is vastly superior to traditional .asmx web services or any of the other previous remote communication technologies such as distributed COM [DCOM]).

EXAM TIP

Although custom bindings are something you need to be familiar with if you are planning on working with WCF, anything more complicated than their simple existence is unlikely to appear on the exam.

- **"C" stands for "contract"** The interface that is defined on the service.

MORE INFO FULL LIST OF WCF BINDINGS

There are several bindings provided for you by the framework. A full list of the out-of-the-box bindings and a discussion about their features and limitations is presented at *http://msdn.microsoft.com/en-us/library/ms730879.aspx*. However, if you find that none of the available bindings is sufficient for your needs, WCF can be extended to employ custom bindings (see Table 3-1).

TABLE 3-1 System-provided binding overview

Binding	Security	Session	Transactions
BasicHttpBinding	None, Transport, Message, Mixed	None	None
WSHttpBinding	None, Transport, Message, Mixed	None, Transport, Reliable session	None, Yes
WS2007HttpBinding	None, Transport, Message, Mixed	None, Transport, Reliable session	None, Yes
WSDualHttpBinding	None, Message	Reliable session	None, Yes
WSFederationHttpBinding	None, Message, Mixed	None, Reliable session	None, Yes
WS2007FederationHttpBinding	None, Message, Mixed	None, Reliable session	None, Yes
NetTcpBinding	None, Transport, Message, Mixed	Reliable session, Transport	None, Yes

Binding	Security	Session	Transactions
NetNamedPipeBinding	None, Transport	None, Transport	None, Yes
NetMsmqBinding	None, Message, Transport, Both	None	None, Yes
NetPeerTcpBinding	None, Message, Transport, Mixed	None	None
MsmqIntegrationBinding	None, Transport	None	None, Yes

If you think about these bindings taken together, it makes perfect sense. To communicate with a service, at some point your client application needs to know where to direct the communication. It needs to know how it will communicate. And it will need to know what it can communicate or do. Remove any one of these elements, and it's hard to imagine how a service could be of much benefit other than to be used as a statically linked class library (which defeats the whole purpose of distributed communication).

WCF processing pipeline

The next thing you need to understand is the WCF pipeline. You know that on one hand you have a service that is being exposed. On the other hand, you have a client that is consuming the service. So what happens in between? Directly or indirectly, a proxy class is created for the client, and the class enables the client application to interact with the service's methods. The request is serialized and transferred through the protocol specified in the binding. It's transported to a dispatcher and then handed off to the service. Any information sent from the client needs to be deserialized for the service to be able to consume it, and the same thing needs to happen in reverse. If your service returns a list of grades for a given exam, it needs to accept some sort of identifier for the exam. After the service's method is called and the parameter is received and deserialized, the method needs to process the application's logic just as any other application does. It accumulates the response or responses, serializes them, and sends them back to the client. The client gets the serialized data, deserializes it, and then does something with it.

If you've worked with distributed communication technologies for long enough that you remember some of the older implementations (think CORBA or DCOM), you might remember that most end up being technology-specific. Imagine that you're a company that has a sizable investment in your services. Just to drive the point home, imagine that it's the equivalent of a total of 500,000 lines of C# code. If your application worked with only one technology, say Microsoft technologies, you would likely run into problems with clients that used some other technology and couldn't consume your service. You would now have to either turn away the business or write a port of your application to the other technology. Anything outside of a simple application would mean a sizable investment in the new development. Every time you made a change to one service set, you would have to make the same changes to the other one or have compatibility problems. You would have to not only run through the development, but the whole QA and testing cycle would also need to be repeated.

Anything of this magnitude would certainly encounter some bugs (even if you somehow wrote the first one without a single bug, the chances of doing it for both technologies are about as slim as writing something of that size without any bugs in the first place). This alone would necessitate much higher support requirements. But then there's the hardware side of things. What if you had everything well suited to handle current loads on one instance of the service but not on the other? You would have big problems with all the customers using the second set. From start to finish, you would have nothing but higher costs and problems.

To be of any commercial use, services need to be technology-agnostic as far as the calling client is concerned. Behind the scenes, things can be as vendor-specific as you want, but the exposed service needs to be visible to anyone with any technology—or at least as many as possible.

The reason for all this background isn't just to discuss the generalities of providing a commercial service; it's to call attention to a few issues. To be agnostic, the serialization format needs to be something that can be read on any operating system and consumed by any technology platform. Does Java or Python know what a System.Data.SqlClient.SqlDataAdapter class is? (If you want to be pedantic, I'll admit that it is possible that someone somewhere created a Java or Python version of the SqlDataAdapter. But the point is that somewhere in the process, if the types employed are pegged to a technology, it will be severely limiting quickly.) Although it's possible that there's some other version of a SqlDataAdapter out there, it's well known that primitives (strings, bytes, integers) are supported almost universally.

A similar issue comes up when dealing with language-specific constructs. Arrays, Stacks, and Queues are examples of data structures that are universal and not vendor-specific. A collection of type System.Collections.Generic.List, on the other hand, is something specific to .NET.

So what are the implications of all this? The more coupled with a vendor that your service is, the more likely you are to run into problems with clients accessing it. These problems are costly to deal with and add cost without adding value, so steps need to be taken to avoid them. To do that, using formats that are universally accepted for serialization, for example, can help ensure that you don't run into such problems. At the same time, the whole reason why objects and object-oriented design are used as a strategy is because it enables modeling real-world entities in programs. If you had only primitives available, that would greatly constrain development flexibility. In this case, there's still a cost with no value; it just shifts the burden to you instead of your clients. It's still undesirable.

The people who created WCF had all this in mind when they created it, so they provided mechanisms to deal with all these associated problems. ServiceContract and OperationContract attributes are the first part of the equation to help solve this problem, but several others exist. Listing 3-3 is a modified version of the project created at the onset of this chapter. The changes are summarized first and then the relevant implementation is shown:

- Default methods were removed in the interface and changed to GetAnswerDetails, GetQuestionAnswers, GetQuestionText, and GetExamOutline.

- The TestQuestion, AnswerSet, and AnswerDetails classes were added.

- Because the actual implementation of each method isn't germane to the exam, the implementation portion of each of the methods has been removed and includes only enough code to ensure that the code compiles. The one exception is with the GetQuestionText method. This method specifically includes code that throws an IndexOutOfRangeException if the caller sends in a value that is less than or equal to 0.

- The ServiceContract defines a specific namespace.

LISTING 3-3 ITestService

```
[ServiceContract(Namespace="http://www.williamgryan.mobi/Books/70-487")]
public interface ITestService
{
  [OperationContract]
  AnswerDetails GetAnswerDetails(Int32 questionNumber);
  [OperationContract]
  AnswerSet[] GetQuestionAnswers(Int32 questionNumber);
  [FaultContract(typeof(IndexOutOfRangeException))]
  [OperationContract]
  String GetQuestionText(Int32 questionNumber);
  [OperationContract]
  String[] GetExamOutline(String examName);
}
```

TestService

```
public class TestService : ITestService
{
  public AnswerDetails GetAnswerDetails(Int32 questionNumber)
  {
    AnswerDetails CurrentDetails = new AnswerDetails();
    // Method implementation
    return CurrentDetails;

  }
  public AnswerSet[] GetQuestionAnswers(Int32 questionNumber)
  {
    AnswerSet[] CurrentAnswers = null;
    // Method implementation
    return CurrentAnswers;
  }

  public String GetQuestionText(Int32 questionNumber)
  {
    if (questionNumber <= 0)
    {
      String OutOfRangeMessage = "Question Ids must be a positive value greater than
0";
      IndexOutOfRangeException InvalidQuestionId =
          new IndexOutOfRangeException(OutOfRangeMessage);
```

```
                throw new FaultException<IndexOutOfRangeException>(InvalidQuestionId,
OutOfRangeMessage);
            }
            String AnswerText = null;
            // Method implementation
            return AnswerText;
        }
    public String[] GetExamOutline(String examName)
    {
        String[] OutlineItems = null;
        // Method implementation
        return OutlineItems;
    }
}
```

TestQuestion

```
[DataContract(Namespace="http://www.williamgryan.mobi/Book/70-487")]
public class TestQuestion
{
  [DataMember]
  public Int32 QuestionId { get; set; }
  [DataMember]
  public Int32 QuestionText { get; set; }
  [DataMember]
  public AnswerSet[] AvailableAnswers { get; set; }
  [DataMember]
  public AnswerDetails Answers { get; set; }

 }
```

AnswerDetails

```
[DataContract(Namespace="http://www.williamgryan.mobi/Book/70-487")]
[Flags]
public enum AnswerDetails
{
    [EnumMember]
    A = 0x0,
    [EnumMember]
    B = 0x1,
    [EnumMember]
    C = 0x2,
    [EnumMember]
    D = 0x4,
    [EnumMember]
    All = 0x8
}
```

AnswerSet

```
[DataContract(Name="Answers", Namespace="http://www.williamgryan.mobi/Book/70-487")]
public class AnswerSet
{
  [DataMember(Name="QuestionId", IsRequired=true)]
  public Int32 QuestionId { get; set; }
  [DataMember]
```

```
  public Guid AnswerId { get; set; }
  [DataMember]
  public String AnswerText { get; set; }
}
```

In the context of this exam as well as in practice, it's important to understand why such changes were made. The following sections go through them individually.

DataContract

If you look at the AnswerSet, AnswerDetails, and TestQuestion items, notice that each is decorated with the DataContractAttribute, which can just be referenced as DataContract, at the top level. Just so it was clear, the AnswerDetails component is implemented as type enum instead of being a class. If data is transferred to or from the service, in most cases, it's going to need the DataContract attribute defined on it. Why? The DataContract explicitly puts forth all necessary information about how the data it represents will be serialized. Precisely because it's a contract, both the client and server can agree and know what's being sent and received, and they can do this without having to share the types.

> **IMPORTANT** DATACONTRACT VERSUS XMLSERIALIZER
>
> Types that participate in WCF operations must be serializable. Although DataContracts are the default serializer in WCF, its predecessor was the XmlSerializer. When using a DataContract, serializations are opt-in. If a member isn't explicitly defined to be serialized, it isn't included in the serialization process. The opposite was the case with the XmlSerializer.

When using DataContracts, you indicate that the .NET type decorated with the DataContract attribute is serialized. You can use the KnownTypeAttribute (or just KnownType) to specify that a given type be included during deserialization. All else being equal, using the DataContract attribute is enough to have a type serialized and deserialized, but there are some exceptions:

- If the item being sent is derived from the expected data contract (as opposed to being of the data contract type), it might not be known.

- If the type of the information being transmitted is an interface versus a class, structure, or enumeration, the actual type might not be known.

- If the declared type being transmitted is typed as an Object, it might not be known in advance. (Just to be clear, this is because every type in the .NET Framework inherits from Object, so an upstream conversion is always possible. This is not a problem when doing the upfront conversion, but can present a serious problem when the type is being deserialized.)

- If a .NET Framework type contains members that meet any of the previous three criteria, there will likely be a problem when attempting to deserialize the type.

Fortunately, all you need to do to let the deserialization engine know about a type is mark the type with the KnownType attribute. Use the KnownType attribute in conjunction with the DataContract attribute, and any ambiguity is removed.

To reinforce the point, let's walk through a sample. Assume (for the sake of brevity and readability) that you have a base class named QuestionBase (the implementation doesn't much matter). To begin with, create two derived types named MathQuestion (with the DataContract.Name property set to Math) and EnglishQuestion (with the DataContract.Name property set to English), respectively:

```
[DataContract(Name="English" Namespace="487Samples")]
public class EnglishQuestion : QuestionBase
{}

[DataContract(Name="Math" Namespace="487Samples")]
public class MathQuestion : QuestionBase
{}
```

With these definitions in mind, assume that you have a DataContract type specified named QuestionManager that had a Guid property and a property of type QuestionBase, as shown here:

```
[DataContract(Namespace="487Sample")]
public class QuestionManager
{
    [DataMember]
    private Guid QuestionSetId;
    [DataMember]
    private QuestionBase ExamQuestion;

}
```

Although there is not a problem on the server side serializing the QuestionManager contract, deserializing it ends up throwing a SerializationException. This can be particularly problematic because the code compiles without error, so you might not even know there's a problem until an attempt is made to access it from a client. The problem can be resolved quite easily using the KnownType attribute. The current class definition simply needs a small change. Currently, it specifies only the DataContract. An addition needs to include a KnownType attribute for each type that can be returned:

```
[DataContract]
[KnownType(typeof(EnglishQuestion))]
[KnownType(typeof(MathQuestion))]
public class QuestionManager{}
```

Although using the DataContract attribute is normally sufficient, it's critical to remember the previous rules, particularly when you're working with polymorphic types.

There are several profound differences between object-oriented design and service-oriented design. Although the two approaches aren't mutually exclusive, good practice in one is frequently ill-advised in the other. A full compare and contrast of the two approaches is well beyond the scope of this book, but polymorphism highlights this issue quite well. There are times when you should use polymorphism, but it's generally something that should be avoided in a well-designed SOA implementation.

.NET Framework primitive types can be communicated back and forth between the client and the service without having to explicitly be decorated with a DataContract attribute. If a type is decorated with the DataContract attribute, the runtime utilizes what's known as the DataContractSerializer as the serialization engine to convert back and forth via XML. The attribute decoration explicitly commands the DataContractSerializer to be used and (generally speaking) the DataContractSerializer expects only DataContract types. MSDN specifically states this, and it's mentioned repeatedly on many message boards and blogs throughout the Internet, but that's a bit of an overgeneralization because many other types are supported by it. This MSDN Article (*http://msdn.microsoft.com/en-us/library/ms731923.aspx*) discusses which types are supported by the DataContractSerializer, but it's more important to understand the big picture here rather than memorize every type natively supported by it.

What you want to remember is that any complex type used as a return type from the service (absent primitives) should be decorated with it. The class or enum can receive the decoration, and you can specify a few different parameters including the Name, the Namespace, and IsReference (which simply indicate whether or not to preserve object reference data).

The Name property is the one optional parameter of the constructor you want to note. If you look at the AnswerSet class defined previously, the Name parameter is specifically used to specify a name that is different from the class name. Internally, any instance of this class is called and referred to as type AnswerSet; from a client perspective, though, it's known as Answers.

The Namespace property isn't required, but it's generally considered a good habit to get into. Although not all that likely, if you don't specify a Namespace, there's a possibility that another item might share the same Name property, which would result in a collision. In practice, the chance of running into a problem by not specifying a Namespace is unlikely, but it's so easy to set that doing so is inexpensive insurance.

Setting the DataContract attribute dictates whether object reference data should be preserved. Outside of the DataContract attribute set on the class or Enumeration value definition, you need to specify either the DataMember attribute or EnumMember in case of enumerations for each property you want serialized. Again, just like the ServiceContract and OperationContract attributes, you are free to have as many properties as you want in the class or enum definition, but only the ones with the respective attributes will be serialized.

DataMember

The DataMember attribute is used to decorate a property that you want serialized. If you mark a class as a DataContract but have no DataMember attributes to go with it, nothing is serialized. The constructor enables you to specify a few optional but potentially important properties (fortunately, each does exactly what you would expect—for the most part), as shown in Table 3-2.

TABLE 3-2 DataMember properties

Name	Description
EmitDefaultValue	If you don't explicitly state it, the default value is true, so it's something you would use only when you want to minimize the amount of data that's serialized. Reference types, which comprise much of what you'll likely decorate with this attribute, have a default value of Null. Int32 has a default value of 0. If you wanted to be a whiz at the next session on ".NET Framework Trivia," you could memorize the default values of every type, but there are few cases in which it makes much sense to set this to false.
Name	Just like its counterpart everywhere else, you can use the Name property to differentiate a name for the clients to consume that's different from what you're defining internally. This is done with the AnswerSet class to show how it's done. Changing the Name value is always considered a breaking change, which is something to keep in mind when considering versioning.
IsRequired	IsRequired does just what the name implies. If it's set to true, the property must have a value, or else a SerializationException is thrown when an attempt is made to serialize it. Adding this to a newer version in which it was not previously in place is considered a breaking change (assuming that you're setting it to true). This is because the default value is false, so no value needs to be specified; by setting this value to true, you're introducing a requirement for a value that was previously unneeded). Uninitialized Reference types have a value of null, whereas Value types have specific default values (Int32 and most numeric types default to 0; Booleans default to false). If you are passing a Value type to a method and it's using its default value, a small performance benefit can be achieved by leaving it out of the parameter list.
Order	Specifies the order of serialization and deserialization of the member type.
TypeId	If defined in a derived class, it will return a unique identifier for the attribute.

EXAM TIP

On the exam, EmitDefaultValue might be used in a question about how the size of the serialized message must be kept to an absolute minimum or about it might be mentioned as part of interoperability issues and the serialization format specifically.

EnumMember

The EnumMember attribute is used to decorate an enumerated value that you want serialized. If you mark an enumeration as a DataContract, but it has no EnumMember attributes to go with it, nothing is serialized. The constructor enables you to specify a Value property but nothing else (see Table 3-3).

TABLE 3-3 EnumMember properties

Name	Description
Name	Returns the name of this enumeration member
Value	Returns the value of this enumeration member
BuiltInTypeKind	Returns the kind of this type
Documentation	Gets or sets the documentation object if one is specified (for example, if there is documentation associated with conceptual model constructs)

The behavior of the serializer is interesting for VALUE. The default behavior is to serialize anything marked with this attribute as the name itself. In the AnswerDetails example, the serialized values are A, B, C, D, as opposed to 0x0, 0x2, 0x4, and so on. If you specify something in the value property, the value you specify will be used in place. Be careful, however, because you could easily cause some accidental problems here. For example, the following compiles and runs, but it might end up creating maintenance problems for someone working downstream:

```
[DataContract(Namespace="http://www.williamgryan.mobi/Book/70-487")]
[Flags]
public enum AnswerDetails : int
{

    [EnumMember(Value="1")]
    A = 0x0,
    [EnumMember(Value = "2")]
    B = 0x1,
    [EnumMember(Value = "3")]
    C = 0x2,
    [EnumMember(Value = "Bill")]
    D = 0x4,
    [EnumMember(Value = "Ryan")]
    All = 0x8
}
```

FaultContracts

System.Exception is the base class for Exception types in the .NET Framework, and structured exception handling is a great feature. As helpful as structured exception handling is, .NET exceptions are technology-specific to the .NET Framework. That means that Java, Python, Visual Basic 6.0, and so on have no idea what a .NET exception is (even if the other language features structured exception handling).

FaultContracts enable services to communicate failures to the client in a safe, intentional, and mutually acceptable fashion. No one who has been hacked (outside of people who create HoneyPots) sits around and plans on his application being hacked. Hackers and malicious users are a creative lot and constantly devise new ways to get access to things they shouldn't be privileged to. One of the ways many systems have been breached is by hackers intentionally inputting bad data and seeing what happens. Sometimes the application does things it shouldn't; other times, it provides information back (usually by someone who provided the information from a well-intentioned perspective).

When an exception is encountered, you have full access to it at the service and can log it and do whatever you want with it. Because you write the service in WCF, you obviously can take advantage of all the tracing and other features provided by it. But there's a lot of information you might be comfortable with people inside your organization seeing that you wouldn't want people outside of your organization seeing. Now, if you specifically decide that certain information can be conveyed, you can use FaultContracts to define when information can be sent and what information is sent. This enables you to give the clients some information they might need for their applications without exposing your service to unnecessary risk. In the example of the TestService's GetQuestionText method, you want to let the client know that an exam id of 0 or less is not valid:

```
public String GetQuestionText(Int32 questionNumber)
{
  if (questionNumber <= 0)
  {
   String OutOfRangeMessage = "Question Ids must be a positive value greater than 0";
   IndexOutOfRangeException InvalidQuestionId =
   new IndexOutOfRangeException(OutOfRangeMessage);
    throw new FaultException<IndexOutOfRangeException>(InvalidQuestionId,
 OutOfRangeMessage);
  }
  String AnswerText = null;
  // Method implementation
   return AnswerText;
}
```

You intentionally throw a validation fault using the IndexOutOfRangeException class. It is used with the FaultException class that you pass back to the client. However, you have to let the client know about it explicitly; to do that, you have to define it in the contract, just like everything else. So in this case, right along the OperationContract attribute, there's an instance of the FaultContract that accepts a type parameter that corresponds to IndexOutOfRange Exception:

```
[FaultContract(typeof(IndexOutOfRangeException))]
[OperationContract]
String GetQuestionText(Int32 questionNumber);
```

To be of any use to the client, the FaultContract needs to be defined explicitly in the contract definition. Before taking the exam, you should definitely review the documentation on

MSDN regarding the FaultContract class: *http://msdn.microsoft.com/en-us/library/ms752208.aspx*.

One of the reasons to use a FaultException is to communicate failure information back to the client. If you want to include additional information about the failure, you can set the Reason property, which accepts a FaultReason type. This enables you to provide a text description of the fault that you are trapping.

FaultCode enables you to specify additional information in a machine-readable manner about the fault, including whether the fault is a SOAP 1.1 or SOAP 1.2 fault type, for example.

SOAP 1.1 provides the following codes: VersionMismatch, MustUnderstand, and Client and Server. SOAP 1.2 provides the following fault codes: VersionMismatch, MustUnderstand, DataEncodingUnknown, Sender, and Receiver.

This distinction might seem trivial, and it's true that many people ignore the use of Fault-Codes in their services. However, this is shortsighted because, as you can see, they provide machine-readable information (which means that your code can more easily react to responses without manual intervention). Keep in mind, though, that the bindings you intend to support have substantial effect on which FaultCodes you should use. The basicHttpBinding messaging specification, for example, is based on SOAP 1.1. The wsHttpBinding, by comparison, uses SOAP 1.2 for both messaging and addressing.

There are cases in which you might want to exert control over fault handling at a much more granular level than what is provided out of the box. As noted previously, you can specify the FaultReason or FaultCode to do this. If you want more control, you can use the Message-Fault class, which gives you an in-memory representation of the fault. It enables you to tailor the details of the fault as specifically as you want. Why would you want to do this?

Assume that you are using an authentication method that compares a user name and password against a custom database. If the user name and password combination isn't found, you want to send a notice back to the client. However, if you see a specific user name or password used, you should throw a specific security-related exception that, when encountered, immediately notifies an administrator of a hack attempt. Locally, you can handle the exception and send the message, but you might not want to tip off the client that you are aware of the hack attempt. So internally you respond to the attempted breach, but you simply inform the calling application that the combination wasn't found. Although this might seem to be an extreme case, generally speaking, you don't want to provide any exception details to the client lest they be used to gather information that expands the attacker's knowledge of your system. End users seldom do anything with exception details other than try again or fail gracefully, so there's little benefit to giving them specific details of the issue.

Focus specifically on how to define a FaultContract, how to throw a FaultException (especially within the context of catching an exception and using it for throwing a FaultException), and the main properties that comprise a FaultException. Finally, keep in mind that FaultException inherits from CommunicationException, so you will catch specific FaultExceptions and then CommunicationException unless you create an unreachable code situation. Table 3-4 shows the available overloads used to create FaultException items.

TABLE 3-4 FaultException overloads

Signature	Description
FaultException()	Creates a new instance of the FaultException class.
FaultException(FaultReason)	Creates a new instance but specifies a specific reason.
FaultException(MessageFault)	Creates a new instance of the FaultException class specifying message fault values.
FaultException(String)	Creates a new instance of the FaultException class using the String parameter to create the FaultReason for it.
FaultException(FaultReason, FaultCode)	Creates a new instance specifying both the FaultReason and Fault Code.
FaultException(MessageFault, String)	Creates a new instance using specified message fault values and providing an action String value.
FaultException(SerializationInfo, StreamingContext)	Creates a new instance specifying serialization information and a corresponding context that the FaultException will be deserialized to. This version of the constructor is one of the more rarely used versions and is mainly intended when you are inheriting. A comprehensive discussion of its use is out of scope for both the book and the exam, but because the other constructors were mentioned, I wanted you to be aware it exists.
FaultException(String, FaultCode)	Creates a new instance of the class and sets both the FaultReason and a specific SOAP fault code.
FaultException(FaultReason, FaultCode, String)	Creates a new instance of the class setting the specified FaultReason, FaultCode, and Action property value. The OperationContext the service operates in contains a RequestMessage property that, in turn, contains a Headers collection that contains an Action property. You can use this value for the Action value, or if you prefer, you can define your own if you believe doing so would provide more useful information.
FaultException(String, FaultCode, String)	Creates a new instance of the class setting the FaultReason, FaultCode, and Action property value. It differs from the previous version only in that the String passed in as the first parameter is automatically turned into a FaultReason.

Implementing inspectors

Using the standard features of WCF more than suffices for most application development scenarios you'll encounter. If you have control over the service being built, you won't typically need to turn to WCF extensibility. But there are cases in which you're working with or building upon another vendor's service, and times when the deployed code is frozen and you can't build upon it without deploying an entirely new version. Figure 3-7 summarizes the WCF processing pipeline.

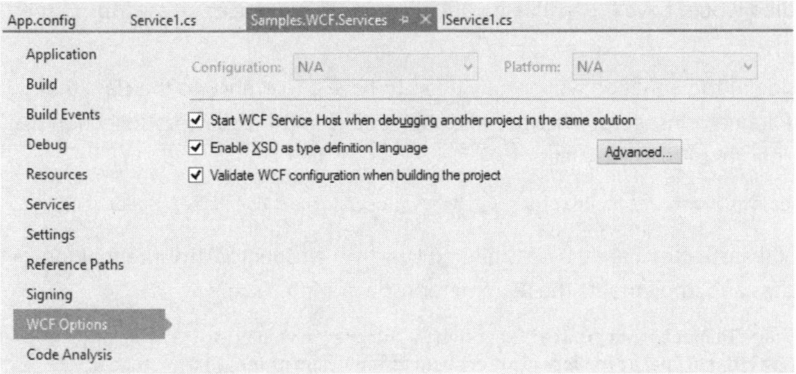

App.config | Service1.cs | Samples.WCF.Services | IService1.cs

Application
Build
Build Events
Debug
Resources
Services
Settings
Reference Paths
Signing
WCF Options
Code Analysis

Configuration: N/A   Platform: N/A

☑ Start WCF Service Host when debugging another project in the same solution
☑ Enable XSD as type definition language   Advanced...
☑ Validate WCF configuration when building the project

FIGURE 3-7 WCF processing pipeline

With the processing pipeline in mind, there are three main opportunities to use WCF extensibility:

- Parameter inspection
- Message formatting
- Message inspecting

When building a multitiered application, you are admonished never to trust user input. It's always advisable to validate input in all your server methods. At the same time, for both security and usability reasons, you should implement client-side parameter valida-tion as well. If you have a case in which you are positive that the input will lead to failure or when processing can never return the desired result, attempting to call the operation with nonconforming parameters is a waste of time and resources. Imagine the following code (simplified for readability):

```
public void VerifyUser(String userName)
{
    if (String.IsNullOrWhiteSpace(userName) ||
      userName.Length < 7)
    {
      throw new ArgumentException("userName", "Parameter is in the incorrect format.");
    }
}
```

If the calling code has a user name value of "Bill," this method will always fail. In this instance, you could implement a parameter inspector, verify that the value is not null or a white space, and that the length of the user name value is at least seven characters long. If it doesn't meet these conditions, you can save a trip to the server, which conserves both client and server resources.

To implement parameter inspection, you can use the IParameterInspector interface. This interface has two methods: BeforeCall and AfterCall. The BeforeCall method is called right before the parameters are serialized into the Message object. The AfterCall method is called, as the name implies, after the call has been processed. In this case, applying validation to the AfterCall method would have little value if your goal was to minimize useless trips to the server.

On the client side of the equation, you simply need to have a reference to the class that implements the IParameterInspector interface and then add it to the Behaviors collection of the Operations property of the proxy class:

```
ProxyInstance.Endpoint.Contract.Operations[0].Behaviors.Add(new UserNameInspector());
```

To implement the inspector, create a class named UserNameInspectorAttribute that inherits the Attribute class and implements the IParameterInspector interface:

```
public class UserNameInspectorAttribute: Attribute, IOperationBehavior{
    public void Validate(OperationDescription operationDescription){}
    public void ApplyDispatchBehavior(OperationDescription operationDescription,
DispatchOperation dispatchOperation){}
    public void ApplyClientBehavior(OperationDescription operationDescription,
ClientOperation clientOperation {}
    public void AddBindingParameters(OperationDescription operationDescription,
BindingParameterCollection bindingParameters){}
}
```

In practice, you need to create the attribute and implementation class prior to adding it to the client-side proxy, but everything will work as long as the item is ultimately added. All that's needed is to implement the logic behind the validator, which matches the validation code shown previously that checks the UserName variable:

```
public class UserNameInspector : IParameterInspector{
    public void AfterCall(string operationName, object[] outputs, object returnValue,
object correlationState){}

    public object BeforeCall(string operationName, object[] inputs){
     //Parameters are passed in the inputs array. We have one parameter
    //we're validating , so it will be index 0.
    String userNameValue = inputs[0] as String;
    if (String.IsNullOrWhiteSpace(userNameValue) ||  userNameValue.Length < 7){
       throw new ArgumentException("userName", "Parameter is in the incorrect
format.");
     }
    return null;
    }
}
```

Implementing message inspectors

There are many different use cases for *message inspectors*, but their main purpose is to enable you to examine the contents of an inbound or outbound message before it gets processed or modify it after the message is serialized and returned to the client. Imagine a case in which you had an involved process for placing an order. You might have some requirements that must be met; otherwise, you would prefer not to waste all the overhead of attempting to process the call just to have it fail. Or perhaps while things are processing, you receive a notification that the credit card used to pay for the order was just stolen and cancelled, so you want to cancel it. There are countless scenarios you can come up with, but if you want to implement message inspection, here's how you do it.

IDispatchMessageInspector interface

On the server side, message inspection functionality can be implemented with the IDispatchMessageInspector interface. Table 3-5 shows the two methods it provides and their purposes.

TABLE 3-5 IDispatchMessageInspector methods

Method	Remarks
AfterReceiveRequest	Called after an inbound message has been received but before the message is forwarded to the target operation
BeforeSendReply	Called after the operation has returned but before the reply is actually relayed

During a presentation not too long ago on this subject, someone complained that MessageInspectors were simply a solution in search of a problem. It was argued that you could essentially get the same results (in practical terms) by calling a function at the beginning and end of any ServiceOperation item that corresponds to each of the previous methods. In many cases, they were right in the sense that you could "do the same thing." You certainly could put in a credit check at the beginning of an order process and perform a stolen credit card check at the absolute end after you've already processed everything. But any changes to the behaviors would need to be done in the method, and each time you had any changes, you would have to rewrite portions of the code and redeploy the whole service.

Using the MessageInspector approach enables you to add, remove, and change the whole inspection process through configuration. You could easily layer these items by simply adding them to the behaviorExtensions element of the Service itself. So although it's true that you can "do it some other way," you almost always can do anything "some other way." This approach provides a clean, intuitive, configurable, and consistent means by which to accomplish such tasks. Assuming that you have a class named ServerInspector to implement the interface, you enable it on the server by using the following configuration information:

```
<extensions>

 <behaviorExtensions>

  <add name="clientSample" type="Samples.WCF.Services.ClientInspector, ClientHost,
Version=1.0.0.0, Culture=neutral,

        PublicKeyToken=null"/>

 </behaviorExtensions>

</extensions>
```

IClientMessageInspector interface

On the client side, the IClientMessageInspector interface (see Table 3-6 for its methods) is the counterpart to the IDispatchMessageInspector.

TABLE 3-6 IClientMessageInspector methods

Method	Remarks
AfterReceiveReply	Fires after a reply message is received prior to it being passed back to the calling method
BeforeSendRequest	Fires before a request message is sent to a service

Assuming that the class was called ClientInspector Version 1.0.0.0, here's what the configuration elements look like (other than the type names, it's virtually indistinguishable from the service-side counterpart):

```
<extensions>

 <behaviorExtensions>

  <add name="clientSample" type="Samples.WCF.Services.ClientInspector, ClientHost,
Version=1.0.0.0, Culture=neutral,

         PublicKeyToken=null"/>

 </behaviorExtensions>

</extensions>
```

In each case, you simply create a class on the client side, the server side, or both, and implement the respective interface if you want to intercept and inspect the message. The type information is added to the <behaviorExtensions> element of the <extensions> element in the client side, server side, or both configuration file(s) using the Add element. From an exam perspective, there's not a lot to know besides the fact that message inspectors exist if you need them, the corresponding interface, and where you specify the inspectors in the configuration file.

Thought experiment

Contract implementation?

In the following thought experiment, apply what you've learned about this objective to message inspection. You can find answers to these questions in the "Answers" section at the end of this chapter.

You are building a WCF Service. There are several methods that you do not want to expose to clients but need to use internally. Several complex types, including enumerations, will be transferred between the client and server. Although the majority of your clients are using .NET, you want to make sure that any decision errs on the side of interoperability. With this in mind, answer the following questions:

1. How should you handle the methods that you don't want publicly exposed?

2. How should you handle the enumeration types and the complex types?

3. Should anything special be done to deal with exceptions?

Objective summary

- At a minimum, a WCF Service consists of a service contract and a service implementation. The service is delineated by the ServiceContract attribute, and the Service's methods are marked by the OperationContract attribute.

- Although it's not technically a requirement, WCF Services generally use an Interface definition for the contract and a standard .NET class to handle the implementation. (In fact, this is the way Visual Studio handles things by default.)

- System.Exception objects and descendants are .NET-specific types that are not usable by other languages/runtimes. To provide an agnostic way of communication failure information, WCF makes use of FaultContracts.

- Items passed to and from a WCF Service must be serializable. The most common way of handling this on custom types is to use DataContracts.

- Each DataContract property that you want exposed should be marked with the DataMember attribute in the case of class definitions or EnumMember attributes in the case of Enumeration types.

Objective review

Answer the following questions to test your knowledge of the information in this objective. You can find the answers to these questions and explanations of why each answer choice is correct or incorrect in the "Answers" section at the end of this chapter.

1. You've implemented a method named GetQuestionText that can throw an IndexOutOfRangeException a SqlException. Which of the following items would correctly expose these exceptions?

   A.
   ```
   [FaultContract(typeof(IndexOutOfRangeException))]
   [FaultContract(typeof(SqlException))]
   [OperationContract]
   String GetQuestionText(Int32 questionNumber);
   ```

   B.
   ```
   [FaultMapping(new FaultMappingCollection[]{IndexOutOfRangeException,
   SqlException})]
   [OperationContract]
   String GetQuestionText(Int32 questionNumber);
   ```

   C.
   ```
   [FaultMapping(new FaultMappingCollection[]{typeof(IndexOutOfRangeExcepti
   on), typeof(SqlException)})]
   [OperationContract]
   String GetQuestionText(Int32 questionNumber);
   ```

   D.
   ```
   [FaultContract(IndexOutOfRangeException)]
   [FaultContract(SqlException)]
   [OperationContract]
   String GetQuestionText(Int32 questionNumber);
   ```

2. Which of the following are true regarding WCF Services and their contracts? (Choose all that apply.)

   A. Each service must have a corresponding Interface class.

   B. The ServiceContract and OperationContract attributes must be applied to the contract, not the implementation.

   C. The ServiceContract and OperationContract attributes can be applied to either the contract or the implementation.

   D. A complex type does not need to be serializable as long as all its properties are serializable.

3. You are tasked with adding a method named GetCurrentStockPrice to an existing service. The Service is named QuoteService and it implements the IQuoteService Contract. How should you go about adding this new method? (Choose all that apply.)

    A. Add the method definition to the IQuoteService Contract.

    B. Add the OperationContract attribute to the method definition.

    C. Add the OperationBehavior attribute to the method definition.

    D. Create a new ServiceContract class and add the GetCurrentStockPrice method to it.

Objective 3.2: Configure WCF services by using configuration settings

It's widely understood that hard-coding values or settings is generally a bad idea and should be avoided whenever possible. This conventional wisdom is particularly true when it comes to WCF Services. You can hard-code everything if you choose. You can specify just about everything needed to make a service operate in code using static values. But doing so deprives you of many of the benefits of WCF and is a guarantee of undesirable outcomes. Furthermore, because hard-coding values generally takes as much or more effort than using configuration, use configuration for your service as much as possible. The exam might well cover implementations using code or hard-coded values, but it's much more likely that you'll encounter configuration file entries and be asked to manipulate them. Configuration in WCF is particularly useful and valuable, and you'll want to be familiar with it both for test taking and real-world reasons.

This objective covers how to:
- Configure service behaviors
- Configure service endpoints
- Configure bindings
- Specify a service contract
- Expose service metadata

As a rule, WCF Services can be set up and managed by coding directly using the API (the subject of the next section) or by using configuration settings. Although there are few times it might make sense to prefer inline code over configuration, configuration is almost always a better option. The reasons for this are beyond the scope of this exam or topic, but if you opt for configuration, you can control just about any aspect of the service or client without having to rebuild it and redeploy it.

Here's a quick example to illustrate this assertion. Assume that you have a WCF Service that's hosted in a Managed Windows Service and it currently uses the basicHttpBinding. You want to either add or change support to employ a wsHttpBinding. If you have the binding configured as opposed to defined in the code, all that's needed is a quick change to the .configuration file. The service doesn't need to be changed, it doesn't need redeployed, and it doesn't need anything else done to it (other than maybe restarted).

Similarly, suppose that a problem crops up, and you want to enable some diagnostics to help discern what the problem is. If you're using configuration, this can be done without touching a line of .NET code and without modifying the service. You can enable the diagnostics you want, let it run for a period long enough to get a feel for the problem, and then turn it off, all without changing the service. If you use the code-centric approach, you have to engage in a new version to add the diagnostic code and then another rollback to undo it. Virtually every aspect of the service's or client's behavior can be manipulated through configuration, so unless you have some specific reason to do otherwise, you should prefer it.

EXAM TIP

There are several questions in the exam that show you a section of a configuration file on one side of the screen, with blank boxes over key elements, and the available choices on the other side of the screen. You are asked to drag and drop those elements in the correct places. You need to get all the items correct in order to get the question right.

Configuring service behaviors

For any given application, you can have it configured as a service, as a client, or both. The Tools menu in Visual Studio provides a tool called the WCF Service Configuration Editor, which enables you to visually manipulate all the XML elements inside the configuration file. Assuming that you're trying to configure a service, start the WCF Service Configuration Editor tool and open your service's configuration file.

Creating a new service

Assuming that you have not yet configured a service, you can open up the WCF Service Configuration Editor (as shown in Figure 3-8) and choose the Create a New Service option. If you created the project as a WCF application, the service already exists, and adding it again obviously results in a clash. If you already have a service defined, select your existing service instead of adding everything as outlined in the following steps.

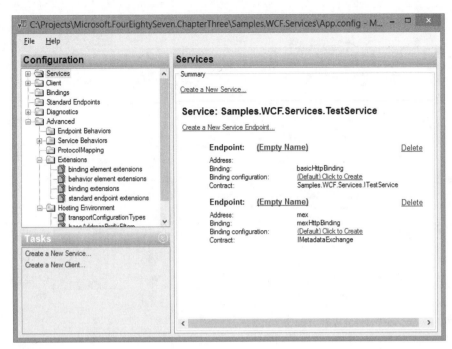

FIGURE 3-8 Create a New Service option

Specifying a new service element (service)

A wizard starts that walks you through the core elements of configuring a WCF Service. The first thing it does is add the <system.ServiceModel> element to the configuration file. It then adds a <services> element. The wizard then presents the New Service Element Wizard page that asks you to browse to the assembly containing the service or services you want to configure (see Figure 3-9).

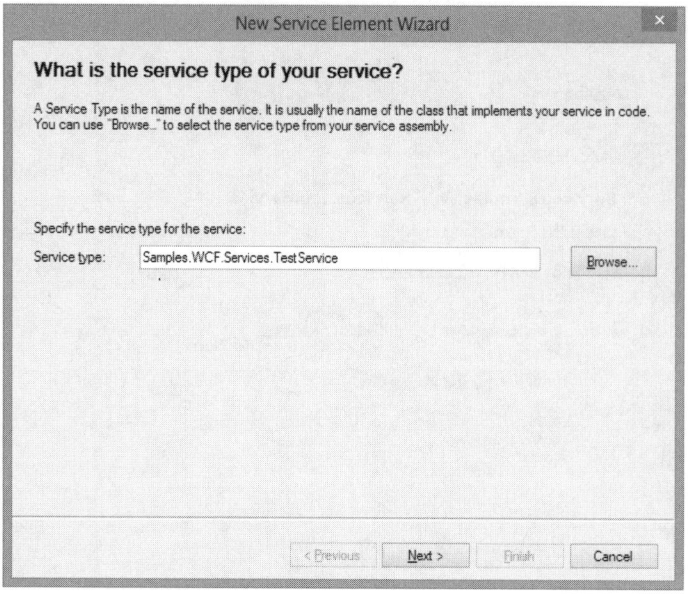

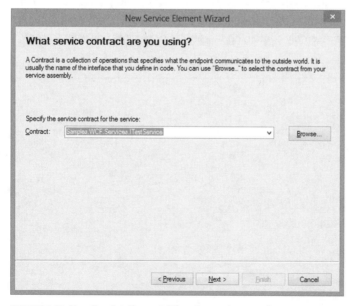

FIGURE 3-9 New Service Element Wizard page (service)

Specifying a new service element (contract)

After you specify the service(s), you need to specify the corresponding contract(s). Unless you keep the interfaces in a separate assembly, the same assembly will contain both items (see Figure 3-10).

FIGURE 3-10 New Service Element Wizard page (contract)

Specifying a new service element (communication mode)

Next, a wizard page asks you to define the communication mode you want to use (see Figure 3-11). Keep in mind that the wizard presents only 5 options; however, there are at least 12 out-of-the-box options available, and you can certainly create your own by making the number of available ones infinite.

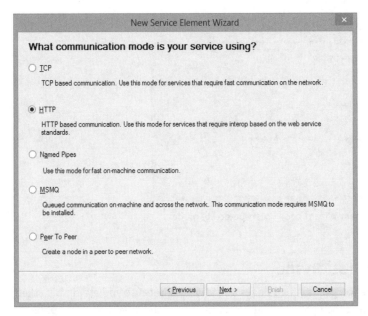

FIGURE 3-11 New Service Element Wizard page (communication mode)

Specifying a new service element (interoperability mode)

The next step asks you to choose between Basic Web Services Interoperability and Advanced Web Services Interoperability. If you choose the Advanced option, you can also specify Duplex or Simplex communication, as shown in Figure 3-12.

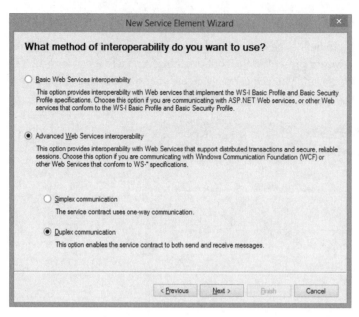

FIGURE 3-12 New Service Element Wizard page (interoperability mode)

Resulting configuration file

Screen shots aren't helpful for the next two pages of the wizard because you are simply asked for the endpoint address and then you see a summary page that shows you all your options. Using the wizard isn't the goal, but showing you how to use configuration for services is. The resulting output is instructional:

```xml
<?xml version="1.0" encoding="utf-8" ?>
<configuration>
    <system.serviceModel>
        <services>
            <service name="Samples.WCF.Services.TestService">
                <endpoint address=http://www.williamgryan.mobi/samples/487
                    binding="wsDualHttpBinding" bindingConfiguration="" name="DualHttp"
                    contract="Samples.WCF.Services.ITestService" />
            </service>
        </services>
    </system.serviceModel>
</configuration>
```

At the outermost level, underneath the <configuration> node, you'll see the <system. ServiceModel> definition. Underneath that node is the <services> node; the pluralization should be enough to indicate that one or more items can be added to it (in this case, service definitions). Underneath that is the <service> node and the main item related to it, the Name attribute. The name is the fully qualified type name of the service, and a matching type needs to be available somewhere along the probing path the runtime uses for assemblies.

Contained in the <service> element is the <endpoint> element, and the ABCs are included: The address, the binding (in this case, I added a name for the binding, although it's not technically necessary), and the contract are all specified. The contract type and the service type are the primary plumbing employed, so both of those types need to be visible to assemblies that the host application can load.

At this point, as simple as it might appear, you have accomplished all the following:

- Configured a service
- Configured an endpoint
- Configured a binding
- Specified a service
- Specified a service contract

The only things left to cover are exposing service metadata and configuring service behaviors.

Exposing service metadata

Metadata endpoints all begin with the prefix "mex," which is an abbreviation for "metadata exchange." Currently, there are four out-of-the-box endpoints:

- *mexHttpBinding*
- *mexHttpsBinding*
- *mexNamedPipeBinding*
- *mexMsmqBinding*

Each corresponds to the underlying binding, and yes, you could certainly opt to expose all of them if the situation necessitated it. Let's use the previous snippet, but change the duplex binding to a more common one (wsHttpBinding) and then add a mexHttpBinding. To do so, add another element under the <service> element of type mexHttpBinding. Unlike bindings for non-mex endpoints, metadata exchange endpoints don't require an address:

```
<service name="Samples.WCF.Services.TestService">
    <endpoint address="http://www.williamgryan.mobi/samples/487"
    binding="wsHttpBinding" bindingConfiguration="" name="WsHttp"
    contract="Samples.WCF.Services.ITestService" />
    <endpoint binding="mexHttpBinding" bindingConfiguration=""
    name="Mex" contract="IMetadataExchange" />
</service>
```

The portion in bold shows the addition of the mex binding. This makes metadata exchange possible, and if you hit the endpoint (which is added by default starting with version 4.0) you'll see the wsdl of the service, which clients can use to gather whatever information you made available about the service.

The last thing you need to know is the BehaviorConfiguration of the service. Many things in WCF can be fine-tuned by using behaviors, the two broad categories being

EndpointBehaviors and ServiceBehaviors. EndpointBehaviors enable you to specify (unsurprisingly) information about endpoints. This information includes clientCredentials, transaction batching, the DataContract serializer, and much more.

There are also ServiceBehaviors that enable you to control several aspects of the service at a granular level. Several examples of these are shown in Figure 3-13.

Like any advanced features, ServiceBehaviors and EndpointBehaviors can be a double-edged sword. There are many problems that require the manipulation of either or both of these behaviors and enable you to do things that would otherwise be awkward and problematic. At the same time, they can be the source of many problems if they aren't understood. The default configuration settings that WCF provides enable you to do quite a bit out of the box, but if your service supports any degree of high volume or requires sophisticated security, you'll almost certainly have to manipulate some of these items.

If you're using the WCF Service Configuration Editor tool, you can simply navigate to the Advanced node, click the Service Behaviors node, and then choose New Service Behavior Configuration. Make sure that you give it a name so you can easily reference it afterward. Figure 3-13 shows a list of the available out-of-the-box behavior extensions you can add to a service.

FIGURE 3-13 Service behavior element extensions

Simply pick the item(s) that you want added, and then click Add. Afterward, you can click the Service node, and any new behaviors you added will be available in the drop-down list. If you don't name the behaviors, the default is to have them named NewBehavior0, NewBehavior1, NewBehavior2, and so on.

When you add a service behavior, it's added to the <behaviors> element and the specifics are included in the <serviceBehaviors> element (which would differentiate it from an endpoint behavior, for example). Again building on the example, the end result would look like the following:

```
<system.serviceModel>
    <behaviors>
        <serviceBehaviors>
            <behavior name="Debug">
                <serviceDebug />
            </behavior>
        </serviceBehaviors>
    </behaviors>
    <services>
            <service behaviorConfiguration="Debug" name="Samples.WCF.Services.
TestService">
            <endpoint address=http://www.williamgryan.mobi/samples/487
                binding="wsHttpBinding" bindingConfiguration="" name="WsHttp"
                contract="Samples.WCF.Services.ITestService" />
            <endpoint binding="mexHttpBinding" bindingConfiguration="" name="Mex"
                contract="IMetadataExchange" />
        </service>
    </services>
</system.serviceModel>
```

The link between the ServiceBehavior and the Service is the Behavior's Name attribute and the Service's BehaviorConfiguration attribute. These need to match in order to be associated.

One item that doesn't exactly fit in the objective set coverage, but will likely be on the exam, is ProtocolMapping, which enables you to specify a relationship between transport protocol schemes (http, net.pipe, and https) and the corresponding WCF bindings. You can define ProtocolMappings so that they apply to all hosted applications by modifying the machine.config file. Conversely, you can limit the scope of the mappings so that they apply only to an individual application. In either case, you do it the same way; the only difference is where you change the values (in the machine.config file to apply the mappings globally, or in app.config/web.config to apply them to a specific application).

```
<protocolMapping>
    <add scheme="http" binding="basicHttpBinding"/>
    <add scheme="net.tcp" binding="netTcpBinding"/>
    <add scheme="net.pipe" binding="netNamedPipeBinding"/>
    <add scheme="net.msmq" binding="netMsmqBinding"/>
</protocolMapping>
```

Configuring service endpoints

As stated earlier, the <behaviors> element enables you to specify both ServiceBehaviors and EndpointBehaviors. A typical EndpointBehavior that you need to configure is one related to security: clientCredentials. (Security is covered later in this chapter; but realize that this is something you might need to do to meet a security requirement.) To facilitate this, a new EndpointBehavior is added through the WCF Service Configuration Editor, which is shown in Figure 3-14. The EndpointBehavior is added, and using wsHttpEndpoint, the BehaviorConfiguration attribute is specified and named. Again, just as with the ServiceBehavior, the Name property is the link between the two.

FIGURE 3-14 Adding an endpoint behavior

The resulting output follows:

```
<system.serviceModel>
    <behaviors>
        <endpointBehaviors>
            <behavior name="wsHttpBehaviorSample">
                <clientCredentials />
            </behavior>
        </endpointBehaviors>
        <serviceBehaviors>
            <behavior name="Debug">
                <serviceDebug />
            </behavior>
        </serviceBehaviors>
    </behaviors>
    <services>
        <service behaviorConfiguration="Debug" name="Samples.WCF.Services.
TestService">
            <endpoint address=http://www.williamgryan.mobi/samples/487
                behaviorConfiguration="wsHttpBehaviorSample" binding="wsHttpBinding"
```

```
                    bindingConfiguration="" name="WsHttp"
contract="Samples.WCF.Services.ITestService" />
                <endpoint binding="mexHttpBinding" bindingConfiguration="" name="Mex"
                    contract="Samples.WCF.Services.ITestService" />
            </service>
        </services>
    </system.serviceModel>
```

Configuring bindings

Next, a new BindingConfiguration is added for the wsHttpBinding. Figure 3-15 illustrates all the available options in the Create a New Binding dialog box (and shows that the wsHttpBinding has been selected):

FIGURE 3-15 Adding a binding configuration

In the current project, there was not a ProtocolMapping defined for the wsHttpBinding, so one was added. Using the editor, you can select the Protocol Mapping node, select New, and choose the Binding, the Binding Configuration, and the Scheme. The resulting configuration items look like the following:

```
<protocolMapping>
 <add scheme="wsHttp" binding="wsHttpBinding"
 bindingConfiguration="wsHttpBindingConfigSample" />
</protocolMapping>
<bindings>

 <wsHttpBinding>
     <binding name="wsHttpBindingConfigSample" />
 </wsHttpBinding>
</bindings>
```

Although this is perfectly valid, it's rather contrived. A more realistic example might be to change the mapping that's already there. For example, as you can see from the original

Protocol Mapping window, the http scheme was mapped to the basicHttpBinding. Perhaps you want the default binding to be the wsHttpBinding instead (and because the configuration is already built, you might as well go ahead and specify it). You simply click the existing scheme, select Edit, and then change the binding, adding in the binding configuration if the requirements dictate the need. The resulting ProtocolMapping looks like this instead:

```
<protocolMapping>
    <remove scheme="http" />
     <add scheme="http" binding="wsHttpBinding"
      bindingConfiguration="wsHttpBindingConfigSample" />
</protocolMapping>
```

So what exactly would happen if you made this last change? If you initially failed to iden-tify an endpoint for the HTTP type base address, one would be created by default (starting with WCF version 4.0; prior to that you had to specify an endpoint), but it would be of type basicHttpBinding. Now, if an endpoint isn't specified, the default for HTTP is wsHttpBinding.

Both basicHttpBinding and wsHttpBinding are similar in that they are both designed to communicate over HTTP. There is nothing stopping you from changing the defaults to some-thing totally different. So the default binding for http when no endpoint is defined could be a netNamedPipeBinding (or any other one you can think of). Although there's nothing stop-ping you from doing this, just because you can do something doesn't mean you necessarily should—or that it makes sense to do so.

The best-case scenario is that you would explicitly define an http endpoint, and no de-faults would be needed. But what if you didn't? Do netNamedPipeBindings have the same addressing scheme as the http bindings do? Do they have the same ones as the tcpBindings or the Msmq bindings? No, they don't. Other than being confusing, the chances of it caus-ing major problems are high, and it's hard to see how there'd be any benefit. If you need a default endpoint for any given binding that isn't already provided, you can add it via ProtocolMapping, but you would want to do it so the scheme corresponds to the binding. Otherwise, you're just as likely to cause some unpredictable behavior in the process.

EXAM TIP

Remember that, even if you don't know the answer to a question, if you can eliminate any wrong choices you immediately increase your chances of getting the item correct. On the new versions of the exam, in which you have all the drag-and-drop items, you have to get several things right in order to get the item correct, and you might find a question that has three empty boxes that need answers, but x (where x > 3) available choices. In the previous item, just by reviewing the resulting items that are created from the configuration file, you can know that the answer will have either binding=somebinding or bindingconfiguration =someconfiguration (or both) because they are the only two possible attributes that are available outside of scheme. If the only bindings you saw were netMsmqBinding or new NamedPipeBinding, that is your answer, even if the use case isn't something that you would typically want to do because no other attributes are allowed to exist there.

Thought experiment
What would you configure?

In the following thought experiment, apply what you've learned about this objective to configure elements of your service. You can find answers to these questions in the "Answers" section at the end of this chapter.

You are building a WCF Service. You expect a tremendous growth in clients and will likely have to support and change quite a few different features. Your service will be hosted internally, so you have full access to it without any real restrictions.

With this in mind, answer the following questions:

1. Would it make sense to use configuration to host custom bindings?

2. What bindings would you choose to configure?

Objective summary

- Each aspect of a service or its operations that can be specified through configuration can also be specified directly in code.
- Each service must have a contract that is defined using the ServiceContract attribute. Typically, an interface definition is used, which is decorated with the ServiceContract attribute.
- The ServiceContract and OperationContract attributes can be defined on the service implementation or the contract, but not both.
- MetadataExchange should be used in conjunction with the ServiceContract and OperationContract attributes to expose information about the service to the client.

Objective review

Answer the following questions to test your knowledge of the information in this objective. You can find the answers to these questions and explanations of why each answer choice is correct or incorrect in the "Answers" section at the end of this chapter.

1. What are the minimum steps that must be performed to configure a service using the WCF Service Configuration Editor? (Choose all that apply.)

   A. Specify a new service.

   B. Specify a MetadataExchange endpoint.

   C. Specify a security configuration.

   D. Specify a contract.

2. Which of the following items can be handled through configuration? (Choose all that apply.)

   A. Defining the service's type.

   B. Defining the service's contract.

   C. Specifying a security configuration.

   D. Adding metadata exchange.

3. Which of the following is not a benefit of configuration?

   A. Ability to change Endpoint URIs

   B. Ability to modify security settings

   C. Ability to redefine metadata exchange

   D. Ability to add new method definitions

Objective 3.3: Configure WCF services by using the API

In the previous objective, you walked through using configuration file items to control the service's behavior. You can do the same thing(s) imperatively in code, although as mentioned before, it's advisable to have a bias toward configuration when choosing between the two. If you understand one approach, though, you can quickly navigate the other should the need arise; after all, they are merely two different vehicles to arrive at the same location. Other than cosmetically, (XML versus C#, VB.NET), they are identical and employ the same functionality.

If you look at the exam outline, you'll notice that the description for this objective is indistinguishable from the previous section with the exception of the title and "WCF routing and discovery features."

You can mix and match between using configuration and code, but in many ways, the more you hard-code, the less flexibility there is. You can define a binding in code, for example, and use a configuration element to specify an endpoint address. Doing this would give you more flexibility than hard-coding all the values, but it would still force your hand in terms of what bindings were used. If you use configuration, you can accomplish most of the same things you would through hard-coding, but not the other way around. Although not WCF-specific, favoring configuration over code is generally advisable unless you're extremely sure that nothing specified in the code will change. It's worth noting, however, that the decision isn't either/or with respect to using the API or configuration. You can use the API and create it so it allows dynamic determination at runtime. Information can be retrieved from a database—for example, an XML file or several other stores—and this information can be used in conjunction with imperative coding. This effectively gives you the benefits of both approaches. The discussion is typically characterized as one approach or the other, and exam questions are likely to have that focus, but in practice, this isn't necessarily the case.

Configuring service endpoints

Remember the whole notion of equating ABCs and endpoints, so when you're programmatically creating an endpoint, you simply decide what type of endpoint you're creating and then you add the respective information to it. Creating an endpoint programmatically works the same way as creating any other class does. The only real trick is knowing how to add it to the service.

Configuring service behaviors

You can configure ServiceBehaviors using the API as well. The ServiceBehaviorAttribute class enables you to programmatically specify the behavior of the service in much the same way you did with the EndpointBehavior.

ServiceBehaviorAttribute

At the beginning of the chapter, a basic service named the TestService that implemented the ITestService contract was created. If you recall, the ServiceContract attribute was defined on the contract definition, and method definitions were decorated with the OperationContract attribute. The ServiceBehaviorAttribute is roughly analogous to the ServiceContract, and the OperationBehaviorAttribute is roughly analogous to the OperationContract. If you want a behavior to apply to an entire service, decorate the service definition with the ServiceBehaviorAttribute; if you want it to apply exclusively to a specific method, use the OperationBehaviorAttribute.

The remarks section of the MSDN coverage highlights most of the important distinctions you need to be aware of regarding this attribute, but there are a few things that people commonly misconstrue that are good candidates for exam questions.

The ServiceContractAttribute includes Name and Namespace properties, and the ServiceBehaviorAttribute also includes Name and Namespace properties. Although the ServiceContractAttribute can be defined on either the interface or the service definition, the ServiceBehaviorAttribute can decorate only the service.

So what happens if you have this situation? You decorate the contract with the ServiceContract attribute and specify one name and namespace; then you decorate the service definition with the ServiceBehavior attribute specifying both the Name and Namespace properties, but you use different values for each:

```
[ServiceContract(Namespace="http://www.williamgryan.mobi/Books/70-487",
Name="RandomText")]
public interface ITestService{}
[ServiceBehavior(Name="Test", Namespace="http://www.williamgryan.mobi/Books/70-487/
Services")]
public class TestService : ITestService
{}
```

Figure 3-16 shows the Request envelope with the Name and Namespace properties set as described previously.

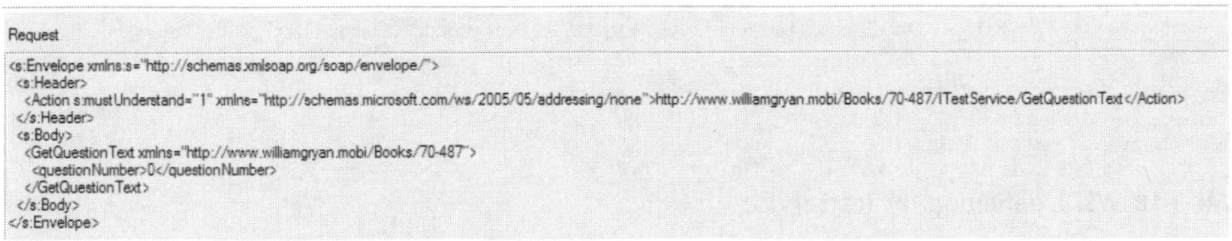

```
Request
<s:Envelope xmlns:s="http://schemas.xmlsoap.org/soap/envelope/">
  <s:Header>
    <Action s:mustUnderstand="1" xmlns="http://schemas.microsoft.com/ws/2005/05/addressing/none">http://www.williamgryan.mobi/Books/70-487/ITestService/GetQuestionText</Action>
  </s:Header>
  <s:Body>
    <GetQuestionText xmlns="http://www.williamgryan.mobi/Books/70-487">
      <questionNumber>0</questionNumber>
    </GetQuestionText>
  </s:Body>
</s:Envelope>
```

FIGURE 3-16 Request envelope definition

Here the namespace (xmlns) matches what was specified in the ServiceContract. But what about MetadataExchange? What happens if you try to add a service reference? The results are shown in Figure 3-17.

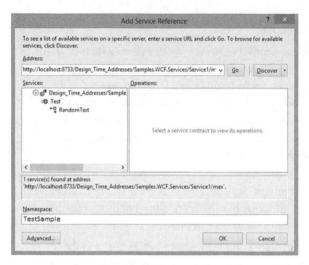

FIGURE 3-17 Service reference with different name and namespace values set

Without giving away the answer yet, it should be clear from Figure 3-17 that the Name and Namespace attributes serve different purposes, even if they seem to accomplish the same thing. Look at the .wsdl file, which should make it all clear (Figure 3-18).

```
<?xml version="1.0" encoding="utf-8"?>
<wsdl:definitions xmlns:wsap="http://schemas.xmlsoap.org/ws/2004/08/addressing/policy" xmlns:wsa10="http://www.w3.org/2005/0
  <wsdl:import namespace="http://www.williamgryan.mobi/Books/70-487" location="" />
  <wsdl:types />
  <wsdl:binding name="BasicHttpBinding_RandomText" type="i0:RandomText">
    <soap:binding transport="http://schemas.xmlsoap.org/soap/http" />
    <wsdl:operation name="GetAnswerDetails">
      <soap:operation soapAction="http://www.williamgryan.mobi/Books/70-487/RandomText/GetAnswerDetails" style="document" />
      <wsdl:input>...</wsdl:input>
      <wsdl:output>...</wsdl:output>
    </wsdl:operation>
    <wsdl:operation name="GetQuestionAnsw">...</wsdl:operation>
    <wsdl:operation name="GetQuestionText">
      <soap:operation soapAction="http://www.williamgryan.mobi/Books/70-487/RandomText/GetQuestionText" style="document" />
      <wsdl:input>...</wsdl:input>
      <wsdl:output>...</wsdl:output>
      <wsdl:fault name="IndexOutOfRangeExceptionFault">
        <soap:fault use="literal" name="IndexOutOfRangeExceptionFault" namespace="" />
      </wsdl:fault>
    </wsdl:operation>
    <wsdl:operation name="GetExamOutline">
      <soap:operation soapAction="http://www.williamgryan.mobi/Books/70-487/RandomText/GetExamOutline" style="document" />
      <wsdl:input>...</wsdl:input>
      <wsdl:output>...</wsdl:output>
    </wsdl:operation>
  </wsdl:binding>
</wsdl:definitions>
```

FIGURE 3-18 WSDL definition for TestService

This code shows that the ServiceBehavior attribute sets the values for Name and Namespace in the Name and Namespace attributes, respectively, in the service element inside the WSDL. When they're defined in the ServiceContract, the Name and Namespace set the value of the <portType> element in the WSDL.

Configuring bindings

There is a substantial library of out-of-the-box bindings available in WCF, and you can further extend things so that you create your own bindings. Some are much more common than others, and each has its respective benefits and relative shortcomings. From a code perspective, the way you use them is identical from binding to binding, but the substantive differences come into play only at a much more granular level.

Binding declarations

There are too many out-of-the-box bindings to go through the nuances of each one in depth, and even if there weren't so many of them, doing so wouldn't add much value. The following sections construct four different bindings and show how they are virtually identical.

The BasicHttpBinding is ostensibly the simplest and most basic binding available out of the box. If you want to communicate over Http, you need to use only the SOAP 1.1 specification, and have minimal security needs, the BasicHttpBinding is well suited for the task. It has three possible constructors:

```
// Default BasicHttpBinding
BasicHttpBinding BasicHttp = new BasicHttpBinding();
// SecurityMode Specified
// SecurityMode values include None, Transport, Message, TransportCredentialOnly
// and TransportWithMessageCredential
BasicHttpBinding BasicHttpSecurity = new BasicHttpBinding(BasicHttpSecurityMode.None);
// Using Binding configured in .config file
BasicHttpBinding BasicHttpConfig = new BasicHttpBinding("BasicHttpBindingConfigSample");
```

You can choose the default constructor that accepts no parameters and let WCF handle all the defaults for you. You can optionally create one by specifying security settings using the BasicHttpSecurityMode enumeration. Finally, you can define the information about the binding in the .config file and just pass in the name of the binding you created to the constructor. (If you have to use the code-based approach, this is probably your best option.) Recall that you need to ensure that you specifically name your bindings if you create any (the same goes for every other item that enables you to name it).

wsHttpBinding

The second common out-of-the-box binding that you can use for Http-based communication is wsHttpBinding. It's much more powerful than the BasicHttpBinding and the main characteristics are these:

- It uses the SOAP 1.2 standard instead of SOAP 1.1.
- It has extensive support for the WS-* standards (hence the name).
- Because of the WS-* support, features such as reliable messaging, transactional support, duplex communication, and much more powerful and granular security support are all readily available.

As you'll see, compared with each of the other bindings illustrated here, one of these things is not like the other—and this is it:

```
// Default wsHttpBinding
WSHttpBinding WsHttp = new WSHttpBinding();
// SecurityMode Specified
// SecurityMode values include None, Transport, Message
// and TransportWithMessageCredential
WSHttpBinding WsHttpSecurity = new WSHttpBinding(SecurityMode.None);
// Uses Binding configured in .config file
WSHttpBinding WsHttpConfig = new WSHttpBinding("wsHttpBindingConfigSample");
// Sets the Security mode and indicates whether or not
// ReliableSessionEnabled should be Enabled or Not
WSHttpBinding WsHttpReliable = new WSHttpBinding(SecurityMode.None, true);
```

So besides the class names, there are two notable distinctions. The first is that the security-based constructor uses the SecurityMode enumeration for the wsHttpBinding, and the BasicHttpBinding uses the BasicHttpSecurityMode enumeration. The second one is that there's an additional overload that enables you to specify whether to use ReliableMessaging.

As you go through the other bindings, you'll see the same distinctions. The different bindings typically have some matching SecurityMode counterpart and, with the exceptions of the wsHttpBinding and the other ones mentioned previously, ReliableMessaging isn't supported on most of the other ones.

NetMsmqBinding

The following snippet shows the constructors available for the NetMsmqBinding. The only notable difference between it and the wsHttpBinding is that it uses the new MsmqSecurityMode enumeration to implement the security-enabled overload, and there's no overload to support reliable messaging:

```
// Default MsmqDefault
NetMsmqBinding MsmqDefault = new NetMsmqBinding();
// NetMsmqSecurityMode includes Transport, Message, Both and None
NetMsmqBinding MsmqSecurity = new NetMsmqBinding(NetMsmqSecurityMode.None);
// Using Binding configured in .config file
NetMsmqBinding MsmgConfig = new NetMsmqBinding("MsmqBindingConfigSample");
```

NetNamedPipeBinding

Named pipes are a mechanism available for intramachine communication. They afford the highest level of performance among the out-of-the-box bindings, but carry with them a huge limitation: Communication needs to happen entirely on the same machine. The following snippet shows the constructors available for the NetNamedPipeBinding. The only notable difference between it and the wsHttpBinding is that it uses the NetNamedPipeSecurityMode enumeration to implement the security-enabled overload, and there's no overload to support reliable messaging.

```
// Default NetNamedPipeBinding
NetNamedPipeBinding NamedPipeDefault = new NetNamedPipeBinding();
// NetNamedPipeSecurityMode includes None and Transport
NetNamedPipeBinding NamedPipeSecurity = new NetNamedPipeBinding(NetNamedPipeSecurity
Mode.None);
// Using Binding Configured in .config file
NetNamedPipeBinding NamedPipeConfig = new NetNamedPipeBinding("NetNamedPipeConfig
Sample");
```

Custom binding

There are definitely times when you will need or want to use a custom binding. Several commercial web services, such as ExactTarget, actually necessitate the use of a custom binding in order to interact with the service. That naturally raises this question: "So when should I use a custom binding?" The answer is any time the system-provided set of bindings doesn't include one that meets your needs.

You have two primary paths when constructing a custom binding. The first entails using one or more of the system-provided bindings and adding to it. The next is to use user-defined custom binding elements exclusively.

In terms of defining a custom binding through configuration, the <customBinding> element is used. However there's an ordered process to properly constructing custom bindings, as described here.

When building a custom binding, you use the CustomBinding constructor that according to MSDN is from "a collection of binding elements that are 'stacked' in a specific order." The process is shown here:

1. The outermost item is the *TransactionFlowBindingElement*. This item is optional and necessary only if you are looking to support flowing transactions.

2. Next is the *ReliableSessionBindingElement,* which is also optional. As you can probably guess, it is used when you want to support reliable sessions.

3. Afterward, you can define a *SecurityBindingElement* that is optional like each of its upstream parents. This requirement is one reasons why custom bindings are used as nuanced security requirements are fairly common. If you need to provide specific functionality around authorization, authentication, protection, or confidentiality, the SecurityBindingElement is the vehicle you can use to get there.

4. If you want to support duplex communication, the next item in the chain is CompositeDuplexBindingElement.

5. In case you want to provide OneWay communication to the service, OneWayBindingElement can be used. As noted in the coverage on the OneWay attribute, there are specific use cases for it, and decisions to use it should not be made lightly. However, if you have a scenario that matches the intended use case, it can be a helpful feature to have. Like the others above it, there's no technical requirement to use it.

6. Further refinement and control can be provided if you choose to support stream security. In the same spirit of the OneWay attribute, the use cases for this functionality are small and clearly defined, but there are definitely times when this functionality is absolutely necessary. It differs from its predecessors because you can define either of two elements (SslStreamSecurityBindingElement, WindowsStreamSecurityBindingElement), instead of just one. You are not required to use either, so implementation is completely optional.

7. Next in the chain is the message encoding binding element. Unlike all the items before it, it is required to correctly create a custom binding. If you choose to implement your own encoding scheme, you can absolutely do so or you can use one of the three available message encoding bindings. These include TextMessageEncodingBindingElement (which has nothing to do with SMS text messaging), BinaryMessageEncodingBindingElement, and MtomMessageEncodingBindingElement.

8. The last item in the chain is the transport element. Like the encoding element, it's absolutely required to properly create a CustomBinding. It provides several options:

    - TcpTransportBindingElement
    - HttpTransportBindingElement
    - HttpsTransportBindingElement
    - NamedPipeTransportBindingElement
    - PeerTransportBindingElement
    - MsmqTransportBindingElement
    - MsmqIntegrationBindingElement
    - ConnectionOrientedTransportBinding element

MORE INFO   CUSTOMBINDINGS

A full discussion of each of these mechanisms is beyond the scope of this book, but a basic familiarity with their relative advantages and disadvantages is helpful to have. A complete discussion of these tradeoffs can be found here: *http://msdn.microsoft.com/en-us/library/aa347793.aspx.*

Specifying a service contract

To be a WCF Service, an item must inherently meet the following criteria:

- Implement a service contract using the ServiceContract attribute. Absent a Service Contract attribute, you have no WCF Service.

- Define the supported operations using the OperationContract attribute. Although you can technically create a service using only the ServiceContract attribute, it wouldn't do anything, making it worthless. So for any practical application, an OperationContract is needed before you would have a service that was of any use.

- If any data types are defined, they must specify a serialization format (the most common being the DataContract attribute on the class, with the DataMember attribute decorating each of the supported members). You might not need to define any types as DataContracts, but unless you're going to work exclusively with primitive types, you'll need to use it (or another serialization counterpart).

If you create a WCF Service using one of the Visual Studio templates, it creates a class definition and a matching interface definition that is pre-applied to the class. Any changes to the definition need to be made to the class, which is not a WCF requirement, but is a runtime/language requirement. If you've worked with .Net for any period of time, you have almost certainly created a class that implemented an interface or multiple interfaces—yet they weren't necessarily WCF Services. Something becomes a WCF Service contract only when the ServiceContract attribute decorates it. You can decorate the implementation class or the interface definition with the ServiceContract attribute, but you can't do both.

ServiceContract attribute defined on the service class

Assume that you have a WCF Service class named ServiceContractSample and IServiceContractSample, respectively. You can define the ServiceContract attribute on the ServiceContractSample as follows:

```
[ServiceContract]
public class ServiceContractSample : IServiceContractSample
{...}
```

ServiceContract attribute defined on the interface definition

You can also define it on the IServiceContractSample interface definition, as shown here:

```
[ServiceContract]
public interface IServiceContractSample
{...}
```

ServiceContract attribute defined on the service class and interface definition

Although both attributes compile and run if defined individually, but defined on both the service and interface as shown here, an InvalidOperationException is thrown when you try to reference the service. (If you were to define the ServiceContract on both items, the project would build without any warnings or errors, however.)

```
[ServiceContract]
public interface IServiceContractSample
{
 ///Operation definitions here
}
[ServiceContract]
public class ServiceContractSample : IServiceContractSample
{
///Operation definitions here
}
```

Defined together, you'll encounter the following message when you try to reference the service: System.InvalidOperationException: The service class of type Samples.WCF.Services. ServiceContractSample both defines a ServiceContract and inherits a ServiceContract from type Samples.WCF.ServicesIServiceContractSample. Contract inheritance can only be used among interface types. If a class is marked with ServiceContractAttribute, it must be the only type in the hierarchy with ServiceContractAttribute..

The same rule applies to the OperationContract attribute, but you'll encounter a different exception and one that might be less obvious when raised. Just like the case with the ServiceContract attribute defined on both, you can define it on both items without encountering a compilation warning or error, but the exception you encounter when trying to reference the service yields the following: System.InvalidOperationException: The OperationContractAttribute declared on method 'DoWork' in type 'Samples.WCF.Services.

ServiceContractSample' is invalid. OperationContractAttributes are only valid on methods that are declared in a type that as ServiceContractAttribute. Either add ServiceContractAttribute to type 'Samples.WCF.Services.ServiceContractSample' or remove OperationContractAttribute from method 'DoWork.'

The reason why it's the place you add the OperationContract and ServiceContract attributes is noteworthy (and an ideal item for a test question differentiator) is precisely because you won't get any assistance from Visual Studio or the compiler; everything will appear fine until you try to actually use the service. Although this isn't necessarily something you would think about at first glance, the problem(s) associated with allowing the definition of either attribute in both places becomes glaring when you think about implementations that don't use the default constructors for either attribute.

If you use just the default constructor on the ServiceContract attribute, the Name property defaults to the class's type name, the Namespace property defaults to *http://tempuri.org*, and the ProtectionLevel property is set to ProtectionLevelNone. Although not necessary, it's strongly advised that you explicitly set these properties so the intent of each is clear.

Consider the following scenario:

```
[ServiceContract(Name = "RightName", Namespace = "RightNamespace")]
public interface IServiceContractSample
{
    /// Implementation details here
}
[ServiceContract(Name="WrongName", Namespace="WrongNamespace")]
public class ServiceContractSample : IServiceContractSample{
    /// Implementation details here
}
```

There would be no way for a client to differentiate or determine which item is the "right" one.

Expose a service's metadata

The ServiceContract identifies a type as a WCF Service, and the OperationContract identifies its methods. However, neither the ServiceContract nor the OperationContract attribute can tell service consumers about the service's details. Fortunately, broadcasting information about the service and its methods is simple, and if you use Visual Studio to build your service, the needed configuration file entries are automatically built in for you.

WCF Services have metadata published by employing one or more metadata exchange endpoints. Recall that endpoints are generally defined by ABC (address, binding, and contract). There are currently four different metadata bindings available, and you can easily identify them by the letters "mex" appearing in their name (a combination of the words "metadata" and "exchange"). The currently available metadata exchange bindings are these:

- mexHttpBinding
- mexHttpsBinding
- mexNamedPipeBinding
- mexTcpBinding

Other than the addition of the endpoint, the only thing noteworthy about using it is speci-fication of the contract. You might assume that the contract that should be used for defin-ing a metadata exchange endpoint is the contract type for the service, but (unlike the other endpoint types) you use a specific and common interface for them. There's an IMetadata Exchange contract already defined in the System.ServiceModel.Description namespace that is used for mex bindings. Enabling it through configuration couldn't be easier; simply add a new endpoint with the corresponding binding type that you want enabled and specify IMetadata-Exchange as the contract. For the sake of illustration, the following snippet shows the ITest-Service host implementation with both a basicHttpBinding and mexHttpBinding enabled:

```
<endpoint address="" binding="basicHttpBinding" contract="Samples.WCF.Services.
ITestService">
</endpoint>
<endpoint address="mex" binding="mexHttpBinding" contract="IMetadataExchange" />
```

If you chose to implement bindings (and metadata bindings in particular), you can use the MetadataExchangeBindings class, calling one of the Create methods that corresponds to the mex bindings shown previously:

- CreateMexHttpBinding
- CreateMexHttpsBinding
- CreateMexNamedPipeBinding
- CreateMexTcpBinding

You can optionally write out the literal "IMetadataExchange" if you wanted to because it's just a String. To verify that it does nothing else but return IMetadatExchange, you can run the following code snippet.

For each sample, assume that a common ServiceHost definition is used, as shown here:

```
String uriString = "http://yourhost/Samples.WCF.Services/TestService/";
Uri[] baseAddresses = new Uri[]{new Uri(uriString)};
 ServiceHost hoster =
     new ServiceHost(typeof(TestService), baseAddresses );
```

CreateMexHttpBinding

```
Hoster.AddServiceEndpoint(ServiceMetadataBehavior.MexContractName,
MetadataExchangeBindings.CreateMexHttpBinding(), "mexBindingHttp");
```

CreateMexHttpsBinding

```
Hoster.AddServiceEndpoint(ServiceMetadataBehavior.MexContractName,
MetadataExchangeBindings.CreateMexHttpsBinding(), "mexBindingHttps");
```

CreateMexTcpBinding

```
Hoster.AddServiceEndpoint(ServiceMetadataBehavior.MexContractName,
MetadataExchangeBindings.CreateMexTcpBinding(), "mexBindingTcp");
```

CreateMexNamedPipeBinding

```
Hoster.AddServiceEndpoint(ServiceMetadataBehavior.MexContractName,
MetadataExchangeBindings.CreateMexNamedPipeBinding(), "mexBindingPipe");
String MexConstant = ServiceMetadataBehavior.MexContractName;
Console.WriteLine(MexConstant);
// Outputs 'IMetadataExchange' literal
```

Thought experiment
Configuration versus using the API

In the following thought experiment, apply what you've learned about this objective to configure a WCF Service. You can find answers to these questions in the "Answers" section at the end of this chapter.

You are building a WCF Service, and you have all the requirements for the service's foreseeable future clearly defined. You have all your options open with respect to implementation.

With this in mind, answer the following questions:

1. Should you lean toward a configuration-based approach, try to define every-thing imperatively, or use a mixed approach?

2. What downside would you experience if you defined everything imperatively?

3. What downside would you experience if you defined everything in configuration?

Objective summary

- You can define the ServiceContract attribute on the actual service class. You can define the ServiceContract on an interface definition and have the service class implement the interface.

- Although you can choose either approach, you cannot define the ServiceContract at-tribute on both the service implementation and an interface that the class implements.

- To fine-tune the behaviors of those items, you can specify the ServiceBehavior or OperationBehavior attributes on the service and its methods. They can also be ma-nipulated through configuration, which is generally considered the preferred way of dealing with them.

- In addition to several out-of-the-box bindings that should cover most traditional needs, you can create custom bindings for when none of them will work. You can also fine-tune the behaviors of your customer bindings, giving you complete control over almost "everything that matters" when it comes to your service.

■ When implementing a CustomBinding, there is a clear hierarchy on how items should be defined. The only two items that are absolutely required for a CustomBinding are the message encoding binding element and the transport element. Somewhat counter intuitively, these two required items are the last two items in the chain of possible item definitions.

Objective review

Answer the following questions to test your knowledge of the information in this objective. You can find the answers to these questions and explanations of why each answer choice is correct or incorrect in the "Answers" section at the end of this chapter.

1. You are creating a CustomBinding that will be consumed only by .NET clients. Performance is the primary concern. Which of the following are true? (Choose all that apply.)

   A. You must define a TextMessageEncodingBindingElement to the binding.

   B. You must define a BinaryMessageEncodingBindingElement to the binding.

   C. You must not define either the TextMessageEncodingBindingElement or the MTOMMessageEncodingBindingElement.

   D. You must define the BinaryMessageEncodingBindingElement.

2. The ServiceOperation attribute is defined on both the service implementation and the interface definition. Each of the property settings is explicitly defined, and each property matches its counterpart in the other definition. Which of the following is true?

   A. As long as the property values are identical or don't conflict with each other, the service will behave as desired.

   B. The items defined on the interface will override the ones on the implementation class.

   C. The items defined in the implementation class will override the ones on the interface definition.

   D. The service will throw an InvalidOperationException because this attribute cannot be defined on both items.

3. Which of the following are valid transport binding elements when defining a custom binding?

   A. TcpTransportBindingElement

   B. TcpBinding

   C. HttpTransportBindingElement

   D. MTOMTransportBindingElement

Objective 3.4: Secure a WCF service

Security is a vital aspect of any commercial software product, but it's particularly important when dealing with services. Many services are exposed to the Internet, which means they are highly visible targets for hackers. When you're building a service, you have no idea who might try to misuse it, and it's highly likely that someone will. Countless people have relied on notions such as security by obscurity or just ignored security because (fill in lame excuse). And day after day, companies, governments, and other entities end up encountering breaches they never anticipated would happen.

In today's environment, it takes only one breach to completely destroy a career or even an entire corporation. Although you can compute the cost of implementing security features with relatively high accuracy, it's next to impossible to predict the damage of a breach.

Fortunately, WCF has powerful security features that are generally quite easy to implement. These features include two primary categories: message level security and transport level security. There's also a third category that is simply a combination of the two.

> **This objective covers how to:**
> - Implement message level security
> - Implement transport level security
> - Implement certificates

Implementing message level security

Message level security is the first primary category of WCF's security infrastructure. With most bindings, it is enabled by default, and starting with later versions of WCF, it runs transparently without any intervention on the developer's part. It is a physical implementation of the WS-Security Specification and essentially augments SOAP messages so that they provide confidentiality, integrity, and authentication (frequently referred to as CIA). Let's just quickly review what each of these elements is and why it matters.

- *Confidentiality* means that only the people or parties are supposed to see the message are the ones see it.
- *Integrity* means that the message cannot be tampered with without being detected.
- *Authentication* ensures the identity of a party viewing the message.

Think of how you interact with your bank. You make deposits and withdrawals that are your business and no one else's (at least no one you don't approve of). Some people don't care about personal privacy, but in general, you wouldn't want just anyone to have access to your bank transactions. By having access to them, they'd know how much money you make, how much you spend, where you shop, what you buy, and a lot of other information that most people consider private.

When you make a deposit, you want to make sure that the correct amount is reflected and that it's credited to your account correctly. You wouldn't want the teller to be able to give you a receipt showing you deposited $10,000 but have only $1,000 of it actually deposited in your account.

Similarly, you expect that the bank ensures that you or authorized parties are the only ones who can conduct transactions with your account. If all someone had to do was go to your bank and say they were you in order to withdraw money, it's pretty much a certainty someone who is less-than-honest would help themselves to your savings.

WCF and its security infrastructure handle these elements if you configure it to do so. However, it's important also to take measures of your own in most cases to ensure each of these objectives—but such measures are to be done in addition to, not in place of these features. This objective isn't concerned with security in general; it is concerned with security specifically related to WCF (and in this section, messages).

To secure the message, you simply need to set the Security.Mode property to the corresponding binding's SecurityMode enumeration indicating that message security should be set. Each of the binding examples illustrated earlier showed one of the constructors that enabled you to set the respective security mode. For the wsHttpBinding, for example, you can use either of these approaches:

```
public void ShowMessageSecurity(){
    // Set Security Mode to Message in Constructor
    WSHttpBinding WsHttpSecurity = new WSHttpBinding(SecurityMode.Message);
    // Use default constructor
    WSHttpBinding wsHttpSecurity2 = new WSHttpBinding();
    // Set the Security property manually
    wsHttpSecurity2.Security.Mode = SecurityMode.Message;
}
```

The actual Mode property type for the wsHttpBinding is the SecurityMode enumeration. If you were trying to accomplish the same goal with the basicHttpBinding, the Mode property is of type BasicHttpSecurityMode. If it's a netNamedPipeBinding, the Mode property is of type NetNamedPipeSecurityMode.

The alternative approach is to specify it through configuration. For any binding that you have configured, the WCF Service Configuration Editor has both a Binding and a Security tab. The Security tab features a Mode drop-down list, and you simply specify Message as the mode for the binding you're configuring. Figure 3-19 shows the value set via the WCF Service Configuration Editor.

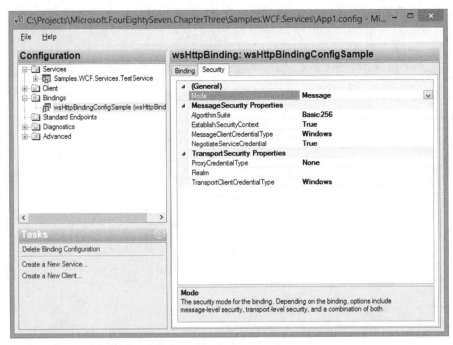

FIGURE 3-19 Configuring message level security

If you examine the configuration file after setting this particular value, you won't see any mention of security, mode, or message because wsHttpBinding enables message level security by default. However, if you want to declare it explicitly, it works just as you expect it to:

```
<wsHttpBinding>
    <binding name="wsHttpBindingConfigSample" >
      <security mode="Message"/>
    </binding>
 </wsHttpBinding>
```

Implementing transport level security

Transport security works virtually identically, except that you need to set the Mode property to Transport instead of Message. Using the same examples as before, the following enables transport level security instead of message security.

```
public void ShowMessageSecurity()
{
    // Set Security Mode to Message in Constructor
    WSHttpBinding WsHttpSecurity = new WSHttpBinding(SecurityMode.Transport);

 // Use default constructor
WSHttpBinding WsHttpSecurity2 = new WSHttpBinding();
 // Set the Security property manually
  WsHttpSecurity2.Security.Mode = SecurityMode.Transport;
}
```

Using the WCF Service Configuration Editor, you simply flip the Mode property from Message to Transport, as shown in Figure 3-20.

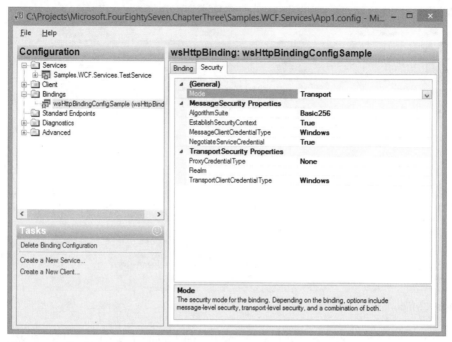

FIGURE 3-20 Configuring transport level security

The resulting XML in the configuration file would look like this:

```
<wsHttpBinding>
        <binding name="wsHttpBindingConfigSample">
                <security mode="Transport" />
        </binding>
</wsHttpBinding>
```

For transport level security to be implemented, you must choose either Transport or TransportWithMessageCredential for the Mode value of the binding. Using the WCF Service Configuration Editor or hard-coding it, it works exactly the same way.

Implementing certificates

To use certificates, you need to add a reference to the System.Security.dll. After a certificate is installed, the rest of the process is all downhill. Assume that you have a netHttpBinding already added to your service. You simply need to tweak the <security> and <message> bindings associated with it so the Mode value of the Security property is "TransportWithMessageCredential," and the ClientCredentialType property of the message element is a certificate. After configuration, the only remaining step is ensuring that the certificate is installed on the client, getting a reference to it, and adding it to the Certificate property of the ClientCertificate property of the Credentials property of your host.

A typical sample looks like this:

```
var MyFactory = new ChannelFactory<ITestService>("*");
MyFactory.Credentials.ClientCredentials.Certificate = X509.CurrentUser.
My.SubjectDistinguishedName.Find("CN=CLIENT").FirstOrDefault();
```

Thought experiment

How much should you secure?

In the following thought experiment, apply what you've learned about this objective to secure a WCF Service. You can find answers to these questions in the "Answers" section at the end of this chapter.

You are building several WCF Services, and some will employ sensitive information. Others transfer information that is completely public and are intended to be as easy to use as possible. Your service will be hosted internally, so you have full access to it without any real restrictions.

With this in mind, answer the following questions:

1. For the secure information, would you choose message level security, transport level security, or both?

2. For the less-sensitive information, would you still want to implement any security?

3. Would certificate-based security be a good fit for either scenario?

Objective summary

- The three goals of security in this context can be remembered by the acronym CIA: confidentiality, integrity, and authentication.

- Messages can be secured. This means that the message is not viewable without the corresponding key, but the cypher text can be viewed directly while it's being transported over the wire.

- The transport can be secured as well. In this case, the message could be left in plain text, but everything transferred across the channel is encrypted, thereby making it difficult (not impossible, but difficult to the point of being impractical) for prying eyes to watch what's going on.

- You have to be careful not to give away information accidentally. Although you want to secure the message or channel or both, don't forget to validate user input, which is often malicious and one of the most open attack vectors.

- Remember that security is always a trade-off. You can spend $1,000,000 on a state-of-the-art safe that guards the contents of your refrigerator. Although it would certainly keep your food safe, the cost far outweighs the value. Most mistakes are made by overlooking security, not overdoing it, but there's a balance that needs to be achieved between user-friendliness and security, and that balance point will likely change dramatically through the life of the application.

Objective review

Answer the following questions to test your knowledge of the information in this objective. You can find the answers to these questions and explanations of why each answer choice is correct or incorrect in the "Answers" section at the end of this chapter.

1. You are using IIS to host a WCF Service. Which of the following would help implement transport security over http (https) without removing previously existing functionality?

   A. The new Https protocol mapping feature

   B. Use of a wsHttpsBinding instead of a wsHttpBinding

   C. Enabling https for the virtual directory that contained the WCF Service items

   D. Ensuring that a metadata is enabled for the service

2. Which of the following are true regarding WCF security? (Choose all that apply.)

   A. You can implement message level security

   B. You can implement transport level security

   C. You can implement both transport level and message level security

   D. Transport security can be enabled, and message security can be enabled, but they cannot both be enabled at the same time

3. You are developing a WCF Service. The service must implement transport security, NTLM authentication, and NetTcpBindings. Which of the following do you need? (Choose all that apply.)

   A. binding value of netTcpBinding

   B. clientCredentialType of netTcpBinding

   C. clientCredentialType of Transport

   D. security mode value of Transport

Objective 3.5: Consume WCF services

To consume a service, you need some basic information about it. That information can come from the vendor, or from the service, or it can be dynamically discovered. From a consumption perspective, though, you typically create a proxy class and communicate with that class. The proxy, in conjunction with information provided about the service details, handles all the communication. Ultimately, dealing with a WCF Service should be no different from dealing with any statically referenced library. There are three ways to interact with the service, two of which accomplish the same task, just doing it slightly differently. The first is using the Svcutil.exe application to generate a proxy class. The next is to generate the proxy using the Add Service Reference feature of Visual Studio. These two do the same thing, but entail different actions on your part. The final way is to use the ChannelFactory class.

> **This objective covers how to:**
>
> - Generate proxies using Svcutil.exe
> - Generate proxies by creating a service reference
> - Create and implement channel factories

Generating proxies using Svcutil.exe

As discussed previously, WCF clients can interact with services by generating a proxy class and interacting with it. Svcutil.exe is a command-line tool that is used for generating proxy classes, among other things.

> **MORE INFO**   RUN SVCUTIL.EXE FROM THE VISUAL STUDIO COMMAND PROMPT
>
> Svcutil.exe is a command-line utility, so it is typically called directly from the command window. However, if you call it from the Windows command window, Windows does not recognize it unless you first navigate to the directory in which it resides. You can set an Environment variable that specifies a path to it, but it's probably not something you'll use frequently enough to necessitate doing so. Instead, just remember to launch it from the Visual Studio command prompt, and it will come right up.

Normally, I recommend doing exactly the opposite of what I recommend here. For one thing, it's something you can always just look up; secondly it's not typically a good way to prepare for an exam. But based on all the certification exams I've taken over the years, I'm making an exception here. Don't just know the "big picture" of what Svcutil.exe does and focus on the conceptual aspects. Look at it in-depth. Create a few different services (they can all be completely basic and even just provide the template functions that Visual Studio generates) and then generate proxies for each of them using Svcutil.exe. Seeing the behavior, seeing the results, and seeing the impact of different switches all help to drive home what the tool does and how it works. Although memorizing command-line switches is not normally a great use of time or energy, other command-line tools, such as aspnet_regiis and similar ones, have featured prominently on exams (likely because they are fairly easy to write questions for).

Before going further, take a look at the following list of items the Svcutil.exe tool can do:

- Generates proxy classes based on existing services or metadata documents. Keep in mind that, if you use the same parameters or supply values that correspond to existing files, vcutil.exe will overwrite the existing items. You can use the /mergeConfig switch to minimize problems associated with it.

- Exports metadata documents from compiled service code.

- Validates service code.

- Downloads metadata documents from existing services.

- Generates serialization code.

Now, take a look at Table 3-7 and pay close attention to each switch and what it accomplishes (note that N/A in the Shortcut section means there is no shortcut available, not that N/A is the shortcut):

TABLE 3-7 Svcutil.exe command-line options

Switch	Behavior	Shortcut
/directory:<directory>	Specifies the output directory in which the generated files will be placed. If no value is specified, it uses the current directory for the output. If the directory has already been used, output will be overwritten if the utility is run with this switch.	/d
/help	Shows the available command-line options. Very unlikely to appear on the test, but if it does, something in the stem will mention "help" or indicate "you need to list the available command-line options for Svcutil.exe, which of the following...."	/?
/noLogo	Suppresses the "Logo" information (copyright and banner message).	N/A
/svcutilConfig:<configFile>	Puts the configuration information in a file other than the default App.config file. You can also use this option to register the <system.ServiceModel> elements without changing the tool's configuration file.	N/A
/target:<output type>	Instructs the tool to create a specific output. You can use one of three options: code metadata xmlSerializer	/t
/asnyc	Creates the proxy class with both standard and asynchronous method signatures. By default, just the standard method signatures are included, so if you see any indication that the asynchronous methods need to be included, anything without the /async option will not be the answer.	/a
/internal	Generates the methods using the internal access modifier instead of generating them as public.	/i

Switch	Behavior	Shortcut
/serializer	Generates data types using a specific serializer. Available options are these: Auto DataContractSerializer XmlSerializer Typically, you'll want to use DataContractSerializer unless you have a specific need to use XmlSerializer.	/ser
/out	Specifies a file name for the generated code.	/o
/language	Causes the output to be generated in a specific language. Available options are the following: c# cs csharp vb visualbasic c++ cpp	/l

Generating proxies by creating a service reference

There's little surface area to test when it comes to this feature. There are only a few things that can be asked besides just knowing that it's an option.

To use it, select your project, right-click the project node, and choose the Add Service Reference option. Or on the Visual Studio menu bar, select the Project menu and then choose the Add Service Reference option. Figure 3-21 shows this menu.

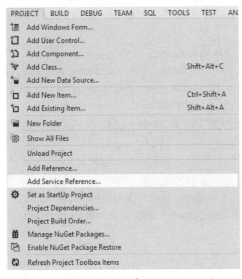

FIGURE 3-21 Add Service Reference menu

You see the dialog box shown in Figure 3-22.

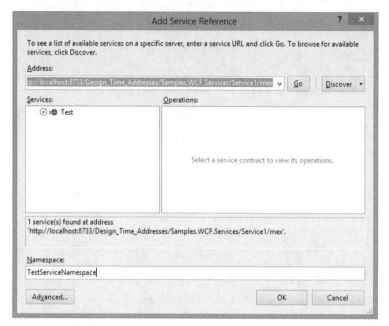

FIGURE 3-22 Add Service Reference dialog box

If the service isn't hosted, but is in the solution, you can use the Discover button on the right side of the dialog box, which gives you the option to use services it finds inside of the current solution. Otherwise, you need to provide a URL that has metadata enabled and then click the Go button.

After you click Go, the services it finds are listed. In many cases, there is just one, but multiple services are possible (particularly if you use the Discover option and have multiple services in your solution). It enables you to specify a namespace, which is something you generally should do. If there's an error (or an authentication requirement, in some cases), you'll either see an error message and the details of the error (if they're available), or you'll see the Authentication dialog box.

EXAM TIP

For test questions, the only things that you might be asked about on this portion are whether to use the Go feature coupled with a URI, the Discover option, or about specifying a specific namespace.

Notice the Advanced button on the bottom. If you need to take control and specify items outside of the default proxy, you can use the Service Reference Settings dialog box, which displays when you click the Advanced button. It's shown in Figure 3-23.

The previous items are the most commonly used values, but there are some others. A complete list is available on MSDN, and yes, it's probably worth the investment to learn the names of each and what they do. The MSDN coverage is available here *http://msdn. microsoft.com/en-us/library/aa347733.aspx*, and you can find more information about it at *http://www.svcutil.com/*. In the simplest form, just open up the Visual Studio command prompt and type the following:

```
svcutil http://service/metadataEndpoint
```

Assuming that the metadata exchange is available, call Svcutil and use the URI of the service. This works without any other command-line parameters because it uses default values for everything. A more common approach involves specifying at least a few of the parameters. Assume that you want to generate the proxy class for the TestService discussed throughout the chapter and have the proxy named TestServiceProxy. Either of the following works:

C#

```
svcutil.exe /language:cs /out:TestServiceProxy.cs /config:app.config
http://www.williamgryan.mobi/487/TestService
svcutil.exe /language:c# /out:TestServiceProxy.cs /config:app.config
http://www.williamgryan.mobi/487/TestService
```

VB.NET

```
svcutil.exe /language:vb /out:TestServiceProxy.vb /config:app.config
http://www.williamgryan.mobi/487/TestService

svcutil.exe /language:visualbasic /out:TestServiceProxy.vb /config:app.
config http://www.williamgryan.mobi/487/TestService
```

It's not possible to cover every single scenario and show you an example of each. Instead, read about the features, and then generate multiple files using different switches. Also, try both mechanisms, generating a proxy based on a live service and generating a proxy based on assembly references.

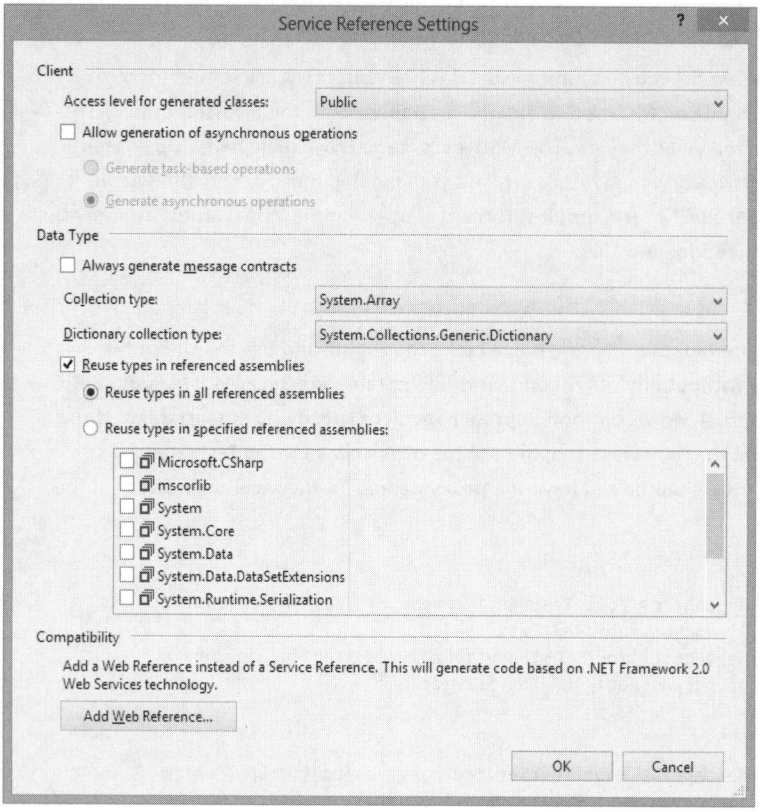

FIGURE 3-23 Service Reference Settings dialog box

At the top you'll notice the option to specify the access modifier. This corresponds to the /internal command-line switch. The next option is the Allow generation of asynchronous operations check box. If you choose it, the proxy class generates methods that contain the methods defined in the service and their asynchronous counterparts.

You have the option to Always Generate Message Contracts, which does what its name implies: generate message contract types.

The Collection Type option enables you to set the default collection type. If you are using a .NET client that's using the .NET Framework 2.0 or later, you can use generic collection types. However, generics are supported only in .NET (there might be counterparts or similar features in other languages, but as implemented in the .NET Framework, generics are a technology-specific feature), so for compatibility, the proxy class generates anything typed as a generic collection as an array. This helps ensure that other technologies can use the service. Many people have used List<Type> in a service, and noticed that the proxy class ends up creating Type[] definitions instead. You can change this behavior, but remember that doing so has consequences. The Reuse Types In Specified Referenced Assemblies option enables type sharing of anything that already exists in a statically referenced assembly on your client. You can opt to do this globally, which is the default behavior, or specify that only some reuse happens.

That leaves the Compatibility section. If you are using an .asmx web service and want to consume it as such (instead of as a WCF Service), you can use the Add Web Reference option (see Figure 3-24).

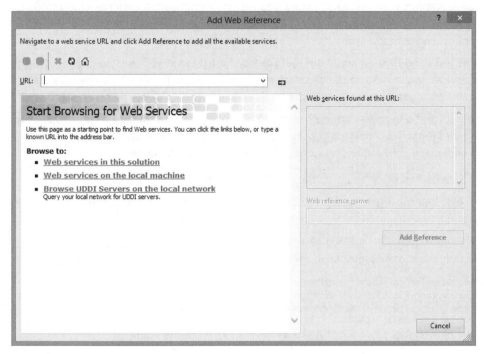

FIGURE 3-24 Add Web Reference dialog box

There are times when you might have to use this option, particularly with older services or services that are not created with Microsoft technologies. If you have to use it, it's there, but you generally shouldn't use this option unless you have specific reasons to do so, and keep in mind that you are definitely limiting quite a bit of functionality. I've heard it likened to having a top-of-the-line GPS at your disposal, one that detects traffic congestion and enables you to select an alternative route, is constantly updated with construction details, and enables you to navigate on virtually every possible option, and then opting to use a paper map that's several years old. If you're forced to do so (like the GPS battery being dead and not having a power supply in your car available), know that it comes with consequences, ones that are likely going to be costly. References created using legacy technology won't provide many of the benefits of WCF, such as ability to specify multiple bindings or use extensibility.

Creating and implementing channel factories

The ChannelFactory class is one of my favorite classes in WCF because it's simple, powerful, and elegant. According to MSDN, the ChannelFactory class "Creates and manages the channels that are used by clients to send messages to service endpoints." In reality, it's a convenient and easy way to let your client interact with WCF Services with extremely minimal effort. It can be used without or in conjunction with your application's configuration file. That means that in some cases you can interact with a service in as little as two lines of code (three if you include the call to close the channel when you're done with it). Even if you use no configuration, however, it's still quick and easy to use. It's such a useful item and lends itself so well to question writing that I can all but assure you that you'll encounter at least one question about it.

The first thing to know about it is that you don't use it alone; you use it in conjunction with the service's contract. So you'll need a reference to the service library or the assembly that contains the interface that serves as the service's contract.

The following samples show each of the constructor overloads for the ChannelFactory class using the ITestService interface. You shouldn't need to memorize each of them, but it helps tremendously if you're at least familiar with what options are available.

```
ChannelFactory<ITestService> Proxy =   new ChannelFactory<ITestService>();
```

The default constructor accepts no parameters, so the information about the endpoint needs to be specified. Similarly, any behaviors need to be specified as well.

The next one accepts a String parameter containing the endpoint configuration name. Obviously the endpoint must be in the configuration file and must have a matching name:

```
String endpointConfigName = "wsHttp_BindingConfig";
ChannelFactory<ITestService> proxy =
    new ChannelFactory<ITestService>(endpointConfigName);
```

The next one accepts a binding as a parameter, but works the same way:

```
String endpointConfigName = "wsHttp_BindingConfig";
WSHttpBinding wSBinding = new WSHttpBinding(EndpointConfigName);

ChannelFactory<ITestService> Proxy = new ChannelFactory<ITestService>(wSBinding);
```

The next one just takes a ServiceEndpoint instance:

```
ServiceEndpoint endpoint = new ServiceEndpoint(new ContractDescription("Endpoint"));
ChannelFactory<ITestService> proxy =
    new ChannelFactory<ITestService>(endpoint);
```

You can go through the other remaining constructors on your own; they are quite easy to understand and work with. In any case, let's go through a real example and one that you're likely to run into on the exam. This would make a perfect candidate for a drag-and-drop type question, so following are the key points:

```
String endpointUri = "http://www.williamgryan.mobi/487/TestService.svc";
String endpointConfigName = "wsHttp_BindingConfig";
WSHttpBinding wSBinding = new WSHttpBinding(EndpointConfigName);
 ChannelFactory<ITestService> proxy =
                new ChannelFactory<ITestService>(wSBinding, new
EndpointAddress(endpointUri));
```

```
ITestService serviceInstance = proxy.CreateChannel();
String[] outlineItems = serviceInstance.GetExamOutline("70-487");
String questionOne = serviceInstance.GetQuestionText(1);
AnswerSet[] answersQuestionOne = serviceInstance.GetQuestionAnswers(1);
AnswerDetails answersDetailsQuestionOne = serviceInstance.GetAnswerDetails(1);
proxy.Close(new TimeSpan(0,0,1,0,0));
```

The first thing is the constructor. It needs to know the contract that's being used.

Next, you used the same interface to declare a variable and then used the CreateChannel method of the ChannelFactory instance to initialize it. Again, it's the contract that is the type used for the return type.

> **MORE INFO** CHANNELFACTORY AND USING STATEMENT
>
> Although it is conventional wisdom that any IDisposable object should be wrapped in a using block, ChannelFactory is one prominent exception. If there's a network-related error (for example, the client loses connectivity), an exception will be encountered when the using statement tries to dispose of the channel. Additionally, if you have an unhandled exception occur within the using block, it will be obscured by the Dispose exception.

From there on, the example shows calls to the various service methods. They vary for every service and the methods (if any) you're instructed to call. The information about these methods is extracted from the contract's details. In a slight digression, you can tell that if you had a version of the interface that didn't match the one the service was currently using, you would run into some problems, especially if it was anything that fell into the breaking change category.

Finally, call the Close method. Though a TimeSpan is specified, it's common to just use the default call. By inserting a TimeSpan, you simply indicate that, if the channel isn't closed within the duration you specify, an exception will be thrown.

You never deal with the actual service class definition (nor do you need it, although it will frequently be in the same assembly as the interface definition, which you do need). Underline, bold, and italicize that point—you never used the service definition. In fact, if you use the code that accompanies this text, the service class was intentionally removed from this sample to draw attention to this fact. You use the interface for both the declaration and instantiation of the ChannelFactory, and they should match as a rule. Now because of language semantics, if you had one interface that implemented another interface, it's possible that they might differ, but that's completely unrelated to WCF, and would definitely fall into the trick question category (which I'm quite sure wouldn't make it through the exam process).

The interface also serves as the type for the variable that is returned from the call to the CreateChannel method, so it will be used repeatedly in any block. The reason I'm driving this point so strongly (other than it's just the way things work, and you need to know it) is that you typically want to use elimination to increase the chances of getting something else right.

In many of the drag-and-drop–style questions, you can reuse certain items (it's indicated when that's the case), so don't be fooled into thinking that, just because you see the interface used somewhere else in the code block, you can't use it again.

Thought experiment
Consuming WCF Services

In the following thought experiment, apply what you've learned about this objective to consume WCF Services. You can find answers to these questions in the "Answers" section at the end of this chapter.

You are building several WCF Services. You have several different clients on several different operating system versions.

With this in mind, answer the following questions:

1. Do you recommend the Add Service Reference feature or Svcutil.exe?

2. Do you recommend that the client proxies support generics or arrays?

3. What other considerations might you find?

Objective summary

- The Svcutil.exe command-line tool is one of the main methods to generate proxy classes and other items relevant to a WCF Service.

- The Add Service Reference is the second way you can directly generate a proxy class in WCF.

- The Add Service Reference enables you to point to a live service (with metadata enabled) and generate the reference from the .wsdl, or you can use the Discover feature to generate proxy classes from services defined in the same solution in which you're building the client application.

- You have the option to specify several other features when using the Service Reference dialog box, including whether to generate message contracts, what access modifiers should be used for methods, whether to generate asynchronous method signatures for each method, and how to handle collections.

- If you don't want to work with a proxy class, you can use the ChannelFactory class, which makes extensive use of the service contract to function and ultimately enables you to do anything you can with proxies generated by other means.

Objective review

Answer the following questions to test your knowledge of the information in this objective. You can find the answers to these questions and explanations of why each answer choice is correct or incorrect in the "Answers" section at the end of this chapter.

1. You need to build a client-side proxy class in VB.NET for a WCF Service named Test-Service that is hosted by one of your vendors. Which of the following options would accomplish that task? (Choose all that apply.)

   A. Use the Svcutil.exe command-line tool with the following command:

   ```
   Svcutil.exe http://www.myvendor.com/TestService.svc
   ```

   B. Use the Svcutil.exe command-line tool with the following command:

   ```
   Svcutil.exe /l:visualbasic http://www.myvendor.com/TestService.svc.
   ```

   C. Use the Add Service Reference dialog box.

   D. Use the ChannelFactory class.

2. You are building a client to consume a WCF Service named TestService, and many of the methods have return types that are generic list collections. You are expecting List<Type> return types for the calls, but the proxy class has implemented each as an array. You want this type implemented specifically as the List<Type>. What should you do? (Choose all that apply.)

   A. Use the ToList<> extension method at the end of each call to the methods that are currently being returned as arrays.

   B. Change the Settings in the Add Service Reference dialog box using the Advanced screen. Change the Collection type to List.

   C. Regenerate the proxy class after changing the settings.

   D. Use the Add Web Reference dialog box to generate the proxy because it automatically respects the return type definitions.

3. Svcutil.exe provides which of the following features? (Choose all that apply.)

   A. Validates compiled service code.

   B. Downloads metadata documents from deployed services.

   C. Generates serialization code.

   D. Adds metadata exchange endpoints to deployed services.

Objective 3.6: Version a WCF service

Unless you deploy a service that has absolutely no bugs or problems and never needs any feature updates, you have to deal with service versioning at one point or another. Versioning is probably not a major feature of the exam, but is certainly fair game as far as questions go, and you should at least be familiar with the concepts before considering taking the exam. Outside of the exam, though, it's something you will have to deal with (probably frequently) and is an area with a small margin for getting things wrong. No one has ever regretted getting versioning and deployment issues "too right" and probably never will.

> **This objective covers how to:**
> - Version different types of contracts (message, service, data)
> - Configure address, binding, and routing service versioning

Versioning different types of contracts

There are four major areas of service changes you are likely to encounter:

- Changes to a contract
- Changes to an address
- Bindings are added or removed
- Implementations change

Although changes are inevitable in most cases, the issues and negatives that arise from mismanaging them can be largely and mostly minimized. These changes fall into two categories:

- *Breaking changes*
- *Nonbreaking changes*

Breaking changes are a necessary evil sometimes, and in some cases can't be avoided, but they are usually costly and inconvenient for all parties involved. Great care should be taken up front to eliminate or minimize the need for breaking changes, and you should have a clear strategy for rolling them up, making consumers aware of them, and informing consumers how to deal with the consequences of such changes. There's quite a bit of literature written on the subject and many different definitions, but the ones that Microsoft uses here are concise and easy to understand.

Nonbreaking changes are the benevolent twin of breaking changes. You make a change, it affects the service in some significant way, but it causes no downstream damage or countermeasures.

If you implement a change to a service, and there is no disruption of service or functionality with any of the consumers, it's a nonbreaking change. Everything else is a breaking change. Make sure that you understand this difference (which is fortunately one you could guess at and get right 99 percent of the time).

Contract versioning

Changes to a contract can include the following:

- Addition or removal of an operation
- Modification of an operation
- Behaviors of the contract changing
- Components of the contract changing
- Elements in the message changing

The contracts used by each party in the communication process do not need to be exactly the same or identical matches; instead, they simply need to be compatible. Say for illustration that Vendor A has a service with Method1, Method2, and Method3. As of right now, every single client has a contract for that service that includes Method1, Method2, and Method3.

Without touching or affecting those methods, let's say the vendor adds Method4, Method5, and Method6. Right now, the contracts the consumers have are not identical to those that the vendor is providing, but they are compatible. That's ultimately what matters.

Say that, instead of adding the three methods, the vendor opts to add a new overload to each of the first three methods. Both vendor and client have a contract that has Method1, Method2, and Method3, but they are absolutely not compatible. The first case could be rolled out without any problem (the worst that could happen is that a client might notice the new methods and ask if they were ready for use or try to use one of the methods on their own, which might not be ready for use). In the second case, unless the consumers were aware of the changes in advance and had already modified their clients to deal with the change, there would be major problems and disruption.

Using the same concept and knowing that data contracts (just like service contracts) need only be compatible, what do you think might break compatibility? The addition of some new types? The modification of an existing DataContract? The removal of an existing DataContract?

The first scenario, adding a type, would present no problems; the latter two absolutely would because changes to the interface will cause compilation to fail. Now that you have covered breaking and nonbreaking change with respect to each service component, you need to understand versioning strategy concepts: *strict versioning* and *lax versioning*.

Strict versioning

The more clients you have, the more damage versioning issues they can potentially cause, and the less control you have over the response. If you have one client, you might be able to offer them a discount for the inconvenience they encounter. You can offer them a free update to their client that they accept. But even with just one customer, they might say "no" and not tolerate it. The more clients you have, though, the more likely it is that you will run into one that has serious issues with version changes.

To make sure that you don't cause any problems, you must ensure that any newly generated messages from your updated service validate against the old schema. The safest way to have this assurance is to never change existing contracts and just create new contracts, ideally ones with new and assuredly distinct XML namespaces.

Lax versioning

WCF and even .asmx web services have support for lax versioning. Lax versioning means that minor changes can often be made without breaking the existing contract. It's possible, for example, that you can add a new member and the data will just be ignored.

Configuring address, binding, and routing service versioning

Changes to an address move from one host to another. Clustering and load balancing all have the possible result of an address change. Ideally, the service is deployed in such a manner that initially that changes of this type can be done transparently without the user even being aware that the change happened, but sometimes that's not possible.

When configuring bindings, they are either added or removed. You might start out just using the basicHttpBinding and find that you need functionality provided by the wsHttpBinding or another binding. You might add features that necessitate behavior that isn't supported by your existing bindings.

Implementation changes might involve using one gateway to process payments and changes to a new gateway that needs different information returns different information. You might have to change the implementation to add caching or include some other optimizations. Implementation changes are almost a certain part of deploying services.

Thought experiment

How should you handle version upgrades?

In the following thought experiment, apply what you've learned about this objective to version a WCF Service. You can find answers to these questions in the "Answers" section at the end of this chapter.

You are building several WCF Services. You have to get the service out immediately, but there's strong reason to believe you're going to have to quickly implement many new features and additional versions.

With this in mind, answer the following questions:

1. How can you avoid breaking changes?

2. If you have breaking changes that you are forced to implement, how would you handle them?

Objective summary

- WCF enables several different aspects of the service to be versioned.
- Modifications fall into two primary categories: breaking and nonbreaking.
- Breaking changes are extremely problematic, and although sometimes unavoidable, great care should be taken to minimize their existence and impact.

Objective review

Answer the following questions to test your knowledge of the information in this objective. You can find the answers to these questions and explanations of why each answer choice is correct or incorrect in the "Answers" section at the end of this chapter.

1. Version 10 of the TestService (which implements the ITestService interface) is about to be updated and deployed. The ITestService interface adds two new methods, both of which are scoped with the public modifier and are decorated with the OperationContract attribute. Which of the following is true?

   A. The two additions will be considered breaking changes unless each assembly includes the correct version number.

   B. The two additions will not be breaking changes because they leave all previous functionality in place and just add new functionality.

   C. As long as the service and contract pairs are both deployed with their respective version numbers (versions 10, 11), clients will not encounter any problems.

   D. Answers B and C.

2. Version 10 of the TestService assembly (which also includes the ITestService interface and implements it) adds two new methods to the interface definition. The new methods use the Protected modifier and do not currently contain the OperationContract attribute (on either the interface or the implementation). Which of the following is true?

   A. There will not be breaking changes on any items that statically link to the assembly.

   B. There will not be breaking changes because the access modifiers are set to Protected.

   C. There will not break changes because they don't implement the OperationContract attribute.

   D. It will be a breaking change to any assembly statically linked to it unless the new methods are also added to the implementation.

3. Which versioning strategies are supported through WCF?

   A. Strict Versioning

   B. Lax Versioning

   C. Mixed-Mode Versioning

   D. Contract Versioning

NOTE MINIMIZING VERSIONING PROBLEMS

To minimize the impact of versioning, make sure that you publicize any changes well in advance; the longer the notice period, the better. Make sure that you document the changes and their known impact as comprehensively as possible. You can't possibly anticipate every possible downstream side-effect, but you can predict many, particularly if you test in as many environments as you feasibly can (particularly ones that you know high-use clients have). Communicate throughout the process, and let clients provide feedback. Many government regulations, for example, involve a "cooling off," or "feedback" period in which they accept feedback about the impact (positive and negative) that the change might cause. You might not be able to accommodate every request, but each one you can accommodate, even partially, minimizes the impact of the change and deflates the charge that the change was forced upon them. Make several reminder announcements as the time period closes on deployment. Have contingency plans and brainstorm about what can go wrong in advance. Test as much as possible, particularly with alpha and beta releases, and welcome users to participate.

Finally, after the change is deployed, make sure that you have adequate support staff to handle the influx of communication you'll likely receive. Much of the communication will be questions you already answered several times. Much will be from those looking for assurances. Much will be complaints or problems (some of which might have nothing to do with your change, but you get to temporarily take the blame because you're the easiest target). And always remember to do as much as possible to consider things from your client's perspective. This might sound like something from a motivational speaker's book instead of a technical one; however, if you win the hearts and minds of your users and convince them that you've done your due diligence, changes are much more likely to be viewed as necessary and problems as costs of doing business. Keep quiet about everything, leave customers out of the loop, and do things in a manner that looks disorganized, and you can bank on a bunch of problems, animosity, and finger pointing. You'll often get that even when you do everything right, so make sure that you limit the surface area as much as you can.

Objective 3.7: Create and configure a WCF service on Windows Azure

Running applications in Azure gives you and your customers a lot of advantages. However, not all customers are willing to deploy their applications to a public cloud. Some have concerns regarding the security of their data or they have local regulations that don't allow them to use the public cloud.

Instead of giving in to those problems and deploying your application as a typical on premise application, you can also choose a hybrid scenario. This means that you create an application that spans both the public cloud and on-premise servers that are under your control.

Connecting these types of applications is the topic of this objective. Azure provides a technology called *Service Bus Relay* to do this. *Relaying* is used to expose services hosted in your own datacenter to the outside world in a secure way.

The term *service bus* is something that doesn't exist only in Azure. Products such as BizTalk also expose service bus functionality. The primary goal is to be a bridge between different applications. The unique point of Azure Service Bus, however, is the capability to not only connect different applications, but to also connect applications on premise and in the cloud in a hybrid fashion. By using Azure Service Bus, you avoid the installation and configuration that typical on-premise service bus products normally need, and you gain all the scalability and availability advantages Azure offers you.

> **This objective covers how to:**
> - Create and configure bindings for WCF services
> - Relay bindings to Azure using service bus endpoints
> - Integrate with the Azure service bus relay

Creating and configuring bindings for WCF services

As you know, WCF is all about ABC: Address, Binding and Contract. When deploying a regular WCF service to Azure you don't have to make any changes and you can just deploy your service to a Web Role or Web Site.

When using the relay feature of the service bus, you can install some additional bindings into your project. The easiest way to do this is by using NuGet.

The NuGet package *Windows Azure Service Bus* contains all the assemblies you need to set up your WCF service for relaying. Take the following service as an example:

```
[ServiceContract(Namespace = "urn:ps")]
interface ISecretService
{
    [OperationContract]
    string GetSecretData(int d);
}
interface ISecretServiceChannel : ISecretService, IClientChannel { }
```

The implementation of this class is simple, but you can imagine using your own, more complex WCF services here:

```
class SecretService : ISecretService
{
    public string GetSecretData(int d)
    {
        return string.Format("You passed: {0}", d);
    }
}
```

Now that you have your WCF service, you need to host it just as you would with any other WCF service. The benefit with using the service bus functionality is that it complements your already existing WCF bindings. This means that you can expose internal endpoints for your service that can be used to integrate with on-premise applications and that you can expose special endpoints to connect to the service bus. To host your service, you create an instance of a ServiceHost, define your endpoints, and then open your server:

```
ServiceHost sh = new ServiceHost(typeof(SecretService));

sh.AddServiceEndpoint(
    typeof(ISecretService), new NetTcpBinding(),
    "net.tcp://localhost:9358/secretservice");

sh.AddServiceEndpoint(
    typeof(ISecretService), new NetTcpRelayBinding(),
    ServiceBusEnvironment.CreateServiceUri("sb", "wcfonazure", "secretservice"))
    .Behaviors.Add(new TransportClientEndpointBehavior
    {
        TokenProvider = TokenProvider.CreateSharedSecretTokenProvider(
        "owner",
        "D1Kmb83CCLrAtz4du9vb3xn99DaM2dH4jQqSec98if4=")
    });

sh.Open();
```

```
Console.WriteLine("Press ENTER to close");
Console.ReadLine();

sh.Close();
```

In this example, both an internal endpoint is created and an endpoint that connects to the Azure Service Bus. By running this code, you automatically create the relay in Azure. When you close the application, the endpoint will be removed from Azure. This means that relaying works only when the server application is online.

> **MORE INFO** BROKERED MESSAGING
>
> If relaying is not suited for your type of application because of the need to be online at all times, you can also look at the brokered messaging capabilities of the Azure Service Bus. To get started with brokered messaging, you can look at *http://msdn.microsoft.com/en-us/library/windowsazure/hh367516.aspx*.

Instead of specifying these endpoints in your code, you can configure them from your App.config just as you can do with other bindings:

```
<services>
  <service name="Service.SecretService">
    <endpoint contract="Service.ISecretService"
              binding="netTcpRelayBinding"
              address="sb://wcfonazure.servicebus.windows.net/secretservice"
              behaviorConfiguration="sbTokenProvider"/>
  </service>
</services>
<behaviors>
  <endpointBehaviors>
    <behavior name="sbTokenProvider">
      <transportClientEndpointBehavior>
        <tokenProvider>
          <sharedSecret issuerName="owner"
                        issuerSecret="D1Kmb83CCLrAtz4du9vb3xn99DaM2dH4jQqSec98if4=" />
        </tokenProvider>
      </transportClientEndpointBehavior>
    </behavior>
  </endpointBehaviors>
</behaviors>
```

As you can see in both the code and the App.config file, you use two important values: the name of your service and the Default Key. How to obtain those values is the topic of the next section.

This example uses the netTcpRelayBinding binding. There are other bindings that you can use depending on the scenarios you want to support. Microsoft recommends using the net-TcpRelayBinding unless you have other specific requirements.

One of the key features of the Azure Service Bus is its capability to create secure connections through a firewall. This means that you won't have to make any changes to your on-premise configuration to allow the Service Bus to communicate with your service. Normally, this is done using TCP ports (both over SSL or unencrypted). If those ports aren't available, relaying can also use the default HTPP (port 80) or HTTPS (port 443) ports.

> **MORE INFO** OTHER BINDINGS
>
> Relayed messaging offers you other bindings that you can use such as BasicHttpRelayBinding, NetOneWayRelayBinding, and NetEventRelayBinding. You can find more information on these bindings at *http://msdn.microsoft.com/en-us/library/windowsazure/hh410102.aspx.*

Relaying bindings to Azure using service bus endpoints

To create a service bus endpoint in Windows Azure, you can go to the management portal to create a new service bus. When creating a service bus, you specify a namespace and the region where you want to deploy your service bus. Just as with other Azure components, it's wise to create them in the same datacenter. This avoids latency issues and additional costs for sending data from one datacenter to another.

The Windows Azure portal gives you detailed connection information that you can use from your server and client services. For example, the connection information for the *wcfonazure* namespace gives you the following connection string:

```
Endpoint=sb://wcfonazure.servicebus.windows.net/;SharedSecretIssuer=owner;
SharedSecretValue=D1Kmb83CCLrAtz4du9vb3xn99DaM2dH4jQqSec98if4=
```

This connection string contains the name of your namespace and the default key. You need to use those values to configure your server and client applications.

When your relaying host is running, you can also use the Windows Azure Management Portal to inspect your relay. You can see the name of your relay and how many listeners are active. When you close the host, the relay disappears from Windows Azure. This also shows why this feature can help clients who are not willing to store data in the public cloud. By using the service bus, they have total control over their services hosted in their own datacenter. If they want, they can shut down their hosts and disconnect themselves from Azure.

Integrating with the Azure service bus relay

After creating a new service bus on Azure and hosting a WCF service with service bus endpoints, you can create a client to communicate with your on-premise service through Azure.

When building a client to communicate with your relay, you need the namespace name that you used for hosting the service and the default key. This also means you shouldn't publicly expose these values because if you do, everyone would be able to access your service.

Using the name of your namespace, the owners name (default: owner), and the Default Key, you use a security mechanism that resembles the idea of a username and password. There are more elaborate security mechanisms if you need them, such as SAML or SimpleWebToken.

MORE INFO   SECURING YOUR CONNECTION

For more information on securing your service bus connection, see *http://msdn.microsoft.com/en-us/library/windowsazure/dd582773.aspx*.

The following code shows how to create a client to call the SecretService that you saw previously:

```
var cf = new ChannelFactory<ISecretServiceChannel>(
    new NetTcpRelayBinding(),
    new EndpointAddress(ServiceBusEnvironment.CreateServiceUri(
        "sb",
        "wcfonazure",
        "secretservice")));

cf.Endpoint.Behaviors.Add(new TransportClientEndpointBehavior
{
    TokenProvider = TokenProvider.CreateSharedSecretTokenProvider(
    "owner",
    "D1Kmb83CCLrAtz4du9vb3xn99DaM2dH4jQqSec98if4=")
});

using (var ch = cf.CreateChannel())
{
    Console.WriteLine(ch.GetSecretData(42));
}

Console.ReadLine();
```

You use the same service interface that you use on the host. By making sure that you use the correct namespace and default key, you can create a channel to the relay and send a message. The relay takes your message and passes it to the hosting service that can run anywhere.

Objective summary

- Azure Service Bus helps you create hybrid applications that span the cloud and on-premise datacenters.

- When working with service bus relay, you need to install the NuGet Package WindowsAzure.ServiceBus into your projects.

- You can host your WCF service on premise. By adding extra bindings that are specifically created for the service bus, you can expose your application securely through firewalls.

- You need to create a service bus with a unique namespace on Azure to relay your messages.

- Client applications can connect to the service bus without knowing where the actual service is hosted. The relaying service authenticates clients and forwards messages to the on-premise service.

Objective review

Answer the following questions to test your knowledge of the information in this objective. You can find the answers to these questions and explanations of why each answer choice is correct or incorrect in the "Answers" section at the end of this chapter.

1. Which elements do you need from the management portal when configuring your host service? (Choose all that apply.)

   A. Namespace

   B. NetTcpRelayBinding

   C. ServiceHost

   D. Default Key

2. You want to use a SharedSecretToken for authentication. Which method and parameters do you use?

   A. TokenProvider.CreateSharedSecretTokenProvider(namespace, key)

   B. TokenProvider.CreateSamlTokenProvider(samltoken)

   C. TokenProvider.CreateSharedSecretTokenProvider(owner, key)

   D. TokenProvider.CreateWindowsTokenProvider(uris)

3. You want to connect a client to the service bus. Which elements do you need? (Choose all that apply.)

   A. Namespace

   B. Service path

   C. Owner name

   D. Default Key

Objective 3.8: Implement messaging patterns

Message exchange patterns (MEPs) are mechanisms that describe how the client and the server should exchange data. There are three primary MEPs to choose from: datagram, request-response, and duplex.

This objective covers how to:

■ Implement one-way, request/reply, streaming, and duplex communication

■ Implement Windows Azure Service Bus and Windows Azure Queues

---

WCF provides communication patterns, so if you're familiar with these concepts in any other version or technology, they will be familiar to you.

Implementing one-way, request/reply, streaming, and duplex communication

Normally, you will call a service's operation and wait for a response. The response might indicate that nothing happened, but it still indicates that the operation completed successfully or an exception was encountered. There are times, (for example with logging), though, when you want to implement so-called fire and forget operations (meaning you call the method, and if an exception is encountered, you don't care or choose to do anything as a result). Fire and forget functionality is implemented in WCF by using the OneWay attribute.

You can define an operation as one way with the IsOneWay parameter in the OperationContract. Here is a quick illustration:

```
[OperationContract(IsOneWay = true)]
void LogMesssage(String messsage);
```

First, to designate an operation as one way, you set the IsOneWay parameter to True. Second, you can't have a return type defined (which should become clear momentarily). So that's the how; here's everything else.

Although few people make a point of memorizing all the current http response codes, chances are you've consciously come across several of them over the years and come across them all the time when working with the web whether or not you realize it.

A request is made to the server, and the server sends back a response. Marking something as OneWay essentially does a pass-fake on the process. It sends back a HttpStatusCode of 202 (if you're wondering, 202 simply echoes back "Accepted"). This code comes back immediately before any processing begins. Here's where things get tricky. Normally, you just get a 202, and that's the end of the story. But you might have a long-running procedure that's marked as OneWay. You get back an immediate 202, but the service is still holding on to and processing your request. Additionally, just because a response is issued doesn't mean the client has it or has accepted it. So it blocks until that response is received and accepted from the service. This can cause problems when multiple requests are made on OneWay methods when using a binding that is configured to use sessions.

Assume that you just called LongRunningMethodThatTakesForever and then called a OneWay method right afterward. You would expect (well, hopefully not after reading this chapter) that the immediate return of the OneWay response would get sent back to the service, and another method could be called on that binding/session. But that's not what will happen. The first request will block the second unless it was specifically called in an asynchronous manner. The 202 response won't be sent back for a long time, at least until after LongRunningMethodThatTakesForever completes, plus a little extra overhead for good measure.

This is one feature that is overused and misused more than just about anything else. The only saving grace is that, even if it had counterparts since the early days of .asmx web services, it's still obscure. The allure of fire and forget functionality makes many developers believe it absolves them of exception handling, callbacks, and all sorts of other things that you have to wait for to get back from the server. In a purely pedantic sense, that's true. But it's true in the same way as closing your eyes absolves you of having to worry about traffic in front of you as you drive. Sure, you don't have to worry about everyone else, but you're going to have to deal with the consequences if you don't.

So what makes a good candidate for a OneWay call? Mainly, it's something you want to be able to execute and forget about. If it doesn't finish or complete correctly, there's little to be concerned about. Logging messages, for example, wouldn't be horrendous consequences in most instances if it didn't get through or wasn't processed correctly. So mainly low-priority, low-importance utility tasks lend themselves to the use of the OneWay attribute. As you can imagine, OneWay methods must not return any value and be typed as void or nothing because one way calls don't return anything other than a status code.

Streaming and duplex

Streaming data and implementing duplex communication (two-way) are likely exam candidates. When implementing streaming in WCF, you have two modes you can work with:

- Buffered
- Streaming

The default is the buffered transfer mode, which means that it must be completely assembled and received before the receiver can start reading or using it. In the streaming mode, the receiver can begin to read the information as soon as it begins transmission and before it's been completely delivered. Not all data can be processed serially, so unless you can do so, streaming won't provide much value. However, particularly in cases where you are dealing with large file sizes (think audio or video files), streaming can be such a big factor that it literally causes people to use or not use your application. If you don't believe me, ask anyone old enough to have been around on the Internet back in the early '90s when streaming media was little more than a pipe dream. More than one person wasted several hours downloading something, only to find out it was not what they wanted or worse.

What about filling a collection or a dataset (which is a collection, but logically a little different)? How many rows will you get back? What is the size of each row? What if you get one more record than the threshold? Well, you'll have a problem. This feature was enabled as a security feature to preempt bad actors from flooding a server with large size payloads and *distributed denial-of-service (DDoS)* attacks. However let's say you bump the setting one order of magnitude and then the database grows and you run into the problem again. So you repeat it. And the process repeats itself. Usually by the second or third time, someone in management says, "Enough of this. I don't want this again. Turn the setting the whole way up," and that ends up being the default setting, which completely defeats the purpose for the value in the first place.

It is not an exaggeration to say that sidestepping the value altogether by using the Max-Value of long (which is syntactical sugar for System.Int64) is common. Just for the record, MaxValue equates to 9,223,372,036,854,775,807 bytes, which is quite large. The answer isn't to just keep increasing it; it is to keep your payload and message sizes tight and under control. Those numbers can be calculated and should be, and you should have a good idea of what capacity a setting can handle. Turning it the whole way up is the exact opposite idea of least privilege: it's like "most privilege," which is ill-advised from a security point of view.

At the contract level, you start the process by defining the return type of a method as a Stream. Next, you need to configure the binding, through code or configuration setting, the TransferMode enumeration value to Streamed. Then you typically want to set the max-ReceivedMessageSize to a value that's the largest value you calculate to need for items you stream. This is a great candidate for one of those drag-and-drop exam items, and I'm guessing that, even if it's not in the exam current version, it will make its way into a future version.

```
<basicHttpBinding>
  <binding name="HttpStreaming" maxReceivedMessageSize="67108864"
          transferMode="Streamed"/>
</basicHttpBinding>
<customBinding>
  <binding name="487CustomBinding">
    <textMessageEncoding messageVersion="Soap12WSAddressing10" />
    <httpTransport transferMode="Streamed"
maxReceivedMessageSize="67108864"/>
  </binding>
</customBinding>
```

There are actually four different values available for the TransferMode enumeration according to MSDN, which are listed in Table 3-8.

TABLE 3-8 TransferMode enumeration values

Member name	Description
Buffered	The request and response messages are both buffered.
Streamed	Both the request and response are streamed.
StreamedRequest	The request message is streamed, and the response message is buffered.
StreamedResponse	The request message is buffered, and the response message is streamed.

There are a few other points to keep in mind. First, enabling streaming (versus buffering) can improve scalability and responsiveness of a service by eliminating the need for large memory buffers. However, just because you set the TransferMode to one of the Streamed mechanisms, you can't just assume that it will automatically fix all that ails you in terms of performance or scalability. You have to keep in mind what's better about it to understand this. If the contents of what you are moving are so small that they easily fit into a buffer, you won't likely see a benefit. If you're dealing with a large object (a *Binary Large Object [BLOB]*, for example) that can span several buffers, you'll likely see a discernible improvement. This is a great feature, but has the same sort of aura that indexes do—those who don't know better automatically suggest that it fix any performance problems in the same way they recommend adding an index to a SQL table because things are running slowly. Like indexes, they can be a great tool when used correctly, but they need to be used in the correct context for the right reasons, and you should have the right expectations about them.

Along those same lines, not all bindings support TransferMode. The following out-of-the-box bindings do support TransferMode and streaming. Keep in mind that this is not the definitive list because you can create custom bindings specifically for this purpose:

- *BasicHttpBinding*
- *NetTcpBinding*
- *NetNamedPipeBinding*

Finally, note the following limitations and restrictions on using streaming:

- Operations that use a streamed transport can have a contract with only one input and one output parameter.
- SOAP headers are always buffered, even if you enable streaming. The headers for the message must not exceed the size of the MaxBufferSize setting.
- Reliable messaging and SOAP message-level security implementations rely on buffering messages for transmission. The overhead you incur by securing the channel can easily offset any benefit you received from streaming. Generally, you should look to

use transport-level security exclusively or mixed-mode security, which simply combines WS-Security claims with transport-level security, making them similar to each other.

Request/reply

The request/reply pattern is technically mentioned as a possibility, but it's something you shouldn't spend too much time studying. In just about every scenario you use in WCF, you're using the request/reply pattern, so you're familiar with it if you've made any WCF calls or written any services, even if you weren't aware of it. The client initiates a request, and the server receives it and processes it, and then commences with a reply. Every one of the Test-Service methods I initially created used this pattern. Request/Reply is the default way you use client-initiated communication, and if you're initiating a request from the client and not using OneWay, you're using it. Said differently, request/reply and OneWay are the only two patterns that have to be initiated by the client. Everything covered so far, other than the OneWay examples, have been using this pattern, so there's not a whole lot to talk about. And other than knowing it must be initiated by the client, there's not a lot more to know that hasn't already been discussed at length.

Duplex

The duplex pattern is much more complex than its counterparts and is not just a nicety; in many cases, it's an absolute necessity. Duplex messaging differs from its siblings in that it enables each established endpoint to send messages to any other endpoint by itself. As MSDN states, "Duplex communication occurs when a client connects to a service and provides the service with a channel on which the service can send messages back to the client." In order for this to happen, all the communication must occur within the context of one session.

Regardless of whether duplexing is being implemented, a WCF Service needs a contract, and the contract requirement is handled by using an interface and the ServiceContract attribute. When using duplexing, an additional interface is required. This necessity entails a callback contract, and this contract must be specified in the service contract by way of the CallbackContract property.

Implementing Windows Azure service bus and Windows Azure queues

A service bus is a component that helps you to connect applications. This could be a connection between on-premise and the cloud or between multiple applications running in the cloud. As you have seen in the previous objective, the service bus relay is one option to connect applications.

However, using a relay is not suitable for all application types. Maybe you want to use a simple queue, possibly extended with a publish/subscribe mechanism. Azure offers all those different communication styles.

A *queue* allows for one-directional communication. The queue stores the messages until another client reads them. A *Topic* extends a queue by adding subscriptions. Each client can specify criteria that are used to filter the messages that it sees.

Relays are already covered. They offer bi-directional communication. They don't store messages. This means that both parties should be online to communicate.

> **MORE INFO** TOPICS
>
> Topics are not explicitly mentioned in the exam objectives. However they are useful for real-world applications and you should definitely read up on them. You can find more information at *http://www.windowsazure.com/en-us/develop/net/fundamentals/hybrid-solutions/*.

When using a queue, you send a message to the service bus. This message has two parts: a set of key/value properties and a binary message body. This message is then stored by the service bus and delivered to a receiver at a later time. This immediately decouples your application, increasing availability and scalability.

To further increase those characteristics, a receiver can choose to remove a message from the queue on read or it can take a lock on the message, process it, and then remove it.

By using multiple receivers, you can distribute the workload of your application. For example, if you have a cloud service that has both a worker and a web role, you can use a queue for communication between both parts. Now let's say you have a lot of read-activity during the day. This would only put load on your web role. By scaling your web role, you can make sure that your application stays responsive. If there is a lot of processing to be done, those messages are sent from the web role to the queue. By using the auto scaling future in Windows Azure, you can configure your worker roles to scale up or down depending on the number of messages in the queue. This way, you scale both parts of your application independently of each other by using a loosely coupled communication mechanism in the form of a queue.

You can find a complete example of how to use a queue at *http://www.windowsazure.com/en-us/develop/net/tutorials/multi-tier-application/*. The important concepts are the use of the QueueClient class that allows you to send and retrieve messages to a queue. For the messages, you can use the BrokeredMessage class. This class takes your data in its constructor and serializes it to a format that can be send to the queue. At the receiving end, you can get the message body and convert it to the type you want.

Objective summary

- Many WCF operations are straightforward in the sense they accept or return, or both, a simple or complex type.

- Many times, items being loaded or retrieved from a WCF Service are large multimedia files. Even though transfer rates have greatly increased over the years, there's still an unnecessarily long wait time, and forcing clients to wait for a download to complete before they can use a file (particularly when it's a media file) will be frustrating for them. For those cases, one should seriously consider using streaming.

- You might have scenarios in which you want to "fire and forget" an operation (typically a logging or low-importance auditing function). For these, use of the OneWay attribute can give you this functionality and limit the blocking behavior of the application.

Objective review

Answer the following questions to test your knowledge of the information in this objective. You can find the answers to these questions and explanations of why each answer choice is correct or incorrect in the "Answers" section at the end of this chapter.

1. You have the following method signature. You are told that it should execute as quickly as possible and advised it would be a good candidate for a OneWay method. Which of the following are true (choose all that apply):

```
[OperationContract(IsOneWay = true)]
Boolean LogMessage(String messsage);
```

   A. This method is not a valid candidate to execute with the OneWay pattern because it has a return type.

   B. This method is not a valid candidate to execute with the OneWay pattern because it accepts a parameter.

   C. Simple logging operations that just accept a String parameter and return a Success or Failure message are ideally suited for the OneWay pattern. However, to work a Callback contract would be needed to work properly.

   D. There's not enough information to know for sure whether this method would be a good candidate to use to implement the OneWay pattern.

2. Your service needs to let clients open a channel to it and allow back and forth communication throughout the session. Which is true?

   A. Any binding that supports streaming would be a work here.

   B. Only bindings with the IsOneWay property set to true would be valid.

   C. As long as the service can stream back to the client, this would work.

   D. Duplex communication cannot be implemented with Http because it's a stateful protocol.

3. Your service needs to support real-time communication between client and service. Which is true?

   A. Streaming should be enabled.

   B. A Binding that supports duplexing must be implemented.

   C. A stateless protocol can be supported but the client must implement threading.

   D. Duplexing and streaming must be implemented together.

Objective 3.9: Host and manage services

Fundamentally, WCF Services are merely a .NET type with a few specific attributes applied to it. You can use a service type just as you would any other class, but that generally defeats the purpose because it adds overhead without adding any value. To be of value, a service needs to be hosted, which places it in a separate process from the client and enables multiple clients to interact with it.

> **This objective covers how to:**
>
> - Manage services concurrency
> - Choose an instancing mode
> - Create service hosts
> - Choose a hosting mechanism
> - Create transactional services
> - Host services in a Windows Azure worker role

Managing services concurrency

Chances are that any service you create will be consumed by more than one consumer at any given time. If you're lucky, your service will be consumed by a substantial number of clients. It's difficult to accurately anticipate the capacity requirements of your service. Noted WCF expert Juval Löwy suggests that a good rule of thumb is planning on one order of magnitude above the highest level you anticipate in the following year. But even then, you might get it wrong, and being wrong can be expensive (not to mention embarrassing). Companies such as Twitter are testimony to achieving levels of success that far surpass anything they initially imagined (enter the term "Fail Whale" into Bing to read up on Twitter's experience).

Through configuration you can change the service's behavior after it has been deployed. Concurrency and instancing are two areas you generally decide up front, though, and are typically defined in code as opposed to configuration (although most other hosting aspects are typically handled through configuration). People frequently confuse *instancing* and *concurrency*, so let's get the distinction out of the way right now. As part of the ServiceBehavior you can define a ConcurrencyMode. The ConcurrencyMode enumeration has three values: single, reentrant, and multiple.

Single

At any given time, only a single request has access to the WCF Service object. The big implication here is that, if multiple requests hit the host at once, each subsequent one is blocked until the one before it is processed:

```
[ServiceBehavior(ConcurrencyMode=ConcurrencyMode.Single)]
public class TestService : ITestService
{}
```

Multiple

At any given time, multiple requests can be processed by the WCF Service object. Subsequent requests are processed on separate threads. This can lead to a tremendously high number of threads being created. Although this will lead to significant throughput compared with a value of single, there are many other considerations you need to take into account to take full advantage of this setting:

```
[ServiceBehavior(ConcurrencyMode=ConcurrencyMode.Multiple)]
public class TestService : ITestService
{}
```

Reentrant

A single request is processed on one thread, but the thread can leave the service to call another service, and it can also communicate backward to a client through a callback without deadlocking:

```
[ServiceBehavior(ConcurrencyMode=ConcurrencyMode.Reentrant)]
public class TestService : ITestService
{}
```

Choosing an instancing mode

The InstanceContextMode setting is another critical item that has a significant impact on the behavior of the service. This setting specifies the number of service instances available for handling calls to the service. There are three possible values for it, coupled with the three values of the ConcurrencyMode, giving you nine different possible combinations.

Single

A single instance of the WCF Service is used for all client requests. This has the benefit of not having to constantly create and destroy instances, but it should be obvious that this has the downside of be limiting in terms of large client request volumes:

```
[ServiceBehavior(InstanceContextMode=InstanceContextMode.Single)]
public class TestService : ITestService
{}
```

PerSession

This is the default setting (remember this!) and creates one or more instance per client:

```
[ServiceBehavior(InstanceContextMode=InstanceContextMode.PerSession)]
public class TestService : ITestService
{}
```

PerCall

This setting creates one instance (or more) for each client request:

```
[ServiceBehavior(InstanceContextMode=InstanceContextMode.PerCall)]
public class TestService : ITestService
{}
```

Creating service hosts

Creating service hosts in WCF entails using the ServiceHost class or using one of the out-of-the-box options (such as IIS or WAS). Hosting is a big part of having a service that can successfully process client requests, so the choice of which mechanism to use should not be taken lightly. We discuss each of the available options and summarize the relative strengths and weaknesses.

Self-hosting

Just like its cousin, the Workflow Foundation, WCF Services have the capability to self-host. They can be hosted in any managed (.NET) application. As we'll discuss shortly, you create an application that you want to use that contains the actual services you want to host. You specify service's configuration information in a .config file or inline in code in conjunction with instance(s) of the ServiceHost class.

There are several benefits of self-hosting, but simplicity has to be at the top of any list. Because you can easily swap out hosts, if you find that your application isn't performing well, you can easily upgrade to another hosting mechanism. This option enables you to use a broad spectrum of bindings as well. It's easy to move such a host application around from machine to machine and location to location. Additionally, because you can access the process without remote debugger privileges, you can easily debug the application and retrieve trace information from it.

There are disadvantages of self-hosting. If you use IIS or WAS (discussed shortly), you have the benefit that they are Microsoft technologies. That means Microsoft not only built them but also supports them. Bugs in these hosts are likely to be discovered early because so many people use IIS/WAS and will usually notify Microsoft immediately when a bug is found. Your self-host, on the other hand, will need to be debugged and tested thoroughly. If you find that you can't support the load, moving to another machine or a major hardware upgrade is usually the only solution. You can't just add nodes or easily implement load balancing. If your application crashes for whatever reason, it's difficult to implement any sort of failover or immediate disaster recovery. For this reason, self-hosting is well suited to peer-to-peer applications and as the development host. It is generally a pretty underpowered choice for production services. Finally, the host will be dependent on a logged-in user in most cases, and if you want it to start automatically if the machine goes down, you'll have to do a lot to make it happen.

Managed Windows Services

Managed services aren't much different from other .NET applications, although they have the capability to run without a logged-in user. You can implement custom logic when the service starts and stops, and you also can implement pause functionality.

Essentially, the benefits include everything that the self-hosted option provides, but it gives you a little more power. It's much better suited to scenarios in which the service will be operating for long periods of time. If the machine restarts, the service can start itself automatically without intervention. It also has the benefit of not necessitating IIS or WAS to be running on the machine (there are many reasons one might not want this, but they are far out of the scope of this book). The last major benefit is that this option is supported by all currently supported versions of Windows.

There are disadvantages of managed services. First, you still have to write code to create the host using the ServiceHost class. You're responsible for starting and stopping the service, and if you don't take steps to add it, you can't pause it successfully. You also have limited ability to scale up or out, and you're responsible for all error reporting and logging. Services also tend to be slightly more challenging to debug.

Internet Information Services (IIS)

IIS is well known to most developers, particularly .NET developers, so not much needs to be said by way of introduction. Suffice it to say that many organizations will already have an IIS instance running, there will probably be personnel dedicated to its maintenance, and most developers have already used it extensively.

IIS is already integrated with ASP.NET. As such, it has out-of-the-box support for many useful features such as isolation of application pools, process recycling, idle shutdown, and process health monitoring. It also enables message-based activation. If your application needs to have high availability and be scalable, IIS is an ideal choice. IIS can easily be clustered. It can be hosted behind a firewall. It can be run behind a load balancer. By nature, it's well suited to processing high request volumes.

Although it is also a strength, IIS has been targeted to many attacks in the past because of publicized security flaws. Its prevalence makes it an attractive attack target for many hackers. But the costs here are more than offset by the benefits provided precisely by its popularity. Most importantly though, IIS limits the bindings you can use and support. IIS only supports message transport via HTTP. As you might recall from the discussion on bindings, the http-based binding set is easy to use, but it's also quite limiting, and because you can use only HTTP, it makes this option unusable for many.

Windows Activation Service (WAS)

Although WAS is generally already present in most organizations, it's still not as widely known or used as IIS. It's a newer technology and still in its adoption curve.

First of all, it's not dependent on IIS and can be run in a standalone manner. It carries with it most of the benefits of IIS, however. It provides process recycling and isolation. It allows for idle shutdown. It provides powerful process health monitoring features. It supports message-based activation. And like IIS, it supports HTTP-based message transfer. But it also supports TCP, named pipes, and MSMQ. It is hard to argue that binding set covers all but rare usage scenarios; it's a fair statement that, compositely, they cover a large swatch of it. All in all, it's a good middle-of-the-road hosting choice that gives you most of hosting features you need without exposing you to excessive costs.

Although widely used, WAS is certainly not as well known as IIS. You might not already have it up and running, and might not have a subject matter expert dedicated to managing it. It still lacks support for several bindings that are commonly used. Although WAS has some distance in terms of adoption, it's still a popular technology, and it's likely to increase substantially over time.

Windows Azure-based hosting

Windows Azure, which is the Microsoft cloud-based offering, is still fairly young but gaining popularity rapidly. Because Windows Azure hasn't been discussed extensively so far (and won't be until Chapter 4, Creating and consuming Web API-based services), the discussion focuses solely on the hosting-based aspects of Windows Azure. If you're not familiar with Windows Azure already, a quick review of it would prove beneficial.

You might argue that there's one big overarching benefit to Windows Azure-based hosting: You are outsourcing all the headaches associated with maintenance and support to Microsoft and technicians whose job it is to know how to make sure that your host application stays running. You currently have three essential options with Windows Azure. You can host in a WebRole, you can host using the AppFabric service bus, and you can host using a WorkerRole. These items are discussed in-depth in the following chapter, but for now, the main takeaway is that these are the available Windows Azure options.

The strength is also a potential downside: Your application is hosted by someone else. That someone else is a group of trained, talented people who are backed by *Service Level Agreements (SLAs)*, but there's still the loss of control that comes with hosting it elsewhere. Using Windows Azure, you can self-host, host in IIS, or host using WAS, but you'll still have to make that decision for yourself, along with choosing the hosting mechanism on Windows Azure (WebRole, WorkerRole, or App Fabric service bus). Additionally, Windows Azure is still a new technology, so many developers are not all that familiar with it. Then there's the one other item that is cited frequently: Windows Azure hosting is not free. People have serious debates about total cost of ownership in the cloud versus in-house hosting, however, you will need to do some homework and figure out which would be more cost-effective for your company and application; unfortunately, there's no simple calculation that derives such numbers.

ServiceHost class

To create a ServiceHost instance is simple. You declare and instantiate an instance of the ServiceHost class, typically passing in the type of the service. To do this, you need a reference to the service class you're implementing. There are several constructor overloads, but hard-coding items in the service host is ill-advised, and for purposes of the exam, it's almost certain you'll be presented with items regarding the configuration of a service if ServiceHost questions are presented.

Upon creation of a ServiceHost, you'll want to call the Open method first and then ultimately the Close method. Both of them should be contained in try/catch blocks because there are several things that can go wrong in calling these operations. How you'll handle the exceptions and what specific items you'll trap depends on you and your application's hosting needs, but in practice you'll want to make sure that the host both opens and closes gracefully. The snippet shown here illustrates the process (minus the exception handlers):

```
using (ServiceHost HostInstance = new ServiceHost(typeof(TestServiceType)))
{
    HostInstance.Open();
    //Put in a Wait Condition so Host stays open
    HostInstance.Close();
}
```

After a channel is opened from a client, the exact behavior depends on the settings you specify (ConcurrencyMode, InstancingMode, endpoint types, and so on), but there's one important takeaway: If there's an unhandled fault, the channel is considered faulted and cannot be used for further operations. So client side, when attempting to establish a connection to a host, you must make sure that it's valid and remains valid throughout the time you are attempting to use it.

Also, you need to understand your choice of options for host applications. WCF Services can be hosted in any valid .NET AppDomain, but if the AppDomain doesn't stay active, it's not of much use. For example, if you had a Windows Forms application, it could definitely serve as a host application. So could a console application. But if the main form closes or you don't have something stopping the console application from closing, the host won't do much good.

If you use a hosting mechanism such as WAS or IIS, you don't need to create a ServiceHost instance because it's already there, per se. Instead, you just need to configure the service and, in older versions of WCF, create an .svc file that pointed to the service assembly. Currently, you don't need to do that.

You can take a slight digression here. Prior to the .NET 4.0 Framework, if you wanted to use IIS to host your application, you would typically create an ASP.NET application, add an assembly reference to the assembly containing your service(s), set up the service settings in the web.config file, and essentially create a text file with the .svc extension. This file just needed one line and would serve as mapping to the service. With the advent of version 4.0, that changed. You can now use the ServiceHostingEnvironment class, which enables you to virtually reference the .svc file. It's generally recommended you do this through configuration; if not, you offset any gain achieved by not needing a physical .svc file in the first place.

The ServiceHostingEnvironment class enables you to reference its ServiceActivations, and you can use the Add method as you use the <connectionStrings> setting in configuration. The following shows you an example:

```
<serviceHostingEnvironment>
  <serviceActivations>
    <add relativeAddress="ServiceOrInterfaceName.svc" service="FullyQualifiedService
Name"/>
  </serviceActivations>
</serviceHostingEnvironment>
```

This feature doesn't do anything that enables you to do things you couldn't do before (other than exclude a file), but it's definitely a convenience and simplification. The inclusion of a one-line text file (and the fact that it had to be created exactly right or else the service hosting would fail) was never a huge burden, but it was something many people found inconvenient. Because it's a new feature, it's likely to come up in one form or another on the exam, and it is something you'll want to take advantage of in practice.

Choosing a hosting mechanism

Services need a host to be of value. In one sense, you have tremendous flexibility in choosing a hosting mechanism; in another it's constrained. You can build a given service and then host it with each of the following:

- Windows Form application
- Console application
- Managed Windows Service
- ASP.NET application
- IIS
- WAS
- Windows Azure

However, you might need to implement specific bindings for your service, and those bindings might force your hand in regard to what mechanism you use. For example, IIS is one of the more common hosting options and by nature was meant to be a web server. Yet it enables you only to expose http bindings. In a similar respect, if you need to use one of the MSMQ bindings or have functionality that requires it, you will need to have MSMQ available. (I realize this is generally an obvious point, but some people are under the impression that adding a binding to a host is all that's needed to get it working.) To that end, there's no way to universally know what the best hosting choice is, and there isn't just one that will be appropriate (or even work) for every use case.

Generally speaking, IIS and WAS are products that have been around a while, are Microsoft products, have a robust user base, and are easy to use in conjunction with WCF. Bugs are a part of new software, so if you write your own host, mistakes will likely be made somewhere along the path. Even if you managed to write a bug-free host, chances are that you might miscalculate the potential load or capacity needs. This isn't to say that you should avoid writing your own hosts; in fact, there are many cases where it's highly advisable. Instead, the service host should not be decided in haste, and you need to understand the bindings, what you are trying to accomplish, and what volumes you are likely to encounter. This is the case with most software architecture decisions; it's just salient in the case of service hosts because the cost of being wrong is so high.

Creating transactional services

Chapter 1 discusses transactions and the use of the TransactionScope class. One of the items mentioned that the TransactionScope can wrap is WCF Services. Enabling transactional capability in WCF Services is straightforward; after it's done, you have little else to do other than manage the operations on the client. You must decorate the operation with a TransactionFlow attribute and also ensure that the TransactionAutoComplete and TransactionScopeRequired properties of the OperationBehavior are set to true.

The TransactionFlow attribute specifies whether the operation supports transactions. It's defined at the operation level and is just marked with an attribute along with the OperationContract attribute. For the record, you define it along with (not as part of) the OperationContract attribute. You have three choices that behave as their names imply.

NotAllowed

This is the default setting for this attribute, so it is the behavior your operation will provide unless you specify otherwise. Any operation marked with this setting cannot participate in a transaction. Just to ensure clarity, both the OperationContract and the TransactionFlow attributes are included:

```
[OperationContract]
[TransactionFlow(TransactionFlowOption.NotAllowed)]
String GetTestSummary(String examId);
```

Allowed

This operation participates in a transaction if the client initiates one. If not, nothing happens:

```
[OperationContract]
[TransactionFlow(TransactionFlowOption.Allowed)]
String GetTestSummary(String examId);
```

Mandatory

For this operation to be invoked, the client must create a transaction:

```
[OperationContract]
[TransactionFlow(TransactionFlowOption.Mandatory)]
String GetTestSummary(String examId);
```

The last thing is to define an OperationBehavior attribute on the service's method and then specify a value of true for both the TransactionAutoComplete and TransactionScopeRequired properties. Assuming that you used the OperationContract definitions implemented in the previous examples, you would need to add the following method implementation:

```
[OperationBehavior(TransactionAutoComplete=true, TransactionScopeRequired=true)]
public  String GetTestSummary(String examId){}
```

The TransactionFlow attribute enables clients to start or participate in a transaction. The TransactionScopeRequired value indicates that the method must be part of a TransactionScope. Setting the TransactionAutoComplete to true tells the runtime to automatically complete if no unhandled exceptions occur. If an unhandled exception is thrown, a rollback operation will happen. The default value is true, but it's a good idea to explicitly set it so that it's obvious to anyone else looking at the code.

Hosting services in a Windows Azure worker role

When you want to run your WCF service on Azure, you normally do this in a web role. However, if you want, you can choose to run your WCF service in a worker role. This way, you avoid using IIS for hosting and you have more control over your service configuration.

Hosting a WCF service in your Azure worker role comes down to initializing your own ServiceHost, configuring endpoints, and opening it. You run this initialization code in your OnStart method and you're done.

The endpoint configuration can be stored in the roles configuration file (the .csdef file). In code, this looks like this:

```
IPEndPoint ip = RoleEnvironment.CurrentRoleInstance.
    InstanceEndpoints["WCFService"].IPEndpoint;

Uri baseAddress = new Uri(String.Format("http://{0}", ip));

try
{
    host = new ServiceHost(typeof(<yourservice>), baseAddress);
    host.Open();
}
catch (Exception ex)
{

    Trace.WriteLine(ex.Message, "Error");
    throw;
}
```

That's all there is to it. It's important to store the host variable outside of your OnStart method so it doesn't get garbage collected when the method finishes and the variable goes out of scope.

Thought experiment
Where should I host my application?

In the following thought experiment, apply what you've learned about this objective to Hosting and Managing Services. You can find answers to these questions in the "Answers" section at the end of this chapter.

You are building several WCF Services. You know that you need to support Http, TCP, and MSMQ. You expect a large number of clients and heavy loads on your services. You might need to move the service host from machine to machine on occasion. Additionally, all your developers are familiar with ASP.NET programming, but are completely new to Windows Azure and WAS.

With this in mind, answer the following questions:

1. Is a console application or a WPF application implemented via self-hosting a viable approach?

2. Is IIS a good candidate here, assuming that there are several instances available internally?

3. What factors shift the equation to one host choice versus another?

Objective summary

- The ConcurrencyMode property and InstanceContextMode are frequently confused. The ConcurrencyMode specifies whether the service supports one thread, supports multiple threads, or allows for reentrant calls. The InstanceContextMode specifies how instances of the service will be created by clients.

- There are several options for hosting a WCF Service: Windows Azure, Windows Forms applications, console applications, Managed Windows Services, web applications, and WCF Services themselves.

- IIS hosting is one of the more common choices, but it has the downside of limiting the bindings that the service can be used. Each hosting choice carries a similar problem. The service hosting mechanism should be carefully thought out.

- Self-hosting is an often overlooked but a powerful feature.

- In addition to making a service accessible to the widest possible audience, making the service discoverable is tremendously beneficial.

Objective review

Answer the following questions to test your knowledge of the information in this objective. You can find the answers to these questions and explanations of why each answer choice is correct or incorrect in the "Answers" section at the end of this chapter.

1. You are developing a new WCF Service. Each time a client initiates a request, you need to create a service instance to support it. What should you do?

   A. Set the InstanceContextMode to Singleton.

   B. Set the ConcurrencyMode to PerCall.

   C. Set the InstanceContextMode to PerCall.

   D. Set the ConcurrencyMode's scope to User and set the InstanceContextMode to PerCall.

2. Which of the following would be appropriate as a WCF Service Host?

   A. Hosted workflow service

   B. .NET console application

   C. Windows Forms application built using Windows Presentation Foundation

   D. IIS

3. You need to develop a WCF Service. The service is supposed to be both self-hosted and discoverable by any client application. Which of the following are needed to support this scenario? (Choose all that apply.)

   A. A DiscoveryEndpoint

   B. A ServiceHost definition

   C. A ServiceBehavior definition

   D. A UpdDiscoveryEndpoint

Chapter summary

A WCF Service is a .NET type that is decorated with the ServiceContract attribute. Methods of the type that are to be exposed to the client should be decorated with the OperationContract attribute.

- The standard approach to creating a service and contract is to create a class that implements an interface. The interface type definition is decorated with the ServiceContract attribute, and each method is decorated with the OperationContract attribute.

- Service specifics can be implemented imperatively in code or through configuration. If desired, a combination of approaches can be used.

- Each feature that can be implemented or manipulated through configuration can also be manipulated or controlled through code.

- Behaviors enable you to control the service's behavior at a granular level. Behaviors come in multiple flavors: operation behaviors, service behaviors, and endpoint behaviors.

- WCF supports a wide variety of bindings, and depending on the host, several bindings can all be supported at once. However, the hosting choice can just as easily become a limitation with respect to what bindings can be supported.

- Instancing and concurrency are two concepts that are frequently confused. They do not have an either/or relationship with each other; they are used in a complementary fashion.

- Depending on the needs of the application, services can interact with the client in a stateful or stateless manner. Bindings in conjunction with the hosting mechanism are the determinants of whether things can be done statefully or will be stateless.

- Almost any .NET application that can "run" can serve as a host to a WCF Service. A .dll/assembly alone lacks an entry point, so it won't work as a host, but it can be referenced by other .NET applications that do have an entry point and can be consumed accordingly.

- Relaying allows you to create a hybrid application that spans both the cloud and an on premise datacenter. The service bus is responsible for forwarding all messages between host and client applications.

Answers

This section contains the solutions to the thought experiments and answers to the lesson review questions in this chapter.

Objective 3.1: Thought experiment

1. You have a few options here. One straightforward method would be to mark only the methods you want publicly exposed with the OperationContract attribute and leave the other ones undefined. You could alternately move all the private methods to another interface and have the service implement both the original interface and the new one.

2. You have several options, but the most straightforward would be to use the DataContract serializer for both the complex types and the enumeration types. This would add a layer of consistency while keeping things simple. On the enumeration values, you would decorate them with the EnumMember attribute. On the members of the complex type you want exposed, you would decorate them with the DataMember attribute.

3. To maximize interoperability, there are several things that can be done including the choice of bindings (however, that's not been covered yet). The main thing so far would be to make sure that you use FaultContracts to wrap exceptions and pass them back to the client.

Objective 3.1: Review

1. **Correct answer:** A

   A. **Correct:** A FaultContract is specified using each of the two types that need to be supported.

   B. **Incorrect:** There is no relevant FaultMapping attribute.

   C. **Incorrect:** There is no relevant FaultMapping attribute.

   D. **Incorrect:** The FaultContract definition attribute is the correct one to use, but the type needs to be specified in conjunction with the Type.

2. **Correct answer:** C

   A. **Incorrect:** A service needs a "contract," and that's usually handled via an interface, but it does not necessarily have to be an interface.

   B. **Incorrect:** The ServiceContract and OperationContract attributes need to be applied to either the interface or the class definition.

   C. **Correct:** The ServiceContract attribute and the OperationContract attribute can be applied to either the interface or the implementation, but not both.

   D. **Incorrect:** Any type transferred through the service must be serializable.

3. **Correct answers:** A, B

  A. **Correct:** The method definition should be added to the service contract .

  B. **Correct:** The OperationContract attribute must be added to the method or the method definition. In this case, it should be the method.

  C. **Incorrect:** Adding an OperationBehavior would be of no benefit here.

  D. **Incorrect:** Adding a new ServiceContract would not do any good without making the service implement the contract as well.

Objective 3.2: Thought experiment

1. It would definitely make sense to use configuration for custom bindings (and any others, for that matter). You could use an imperative approach for items you are absolutely sure of, but you can do everything discussed here through configuration, so there's probably a big benefit to keeping things consistent.

2. You could certainly go ahead and add every binding you can imagine that you'll need. Multiple bindings can be supported, although the particular host can limit what is supported. The best approach, however, is to go ahead and set up the items that you know for sure you need now. You can easily add new bindings and tweak the configuration as you go along and find out about new requirements. Configuring everything up-front has many downsides, and the cost of adding a new configuration binding is relatively small.

Objective 3.2: Review

1. **Correct answers:** A, D

  A. **Correct:** A new service must be specified.

  B. **Incorrect:** Although useful, particularly for discovery, a MetadataExchange endpoint does not need to be configured for a service to correctly operate.

  C. **Incorrect:** Not specifying security is ill-advised, but the default settings work if no security values are configured. Hence, it is not absolutely necessary to operate.

  D. **Correct:** A contract absolutely must be specified, along with defining the service itself.

2. **Correct answers:** A, B, C, D

  A. **Correct:** A new service can be defined through configuration.

  B. **Correct:** A service's contract type can be defined through configuration.

  C. **Correct:** A service's security configuration can be defined through configuration.

  D. **Correct:** Adding metadata exchange can be implemented through configuration.

3. **Correct answer:** D

   A. **Incorrect:** Endpoint URIs can be easily changed through configuration.

   B. **Incorrect:** A service's security settings can be easily changed through configuration.

   C. **Incorrect:** Metadata exchange can be added, removed, or modified through configuration.

   D. **Correct:** Changes to a method definition or implementation can be made cited through code.

Objective 3.3: Thought experiment

1. There are good reasons to use every one of the mentioned approaches. The more well-defined the application requirements, the less risk there is to using a completely imperative approach. The less clear the requirements, the more likely you are to benefit from using configuration. Using a hybrid approach can enable you to have the best of both worlds, and you don't have to make a definitive choice one way or the other. If you're hosting the service internally and have full access to it, configuration carries little cost or risk. In some Windows Azure-based hosting scenarios, you have to use a more imperative approach, although you can still use a hybrid approach here.

Objective 3.3: Review

1. **Correct answer:** D

   A. **Incorrect:** If they were both included, there would be a conflict, and one wouldn't take precedence or overwrite the other.

   B. **Incorrect:** Defining the same binding twice would not cause any compilation issues.

   C. **Incorrect:** The service would compile, but the conflict would cause a problem immediately.

   D. **Correct:** An InvalidOperationException would be thrown when the application started.

2. **Correct answer:** D

   A. **Incorrect:** Even if they're defined in an identical manner, there would be a conflict and resulting exception.

   B. **Incorrect:** There would be a conflict; they can't co-exist without a problem.

   C. **Incorrect:** There would be a conflict; they can't co-exist without a problem.

   D. **Correct:** The service would definitely throw an InvalidOperationException, as indicated.

3. **Correct answers:** A, C

   A. **Correct:** A TcpTransportBindingElement can be used with a CustomBinding.

   B. **Incorrect:** A TcpBinding can be used, but it is not a binding element; it is an actual binding.

   C. **Correct:** A HttpTransportBindingElement can be used with a CustomBinding.

   D. **Incorrect:** While MTOM can be used, it is not a specific BindingElement that can be used with a CustomBinding.

Objective 3.4: Thought experiment

1. Message and transport security aren't mutually exclusive; they are complementary, in fact. There is additional overhead with more security implemented, but that overhead can be worked around. Getting it wrong can destroy your company and cause many problems for your clients, and estimating the full scope of damage is difficult to do. Generally speaking, people are much more tolerant of a slight performance loss (especially if they understand why) than they are of a data breach.

2. You can go overboard with anything, but there is little inconvenience to implementing either approach. Moreover, even if something is intended to be public, you still would have an incentive to keep some level of control over it. Many people are inherently concerned about any insecure communication. You have complete control here, so there's quite a bit of flexibility in terms of what you want to identify.

3. Certificate-based security has many upsides and it's desirable in many circumstances, but it does add a level of implementation complexity that many find inconvenient and cumbersome. If it's not necessary, it's probably more hassle than benefit.

Objective 3.4: Review

1. **1. Correct answers:** A, B, C

   A. **Correct:** Using protocol mapping will help in this situation.

   B. **Correct:** Using a secure binding will help in this situation.

   C. **Correct:** Enabling https on the virtual directory will help in this situation.

   D. **Incorrect:** Enabling metadata will do nothing to help facilitate transport security.

2. **Correct answers:** A, B, C

   A. **Correct:** You can implement message level security in WCF.

   B. **Correct:** Transport level security can be implemented.

   C. **Correct:** Message and transport security can be implemented together.

   D. **Incorrect:** Both can be implemented together and often are; they are not in conflict with each other.

3. **Correct answers:** A, B, D

   A. **Correct:** A netTcpBinding must be defined.

   B. **Correct:** A clientCredentialType of netTcpBinding must be defined.

   C. **Incorrect:** A clientCredentialType of Transport is not needed.

   D. **Correct:** A SecurityMode value of Transport must be specified.

Objective 3.5: Thought experiment

1. Both can get you to the same place, but the Add Service Reference dialog box has a few restrictions. First, it necessitates having Visual Studio, which won't be a problem for clients using .NET, but might be a problem for others. Similarly, the Add Service Reference dialog box walks you through the nuances of creating a proxy class, but its strength is its weakness. Because it is visual, it is a manual process and cannot be easily called in a build script or through process automation.

2. Generics are powerful and make development a lot more attractive. However, only .NET languages support generics. Using arrays maximizes interoperability. Moreover, converting an array to a generic is simple to do, particularly if you're using a .NET language.

3. Older versions of the .NET Framework did not support generics. LINQ was introduced in version 3.0 of the Framework as well. You have the power to use Svcutil.exe to generate several different languages, which is beneficial. Additionally, if you need to work with a WCF Service as a traditional web service, you can easily have that done.

Objective 3.5: Review

1. **Correct answers:** B, C, D

   A. **Incorrect:** Although the proxy would be successfully generated, absent a specific switch for Visual Basic, C# code would be generated.

   B. **Correct:** Using Svcutil with the I switch and indicating a valid language works.

   C. **Correct:** Using the Add Service Reference dialog box works because it's designed to handle this use case in particular.

   D. **Correct:** ChannelFactory works in this case.

2. **Correct answer:** B

   A. **Incorrect:** Calling ToList works, but it's an extra step and doesn't directly address the problem.

   B. **Correct:** This is the feature designed specifically to handle this situation.

   C. **Incorrect:** Regenerating the proxy alone does nothing.

D.   Incorrect: The default behavior of the Add Web Reference dialog box is used to add an older form of the service; it does not handle the conversions correctly.

3.   **Correct answers:** A, B, C

   A.   Correct: Svcutil.exe can be used to validate compiled service code.

   B.   Correct: Downloading metadata documents from deployed services is one of the features of Svcutil.exe.

   C.   Correct: .Generating serialization code is one of the features of SvcUtil.exe.

   D.   Incorrect: Svcutil.exe does not add metadata exchange to running services.

Objective 3.6: Thought experiment

1.   Breaking changes are a part of life. There's often no way to avoid them, particularly when you have to deploy something immediately that you know will change frequently. Breaking changes are inconvenient, and many people refuse to move to new products because of them. Planning and thinking about future features helps reduce the probability that you'll run into them, but it's no guarantee that you won't have to implement them. In some cases, it might be advisable to try to consolidate breaking changes in another service and have the existing service make calls to it. The more you can consolidate and obscure from clients, the less of a problem they'll be. You are always in a position to deal with internal breaking changes more easily than your clients will be.

2.   Communication is the only way to mitigate problems associated with breaking changes. An extensive testing plan is needed to avoid breaking changes and the problems associated with them. Breaking changes are bad enough, but coupled with bugs, you'll have angry customers in all likelihood. There are several articles that deal with the issue, and becoming familiar with the process is absolutely critical. Telling clients of the breaking changes with as much advance notice as possible is one mitigation strategy. Making sure that everyone knows about them so no one is surprised will also help. Precise details about what the changes will be; what will be affected; and, ideally, suggestions on how best to deal the changes will also help. If you have to deal with a breaking change, it's much easier to do with a clear definition of what's changing and a six-month planning window. Flip it around and imagine that you find out the changes have already been made and your users are already dealing with problems. Imagine that you get an early notice, but you get several updates that change the nature of what you've already changed. In the final analysis, the fewer interruptions, the more predictability, and the more certainty clients have, the easier it will be for them to deal with the changes.

Objective 3.6: Review

1. **Correct answers:** A, C

   A. **Correct:** Contract changes are a breaking change.

   B. **Incorrect:** Additions don't remove functionality, but are still a breaking change.

   C. **Correct:** As long as the old service with its old definitions is still in place, the addition of a new service will not cause a problem.

   D. **Incorrect:** Because B is incorrect, this item is incorrect.

2. **Correct answers:** A, B, D

   A. **Correct:** Strict versioning can be implemented with WCF.

   B. **Correct:** Lax versioning can be implemented with WCF.

   C. **Incorrect:** Mixed-mode versioning would defeat the purpose or either approach.

   D. **Correct:** Contract versioning is supported and necessary in most cases.

Objective 3.7: Thought experiment

1. Because the customer is dealing with private and confidential data, a cloud-only solution will probably not appeal to them. By offering a hybrid solution, he can control the data while having all the benefits of a secure public interface hosted in Azure.

2. The service bus can offer a relaying endpoint to client applications that run on the devices of the employees The relay then securely forwards messages to the on-premise datacenter. This creates a secured way of exposing data.

Objective 3.7: Review

3. **Correct answers:** A, D

   A. **Correct:** The namespace is required to access your service. You specify the namespace when creating your bindings and addresses.

   B. **Incorrect:** The binding is specified at the host side for connecting to Azure Service Bus. This is not something that you configure in the Management Portal.

   C. **Incorrect:** ServiceHost is required to host your WCF service. It's not something that you configure in the Management Portal.

   D. **Correct:** The Default Key is used for authentication both your server and client applications to the service bus.

4. **Correct answer:** C

    A. **Incorrect:** You do need the CreateSharedSecretTokenProvider method. However, you need to pass it the owner and key. The namespace is used in the service URI.

    B. **Incorrect:** This method creates a SAML token.

    C. **Correct:** CreateSharedSecretTokenProvider with the owner and key creates the correct token.

    D. **Incorrect:** This creates a Windows token.

5. **Correct answers:** A, B, C, D

    A. **Correct:** The namespace is required to access your service. You specify the namespace.

    B. **Correct:** The service path is required as a part of your endpoint address.

    C. **Correct:** The owner name is required when creating your SharedSecretToken.

    D. **Correct:** The Default Key is also used for authentication and is required to create your SharedSecretToken.

Objective 3.8: Thought experiment

1. Logging calls are great candidates for OneWay implementation. The less important the data is, the better candidate it is for a OneWay call. You lose the ability to have return types on OneWay calls, but for logging operations, particularly ones that fire frequently, if a few don't make it to the server, it will likely have little impact. On the other hand, the time it takes just to deal with a response type can exacerbate the problems associated with chatty applications.

2. Duplex communication is useful and, in some cases, it is the only option you have. However, it is neither free nor cheap. Although WCF makes duplex communication appear simple, quite a bit has to happen to make it work right. This happens largely out of the user's view, but it still happens. Implementing duplexing when it's not needed is the logical inverse of using a OneWay call. It adds overhead with no benefit and can greatly hinder scalability. Although it's powerful and useful, it should be used judiciously and only when necessary.

Objective 3.8: Review

1. **Correct answer:** B

    A. **Incorrect:** Having a return type negates the use of the OneWay attribute.

    B. **Correct:** OneWay can be used in conjunction with an input parameter.

    C. **Incorrect:** Simple operations might be good candidates, but not if they return a message.

    D. **Incorrect:** The method has a return type that automatically disqualifies it.

2. **Correct answers:** A, C

   A. **Correct:** Any binding that enables clients to open a channel with it and have back-and-forth communication would work here.

   B. **Incorrect:** *OneWay* goes completely against the desired goal here.

   C. **Correct:** As long as the service can call back to the client, it should work.

   D. **Incorrect:** Http is a stateless protocol, so it can't be used.

3. **Correct answer:** B

   A. **Incorrect:** Streaming alone would not solve any of the stated problems.

   B. **Correct:** Duplexing must be implemented, and as such, a binding that supports duplexing must be enabled.

   C. **Incorrect:** A stateless protocol by definition would be inadequate here, irrespective of multi-threaded clients.

   D. **Incorrect:** Duplexing alone suffices; there is no need for streaming.

Objective 3.9: Thought experiment

1. Self-hosting with a console or WPF application would most likely be the worst of the possible approaches. Self-hosted services are easy to move from machine to machine, and you can support each of the required bindings. However, heavy loads make it a bad choice. The fact that most self-hosted services have to run under a dedicated account makes it a bad choice. Someone could accidentally click the mouse over the close button or erroneously hit an enter button and possibly shut down the entire host.

2. IIS would be a great choice except for one major issue: It simply doesn't support any of the bindings other than HTTP, so it clearly wouldn't work here. The fact that developers are familiar with it and that it scales well is irrelevant because of the bindings issue.

3. Windows Azure might be a decent approach, although the fact that the developers are unfamiliar with it would necessitate them gaining that expertise quickly. That's not a huge hurdle, but it is a hurdle nonetheless. WAS supports all the bindings needed. The services can move from one WAS instance to another with relative ease; in fact, the move could even be scripted. WAS on Windows Azure could meet all the criteria, but internally hosted WAS would seem in this case to be the most appropriate hosting choice.

Objective 3.9: Review

1. **Correct answer:** C

    A. Incorrect: There's no Singleton enumeration value but even if there was, it would make no sense here.

    B. Incorrect: ConcurrencyMode doesn't have a PerCall value.

    C. Correct: InstanceContextMode needs to be set to PerCall to work.

    D. Incorrect: There is no way to set the ConcurrencyMode's scope to User.

2. **Correct answers:** A, B, C, D

    A. Correct: A hosted workflow service has an appDomain and an entry point, so it would work.

    B. Correct: A Managed Windows Service has an entry point and is an ideal candidate as a host.

    C. Correct: A console application has an entry point and would work fine in this scenario.

    D. Correct: IIS is well suited to WCF hosting.

3. **Correct answers:** A, B

    A. Correct: A DiscoveryEndpoint would be necessary to meet the discovery requirement.

    B. Correct: Without a servicehost definition, it would be impossible to create this application as a self-hosted service.

    C. Incorrect: A ServiceBehavior definition might be beneficial, but it's not required as the item is stated.

    D. Incorrect: While a DiscoveryEndpoint is necessary to meet the application requirements, there is no need for a UdpDiscoveryEndpoint specifically.

CHAPTER 4

Creating and consuming Web API-based services

Today applications are more connected. Exposing your application through a set of services is important to achieve such interconnectivity.

When building a service, the more limitations and constraints it comes with, the more likely you are to encounter resistance during adoption. There are certainly cases in which clients are well-defined, and you can control who is consuming your services and how they are used, but such an approach will likely cause you some problems.

HTTP is established and ubiquitous. As such, it's well-suited for many purposes, among which is creating an ASP.NET Web API. These HTTP services are also known as *Representational State Transfer (RESTful services, or REST* for short). This chapter focuses on building and utilizing Web APIs to expose your application over HTTP.

According to the exam topics, Web API makes up 18 percent of the exam. You will need to know how to create a Web API and how to consume it. Understanding REST is also an important aspect of the exam because it is the conceptual basis for Web API.

Objectives in this chapter:
- Objective 4.1: Design a Web API
- Objective 4.2: Implement a Web API
- Objective 4.3: Secure a Web API
- Objective 4.4: Host and manage a Web API
- Objective 4.5: Consume Web API Web Services

Objective 4.1: Design a Web API

Through Windows Communication Foundation (WCF), you should already be familiar with creating services and exposing them to the outside world. When creating a WCF Service, you focus on the acronym ABC: address, binding, contract.

Creating a Web API is different. Because Web API is focused on using HTTP to expose your service, you remove a lot of configuration that would be required for a WCF service.

Web API builds upon the standard HTTP verbs, routing to define your URLs and content negotiation to exchange data with clients.

The focus of this objective is on making sure you understand the conceptual idea behind the Web API, which is important for the exam. For example, you can expect questions on choosing the correct HTTP methods and creating a URL scheme for your Web API.

> **This objective covers how to:**
> - Choose appropriate HTTP method (get, put, post, delete) to meet requirements
> - Define HTTP resources with HTTP actions
> - Plan appropriate URI space and map URI space using routing
> - Choose appropriate format (Web API formats) for responses to meet requirements
> - Plan when to make HTTP actions asynchronous

Choosing appropriate HTTP methods

To understand Web API, you need to understand how HTTP works. Representational State Transfer (REST) services are built upon HTTP. Instead of calling a specific method, you access a URL in combination with an HTTP method. Because Web API is a RESTful solution, it's very important (both in the real world and for the exam) to understand the various HTTP methods and what they do. When accessing a Web API, you do this by requesting a URL. The HTTP method that you use on that URL determines what will happen.

Because you're working with HTTP, it's also important to know what to return to the client. Status codes such as 200 (OK), 201 (Created), 400 (Bad Request), and 404 (Not Found) are often used. They inform the caller of your service of what happened. Next to using the correct HTTP method, it's equally important to use the correct status code.

There are seven items of primary concern and they are shown in Table 4-1.

TABLE 4-1 HTTP Verbs

Verb	CRUD action	Behavior
Delete	Delete	Specifies that a given URI be deleted.
Get	Read	Retrieves one or more entities or some other data that is identified by the URI of the request.
Put	Update	Replaces an entity that is identified by the URI. By standards, this verb requires all fields on the entity be specified, regardless of how many change.
Post	Create	Inserts a new entity to the URI.
Head	N/A	Retrieves just the message headers identified by the URI.

Verb	CRUD action	Behavior
Patch	Update	Transmits a partial change to the entity identified by the URI where only identifiers and modified fields are specified.
Options	N/A	Represents requests for information about the communication options available on the target resource.

Each value has its own purpose and need, but for the most part, you'll want to focus on how each is used with respect to common data operations frequently referred to as Create, Read, Update, and Delete (CRUD).

HttpGet

Just about all query or retrieval operations are implemented as HttpGet actions. Although not always the case, the number of methods that are implemented as HttpGet actions are usually the highest. For any given object that's represented by a model, there is typically at least the need to retrieve all the items in the dataset and then one that allows for individual retrieval by the key. Table 4-2 shows a basic REST scheme for retrieval centered on a given model (in practice, you have several different models represented and as such, you likely have several different HttpGet methods).

TABLE 4-2 HttpGet retrieval

Action	URI
Get a list of all Foos	/api/Foos
Get an instance of Foo by key field	/api/Foos/keyvalue
Get an instance of Foo by an attribute	/api/Foos?attributename=attributevalue

Although not a strict requirement, generally you need to differentiate between a request that is malformed or points to something that doesn't exist, and one that simply doesn't contain matching values. If you search for a hard-coded set of customers for one who has the last name of Doe, and none is found, it is a different scenario from one in which a request is made for race car drivers.

Checking for a valid result inside the method implementation and throwing an HttpResponseException with an HttpStatusCode of NotFound accomplishes this in a direct manner. Although both would result in a 404, the unhandled 404 also comes with an error message stating that it was unhandled to provide an additional explanation.

HttpDelete

Arguably the easiest of the set to identify, HttpDelete requests are straightforward to both identify and implement. The most common way to accomplish the deletion of a record is to specify the dataset key and use it to identify and delete the record. For the sake of clarity, it's advisable to name any such operations with a prefix of *Delete*.

As is the case with retrieval operations, it's desirable to provide some sort of feedback to the end user indicating that the operation was successful. There are three possible outcomes, assuming that the request is correctly formed and processed:

- The first is a successfully processed request that has an HttpStatusCode of OK (200). A valid response is returned to the client, and information from the request can be included.

- The next outcome is an HttpStatusCode of Accepted (202), which indicates that the request was processed and accepted, but is still pending.

- The last outcome is an HttpStatusCode of No Response (204). It's important to note that the method return type can directly affect this value. When the type has a void return type, a value of 204 is automatically transmitted back to the client.

HttpPost

When you want to insert new data, the HttpPost verb is typically used. In accord with the method's behavior, Post operations should be named with a prefix of *Post*. If any exam question or requirement specifies that a new record be created, it will probably necessitate an HttpPost operation.

A method that maps to an HttpPost request can have various return types (including void). It almost always requires an input parameter corresponding to the type that's being inserted or created.

If you're attempting to insert a new record, it makes sense to get some feedback that the operation was successful. (If you think back to ADO.NET, for instance, when performing an INSERT operation, the ExecuteNonQuery method has a RecordsAffected property indicating how many records were just inserted.) Although this makes sense, and there's nothing stopping you from doing it, the HTTP 1.1 protocol stipulates that when a resource is created, the server responds with an HttpStatusCode of Created (201). If you don't specify otherwise, though, when the operation is processed, the framework returns an HttpStatusCode of OK (200), so you have to put effort into returning a 201.

Additionally, when a new resource is created, it's advisable that the location of the new resource be included in the response. This enables a user of your API to immediately get the feedback where it can find any details on the entity that was just added. For both of these reasons, the following method would compile and run:

```
// Don't use this
public int PostAccount(Account account)
{
    return 0;
}
```

Even though it would technically work, it's equally a bad idea for precisely the two reasons stated previously. A better implementation and one that would use the System.Net.Http. HttpResponseMessage as the return type and would provide information about the operation is the HttpResponseMessage:

```
[HttpPost]
public HttpResponseMessage PostAccount(Account account)
{
    HttpResponseMessage response =
        Request.CreateResponse<Account>(HttpStatusCode.Created, account);
    string newUri = Url.Link("NamedApi", new { accountId = account.AccountId });
    response.Headers.Location = new Uri(newUri);
    return response;
}
```

This implementation returns a 201 status code and points to the location of the newly created item.

HttpPut

The HttpPut is used for operations that correspond to upserts, inserting for new records and updating for existing records. An interesting side effect of supporting upserts is that the method should be idempotent (that is, if you call the method once or 100 times with the same data, there should be no meaningful difference in the side effects of calling it one or 100 times).

Any methods that execute update operations should use the *Put* prefix. Following along with the examples, to have an update for an Account, you'd need to specify a key to look up the record and then a container to hold the new values. Implementation is simple, and the only noteworthy component is prefixing the method name with Put:

```
[HttpPut]
public HttpResponseMessage PutAccount(int id, Account account)
{
    // perform insert and/or edit here.
}
```

> **NOTE SOURCE VALUES**
>
> Just as with the ASP.NET Model-View-Controller (MVC), Web API uses model binding to create the arguments necessary for your method. For example, the ID parameter to the PutAccount method can be extracted from the corresponding value if that's specified in the RouteTemplate. The account parameter is extracted by deserializing the request body. Being able to send data both in the URL and the request body makes sense if you think about it with respect to how it's being processed. A typical request often involves more than one value, and in many cases, it will involve several values. A key, on the other hand, is exclusive and must by definition be a scalar value. As such, the key lends itself to intuitive representation via the URI, but trying to specify 20 values would be quite convoluted. Using simple parameter types extracted from the Route while extracting complex types from the Request body not only makes sense but also allows for items being addressable by URI without making them impossible to understand or build.

Defining HTTP resources with HTTP actions

Now that you understand the HTTP methods involved in creating a Web API service, it's time to start looking at how to use them in Web API.

First, let's contrast a Web API service with a WCF service. If you think back to a traditional WCF Service, you need to follow the ABC pattern: address, binding, and contract. The address specifies the location of your service, the binding configures how you can call the service, and the contract defines your actual service.

Items you create to transfer the data need to be serialized, and the most common mechanism is to decorate the type with the DataContract attribute. Each property that you want exposed should be decorated with the DataMember attribute.

You have complete freedom in how you create your service. This gives you a lot of flexibility and power, but it also introduces complexity. Another problem with the complexity of WCF is that it often creates a strong coupling between the client and the server. In today's world, more and more devices need to access your services. Not all those devices are running on the .NET platform. The only ubiquitous feature is HTTP. All modern devices are capable of executing HTPP requests and retrieving the results.

This is why Web API is built upon HTTP. When building a service with a Web API, you build an application that uses controllers and action methods that map to specific URLs and HTTP actions.

After you choose to create the application, you'll be prompted to specify the template you want to use when the project is created. Unsurprisingly, you should choose the Web API option shown in Figure 4-1.

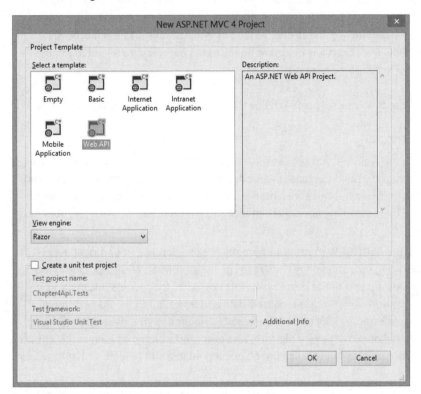

FIGURE 4-1 Web API template dialog box

With the application in place, you can define the resources and corresponding actions.

Creating the model

When designing your Web API, you probably have some data that you want to expose. This is why you don't technically need to create the model first, but it is the logical way to proceed. The model you define is a physical representation of the data you want to transfer. Unlike its WCF counterpart, there's nothing special about creating a model; you define it just like any other .NET Class.

Once defined, the ASP.NET Web API transparently handles sending your model over HTTP. It does so by serializing your model's members to the target format. JavaScript Object Notation (JSON) and XML are two of the best-known formats. After the model's information is serialized, the framework will take the serialized data and insert it into the Body element of the HTTP response message. JSON and XML are both ubiquitous in the development world, and both can be read on almost every platform and every technology. As long as a client can read the chosen format, it can deserialize the object and enable you to work with it however you desire.

When the project is created for you by Visual Studio, it creates several project folders for you that allow convenient and intuitive locations to store the components of the service. For more complex applications, you probably store your model in a separate assembly. But in this case, create each item that serves as a model in the Models folder in the Solution Explorer. To illustrate how this works (and how simple it is), define two items like this:

Account.cs in the Models folder

```
public class Account
{
    public int AccountId { get; set; }
    public string AccountAlias { get; set; }
    public DateTime CreatedDate { get; set; }
}
```

Customer.cs in the Models folder

```
public class Customer
{
    public int CustomerId { get; set; }
    public int AccountId { get; set; }
    public string FirstName { get; set; }
    public string LastName { get; set; }
}
```

The only thing noteworthy about either of these two class definitions is that there is nothing noteworthy about them! They have no special constructor that needs to be implemented. There is no requirement to inherit from a base class or to implement an interface. A special attribute decoration is not needed. To that end, each of these classes looks like any other .NET class. The only requirement worth mentioning is that the model definition must provide for a nonprivate default constructor.

Creating the controller

Controller classes are the most important part of your Web API. They define the actual service that you expose to users. The primary purpose of the controller is to handle HTTP requests. The controller implementation you create needs to inherit from the ApiController class. The members that manipulate the model types are known as *action methods*, *action handlers*, or simply *actions*. No extra attributes are needed on a method to facilitate it becoming an action; it simply needs to be a public method defined as part of the controller instance.

To expose the Account and Customer class that you just created, create a class derived from the System.Web.Http.ApiController base class in the Controllers folder. Define an array of Account items and prepopulate the array with data. In a real-world scenario, instead of using hard-coded data, the data would be retrieved from a Web Service, XML file, SQL Server database, or other store. In fact, you can very easily hook this up to a database by using the Entity Framework or any other data access technology you choose.

In this example, you'll build the following retrieval methods:

- Return all available Accounts
- Return a specific Account based on the AccountId
- Return all Customers on a specific AccountId
- Search all Customers on a specific AccountId by Last Name

The first step is to create the controller objects in the Controllers folder. Following the REST pattern, you expose a service for each model type that you have. In this case, you add a controller for both Accounts and Customers. The following uses stub in the action handlers:

AccountController.cs

```csharp
public class AccountController : ApiController
{
    public IEnumerable<Account> GetAccounts()
    {
        throw new NotImplementedException("You still need to write this logic");
    }
    public Account GetAccount(int accountId)
    {
        throw new NotImplementedException("You still need to write this logic");
    }
}
```

CustomerController.cs

```csharp
public class CustomerController : ApiController
{
    public IEnumerable<Customer> GetCustomers(int accountId)
    {
        throw new NotImplementedException("You still need to write this logic");
    }
    public IEnumerable<Customer> SearchCustomers(int accountId, string lastName)
    {
        throw new NotImplementedException("You still need to write this logic");
    }
}
```

Next, prepopulate an array of Accounts and an array of Customers so you have data to work with. Place them in a new class file named DataRepository in the Web API project's root directory:

DataRepository.cs in MyWebApi's root directory

```csharp
public static class DataRepository
{
    public static Account[] Accounts = new Account[]
    {
        new Account{ AccountId = 1, AccountAlias = "Disney"},
        new Account{ AccountId = 2, AccountAlias = "Marvel"},
        new Account{ AccountId = 3, AccountAlias = "McDonald's"},
        new Account{ AccountId = 4, AccountAlias = "Flintstones"}
    };
    public static Customer[] Customers = new Customer[]
    {
        new Customer{ AccountId = 1, CustomerId = 1,
            FirstName = "Mickey", LastName = "Mouse"},
        new Customer{ AccountId = 1, CustomerId = 2,
            FirstName = "Minnie", LastName = "Mouse"},
        new Customer{ AccountId = 1, CustomerId = 3,
            FirstName = "Donald", LastName = "Duck"},
        new Customer{ AccountId = 2, CustomerId = 4,
```

```
            FirstName = "Captain", LastName = "America"},
        new Customer{ AccountId = 2, CustomerId = 5,
            FirstName = "Spider", LastName = "Man"},
        new Customer{ AccountId = 2, CustomerId = 6,
            FirstName = "Wolverine", LastName = "N/A"},
        new Customer{ AccountId = 3, CustomerId = 7,
            FirstName = "Ronald", LastName = "McDonald"},
        new Customer{ AccountId = 3, CustomerId = 8,
            FirstName = "Ham", LastName = "Burgler"},
        new Customer{ AccountId = 4, CustomerId = 9,
            FirstName = "Fred", LastName = "Flintstone"},
        new Customer{ AccountId = 4, CustomerId = 10,
            FirstName = "Wilma", LastName = "Flintstone"},
        new Customer{ AccountId = 4, CustomerId = 11,
            FirstName = "Betty", LastName = "Rubble"},
        new Customer{ AccountId = 4, CustomerId = 12,
            FirstName = "Barney", LastName = "Rubble"}
    };
}
```

> **NOTE MVC AND WEB API**
>
> For organizational purposes, it is helpful to store controllers in the predefined Controllers
> folder, but it's not an absolute requirement. Also, when you go to create a new controller,
> you can add a controller in the Solution Explorer's context menus for the Controllers folder.
> However, this adds an MVC controller, not a Web API controller (this will be fixed in Visual
> Studio 2013). It is actually easier to just add a new Class because you have to remove the
> majority of what is in the initial controller template. Finally, be sure to include the System.
> Web.Http namespace so the ApiController base class can be resolved.

The only remaining task is to implement the functionality in each action handler:

AccountController.cs

```
public class AccountController : ApiController
{
    public IEnumerable<Account> GetAccounts()
    {
        return DataRepository.Accounts;
    }
    public Account GetAccount(int accountId)
    {
        Account result = DataRepository.Accounts.SingleOrDefault(acc =>
            acc.AccountId == accountId);

        if (result == null)
        {
            throw new HttpResponseException(HttpStatusCode.NotFound);
        }

        return result;
    }
}
```

CustomerController.cs

```
public class CustomerController : ApiController
{
    public IEnumerable<Customer> GetCustomers(int accountId)
    {
        return DataRepository.Customers.Where(cust =>
            cust.AccountId == accountId);
    }
    public IEnumerable<Customer> SearchCustomers(string lastName)
    {
        return DataRepository.Customers.Where(cust =>
            cust.LastName.ToLower().Contains(lastName.ToLower()));
    }
}
```

EXAM TIP

If the query parameters don't return a matching value, you have several ways to respond, just as you would any other query. Although you can opt to return a null value, a more elegant and expressive means is to throw an HttpResponseException. The HttpResponseException class has two overloads you can use: The first is to specify an HttpStatusCode enumeration value, and the second is an HttpResponseMessage. The HttpStatusCode enumeration provides several common and intuitive codes, and in this case, the value of NotFound fits both logically and mechanically. Make sure that you understand how to use HttpStatusCode for the exam to return meaningful responses to the client.

The choice about which methods to support and how methods return data depends on the requirements of the application. After this is all in place, everything is ready to be used. To access one of the model items, you simply need to reference it by a uniform resource identifier (URI). In this example, assuming that you host your Web API in the development web server that is installed with Visual Studio, you can retrieve the Accounts by navigating to *http://localhost:PORTNUMBER/api/Account* in your browser. Alternatively, you can also configure IIS to host these services as you would any other web application. You can navigate to *http://localhost:PORTNUMBER/api/Account?accountId=1* to use querystring parameters to pass values in for the parameters of your methods.

EXAM TIP

Experiment with calling your Web API by accessing all action methods through their URL. Try passing different values for parameters such as accountId. Also pass an invalid value so you get back an HTTP 404 error (the result of HttpResponseException's HttpStatusCode).

Browser functionality and support

Different browsers, and even different versions of some browsers, behave differently when you attempt to test these services. At the time this section of the book was being written, the latest version of Chrome and Firefox displayed the data as in-page XML, whereas the latest version of Internet Explorer prompted you to download JSON data. Some browsers even have settings to help control this behavior. The reason you sometimes get XML and sometimes get JSON is because different values are sent in the Accept header.

Following are the headers sent from a few browsers that can be obtained by using a tool such as Fiddler (*http://fiddler2.com/*):

Internet Explorer 10

```
Accept: text/html, application/xhtml+xml, */*
```

Chrome 28

```
Accept: text/html,application/xhtml+xml,application/xml;q=0.9,*/*;q=0.8
```

Firefox 22

```
Accept: text/html,application/xhtml+xml,application/xml;q=0.9,*/*;q=0.8
```

As you can see, Chrome and Firefox send an identical Accept header, so it's no surprise that they both behave similarly. Specifically, it's the application/xml portion of the header that's causing the XML to come back for those versions of those browsers.

Fortunately, this is only a problem with web browsers. If you were consuming these services with a custom client, you would easily be able to specify whether you wanted the services to return the data as JSON or XML.

Mapping URI space using routing

If you followed along with the example, you likely noticed that other than the model and the controller definitions and some fake data, there wasn't anything else that needed to be done. Yet somehow, a few class definitions in an application turn into a URI-accessible mechanism for handling data. The way this happens is via a *Routing Table*.

If you examine the contents of the App_Start folder, you should see a structure similar to what's shown in Figure 4-2.

FIGURE 4-2 App_Start folder contents

A Routing Table is a class that implements the System.Web.Http.Routing.IHttpRoute interface and performs the simple task of mapping an incoming HttpRequestMessage to a specified controller and action. If you select the WebApiConfig.cs file, you'll see the following definition (or perhaps something similar to it with some additional comments):

WebApiConfig.cs

```
namespace MyWebApi
{
    public static class WebApiConfig
    {
        public static void Register(HttpConfiguration config)
        {
            config.Routes.MapHttpRoute(
                name: "DefaultApi",
                routeTemplate: "api/{controller}/{id}",
                defaults: new { id = RouteParameter.Optional }
            );
            config.EnableSystemDiagnosticsTracing();
        }
    }
}
```

Because this class is created by the project template, you don't need to actually be concerned about creating it, but you should become familiar with what it does and how it does it because it will be covered on the exam. To make sure that you understand how it affects the application, navigate to *http://localhost:PORTNUMBER/api/Account*. Depending on the browser and version, you are presented with a .json file containing each of the items in the Accounts array defined earlier.

Now experiment with this routing configuration. To do so, change the routeTemplate property value in the WebApiConfig.cs file from "api/{controller}/{id}" to "data/{controller}/{id}".

Build and run it after you've made the change and then navigate to the same URI; just replace the word "api" with "data" in the browser's address bar. Let's review what happens when you execute a request for a given method by typing the URI into a browser.

Navigating to the URI executes an HTTP request that starts the processing pipeline. The request is received, and the Web API framework tries to match it to one of the route templates defined in the Routing Table. If a match is found, the request is forwarded and processed as expected; if not, an HttpStatusCode of 404 is returned to the client. If a matching route is present, the Web API maps an appropriate controller and/or action to the request. Per MSDN, the following actions are performed when a match is found:

1. To match the correct controller, the Web API adds the literal *Controller* to the controller variable.

2. To match an action, the Web API examines the HTTP method and tries to match it to an action whose name corresponds to the HTTP method name.

3. By default, the action names used correspond to four specific HTTP methods: GET, POST, PUT, and DELETE. It's important to note, however, that this mechanism works specifically only for these four methods. You can define and enable other HTTP methods, but a different convention is used for processing.

4. Finally, placeholder variables in the route template are mapped specifically to the corresponding action parameters.

In addition to using the default naming convention for these HTTP methods, you can also explicitly set them. Especially when working with custom names, this is important and something you should remember for the exam. To do this, decorate each method you want exposed with a matching System.Web.Http.ActionMethodSelectorAttribute class:

- HttpGet
- HttpPost
- HttpDelete
- HttpPut

To see this work, decorate the GetAccount method. In this instance, decorate it with the HttpGet attribute, as shown in the following example:

```
[HttpGet]
public Account GetAccount(int accountId)
{
    Account result = DataRepo.Accounts.SingleOrDefault(acc =>
        acc.AccountId == accountId);

    if (result == null)
    {
        throw new HttpResponseException(HttpStatusCode.NotFound);
    }

    return result;
}
```

If you plan to use the default naming conventions, you don't necessarily need to do anything. For each method that corresponds to the HTTP action, you just define the HTTP action you want to employ.

EXAM TIP

There are HTTP actions defined in two obvious namespaces: System.Web.Http and System.Web.Mvc. They both have their use and place in the application, but in this sample, the one in the System.Web.Http namespace is the one that should be used. Because there are some other classes in the System.Web.Mvc namespace, it is incredibly easy to accidentally use the incorrect one, so be careful here!

Equally as confusing is the AcceptVerbsAttribute, which also exists in both places. Yet it is important to use the one in the System.Web.Http namespace. So how do you know when to use one versus the other? It's quite simple! Look at your controller and see what the base class is. If it's ApiController, you should use the System.Web.Http namespace. If it's not, use the System.Web.Mvc namespace for them. It's certainly possible for both to exist within the same project!

System.Web.Http.AcceptVerbsAttribute

There are cases for which you will want to define multiple actions on a given method or to define an action other than the four default ones. To support these scenarios, use the System.Web.Http.AcceptVerbsAttribute class.

There is only one constructor for the AcceptVerbsAttribute class, which lets you pass in an array of strings corresponding to each action the method should be mapped to:

```
[System.Web.Http.AcceptVerbs("GET", "HEAD")]
public IEnumerable<Customer> GetCustomers(int accountId)
{
    return DataRepo.Customers.Where(cust =>
        cust.AccountId == accountId);
}
```

NOTE DEVELOPER TYPO ERRORS

Unfortunately, there are currently no framework constants that include all the typical HTTP verbs you would likely want to use in the constructor for AcceptVerbs. There is a partial set in System.Net.WebRequestMethods.Http, but it lacks an important one: Delete. Instead, you should definitely create constants for the verbs your system needs to support in order to avoid runtime errors caused by developer typos. This book uses hard-coded strings.

ActionNameAttribute

If you have the need or desire to create a route in which the action name is indicated in the URI, you can change the routing to explicitly mention the action name. To do this, you need to change the MapHttpRoute value. Doing so is quite simple:

```
public static void Register(HttpConfiguration config)
{
    config.Routes.MapHttpRoute(
        name: "NamedApi",
        routeTemplate: "api/{controller}/{action}/{id}",
        defaults: new { id = RouteParameter.Optional }
    );

    config.EnableSystemDiagnosticsTracing();
}
```

To make sure that the differentiation is clear, the name property here is renamed to NamedApi, and a token of {action} is added in between the controller and Id tokens. After this is defined, you can name your method whatever you want and thereafter reference it in the URI. So instead of calling *http://localhost:PORTNUMBER/api/Controller/Customers/1*, you now call *http://localhost:PORTNUMBER/api/Controller/Customers/GetCustomers/1*.

You can also change the name of the action method by using the ActionNameAttribute. Using the previous SearchCustomers method implementation, you can change the name to FindCustomers:

```
[HttpGet]
[ActionName("FindCustomers")]
public IEnumerable<Customer> SearchCustomers(string lastName)
{
    return DataRepository.Customers.Where(cust =>
        cust.LastName.ToLower().Contains(lastName.ToLower()));
}
```

After you alter this action handler, navigate to *http://localhost:PORTNUMBER/ data/Customer/SearchCustomers?lastName=r,* and you'll notice that you receive an error stating that this service does not exist. However, if you now attempt to navigate to *http://localhost:PORTNUMBER/data/Customer/FindCustomers?lastName=r,* you should see some data.

NonActions

Any Controller method defined with the public access modifier is accessible by default. There are certainly times when you might need to have the member typed with the public modifier but don't want it exposed to clients. In these cases, simply annotate each such method with the NonAction attribute, and it will be explicitly prevented from being invoked.

Choosing appropriate formats for responses to meet requirements

If you access your Web API service from a browser, you execute a request to your service. This request contains something called an *Accept header*, which specifies the type of data that you as a client expect from the server:

```
Accept: text/html,application/xhtml+xml,application/xml
```

By default, Web API works with both JSON and XML data. Returning the correct format is done by an object called a *media-type formatter*. These classes are capable of both reading and writing objects to and from the HTTP message body.

The process of returning your data in the format requested by the client is called *content negotiation*. As you can understand, separating the way your data is serialized from your actual code gives you a very flexible solution. If you want, you can even add media-type formatters of your own. You do this by adding a class that inherits from MediaTypeFormatter or BufferedMediaTypeFormatter (a wrapper around the asynchronous methods of MediaTypeFormatter).

> **MORE INFO** **CUSTOM MEDIA-TYPE FORMATTER**
>
> For a complete example of how to implement a custom media-type formatter, see
> *http://www.asp.net/web-api/overview/formats-and-model-binding/media-formatters*.

Planning when to make HTTP actions asynchronous

Users expect a fast website, and you want to scale to as many requests as possible on your server. This is why asynchronous code is becoming more and more important. When a user issues a request to your Web API, a thread is used to process the request. Your web server only has a limited number of threads.

Now, when a request takes a long time and a lot of requests are coming in, it could be that your server runs out of threads. This will start queuing requests, and it might even lead to your server coming to a halt.

Now, take a look at what a thread actually does when it executes a request. In most applications, a lot of time is spent waiting for other code to finish, be it a request to a database, another web service, or some data on disk. These types of I/O requests can take a relatively long time to finish. In the meantime, your thread is just waiting for the result.

Asynchronous code is all about freeing your thread to process other requests while the I/O is being processed. This lets your server process more requests with fewer threads.

When deciding whether you want to make an HTTP action asynchronous, first ask yourself whether the work you are doing is CPU- or I/O-bound. CPU-bound work means that your thread is very busy executing calculations, processing results, or doing something else that is CPU-intensive. If you execute CPU-bound work asynchronously, you are freeing the current thread to do some other work and then immediately claiming another thread to execute your CPU work. This doesn't give you a performance benefit. Instead, managing different threads and switching between them can hurt your performance.

So make sure, both for the exam and in real world, that you use asynchronous code only for I/O-bound work. That will free your thread to really work on something else until your I/O work is done, and a thread will be asked to continue working with it. (This is different in client applications such as WPF or Winforms. There, it's a good idea to move long-running code to a different thread to make sure that you don't block the user interface. For a server application, however, you should do this only with I/O-bound code.)

Because Web API can be used with C# 5, you have an easy mechanism to make your code asynchronous: async/await. The async and await keywords were added to C# to make writing asynchronous code easier (which shows how important asynchronous code is becoming). In combination with the Task Parallel Library (TPL), you can now create asynchronous code that almost looks like its regular synchronous code.

Take the following synchronous Web API method:

```
public string Get()
{
    WebClient webClient = new WebClient();
    string result = webClient.DownloadString("http://microsoft.com");
    return result;
}
```

This method uses the WebClient to download the HTML of microsoft.com. The thread executing this code spends most of its time waiting for the external IO request. Now by using async/await, you can easily convert this to an asynchronous request:

```
public async Task<string> Get()
{
    WebClient webClient = new WebClient();
    string result = await webClient.DownloadStringTaskAsync("http://microsoft.com");

    return result;
}
```

As you can see, the async keyword was added to the method definition. The return type is changed from string to Task<string>. Task<string> signals to the Web API framework that this code will return a string somewhere in the future. The call to DownloadString is also replaced with a call to DownloadStringTaskAsync, and the await keyword is used on it.

Behind the scenes, the compiler will translate your code into a complex state machine that keeps track of all asynchronous operations and exception handling to make your code look as if it is synchronous.

Thought experiment
Understanding Web API

In this thought experiment, apply what you've learned about this objective. You can find answers to these questions in the "Answers" section at the end of this chapter.

You are explaining Web API to your colleagues. You think it's a nice and elegant solution, but they don't see the advantages of Web API over Windows Communication Foundation (WCF). They come with up with the following questions:

1. Why should we depend on HTTP verbs instead of calling a method by name?

2. What's the advantage of content negotiation? Isn't the service the one that should declare the return type?

Objective summary

- Using Web API, you can build an intuitive and consistent service that can be accessed by just about any type of client.

- Web API is an implementation of a RESTful service. You use URIs with HTTP verbs to expose your service. A Web API consists of a controller class that inherits from ApiController and several model classes that you want to expose.

- The most-used HTTP verbs are HttpGet (to handle the retrieval of data), HttpPost (for the creation and insertion of new data), HttpPut (for updating data), and HttpDelete (for deleting data).

- By default, the mapping of the controller and models is facilitated via the WebApiConfig.cs. This class defines the routing for your Web API.

- Content negotiation uses media-type formatters to return the requested format to a client.

- Asynchronous methods are made possible by using the new async and await keywords. In Web API, you should use async and await only on I/O-bound code.

Objective review

Answer the following questions to test your knowledge of the information in this objective. You can find the answers to these questions and explanations of why each answer choice is correct or incorrect in the "Answers" section at the end of this chapter.

1. You have been asked to create an ASP.NET Web API application. The current site enables users to post comments on newly posted articles. There's been an increasing problem of inappropriate and spam comments. Editors need to be able to edit the inappropriate content after reviewing it and finding it in violation with the terms of service. Editors also need to be able to permanently delete any comments that are considered spam. Which operations accomplish these goals? (Choose all that apply.)

   A. HttpGet

   B. HttpPost

   C. HttpDelete

   D. HttpPut

2. You have an ASP.NET MVC Web API that processes new customer inquiries. The client applications are intended to be very focused in scope and centered on just a few operations. A decision was just made that, for now, the API needs to simply allow data collected from a Web Form to be submitted to a SQL Server database. Which of the following is needed to allow form data to be submitted to the server?

   A. HttpGet

   B. HttpHead

   C. HttpPost

   D. HttpPut

3. Your ASP.NET Web API application needs to be able to allow action methods to operate through multiple HTTP Actions (namely HttpPost and HttpPut). How should this be accomplished?

   A. Decorate the method with both the HttpGet and the HttpPost attribute.

   B. Decorate the method with an HttpGet and an HttpPut attribute.

   C. Decorate the method with the ActionNames attribute using the values of HttpPut and HttpPost.

   D. Decorate the method with the AcceptVerbs attributes, including HttpPut and HttpPost.

Objective 4.2: Implement a Web API

The previous objective discussed the design aspects of creating a Web API. The next step in the logical progression is to cover the implementation of a Web API to provide a richer experience.

> **This objective covers how to:**
> - Accept data in JSON format
> - Using content negotiation to deliver different data formats to clients
> - Define actions and parameters to handle data binding
> - Use HttpMessageHandler to process client requests and server responses
> - Implement dependency injection
> - Implement action filters and exception filters
> - Implement asynchronous and synchronous actions
> - Implement streaming actions

Accepting data in JSON format

In the last objective, you created a basic Web API for an AccountService and verified that the methods were working correctly by referencing them in browsers. Each query returned different results, but if you look at the following content, it's typical of what a fully executed query would return:

```
[{"AccountId":1,"AccountAlias":"Disney","CreatedDate":"0001-01-01T00:00:00"}, {"AccountId":2,"AccountAlias":"Marvel","CreatedDate":"0001-01-01T00:00:00"}, {"AccountId":3,"AccountAlias":"McDonald's","CreatedDate":"0001-01-01T00:00:00"}, {"AccountId":4,"AccountAlias":"Flintstones","CreatedDate":"0001-01-01T00:00:00"}]
```

This serves an illustrative purpose well, but from an application development perspective, it leaves much to be desired. That's simply because most users are not looking for anywhere near that technical sort of output. Instead, they tend to want an application interface that consumes the data and enables them to do things with it.

Building a Razor page

When creating a new Web API application, the Razor view engine is used by default. By specifying Razor, several views are automatically defined for you and stored in the Home folder of the Views folder in the Index.cshtml file. When the application is run, if nothing is modified in the Index.cshtml file, the default output will match or closely resemble that of Figure 4-3.

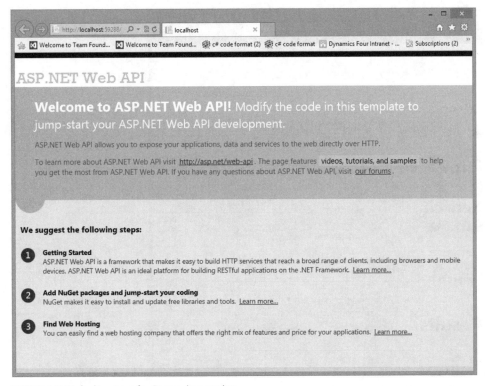

FIGURE 4-3 Default output for Razor view engine

To illustrate how this works, first let's make some basic layout changes to the underlying HTML structure so that it displays a form related to the defined scenario. If you replace the entire contents of Index.cshtml with the following markup, the output changes to what's shown in Figure 4-4:

```
<body id="body" >
    <div class="main-content">
        <div>
            <h1>Flintstone Customers</h1>
            <ul id="customers"/>
        </div>
        <div>
            <h1>Search</h1>
            <label for="lastName">Last Name:</label>
            <input type="text" id="lastName" size="5"/>
            <input type="button" value="Search" onclick="find();" />
        </div>
        <div>
            <h1>Results</h1>
            <ul id="results" />
        </div>
    </div>
</body>
```

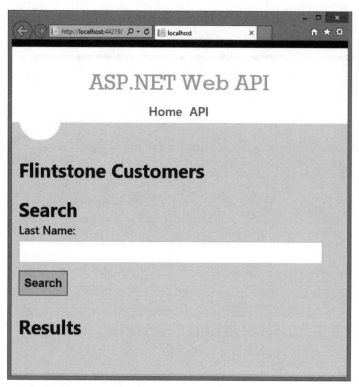

FIGURE 4-4 Modified Index.cshtml form

The plan for this page is to list all the customers under the Flintstone account at the top of the page, but at the bottom of the page you get to search for all customers by last name and see the results. When the page initially loads, it should be loaded with no data in it and will make some AJAX calls to both initially populate the top of the page as well as to perform the search functionality.

AJAX stands for Asynchronous JavaScript and XML. Normally, when executing a request to the server from your browser, the complete page is refreshed. When executing an AJAX call, the browser sends this call in the background to the server. The server responds to this request and returns some data to the client. This data is then processed by some JavaScript running on the client. This way, you can make fluent updates to the page shown in the browser without updating the complete page. If your clients support JavaScript, using AJAX creates a better user experience for them.

Adding client-side functionality

To wire this form up to accept and consume JSON data, very little additional modification needs to be done. Essentially, you need to create a <script> block defined as type in a special Razor Section (defined in _Layout.cshtml under the Shared folder in Views) to invoke this client script. Without getting too deeply into explaining the Razor or jQuery syntax, add the following code at the end of your Index.cshtml file after the </body> tag:

```
@section Scripts {
    <script type="text/javascript">
        $(document).ready(function () {
            // Populate the "All" list for the Flintstones
            $.getJSON('data/Customer/GetCustomers?accountId=4')
                .success(
                    function (data) {
                        // If successful, 'data' contains our Customers
                        $.each(data, function (key, val) {
                            var displayValue = val.FirstName + ' ' + val.LastName;

                            $('<li/>', { text: displayValue })
                                .appendTo($('#customers'));
                        });
                    });
        });

        function find() {
            $('#results').empty();
            var searchString = $('#lastName').val();
            $.getJSON('api/Customer/FindCustomers?lastName=' + searchString)
                .success(
                    function (data) {
                        $.each(data, function (key, val) {
                            var displayValue = val.FirstName + ' ' + val.LastName
                                + ' [' + val.CustomerId + ']';

                            $('<li/>', { text: displayValue }).appendTo($('#results'));
                        });
                    })
                .fail(
                    function (jqXHR, textStatus, err) {
                        $('#results').text('Error: ' + err);
                    });
        }
    </script>
}
```

After adding this code, you should be able to refresh your page and get full functionality. With the test data that you have hard-coded, you should see something like what you see in Figure 4-5.

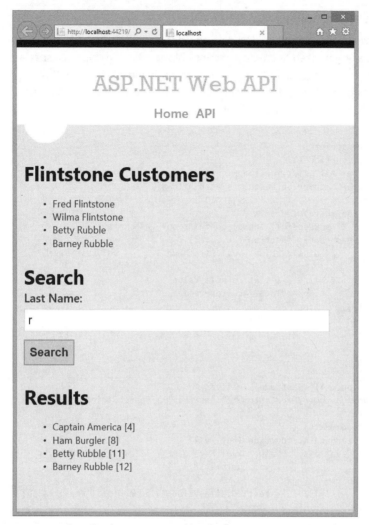

FIGURE 4-5 Functional customer searching form

You don't have to change anything on the server to accept data in JSON format. By default, your server can process both JSON and XML data without any changes. The most important step on the client is to explicitly state whether you are sending XML, JSON, or some other type of data so the server can process it.

Using content negotiation to deliver different data formats

Content negotiation is the process by which a response format is selected for a given response when there are multiple representations available. Content negotiation can happen multiple ways, but the primary way it happens is via the HttpRequest header (see Table 4-3).

TABLE 4-3 HTTP request headers

Item	Details
Accept	Specifies the media types that are acceptable in the response. Common formats are "application/json", "application/xml", or "text/xml".
Accept-Charset	Specifies which character sets are allowed. Common examples include UTF-8 or ISO-8859-1.
Accept-Encoding	Specifies which encodings are acceptable.
Accept-Language	Specifies the preferred language.

These aren't the only portions of the request that can be examined or utilized in content negotiation. In an AJAX request, for instance, the request might contain an X-Requested-With header. If no Accept header value is indicated, a request defaults to JSON.

To understand how your HTTP traffic works, it helps to use a tool called Fiddler (*http://fiddler2.com/*) to inspect the HTTP traffic. For the exam, it definitely helps to run Fiddler while surfing the web and accessing your Web API. Look at the header values that are sent and the values returned from the server to really understand what's happening.

Using the CustomerController sample, you have the following implementation:

CustomerController.cs

```
public class CustomerController : ApiController
{
    [System.Web.Http.AcceptVerbs("GET", "HEAD")]
    public IEnumerable<Customer> GetCustomers(int accountId)
    {
        return DataRepo.Customers.Where(cust =>
            cust.AccountId == accountId);
    }
    [HttpGet]
    [ActionName("FindCustomers")]
    public IEnumerable<Customer> SearchCustomers(string lastName)
    {
        return DataRepo.Customers.Where(cust =>
            cust.LastName.ToLower().Contains(lastName.ToLower()));
    }
}
```

The page implemented in the previous section is driven entirely by the services hosted in these two action handlers. The top of the page is populated by GetCustomers, whereas the bottom of the page is populated by SearchCustomers (or FindCustomers, depending on how you want to look at it). When viewed in Internet Explorer 10, a raw HTTP request is similar to the following:

Raw Client HTTP request

```
GET http://localhost:53366/data/Customer/FindCustomers?lastName=r HTTP/1.1
X-Requested-With: XMLHttpRequest
Accept: application/json, text/javascript, */*; q=0.01
Referer: http://localhost:53366/
```

```
Accept-Language: en-US,en;q=0.5
Accept-Encoding: gzip, deflate
User-Agent: Mozilla/5.0 (compatible; MSIE 10.0; Windows NT 6.2; WOW64; Trident/6.0)
Host: localhost:53366
DNT: 1
Connection: Keep-Alive
```

After processing the request, the server should return something similar to the following raw response (some white space was added to the body for readability):

Raw server response

```
HTTP/1.1 200 OK
Cache-Control: no-cache
Pragma: no-cache
Content-Type: application/json; charset=utf-8
Expires: -1
Server: Microsoft-IIS/8.0
X-AspNet-Version: 4.0.30319
X-SourceFiles: =?UTF-8?B?QzpcUHJvamVjdHNcTX1Tb2x1dGlvblxNeVdlYkFwaVxkYXRhXEN1c3RvbWVyyXEZ
pbmRDdXN0b21lcnM=?=
X-Powered-By: ASP.NET
Date: Mon, 15 Jul 2013 15:52:20 GMT
Content-Length: 290
```

```
[{"CustomerId":4,"AccountId":2,"FirstName":"Captain","LastName":"America"},
{"CustomerId":8,"AccountId":3,"FirstName":"Ham","LastName":"Burgler"},
{"CustomerId":11,"AccountId":4,"FirstName":"Betty","LastName":"Rubble"},
{"CustomerId":12,"AccountId":4,"FirstName":"Barney","LastName":"Rubble"}]
```

In this cycle, the client initiates a request requesting the results in JSON (application/json), JavaScript (text/javascript), or anything else (*/*). The server's response makes it clear that the request was processed and the response was created using JSON.

Try performing the search again with no input as well as an invalid input. Although one of the Account's action handlers threw an explicit error when there were no results, this Search implementation does not. So if you search for an invalid string, you get an empty collection returned to you with a status code of 200. However, if you provide no input, this equates to NULL being passed into the SearchCustomers function and ultimately results in a NullReferenceException being thrown when lastName.ToLower() is called, which comes back with a response with a status code of 500 Internal Server Error. Even so, the body of the response with an error message, as indicated by the headers, is still in JSON and not HTML or anything else.

Content negotiation happens in the following sequence. Processing begins when the request is received by the server. The pipeline extracts an instance of the IContentNegotiator service from the HttpConfiguration instance. The HttpConfiguration includes a Formatters collection that provides a list of all available media formatters.

The next step in the pipeline calls the Negotiate method of the IContentNegotiator service. This accepts each of the following:

- The type of object being serialized
- A collection of the media formatters
- The HTTP request

The Negotiate method accepts these input parameters and returns two separate pieces of information:

- The formatter being used
- The media type for the HTTP response

If no formatter can be found, the Negotiate method will return a value of null, which results in the client receiving an HttpStatus code of Not Acceptable (406).

MORE INFO   CONTENT NEGOTIATION

For a detailed look at content negotiation, see *http://www.asp.net/web-api/overview/formats-and-model-binding/content-negotiation*.

Defining actions and parameters to handle data binding

One of the features of Web API is a process called *binding*. When creating an action method on your Web API controller, you can specify arguments that you want to use in your method.

You can use simple types (such as int, string, bool, DateTime, and so forth) or complex types. Simple types are filled with data from your URL. This means that you can pass a property such as id by putting it in the URL and making sure that routing knows about it.

Complex types are read from the message body using a media-type formatter. This is a key principle of HTTP: Resources are sent in the message body. Content negotiation enables you to convert the message body to the correct type and use it in your code.

However, you can influence the default binding process. One attribute that you can use is the FromUri attribute. This attribute specifies that a complex type should be read from the URI instead of the message body. For example, take the following complex type:

```
public class Person
{
    public string FirstName { get; set; }
    public string LastName { get; set; }
}
```

You can use this class as a parameter to your action method:

```
public HttpResponseMessage Get([FromUri] Person person) { /* implementation */}
```

You can now call this method and specify the name of the person in the URL:

```
http://localhost/api/Persons/?FirstName=John&LastName=Doe
```

You can also configure the binding process to get a simple type not from the URI but from the body. You do this by using the FromBody attribute.

By using more complex features such as TypeConverters and ModelBinders, you can extend Web API to read your custom types from the body of your request, route data, or other values.

MORE INFO   PARAMETER BINDING

If you want to know more about extending Web API with TypeConverters and ModelBinders, have a look at *http://www.asp.net/web-api/overview/formats-and-model-binding/parameter-binding-in-aspnet-web-api*.

Using HttpMessageHandler to process client requests and server responses

The Web API pipeline is very flexible: An incoming request is matched to a route and then sent to a specific Web API controller.

Those steps are performed by what's called a *message handler*. These method handlers are chained together and are called when a request comes in and when the response is returned to the client.

Message handlers can be used when you want to execute some cross-cutting concern. A cross-cutting concern is something that doesn't really fit in one logical place in your code, but instead should be executed at multiple places in your code. For example, logging a request or authenticating a request is a cross-cutting concern. You don't want to add logging or authentication code to each and every action method. Instead, you want to define this in one single place and then attach the code to each request.

This is where message handlers can be used. You can create a custom message handler by deriving from System.Net.Http.DelegatingHandler and overriding the SendAsync method. For example, you could create a handler that would log the beginning and end of every request:

```
public class LoggingMessageHandler: DelegatingHandler
{
    protected async override Task<HttpResponseMessage> SendAsync(
        HttpRequestMessage request, CancellationToken cancellationToken)
    {
        Debug.WriteLine("Process request");
        var response = await base.SendAsync(request, cancellationToken);
        Debug.WriteLine("Process response");
        return response;
    }
}
```

To add this handler to your Web API pipeline, you need to add it to the HttpConfiguration object that's passed to the Register method of the WebApiConfig class:

```
config.MessageHandlers.Add(new LoggingMessageHandler());
```

You can also choose to not call the other handlers. This way, you can break off a request and immediately return a response. This can be useful when the request is invalid or authentication fails.

When you add a handler to the HttpConfiguration object, the handler applies globally. This means that it will run for every request. You can also add a handler to a specific route. That way, the handler will execute only when the request matches your route:

```
config.Routes.MapHttpRoute(
        name: "LoggingRoute",
        routeTemplate: "api/sensitive/{id}",
        defaults: new { controller = "sensitive" id = RouteParameter.Optional },
        constraints: null,
        handler: new LoggingMessageHandler()
    );
```

Using handlers can be a powerful technique. When you get questions on the exam about code that should execute on each and every request, think of handlers and see whether they can solve the problem in an elegant way.

Implementing dependency injection

When building an application, you always deal with dependencies. Those dependencies could be a database or a web service, but also a class that implements a complex algorithm.

Without dependencies, applications don't offer much value. However, dependencies can make your code harder to use. If you study object-oriented programming (OOP) and design, you will come across the acronym SOLID:

- Single responsibility principle
- Open/closed principle
- Liskov substitution principle
- Interface segregation principle
- Dependency inversion principle

These principles help you to build an application that can easily be extended and maintained. Dependency injection is a method following the last principle: dependency inversion.

Dependency inversion states that your code shouldn't depend on concrete objects but upon abstractions. Why? Because it creates code that is less coupled and, as such, is easier to maintain.

Take the following code for example:

```
public string Get()
{
    WebClient webClient = new WebClient();
    string result = webClient.DownloadString("http://microsoft.com");
    return result;
}
```

This code uses a concrete class, WebClient, to get the content of microsoft.com. But what if you want to change this code to retrieve the data from a cache? Because you are programming against a concrete class, you have to change each and every line of code that uses WebClient.

Now, what if you don't depend upon a concrete class, but an abstraction instead? Let's say you have the following interface:

```
public interface IContentRepository
{
    string GetContent(string uri);
}
```

This interface doesn't reveal anything about its implementation. You don't know whether it uses a WebClient, Entity Framework, XML file, or some other kind of magic to load the content. You can now create an implementation that uses WebClient:

```
public class WebClientContentRepository : IContentRepository
{
    public string GetContent(string uri)
    {
        WebClient webClient = new WebClient();
        string result = webClient.DownloadString("http://microsoft.com");
        return result;
    }
}
```

But how do you get this class into your Web API controller? You could add a constructor like this:

```
public ContentController()
{
    contentRepository = new WebClientContentRepository();
}
```

But this still couples your class to a concrete implementation, although in a different place. Instead, you can use dependency injection, meaning that you ask for the objects you need, and they are injected into your class at construction. You do this by first changing your constructor:

```
public ContentController(IContentRepository contentRepository)
{
    _contentRepository = new WebClientContentRepository();
}
```

If you now run your application and navigate to *http://localhost/api/content*, you get an error stating that your class doesn't have a default constructor (meaning a constructor that doesn't take any arguments). To help the Web API framework, create the class and resolve all dependencies you need to implement an interface called IDependencyResolver. This class is used by Web API to create objects that have dependencies, such as the ContentController.

You can create your own implementation like this:

```
public class ResolveController : IDependencyResolver
{
    public object GetService(Type serviceType)
    {
        return serviceType == typeof(ContentController) ?
                    new ContentController(new WebClientContentRepository())
```

```
                            : null;
    }

    public IEnumerable<object> GetServices(Type serviceType)
    {
        return new List<object>();
    }

    public IDependencyScope BeginScope()
    {
        return this;
    }

    public void Dispose() { }
}
```

If this class is asked for an instance of type ContentController, it returns a new Content-Controller initialized with an instance of WebClientContentRepository. To start using this class, you need to configure the HttpConfiguration object:

```
config.DependencyResolver = new ResolveController();
```

After adding this code, your ContentController starts functioning again, and you can use the IContentRepository to get the data for the specified URI.

Of course, doing all this by hand isn't a really elegant and flexible solution. Fortunately, there are a couple of great open source projects that help you with implementing dependency injection. One such a tool is Unity. You can easily install Unity into your Web API project by using the NuGet package Unity.WebApi.

> **MORE INFO** **NUGET PACKAGE MANAGER**
>
> NuGet is a great way to install packages into your projects. You can find a detailed description on NuGet in Chapter 5.

After installing this package, a Bootstrapper.cs file is added to your project. Make sure that you call the BootStrapper.Initialize from your Global.asax. You can then register all the types you want to construct to Unity like this:

```
container.RegisterType<IContentRepository, WebClientContentRepository>();
```

If you now run your program, Unity will take care of constructing your ContentController and making sure that all dependencies are created. Dependency injection tools like Unity help you a lot with implementing dependency injection in your application. A lot of those tools enable you to specify the scope of a dependency (for example, a singleton or per-session object). Dependency injection tools are also capable of building complex hierarchies of objects where objects depend on other objects.

Implementing action filters and exception filters

Filters are used in Web API to decorate a controller or an action method. The filter modifies the way in which the action is executed. Take the following code, for example:

```
public class XmlOutputAttribute : ActionFilterAttribute
{
    public override void OnActionExecuted(
        HttpActionExecutedContextactionExecutedContext)
    {
        ObjectContent content = actionExecutedContext.Response.Content as ObjectContent;

        var value = content.Value;
        Type targetType = actionExecutedContext.Response.Content.
                            GetType().GetGenericArguments()[0];

        var httpResponseMessage = new HttpResponseMessage
        {
            StatusCode = HttpStatusCode.OK,
            RequestMessage = actionExecutedContext.Request,
            Content = new ObjectContent(targetType, value,
                                        newXmlMediaTypeFormatter(), (string)null)
        };

        actionExecutedContext.Response = httpResponseMessage;
        base.OnActionExecuted(actionExecutedContext);
    }
}
```

This attribute can be applied to a method to force it to return XML. This completely replaces the default behavior of content negotiation, and it's something you should only use in special circumstances. In this case, I once used this code to return XML to a client who expected XML but didn't use the correct Accept header.

As you can see, a custom action filter should inherit from ActionFilterAttribute. You can override several methods that execute before or after the code in the controller.

In addition to action filters, you can also create exception filters, which execute whenever an exception happens in your code. You can use them to return a nice response to the user, log the error, or execute other code in case of an error. Exception filters should inherit from ExceptionFilterAttribute.

You can apply a filter to a controller or a method by placing the attribute above the method or class definition. You can also apply an attribute globally by adding it to HttpConfiguration.Filters. This can be useful when you have an attribute, such as a RequireHttps attribute, that should be used in all requests.

Implementing asynchronous and synchronous actions

Your Web API will probably be distributed as a publicly facing API. This means you want to build your service in such a way that it can potentially serve a huge number of users.

Of course, you shouldn't fall into the trap of premature optimization. When you don't have an actual problem, why waste time on optimizing your code? However, when designing for scalability, you should think about synchronous and asynchronous methods.

The code you normally see is synchronous. It runs from top to bottom and executes your statements one at a time. When looking at a piece of code, you can't predict how long things will take. Some operations, such as incrementing an integer, can execute very quickly. Other operations, such as calling an external web service or database, can potentially take a long time.

Because your web server has a limited amount of threads to service incoming requests, you want to use your threads wisely. Making a thread wait for an external call to come back is a waste of resources. This is where asynchronous code can help you. When you make an asynchronous call to an external dependency, such as a database or a file, the thread is immediately returned so it can serve other incoming requests. When the external call finishes, an available thread is used to process the remainder of the request.

This way, you can improve the scalability of your service dramatically. Please be aware however, both for the exam and on the job, that you should use asynchronous calls only for I/O-bound operations. Using it on CPU-bound operations is a waste of resources on your server. Because CPU-bound operations require a thread to process, an asynchronous call would just pick a different thread and then switch back to another thread when it finishes.

> **MORE INFO** **ASYNCHRONOUS METHODS**
>
> Objective 4.1 gives you more information on how to create asynchronous calls. This is an important part of the exam, and you should make sure that you understand it.

Implementing streaming actions

When working with Web API, you will definitely encounter a situation in which you want to return a large amount of data. Maybe you need to return a lot of data from a database or binary data.

What you want to do is return a stream to the client so the client can fetch data as needed. The server will respond to this request and send the data to the client. You do this by using a special class called PushStreamContent. This method enables you to progressively push data to the client.

Listing 4-1 shows an example. This code uses a timer to send some data to the connected clients every second. The PushStreamContent class is used and is initialized with the OnStreamAvailable method.

LISTING 4-1 Using PushStreamContent

```
using System;
using System.Collections.Concurrent;
using System.IO;
using System.Net;
using System.Net.Http;
using System.Threading;
using System.Web.Http;

namespace StreamingApp.Controllers
{
    public class PushContentController : ApiController
    {
        private static readonly Lazy<Timer> _timer =
                new Lazy<Timer>(() => new Timer(TimerCallback, null, 0, 1000));
        private static readonly ConcurrentDictionary<StreamWriter, StreamWriter>
            _outputs = new ConcurrentDictionary<StreamWriter, StreamWriter>();

        public HttpResponseMessage GetUpdates(HttpRequestMessage request)
        {
            Timer t = _timer.Value;
            request.Headers.AcceptEncoding.Clear();
            HttpResponseMessage response = request.CreateResponse();
            response.Content = new PushStreamContent(OnStreamAvailable, "text/plain");
            return response;
        }

        private static void OnStreamAvailable(Stream stream, HttpContent headers,
                                                TransportContext context)
        {
            StreamWriter sWriter = new StreamWriter(stream);
            _outputs.TryAdd(sWriter, sWriter);
        }

        private static void TimerCallback(object state)
        {
            foreach (var kvp in _outputs.ToArray())
            {
                try
                {
                    kvp.Value.Write(DateTime.Now);
                    kvp.Value.Flush();
                }
                catch
                {
                    StreamWriter sWriter;
                    _outputs.TryRemove(kvp.Value, out sWriter);
                }
            }
        }
    }
}
```

If you run this code, you get a request that ends only when you close the browser. This way, you can send a lot of data in packages to the client.

Thought experiment

Implementing a Web API

In this thought experiment, apply what you've learned about this objective. You can find answers to these questions in the "Answers" section at the end of this chapter.

You are the architect and lead developer on a new project. You are going to build the back end for a new app. The app will be used by health care services to track patient records. Depending on the access privileges of the users, they can view and edit patient status, such as notes and images like x-rays or other scans. To support the bring-your-own-device policy, the app will be distributed to a multitude of devices running on Windows, Windows Phone, iOS, and Android, and on the web. You already have two hospitals with thousands of staff members who are going to beta test your app.

1. Why is Web API well-suited for this scenario?

2. Are you planning to use any of the following techniques?

- Content negotiation
- HttpMessageHandler
- Dependency injection
- Action filters
- Streaming

Objective summary

- Through content negotiation, a Web API service can both retrieve and send data in different formats. The format the client expects is specified in the Accept header.
- Actions can use parameters. The value for these parameters can come from the URL or from the request body.
- HttpMessageHandler can be used to create message handlers that are added to the request pipeline. They can inspect and modify the current request and response.
- Dependency injection is implemented through an IDependencyResolver. A lot of open source tools can help you with this.
- Action filters and exception filters can be used to execute code before or after an action or in case of an exception.
- Streaming can be used when you need to send a large amount of data to a client. You use the PushStreamContent class to stream data.

Objective review

Answer the following questions to test your knowledge of the information in this objective. You can find the answers to these questions and explanations of why each answer choice is correct or incorrect in the "Answers" section at the end of this chapter.

1. Which of the following media types are valid default options for an Accept request header? (Choose all that apply.)

   A. application/json

   B. application/xml

   C. gzip

   D. en-us

2. Which of the following request headers can be sent to help perform content negotiation? (Choose all that apply.)

   A. Accept

   B. Accept-Charset

   C. Accept-Request

   D. Accept-Language

3. You want to create an attribute that executes when an exception happens anywhere in your application. Which steps do you take? (Choose all that apply.)

   A. Inherit from ActionFilterAttribute.

   B. Inherit from ExceptionFilterAttribute.

   C. Add the custom attribute to your controllers.

   D. Add the custom attribute to HttpConfiguration.Filters.

Objective 4.3: Secure a Web API

Although making a Web API available and ubiquitous has obvious benefits, like any other service or application, correctly securing resources is of the utmost importance. It's easy to take security for granted or assume that security through obscurity can keep your resources safe. Some people are overly concerned with security, and their careers suffer as a result. The number of such cases and the magnitude of the damage done, however, pale in comparison with that of people who don't take it seriously and assume that obscurity can keep their resources safe.

Security needs should be determined by carefully weighing the costs and the benefits, and those needs usually exist in a rather delicate balance. Web APIs expose corporate resources to the Internet, which makes security a broader concern than more limited or sandboxed applications. The fact that you can access Web APIs by simple use of a web browser makes them particularly useful and opens them up to just about every technology and platform out there. At the same time, this openness carries with it an increased attack vector precisely because access is so simple. There are many very useful features to make sure that your Web API is only used by people you want to use it and that they use it in ways you intend for them to.

Fortunately, the leading authentication mechanisms employed by Web API developers are the standard ones built into IIS that you are mostly likely familiar with if you have implemented secure web applications over the years.

For the exam, it's important to understand the different authentication strategies you can use. You also need to understand the threats, such as cross-site request forgery (XSFR), that face your Web API and that you need to protect against.

This objective covers how to:

- Authenticate and authorize users
- Implement HTTP Basic authentication over SSL
- Implement Windows Authentication
- Enable cross-domain requests
- Prevent cross-site request forgery
- Implement and extend authorization filters

Authenticating and authorizing users

Although Web APIs are usually designed to allow easy access to the services, there will be people you specifically want to access the service and people you want to prohibit from accessing it. You'll want customers, licensed users, and perhaps other employees to be able to access the service. People who have been blocked, spammers, license violators, and other random miscreants should be restricted.

Even though you might specifically allow someone to use your service, there are things you'll probably want to restrict them from doing (even if you assume that no one has any malevolent intentions, there are still reasons you want to restrict what can be done).

Authentication

Authentication is the process of knowing the identity of a given user. If you have a subscription service, you want to make sure that the subscriber is the one who's using the service. Your exact needs will vary from application to application and company to company. In some cases, you might be comfortable with validating a user's identity via a user name and password combination. Sometimes your needs are much more specific, however.

If you have a subscription service in which a user name and password are the only requirements for authentication, someone could post the credentials to a public forum, and several people could use the account in direct violation of your license policy. There are well-known and well-meaning services that provide such information so that people can bypass registration systems to read content. If it's important to you that only one user employs a given account/password combination, you need to take many more steps to ensure they are authenticated correctly. Fortunately, the Web API framework has a rich set of tools to employ authentication, so the scheme you use for your given service can range from nonexistent to quite sophisticated.

Authorization

Authorization is the process of deciding whether a given user can perform a given action. You might allow a given user to access your service, but limit the number of requests the user can make in a given time period. You might want to restrict the operations the user can perform (for instance, executing read-only queries as an anonymous user, inserts as an authenticated user, and updates as an administrative user).

The degree of control you exert over each of these can and will vary with the application; experience with the users; resources you have available; and many, many more factors.

Implementing HttpBasic authentication

HttpBasic authentication is the simplest and easiest to use of each of the available mechanisms. Basic authentication provides a simple user name/password authentication mechanism over plaintext. They are Base64–encoded header values that most web technologies that require authentication can work with. Table 4-4 lists some of the advantages and disadvantages of HttpBasic authentication.

> **MORE INFO** **BASIC AND DIGEST ACCESS AUTHENTICATION**
>
> Basic authentication is defined in RFC 2617. It's a mature and well-known mechanism, so it can be easily used for most authentication scenarios that aren't overly complicated. To read the RFC and learn more of the generic details, see *http://www.ietf.org/rfc/rfc2617.txt*.
>
> Digest authentication is the next simplest form of authentication. However, instead of credentials being sent in plaintext, they are encrypted with some input from the server.

TABLE 4-4 Trade-offs related to HttpBasic authentication

Advantage	Disadvantage
Well known, mature internet standard	User credentials are transmitted in the request.
All major browsers support it (Internet Explorer, Safari, Firefox, Chrome, Opera, etc.)	The credentials are not just part of the request; by default they are transmitted in plaintext. This makes them vulnerable to interception unless additional steps are measured.
Simplest of the currently implemented protocols	User credentials continue to be sent in subsequent requests.
Natively supported by Internet Information Services (IIS)	There is no way to explicitly log out after authentication except by explicitly ending the browser session.
	Highly vulnerable to XSRF unless additional measures are taken.

Server-side processing

The list of strengths and weaknesses of Basic authentication in Table 4-4 helps to set the context for how Basic authentication works. Processing a request for a resource protected with Basic authentication proceeds as follows:

1. An initial request is executed. If the resource necessitates Basic authentication, a response code of Unauthorized (401) is returned. This response includes a WWW-Authentication header that specifies that the server supports Basic authentication.

2. A subsequent request is sent to the server, this time with the client credentials contained in the Authorization header.

   The WWW-Authentication header for basic authentication resembles the following:

```
WWW-Authenticate: Basic realm="Realm Name"
```

Client-side processing

After the 401 response code is returned with the authentication header, the client begins to assemble an authorization header. Construction of this header proceeds in the following steps:

1. The indicated Username and Password combination are concatenated into one scalar value. The Username and Password combination are separated by a colon. If a Username value of JohnQPublic had a corresponding Password value of !*MyPa55w0rd*!, the value sent would be the following:

```
JohnQPublic:!*MyPa55w0rd*!
```

2. The combined string literal referenced in the first step is encoded using a Base64 encoding. Assuming the concatenated value in Step 1, the encoded Base64 representation would be the following:

```
Sm9oblFQdWJsaWM6ISpNeVBhNTV3MHJkKiE=
```

3. A final value is constructed by adding the authentication method, the literal Basic, and then the encoded string specified in the previous step. The resulting value looks like the following:

```
Authorization: Basic Sm9ob1FQdWJsaWM6ISpNeVBhNTV3MHJkKiE=
```

There are two extremely noteworthy items to keep in mind. First, although the encoded user name and password string isn't easily readable at first glance, encoded does not mean encrypted. Any application that monitors traffic to and from a client is also very capable of instantaneously decoding the Base64 value. Absent encryption or hashing, the user name and password are completely exposed to unwanted monitoring. To be blunt about it, unless the transfer happens via HTTPS, Basic authentication is *not* secure. Remember for the exam that you should never use Basic authentication without SSL.

Second, the entire authentication process is valid only within the context of a realm. If you examine the initial response shown in the Server Side Processing section, a core component of the header is the realm name. After the credentials are authenticated, they are valid only within the specified realm.

Enabling SSL

To make your Basic authentication secure, you need to enable SSL. For local testing, you can just enable SSL in ISS Express from Visual Studio by setting the SSL Enabled to True in the properties window of Visual Studio. The value of the SSL URL can then be used for testing.

To enforce HTTPS in your Web API service, you can use the following attribute:

```
public class RequireHttpsAttribute : AuthorizationFilterAttribute
{
    public override void OnAuthorization(HttpActionContext actionContext)
    {
        if (actionContext.Request.RequestUri.Scheme != Uri.UriSchemeHttps)
        {
            actionContext.Response = new HttpResponseMessage
                            (System.Net.HttpStatusCode.Forbidden)
            {
                ReasonPhrase = "HTTPS Required"
            };
        }
        else
        {
            base.OnAuthorization(actionContext);
        }
    }
}
```

This attribute inspects a request and checks to see whether it is using HTTPS. If not, an error is returned to the client stating that HTTPS is required.

You can now add this attribute to specific controllers or even as a global attribute to make sure that HTTPS is used to secure your Web API.

When moving to a production environment, you require a certificate to enable SSL. For testing, you can create such a certificate by using the MakeCert.exe tool.

> **MORE INFO** **USING MAKECERT**
>
> For more information on how to use MakeCert to create certificates, see *http://msdn. microsoft.com/en-us/library/bfsktky3.aspx.*

Implementing Windows Authentication

When Basic authentication is not sufficient or appropriate (for intranet applications, for example), it might be beneficial to use Windows Authentication. Windows Authentication enables users to be authenticated using their Windows login credentials, Kerberos, or NTLM. Windows Authentication is easy to use from both a client and server perspective, but it has clearly defined boundaries that might immediately exclude it as an authentication mechanism (see Table 4-5).

TABLE 4-5 Trade-offs related to Windows Authentication

Advantage	Disadvantage
Natively supported by Internet Information Services (IIS).	Requires client-side NTLM or Kerberos support.
Client credentials are not transmitted in the request.	This is a poor choice to use for consumer-facing systems.
If the client is a member of the same domain as the server, the client does not need to enter credentials.	This is a poor choice to use for consumer-facing systems.

Server-side processing

Very little needs to be done on the service side portion of the application. Inside the Web API's web.config file, the Authentication element's Mode property should simply be set to Windows. In your actual application, there will be several other elements inside the <system.web> element, but the following snippet shows what's needed to enable Windows Authentication:

```
<system.web>
    <authentication mode="Windows" />
</system.web>
```

Client-side processing

To operate correctly, requests made using the web browser necessitate browser support of the Negotiation authentication scheme. Virtually all popular web browsers and their currently supported versions support Negotiation, so there's not much else needed if access will be performed through the browser exclusively.

If a .NET client application is being used instead of the browser, use of the HttpClient class enables the use of Windows Authentication. Doing this via the HttpClient class is extremely easy, and a working example is shown here. All that's needed is the creation of an HttpClientHandler class. The UseDefaultCredentials property should then be set to true. This can all be done in one operation:

```
HttpClientHandler ClientHandler = new HttpClientHandler
{
    UseDefaultCredentials = true
};
```

After the HttpClientHandler instance is created, simply pass it to the constructor of the new HttpClient instance used in your application and you are done!

Preventing cross-site request forgery

Cross-site request forgery (referred to both as CSRF and XSRF), can be a very serious problem for developers of Web API services. XSRF is a known attack vector for many of the authentication methods used with Web API and is something that you absolutely must understand (just like SQL injection with data access technologies) to make sure that you don't open your system up unsuspectingly to the wrong people. However, preventing XSRF from being a problem is not a terribly difficult task.

Before you learn about preventing XSRF from happening, you need to understand what it is, when it can happen, and when you need to protect against it.

What is XSRF?

Many attacks (such as SQL injection, cross-site scripting or cross-site request forgery attacks) are well known and have been documented for a long time. SQL injection attacks have been widely discussed in security and application development literature for many years, yet many sites are still successfully attacked by using it because the original vulnerability was never covered or hardened. It's understandable that a site might be vulnerable to a newly found attack, but leaving unpatched holes around well-known vulnerabilities is a recipe for disaster and is simply irresponsible behavior of the IT staff deploying such vulnerabilities.

There are many automated tools that enable relatively unsophisticated users to probe and launch an attack around almost every well-known vulnerability, and there is no shortage of people willing to employ them. Attackers span a very large profile number, including each of the following: state-sponsored hackers, people engaged in industrial and/or sovereign espionage, people seeking retribution with a company or entity for some perceived wrong, "script-kiddies" (novice hackers who know enough to use an automated tool, but little more), disgruntled former employees, and many more.

Here's an example of an XSRF: You are logged into the Windows Azure Management Portal and, while reading your email, you click what you think is a link for a discount for additional servers in Windows Azure, but ultimately causes your browser to navigate to *https://manage.windowsazure.com/api/DeleteAllData* without your realizing it. Although this path doesn't really exist in the Management Portal, such a path could exist; if it did, you could be in some real trouble! This is one reason why such a delete via a Web API service should be done via an HttpDelete instead of an HttpGet because clicking that link performs a GET, not a DELETE request. Even so, you are still not immune if the link comes from another web page that actually sends a DELETE request!

EXAM TIP

If you're unfamiliar with XSRF, *https://www.owasp.org/index.php/Cross-Site_Request_Forgery* provides a wonderful and very thorough description of it. A summary description of XSRF is simply when a different website or application (even email links) attempts to access a resource that requires authentication to trigger some action that has some side effect.

When are you vulnerable?

It is great to know that potential vulnerabilities exist but it's even better to know whether your system is at risk or not to these vulnerabilities, and XSRF is no exception. XSRF can be a valid attack vector to your system when you use an authentication mechanism in which your web browser "keeps you logged in" or when you allow cross-site communication.

Authentication mechanisms such as Basic authentication or cookie-based authentication are vulnerable. XSRF is about the browser implicitly trusting a URL and sending the credentials it has stored with a request to that website.

Imagine that you are browsing a page at *http://malicious.com/haha* while you are waiting for a Windows Azure deployment to finish, when all of a sudden some JavaScript code makes an attempt to send an AJAX DELETE request to *https://manage.windowsazure.com/api/DeleteAllData*. Because your browser trusts windowsazure.com and has credentials for the Management Portal, those credentials are used when the website malicious.com sends a request to the Management Portal. If Microsoft didn't attempt to protect the request against XSRF, you would have a bad day!

This also means that native applications that send the user credentials on each request are not vulnerable for XSRF attacks on your Web API. Only browser-based clients that cache user credentials are vulnerable.

How to protect from XSRF

Okay, you know all about what XSRF is and when it is likely to be a problem. But what do you do about it? Fortunately, this isn't a terribly difficult problem and is something you can fairly easily implement.

First of all, with authentication mechanisms, you are vulnerable when using systems where you are authenticated and that state is effectively a flag. This is a problem with Basic authentication because normally the browser stores your authentication token, which is to avoid prompting the user for authentication on each request. This stored token can be used by other sites to execute requests on your service.

Protecting an MVC web application is fairly easy using the Html.AntiForgeryToken method in a view and the ValidateAntiForgeryToken attribute on your action method.

An AntiForgeryToken is a hidden field in your HTML that looks something like this:

```
<input name="__RequestVerificationToken" type="hidden"
value="saTFWpkKNOBYazFtN6c4YbZAmsEwGOsrqlUqqloi/fVgeV2ciIFVmelvzwRZpArs" />
```

This value is randomly generated and is also stored in a cookie that is passed to the user. The attribute on your action method makes sure that the value in the cookie and the one submitted in the form data from the client match. This is secure because a potential attacker won't know the value from the cookie and can't use this value to forge a valid form post.

For Web API, you can follow the same principle. You want to send a value both in a cookie and in the generated HTML. Then on the server, you compare these two values and make sure that they match. You can send the antiforgery token by using the Html.AntiForgeryToken in your HTML.

Checking the token in your Web API controller takes a couple of steps:

1. Get the token from the cookie.

2. Get the token from the form data.

3. Pass the values for the token from both sources to AntiForgery.Validate.

4. Send an Unauthorized when validation fails.

5. In code, this process would look something like this:

```
CookieHeaderValue cookie = Request.Headers
  .GetCookies(AntiForgeryConfig.CookieName)
  .FirstOrDefault();

if (cookie == null) return;

Stream requestBufferedStream = Request.Content.ReadAsStreamAsync().Result;
requestBufferedStream.Position = 0;
NameValueCollection myform = Request.Content.ReadAsFormDataAsync().Result;
try
{
    AntiForgery.Validate(cookie[AntiForgeryConfig.CookieName].Value,
        myform[AntiForgeryConfig.CookieName]);
}
catch
{
    throw new HttpResponseException(
        new HttpResponseMessage(HttpStatusCode.Unauthorized));
}
```

Of course, you can move this code to an attribute or handler to avoid repeating it in each action method.

There are some nuances to this solution if your client is not an MVC application or if you have the content type set to Streaming instead of the default Buffered setting. With other client types, you need an equivalent to the Html.AntiForgeryToken method to persist the tokens and send them back to the server. The solution to the content type setting is an even more complicated topic that is beyond the scope of this book and the exam, but you are encouraged to investigate that topic on your own.

EXAM TIP

Of course, it's not required to memorize all the code involved in checking the antiforgery tokens. You do need to make sure that you understand the ideas behind it. Sending two values, one in a cookie and one in the form data, and making sure these values match is the basic idea for protecting against XSRF. A good practice is to create a simple Web API that is vulnerable to XSRF and then protecting it so you understand all steps involved. An example can be found at *http://www.dotnetcurry.com/ShowArticle.aspx?ID=890*.

Enabling cross-domain requests

For security reasons, browsers prohibit AJAX calls to resources residing outside the current origin. This is called the same-origin policy. The origin refers to the URL of your website. For example, if your website is located at *http://www.contoso.com*, you can't make an AJAX request to *http://www.someotherwebsite.com*. You also can't make request to your domain with another protocol (such as https instead of http) or on a different port (81 instead of 80 for example).

With websites storing authentication data in cookies that are maintained by the browser, this policy is important for avoiding XSRF attacks.

But sometimes you want to explicitly allow a cross-domain AJAX call. This is called cross-origin resource sharing (CORS).

A simple way to allow CORS is to add a setting to your web.config file:

```
<system.webServer>
    <httpProtocol>
        <customHeaders>
            <add name="Access-Control-Allow-Origin" value="*"/>
            <add name="Access-Control-Allow-Headers" value="Origin, X-Requested-With,
Content-Type, Accept" />
        </customHeaders>
    </httpProtocol>
</system.webServer>
```

This code adds a special header to your request, stating that CORS is allowed. However, this will allow CORS for all your Web API services and for all clients that are calling it, so this is not the most secure way to enable CORS. Microsoft created a NuGet package to allow CORS in Web API on a more granular level.

You can install this package by executing the following line in your Package Manager Console (the -pre flag is required at this time because the package is still prerelease):

```
Install-Package Microsoft.AspNet.WebApi.Cors -pre
```

You now get a new extension method on your HttpConfiguration object:

```
config.EnableCors();
```

By calling this method in the static WebApiConfig.Register method, you enable CORS support for your application. Now you can add attributes to controllers or action methods to enable CORS like this:

```
public class ValuesController : ApiController
{
    [EnableCors(origins: "http://localhost:26891", headers: "*", methods: "*")]
    public IEnumerable<string> Get()
    {
        return new[] { "Value1", "Value2" };
    }
}
```

In this case, you allow CORS access to the Get method from *http://localhost:26891*. All other domains don't have access. You can also apply this attribute to a complete controller or even globally to your Web API configuration.

Implementing and extending authorization filters

Web API offers the default AuthorizeAttribute to make sure that all users who access your controller or action method are authenticated. After applying this attribute, users who are not authenticated can't access your service.

If the default behavior of the AuthorizeAttribute is not sufficient, you have a couple of options for extending it:

- **AuthorizeAttribute** Extend this class to perform authorization logic based on the current user and the user's roles.

- **AuthorizationFilterAttribute** Extend this class to perform synchronous authorization logic that is not necessarily based on the current user or role.

- **IAuthorizationFilter** Implement this interface to perform asynchronous authorization logic—for example, if your authorization logic makes asynchronous I/O or network calls. (If your authorization logic is CPU-bound, it is simpler to derive from AuthorizationFilterAttribute because then you don't need to write an asynchronous method.)

The default AuthorizeAttribute works on white listing, meaning that you pass it the roles for users and roles that are explicitly allowed to access a resource. You can create a custom attribute for black listing, as Listing 4-2 shows.

LISTING 4-2 A BlackListAuthorizationAttribute

```
public class BlackListAuthorizationAttribute : AuthorizeAttribute
{
    protected override bool IsAuthorized(HttpActionContext actionContext)
    {
        IPrincipal user = Thread.CurrentPrincipal;

        if (user == null) return true;

        var splitUsers = SplitString(Users);

        if (splitUsers.Contains(user.Identity.Name, StringComparer.OrdinalIgnoreCase))
            return false;
        var splitRoles = SplitString(Roles);

        if (splitRoles.Any(user.IsInRole)) return false;

        return true;
    }

    private static string[] SplitString(string original)
    {
        if (String.IsNullOrEmpty(original))
        {
            return new string[0];
        }

        var split = from piece in original.Split(',')
                    let trimmed = piece.Trim()
                    where !String.IsNullOrEmpty(trimmed)
                    select trimmed;
        return split.ToArray();
    }
}
```

By overriding the IsAuthorized method, you can implement your own custom authorization logic.

Deriving from IAuthorizationFilter or the AuthorizationFilterAttribute is also possible, but is also more difficult. If you need to implement some basic authorization logic on the exam, you can almost always derive from AuthorizeAttribute and override the IsAuthorized method. Only when you have authorization logic that's not based on the current user or role should you look at the other classes.

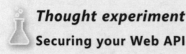
Objective summary

- Authentication is the act of making sure that a user is logged in. Authorization determines the specific rights of an authenticated user.

- HttpBasic authentication is an easy way to implement authentication for your Web API. Because it submits credentials in plaintext, you should never use it without SSL.

- Windows Authentication is well-suited for intranet scenarios. Users can log in with their Windows account.

- XSRF is an attack on your Web API in which the attacker uses the cookies stored in the browser to trick the service into processing requests under the identity of the user. You protect yourself against XSRF by using antiforgery tokens in both a cookie and the form data.

- Cross-domain requests can be enabled for a Web API by settings in the web.config file or by using the Microsoft.AspNet.WebApi.Cors NuGet package.

- Authorization is normally handled by the AuthorizeAttribute. You can extend authentication by deriving from this attribute or from low-level classes such as AuthorizationFilterAttribute or IAuthorizationFilter.

Objective review

Answer the following questions to test your knowledge of the information in this objective. You can find the answers to these questions and explanations of why each answer choice is correct or incorrect in the "Answers" section at the end of this chapter.

1. You want to enable HTTPS for your Web API, and you want to make sure that none of the developers forgets about this requirement. How do you do this?

A. Create a custom ApiController base class from which all developers need to inherit.

B. Create an HttpsRequiredAttribute and add it to each controller.

C. Create an HttpsRequiredAttribute and add it to the global collection of attributes.

D. Use MakeCert.exe to create an HTTPS certificate.

2. You are building a Web API to be used by third-party websites, and you want to reach as many users as possible. You want to protect your service from XSRF attacks. Which requirement do you state for your third parties?

A. Force them to use ASP.NET MVC so you can easily authenticate requests.

B. Require them to include both a cookie and a form value with a unique token.

C. Use the ValidateAntiForgeryToken attribute on your Web API service.

D. Use Windows Authentication.

3. You want to extend the default authentication mechanism of Web API. You want to have an attribute that you can place on a couple of action methods to log nonauthenticated requests. What do you do?

A. Inherit from IAuthorizationFilter to implement the custom logic.

B. Inherit from AuthorizeAttribute to implement the custom logic.

C. Inherit from AuthorizeFilterAttribute to implement the custom logic.

D. Create an HttpMessageHandler that you attach to specific routes.

Objective 4.4: Host and manage a Web API

Conceptually similar to a WCF Service or Workflow, a Web API needs to be made accessible to clients. There are two primary mechanisms available for hosting a Web API: IIS and self-hosting. This objective covers both of these hosting options. For the exam, you should understand the possibilities in hosting your Web API. You should also understand the classes involved in self-hosting your Web API.

This objective covers how to:
- Self-host a Web API
- Host Web API in an ASP.NET app
- Host ASP.NET Web API on Windows Azure platform
- Restrict message size
- Configure the host server for streaming

Self-hosting a Web API

To self-host a Web API, you can use any of the project templates that create an executable application (Windows Service, Windows Forms application, console application, and so on). There are two essential steps to the process:

1. Create an instance of the HttpSelfHostConfiguration class.

2. Create an instance of the HttpSelfHostServer.

First, you need a project, and then you need the proper assemblies.

Installing Web API self-hosting

Even if you have installed ASP.NET Web API, you still need to install the self-hosting framework if you have not already done so. In Visual Studio 2012, this process is simple using NuGet.

The NuGet package is called Microsoft ASP.NET Web API Self Host (see Figure 4-6). After it is installed, you have references to both System.Web.Http and System.Web.Http.SelfHost assemblies.

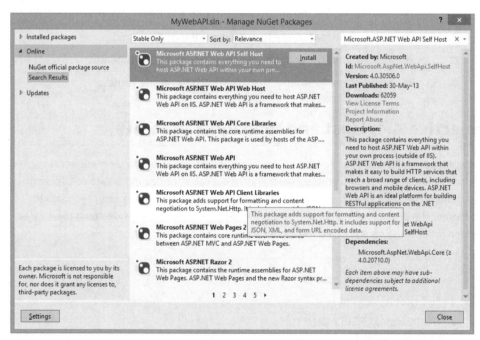

FIGURE 4-6 Installing Microsoft ASP.NET Web API Self Host package

Creating your Web API hosting server

After installing the package, you can create your own hosting server. Assuming that you have a Web API project called MyWebApi with a ValuesController, the following code shows how to host this in a simple console application. (Note that you might have to run Visual Studio as Administrator in order to successfully open up the port you specify here.)

```
class Program
{
    static void Main(string[] args)
    {
        Console.WriteLine("Starting Web API Server. Please wait...");
        if (typeof(MyWebApi.Controllers.ValuesController) == null)
        {
            // work-around
            return;
        }

        var hostConfig = new HttpSelfHostConfiguration("http://localhost:8080");
        hostConfig.Routes.MapHttpRoute("API Name",
            "api/{controller}/{action}/{id}",
            new { id = RouteParameter.Optional });

        using (HttpSelfHostServer server = new HttpSelfHostServer(hostConfig))
        {
            server.OpenAsync().Wait();
            Console.WriteLine("Press [ENTER] to close");
            Console.ReadLine();
            server.CloseAsync().Wait();
        }
    }
}
```

That's all you need; now run it. With the application running, navigate your browser to *http://localhost:8080/api/Values/* to call your Web API.

In this code, there are three significant things going on: the workaround, the hosting configuration, and the server.

The workaround is important though uninteresting. If you don't forcefully do something to load a type from your Web API project, the self-hosting framework will not actually host the controllers in that project. Load a single type from the assembly, as the previous code does, and then all your controllers should be loaded into the self-hosting framework. An alternative option is to never use an MVC Web API project and to simply build your models and controllers in your hosting project (they aren't much more than simple classes). This workaround is required only when the controllers exist in a separate assembly.

The HttpSelfHostConfiguration class has two constructor overloads, both of which accomplish the same task. The first accepts a string parameter representing the base address where the service will be accessed. The second accepts a value of type Uri. Simply declare and instantiate a new instance using either of the constructors, as shown here:

```
var hostConfig = new HttpSelfHostConfiguration("http://host:Port");
```

If you think back to earlier coverage, the template used automatically created a file named WebApiConfig.cs in the App_Start folder, which added a Register method that called the MapHttpRoute method of the Routes property of the HttpConfiguration class. The same thing needs to be done here, except you call the method on the Routes property of the HttpSelfHostConfiguration instance:

```
HostConfig.Routes.MapHttpRoute("API Name",
    "api/{controller}/{id}",
    new { id = RouteParameter.Optional });
```

For all practical purposes, the configuration works the same way it did in the autogenerated instance.

EXAM TIP

Remember to add the default route when self-hosting your Web API. In a web application, this configuration is automatically created for you, but you should add it yourself when self-hosting.

After the HttpSelfHostConfiguration class is created, you just need to create a new instance of the HttpSelfHostServer class, passing the configuration to the constructor. After it is created, the OpenAsync method needs to be called, and the rest is taken care of for you.

```
using (HttpSelfHostServer SelfServer = new HttpSelfHostServer (HostConfig))
{
    SelfServer.OpenAsync().Wait();
    Console.WriteLine("Press any key to close");
    Console.ReadLine();
}
```

Hosting Web API in an ASP.NET app

In terms of ASP.NET, IIS hosting has been around the longest and is the most mature. There's not much surprise in terms of hosting in IIS, but it's necessary to cover just because of its prevalence both on the exam and in the real world.

To start the process, open up Internet Information Services Manager. You can navigate to it directly or run **inetmgr** from the command prompt. Although not absolutely necessary, it is generally advisable to create a separate application pool in which the service will be hosted. The configuration is shown in Figure 4-7.

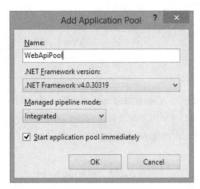

FIGURE 4-7 Add Application Pool dialog box

Next, you need to either create a new website under the Sites node or add an application or virtual directory under an existing one. From there, create a new application or virtual directory, as shown in Figure 4-8. (If you create a new application, make sure that you select the application pool created in the previous step.)

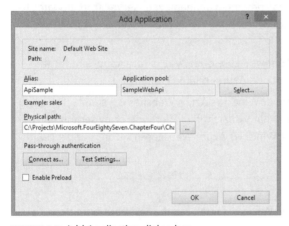

FIGURE 4-8 Add Application dialog box

After it is in place, the application should be live, and you can access it by referencing the website, application, or virtual directory.

Hosting services in a Windows Azure worker role

In addition to self-hosting or using IIS, you can use the Windows Azure platform to host your application. By hosting your Web API in Windows Azure, you get all the benefits of Windows Azure, such as scalability and availability, without having to worry about the underlying infrastructure.

When deploying to Windows Azure, you have three options:

- Windows Azure Websites
- Windows Azure Cloud Services
- Windows Azure Virtual Machines (VMs)

Windows Azure Websites enable you to create highly scalable websites quickly. You don't need to learn a new application model or manage machines. If you don't have specialized requirements that require you to use cloud services or VMs, Windows Azure Websites is a great choice.

Windows Azure cloud services offer you greater control. You have more instance sizes to choose from and you can create a more complex multitier architecture. For example, you can have your Web API as a public-facing Web Role that communicates with a Worker Role through a queue to achieve maximum scalability. It also offers you ways to configure IIS and other machine configurations when your role starts. You can even remote desktop to your machine.

Using a VM on Windows Azure gives you complete control. You use only the underlying Windows Azure infrastructure. You need to completely manage your server, from updates to configuration. Although this gives you a lot of freedom, for a Web API service, it isn't usually required.

Knowing the different models that Windows Azure offers you is very important for the exam, not only for Web API but for all Windows Azure–related content.

Deploying a Web API to a cloud service or Windows Azure Websites is a simple task using Visual Studio. By using the publish options that Visual Studio offers you or by setting up continuous deployment, you can deploy your Windows Azure Websites in seconds and a cloud service in minutes.

EXAM TIP

Deploying a Web API to Windows Azure Websites doesn't require any more extra steps than deploying it to an on-premises IIS.

MORE INFO **DEPLOYMENT OPTIONS**

For more information on the different deployment options and how to use them, see Chapter 5, "Deploying web applications and services."

Restricting message size

When hosting your Web API, you want to make sure that your services won't go down when extremely large messages are sent to your service. Sometimes attackers try to send extremely large messages to attack your servers. This is called a denial of service (DoS) attack, and you want to protect yourself against this.

When self-hosting your Web API, you can do protect yourself by using the MaxReceivedMessageSize and MaxBufferSize properties on the HttpSelfHostConfiguration object:

```
var config = new HttpSelfHostConfiguration(baseAddress);
config.MaxReceivedMessageSize = 1024;
config.MaxBufferSize = 1024;
```

When hosting your Web API in IIS, you can use the default web.config configuration for setting the maximum length of your request:

```
<httpRuntime maxRequestLength="1024" />
```

Configuring the host server for streaming

Sometimes you do want to allow large files to be sent to your Web API. Maybe you have a controller that's used for uploading files or some other requirement that can lead to a large amount of data being submitted.

When hosting your service on IIS, you can configure your service to allow large files to be sent to a particular controller.

You do this by making sure that your controller is not using the default buffered mode that Web API uses. Buffering the data that it receives can use a lot of memory when receiving large files. Instead, you want to use a streaming mode.

The decision to switch from buffered to streaming mode is made by an implementation of the IHostBufferPolicySelector class. This class has a method, UseBufferedInputStream, that can return true or false. Currently, there is one default implementation for this interface: WebHostBufferPolicySelector. For incoming requests, this class just returns true, meaning that all requests are buffered.

The easiest way to change this behavior is to inherit from the WebHostBufferPolicySelector class and override the UseBufferedInputStream method like this:

```
public class StreamingPolicySelector : WebHostBufferPolicySelector
{
    public override bool UseBufferedInputStream(object hostContext)
    {
        var context = hostContext as HttpContextBase;

        if (context == null) return true;

        return !string.Equals(
            context.Request.RequestContext.RouteData.Values["controller"].ToString(),
            "uploading",
            StringComparison.InvariantCultureIgnoreCase);
    }
}
```

This policy sees whether the request targets the uploading controller to determine whether streaming should be used. You can now use the StreamingPolicySelector like this:

```
config.Services.Replace(typeof(IHostBufferPolicySelector),
                        new StreamingPolicySelector());
```

Next to switching from buffered to streaming input, you also have to configure the regular
ASP.NET properties such as maxAllowedContentLength and maxRequestLength in your
web.config file. This will make sure that large requests are not rejected by IIS before reaching
your controller. You configure these properties like this:

```
<system.webServer>
  <security>
    <requestFiltering>
      <requestLimits maxAllowedContentLength="2147483648" />
    </requestFiltering>
  </security>
</system.webServer>
<system.web>
  <httpRuntime maxRequestLength="2097152" />
</system.web>
```

Configuring streaming for self-hosting is not so elegant. Instead of being able to use
streaming on a per-controller basis, you need to enable streaming for all requests. You do this
by using the TransferMode property on the HttpSelfHostConfiguration object. You can enable
request streaming, response streaming, or both:

```
selfHostConf.TransferMode = TransferMode.StreamedRequest;
//responses only
selfHostConf.TransferMode = TransferMode.StreamedResponse;
//both
selfHostConf.TransferMode = TransferMode.Streamed;
```

Thought experiment
Choosing your hosting options

In this thought experiment, apply what you've learned about this objective. You can
find answers to these questions in the "Answers" section at the end of this chapter.

You can find answers to these questions in the "Answers" section at the end of this
chapter.

You are planning the deployment of your Web API and you are looking at the various options you have. You are looking at self-hosting, hosting in IIS on your own
server, and hosting on Windows Azure Websites.

1. What are the pros and cons for self-hosting?

2. If you choose to use IIS, do you want to use an on premise IIS or Windows Azure
   Websites?

Objective summary

- After the service is built, it needs to be hosted before clients can consume it.
- IIS, self-hosting, and Windows Azure are currently viable and fairly simple options, each with its respective costs and benefits.
- Self-hosting has two core components: the configuration (implemented through the HttpSelfHostConfiguration class) and the server (implemented through the HttpSelfHostServer). The NuGet package Microsoft ASP.NET Web API Self Host helps you with configuring self-hosting.
- ASP.NET Web API can also be hosted in IIS. When you create a default ASP.NET MVC project with the Web API template, you get an ASP.NET project that's ready for IIS hosting.
- You can also host your service on Windows Azure. Windows Azure Websites is a quick and easy way. If you need more control, you can use cloud services or a VM.
- Restricting the message size for your service protects you against denial of service attacks. You can use the HttpSelfHostConfiguration to configure the MaxReceivedMessageSize and MaxBufferSize when self-hosting or the httpRuntime element in the web.config when hosting in IIS.
- Streaming is important when dealing with large request or response sizes. In a web environment, you have fine-grained control for enabling streaming. For a self-host, you can enable streaming for the complete service.

Objective review

Answer the following questions to test your knowledge of the information in this objective. You can find the answers to these questions and explanations of why each answer choice is correct or incorrect in the "Answers" section at the end of this chapter.

1. Which of the following items must be provided to use the self-host option? (Choose all that apply.)

   A. AspnetSelfHostConfiguration

   B. HttpSelfHostConfiguration

   C. AspnetSelfHostServer

   D. HttpSelfHostServer

2. You are changing the hosting of your Web API to use a Windows Service. Originally, the configuration was automatically generated by the Visual Studio template. What do you need to do to make this work?

   A. Nothing; the existing configuration will work.

   B. Copy the existing configuration to a new class in the host project.

C. Add a new class of type HttpSelfHostConfiguration. Use the Initialize method to call the MapHttpRoute method.

D. Add a new class of type HttpSelfHostConfiguration. Use the Routes property to call the MapHttpRoute method.

3. You are working for a large company that has a lot of maintenance engineers on the road. You are going to develop an app to support their work remotely with publicly available data. You are looking at your deployment options. You know the app will be used during office times. Throughout the day, you will have five thousand users of your service. What deployment option do you choose?

A. You buy extra servers for your on-premise data center.

B. You use Azure Cloud Services to host your Web API as a Web Role.

C. You use Azure websites.

D. You deploy Azure Virtual Machines to host your Web API.

Objective 4.5: Consume Web API web services

At the risk of pointing out the obvious, the main reason to create Web API web services is so that they can be consumed. Building a service and hosting it provides no real value unless it's consumed. When thinking about services, you probably think about using some kind of AJAX to call your service from a web page. However, that's definitely not the only option to call a service.

When other applications start integrating with your service, they want to call your service from their own code. This is why the exam also focuses on using HttpClient. It's important to understand how this class works and when you should use it, both in the real world and for the exam.

This objective covers how to:

- Consume Web API Services using HttpClient
- Send and receive requests in different formats

Consuming Web API services

When consuming a Web API from code, you can use the HttpClient class. This class enables you to send requests to a service and work with the results. You set up an HttpClient like this:

```
/// <summary>
/// This should be whatever the port number is that your
/// Web Server is hosting the Web API project on
/// </summary>
private const int port = 30930;
private HttpClient GetClient(string mediaType)
```

```
{
    String baseUri = @"http://localhost:" + port;
    HttpClient apiClient = new HttpClient();
    apiClient.BaseAddress = new Uri(baseUri);
    apiClient.DefaultRequestHeaders.Accept.Add(
            new MediaTypeWithQualityHeaderValue(mediaType));

    return apiClient;
}
```

Depending on the media type that you pass to this method, you receive data in a format such as JSON or XML. This is not the easiest format to work with. If you have access to the Web API project, you can reuse the models (for example, by moving them to a separate assembly and referencing the assembly from both projects). If you don't have access to the original class definitions, it pays to create them yourself so you can easily work with the data returned from the service.

There are several methods available, but there are four specific ones you will use regularly: HttpGet, HttpPost, HttpPut, and HttpDelete.

HttpGet via GetAsync

To execute an HttpGet operation, you can use the GetAsync method of the HttpResponseMessage class. Although the call seems completely intuitive and operates as you'd expect, it's important to understand the nuances of it. There is no synchronous Get method defined in the HttpResponseMessage class—only GetAsync.

```
Task<HttpResponseMessage> GetResponse = client.GetAsync("api/values/1");
```

It's easy to use this method with the new async and await features that were added to C# 5:

```
HttpResponseMessage GetResponse = await client.GetAsync("api/values/1");
```

EXAM TIP

Make sure that you understand how async and await work. Although they're not explicitly mentioned in the exam objectives, they're a fundamental part of C# 5. If you haven't studied async and await yet, see *Exam Ref 70-483: Programming in C#*, by Wouter de Kort, or start at *http://msdn.microsoft.com/en-us/library/vstudio/hh191443.aspx*.

After the first operation completes, the response has an IsSuccessStatusCode property populated. As you'd expect, if the request was successful, this value will be true. You can now read the content body of the request like this:

```
using (var client = GetClient("application/json"))
{
    HttpResponseMessage message = await client.GetAsync("/api/values/1");
    if (message.IsSuccessStatusCode)
    {
        Foo  result = await message.Content.ReadAsAsync<Foo>();
    }
}
```

In this case, the service returns an object of type Foo, which is just a simple class with two properties:

```
public class Foo
{
    public string Value1 { get; set; }
    public int Value2 { get; set; }
}
```

> **NOTE** **READASASYNC**
>
> ReadAsAsync, as used in the previous tests, is actually not a method off of the Content property, but an extension method. Although it might not be obvious, you can find it if you reference and include the System.Net.Http.Formatting assembly and namespace.

HttpPost via PostAsync and PostAsJsonAsync

To execute an HttpPost, you can use the PostAsync method or the PostAsJsonAsync method, which simplifies things a little. To use the PostAsJsonAsync method, simply use an instance of the data transfer class and a MediaTypeFormatter. The MediaTypeFormatter is an abstract class, so you need to use one of the derivations. If you want to use the Json implementation, the JsonMediaTypeFormatter class is available:

```
using (var client = GetClient("application/json"))
{
    var message = await client.PostAsJsonAsync<Foo>("api/values",
        new Foo
        {
            Value1 = "Bar",
            Value2 = 42
        });
}
```

HttpPut via PutAsync and PutAsJsonAsync

Executing an HttpPut request can be accomplished using the PutAsync method or the PutAsJsonAsync method. Performing a Put is nearly identical to performing a Post.

```
using (var client = GetClient("application/json"))
{
    var message = await client.PutAsJsonAsync<Foo>("api/values",
        new Foo
        {
            Value1 = "Bar",
            Value2 = 42
        });
}
```

HttpDelete via DeleteAsync

The last of the set is the DeleteAsync method to execute an HttpDelete. It requires only a reference to the URI for the operation. There is no payload as there is with PostAsync and PutAsync. Also, there are no JSON or XML equivalents. Simply call the DeleteAsync method specifying the URI. Web API extracts the id property from the route and maps the call to the Delete method based on the HTTP verb:

```
using (var client = GetClient("application/json"))
{
    message = await client.DeleteAsync("api/values/1");

}
```

Exception handling

When calling methods on a Web API service, you sometimes get an error back. Any responses that contain an HTTP error code are simply returned like any other request unless you specify otherwise. If the request did not process correctly, there's nothing you can do with respect to processing of the expected business logic (unless that happens to be exception code).

As such, you have two options. The first is to parse each response and try to extract the status code token each time. If you find one of the error codes returned (any code in the 500–599 range), you can run your error logic. This generally creates a lot of work and is error prone. The HttpClient class allows a very convenient shortcut here, but you have to specifically opt in. If you set the EnsureSuccessStatusCode property of the client instance, the framework throws a specific HttpRequestException if any of the error codes are encountered. In the following code, the first sample just processes normally, and no exception is thrown. The second sample traps the exception and enables you to respond accordingly.

```
try
{
    message = await client1.GetAsync("BadUri");
}
catch (HttpRequestException errorCode)
{
    Debug.WriteLine(errorCode.Message);
}

try
{
    message = await client2.GetAsync("BadUri");
    message.EnsureSuccessStatusCode();
}
catch (HttpRequestException errorCode)
{
    Debug.WriteLine(errorCode.Message);
}
```

Sending and receiving requests in different formats

There are several current options with respect to media type (MIME) formats. Supported types include the following

- application/xml
- text/html
- image/png
- application/json
- Custom format

When a request is processed, and the message contains a valid body, the format of the message body is contained in the Content-Type. If a request is processed and contains text/html, the following response header is returned:

```
HTTP/1.1 200 OK
Content-Length: 952
Content-Type: text/html
```

On the other end, the client can specify a specific value(s) in the Accept header. This request simply instructs the server which type or types it is expecting. To specify text/html, the following is sent:

```
Accept: text/html
```

Multiple formats can be specified by simply separating the values with a comma. There is out-of-the-box support for XML, JSON, and form-urlencoded data. These can be expanded upon by writing your own custom formatters. There are two base classes that you can inherit from to create your own formatters:

- MediaTypeFormatter
- BufferedMediaTypeFormatter

The main difference between these two options is whether they'll support asynchronous operations. The MediaTypeFormatter should be used if asynchronous support is needed; the BufferedMediaTypeFormatter otherwise.

To use either, first you create a class that inherits from the respective type:

```
public class CustomerCsvFormatter : BufferedMediaTypeFormatter
{
    public class CustomerCsvFormatter()
    {
      SupportedMediaTypes.Add(new MediaTypeHeaderValue("text/csv");
    }

}
```

The constructor necessitates the use of the Add method of the SupportedMediaTypes class. The method should be called, specifying a MediaTypeHeaderValue, as shown here:

```
public class CustomerCsvFormatter : BufferedMediaTypeFormatter
{
    public class CustomerCsvFormatter()
    {
        SupportedMediaTypes.Add(new MediaTypeHeaderValue("text/csv");
    }
}
```

Next, you need to override the CanWriteType and CanReadType for each of the types that you want to support. If the type supports deserialization, CanReadType should return true; otherwise, it needs to be set to false. With this in place, one last step needs to be performed on the formatter. The WriteToStream method needs to be implemented in either case (otherwise, the type can't be transmitted). If the formatter needs to support deserialization, the ReadFromStream method needs to be overridden and implemented as well. There is ample documentation on MSDN, but the implementation is both straightforward and dependent on the type you are supporting.

After creating your formatter, you need to add it to the configuration for Web API. You do this by calling the following:

```
config.Formatters.Add(new CustomerCsvFormatter());
```

EXAM TIP

To prepare for the exam, you can follow the example at *http://www.asp.net/web-api/ overview/formats-and-model-binding/media-formatters*. It shows you how to create your own formatter and how to use it.

Thought experiment
Consuming a Web API

In this thought experiment, apply what you've learned about this objective. You can find answers to these questions in the "Answers" section at the end of this chapter.

You are integrating with a third-party Web API service. The service enables you to execute CRUD operations to work with time records.

1. How can you map the HttpClient methods to the standard CRUD operations?

2. Why is it useful to create classes that map to the return values of the service?

Objective summary

- All operations (Get, Post, Put, Delete, and more) are supported by the HttpClient class.
- Each standard operation is suffixed with Async. You should use async and await to work with these operations.
- The Result property of the HttpResponseMessage returns the entirety of the response, including the status code and message details.
- Unless the EnsureSuccessStatusCode method is called, any requests that receive an error code in the response will not throw any exceptions.
- The format of the data in the response is directly governed by what the client requests. This can be JSON, XML, HTML, or even custom things such as CSV or other formats.

Objective review

Answer the following questions to test your knowledge of the information in this objective. You can find the answers to these questions and explanations of why each answer choice is correct or incorrect in the "Answers" section at the end of this chapter.

1. The HttpClient class you have implemented frequently receives error codes, but the application is not responding to them. What should you do?

   A. Trap the OnError event of the request.

   B. Set the EnsureSuccessStatusCode property to true and implement an exception handler in the OnError event.

   C. Call the EnsureSuccessStatusCode method and trap the HttpRequestException exception.

   D. Check the ResultStatusCode property and throw an exception if one of the error values is present.

2. You need to create a custom media type for vCards. The media formatter needs to access an XML file to get the format for specific vCards. What should you do? (Choose all that apply.)

   A. Create a formatter using the MediaTypeFormatter class.

   B. Create a formatter using the BufferedMediaTypeFormatter class.

   C. Add the formatter to each request at the client.

   D. Add the formatter to the Web API configuration on the server.

3. You have multiple HttpClient calls that can run independently of each other. You want to execute them as fast as possible. What should you do?

   A. Use the Result property of each HttpClient call to get the result as fast as possible.

   B. Use async/await to make sure that the calls run asynchronously.

   C. Use Task.WaitAll to execute the tasks in parallel.

   D. You can't execute asynchronous tasks in parallel.

Chapter summary

- Web API is built on top of HTTP. HTTP verbs are mapped to action methods on controllers.
- CRUD operations are supported by using HttpPost, HttpGet, HttpPut, and HttpDelete.
- Routing is used to map URLs to controllers.
- Web API supports content negotiation, so a user of your service can specify both the format of the request and the desired response format. By default, JSON and XML are supported.
- You can secure Web APIs by using Basic authentication and Windows Authentication.
- When using Basic authentication, you should use SSL to secure user credentials.
- XSFR is an important thread to protect yourself from by using specialized tokens.
- Services can be hosted in several different ways, including self-hosting, IIS, and Windows Azure.
- Self-hosting is facilitated by using the HttpSelfHostConfiguration and HttpSelfHostServer classes.
- The HttpClient class can be used to call a Web API.

Answers

This section contains the solutions to the thought experiments and answers to the objective review questions in this chapter.

Objective 4.1: Thought experiment

1. By using the HTTP verbs, you use HTTP as the foundation of your service. The HTTP verbs are supported by browser and by the HttpClient and by all other platforms. This way, you can use a single URL and use the verb to specify what action you want to take. This decouples the client code from implementation details such as method names.

2. By using content negotiation, you don't couple your service to a specific technology. Instead, you support multiple clients, all with their own requirements. The clients can then choose the format to work with.

Objective 4.1: Review

1. **Correct answers:** A, C, D

   A. **Correct:** HttpGet requests are necessary to view the data to moderate it.

   B. **Incorrect:** HttpPost is used to add new items. Editors don't need to add new items (but users do).

   C. **Correct:** Deletions should be done through the HttpDelete operation.

   D. **Correct:** HttpPut can be used for modifying posts.

2. **Correct answer:** C

   A. **Incorrect:** HttpGet should be used only to retrieve data, not to insert it.

   B. **Incorrect:** HttpHead can be used to retrieve information about the request, but not to insert records.

   C. **Correct:** To insert a new record, the HttpPost operation should be called.

   D. **Incorrect:** The HttpPut operation should be used for modifying data. HttpPost is a better candidate for inserting data.

3. **Correct answer:** D

   A. Incorrect: HttpPost and HttpPut need to be implemented here; an HttpGet does not solve the core requirement. You also need to use the AcceptVerbs attribute to allow multiple verbs to be used.

   B. Incorrect: HttpPost and HttpPut need to be implemented here; an HttpGet does not solve the core requirement. You also need to use the AcceptVerbs attribute to allow multiple verbs to be used.

   C. Incorrect: The operations are correct but need to be implemented with the AcceptVerbs attribute.

   D. Correct: The AcceptVerbs attribute should be implemented as indicated here, and both the HttpPut and HttpPost operation should be supported.

Objective 4.2: Thought experiment

1. All devices are capable of executing web requests. By using Web API, you open your service to all devices that you want to support.

2. The following explains what you should use:

   - Through content-negotiation, all clients can work with data in a format that's suitable for the device. It's one of the foundational features of Web API.

   - You can use an HttpMessageHandler if you have any cross-cutting concerns that should apply to all requests or to specific routes. At this moment, you have no use for handlers, but that could change.

   - Dependency injection is an important part of each modern architecture. You can use it to create a loosely coupled system that can easily be unit tested.

   - You should use the AuthorizeAttribute, which is an implementation of an action filter. You can also create your own attributes if you want to run code before or after an action runs.

   - Streaming is important because you are supporting thousands of users, and you need to transmit large amounts of data for the images.

Objective 4.2: Review

1. **Correct answers:** A, B

   A. Correct: application/json is a supported format type.

   B. Correct: application/xml is a supported format type.

   C. Incorrect: gzip could be supported, but would require special implementation.

   D. Incorrect: en-us is a culture and region formatter, not a media type.

2. **Correct answers:** A, B, C, D

   A. **Correct:** Accept is a valid request header type.

   B. **Correct:** Accept-Charset is a valid header value.

   C. **Correct:** Accept-Encoding is a valid encoding.

   D. **Correct:** The Accept-Language corresponds to the natural language and is supported.

3. **Correct answers:** B, D

   A. **Incorrect:** For exception handling, you shouldn't inherit from ActionFilterAttribute. Those filters execute on each request, independently of an exception happening.

   B. **Correct:** ExceptionFilterAttribute is the correct base class for filters that should execute whenever an exception happens.

   C. **Incorrect:** Adding the attribute to all your controllers is error prone. Instead, you can apply the attribute globally.

   D. **Correct:** By adding the attribute to the global collection of filters, you apply it to all controllers and action methods in one step.

Objective 4.3: Thought experiment

1. No. Windows Authentication is not suited for consumer-facing applications. It should be used for intranet applications.

2. Yes. Because you are storing user credentials in a cookie for the web application, your application is vulnerable for XSRF attacks.

3. Because your back end won't be called by other websites through AJAX, CORS is not important. Only when you have AJAX calls coming from other origins should you enable CORS.

Objective 4.3: Review

1. **Correct answer:** C

   A. **Incorrect:** Developers can forget to inherit from the custom controller. This is no safe way to implement the requirement.

   B. **Incorrect:** If a developer forgets to add the attribute to a controller, the controller will be accessible through HTTP.

   C. **Correct:** Adding the attribute to the global collection of attributes makes sure that it is automatically applied to all controllers.

   D. **Incorrect:** MakeCert is used to create a test certificate that you can use on your development machine. It doesn't force your application to HTTPS.

2. **Correct answer:** B

   A. **Incorrect:** Forcing your customers to use ASP.NET MVC to develop their websites doesn't increase your user base. This is not something you can state as a requirement in the real world.

   B. **Correct:** This is the basic idea behind the antiforgery token solution that ASP.NET MVC offers. By comparing the two values, you can validate the request origin.

   C. **Incorrect:** ValidateAntiForgeryToken can be used only with ASP.NET MVC.

   D. **Incorrect:** Windows Authentication isn't possible with a consumer-facing application.

3. **Correct answer:** B

   A. **Incorrect:** IAuthorizationFilter is a very low-level interface. You should inherit from this interface only if you have any asynchronous work that doesn't involve the current user or role.

   B. **Correct:** By inheriting from this attribute, you get a fully implemented authorization attribute that you can easily extend.

   C. **Incorrect:** You should extend this class only to perform synchronous authorization logic that is not necessarily based on the current user or role.

   D. **Incorrect:** It's easier to inherit from the AuthorizeAttribute. By directly adding the attribute to specific methods, you can control when to run the code.

Objective 4.4: Thought experiment

1. Self-hosting is really easy to set up. You can use it for things such as integration tests or for hosting your Web API on a server that doesn't have IIS installed. However, ASP.NET hosting offers you all the mature features that IIS has, which is a big plus.

2. Windows Azure Websites has the big advantage of completely outsourcing the infrastructure. You get a robust infrastructure with easy scalability options. You pay only for what you use. However, an on-premises server is totally under your control. Sometimes this is a requirement for data security.

Objective 4.4: Review

1. **Correct answers:** B, D

   A. **Incorrect:** AspNetSelfHostConfiguration does not exist and is not a valid option.

   B. **Correct:** HttpSelfHostConfiguration is one of the two required classes needed to self-host.

   C. **Incorrect:** AspNetSelfHostServer does not exist and is not a valid option.

   D. **Correct:** HttpSelfHostServer is the second of the two required classes needed to self-host.

2. **Correct answer:** D

    A. Incorrect: Without specifying a configuration, the host will not operate correctly. You need the HttpSelfHostConfiguration class to start the host and set up the api route.

    B. Incorrect: As it stands, a copy of the existing configuration does not work because the HttpSelfHostConfiguration class needs to be used.

    C. Incorrect: Although the HttpSelfHostConfiguration should be used, the Routes property is what you use to access the MapHttpRoute method.

    D. Correct: The Routes property on the HttpSelfHostConfiguration class has the MapHttpRoute method necessary to configure Routes.

3. **Correct answer:** C

    A. Incorrect: Because your data is publicly available, you don't face any security issues when moving your service to the cloud. Because you have a fluctuating user load, the elasticity of the cloud can help you. Deploying to Azure websites is the easiest solution.

    B. Incorrect: Cloud Services are an option, but because you are only deploying a Web API service, it's much easier to use Azure websites.

    C. Correct: Azure websites saves a lot of time and cost upfront. Because you pay for each minute you use, you can save costs by scaling your service down outside office times. When you have a high user load, you can automatically add extra servers to make sure your service performs.

    D. Incorrect: Azure virtual machines require you to manage all servers yourself. You get the hardware from Azure, but it still requires configuring and updating your operating systems. Azure websites is a much easier solution to host a Web API.

Objective 4.5: Thought experiment

1. CRUD stands for Create, Read, Update and Delete. Create can be done with Post, Read with Get, Update with Put, and Delete with the Delete verb.

2. This way, you don't have to work with raw JSON or XML data. By deserializing the results to classes, you can easily use them in the rest of your code.

Objective 4.5: Review

1. **Correct answer:** C

   A. **Incorrect:** There is no OnError event, so trapping it would not work.

   B. **Incorrect:** The EnsureSuccessStatusCode is a method, not a property. You also need to catch an exception directly with a try/catch statement.

   C. **Correct:** The EnsureSuccessStatusCode method should be called, and an exception should be trapped of type HttpRequestException.

   D. **Incorrect:** Checking the status code would work, but you would need to check each value in the range of 500–599. The EnsureSuccessStatusCode method is a better way to do this.

2. **Correct answers:** A, D

   A. **Correct:** You should inherit from the MediaTypeFormatter class if you want to execute any I/O or other asynchronous operation.

   B. **Incorrect:** You should use the MediaTypeFormatter base class so you can implement asynchronous I/O.

   C. **Incorrect:** The formatter should be added to the server configuration.

   D. **Correct:** You activate the formatter by adding it to the global Web API configuration on the server.

3. **Correct answer:** C

   A. **Incorrect:** Using the Result property blocks the asynchronous call until it's finished. This is not the fastest way.

   B. **Incorrect:** Although it runs the requests asynchronously, it doesn't run them in parallel.

   C. **Correct:** Task.WaitAll can be used to run multiple asynchronous requests in parallel.

   D. **Incorrect:** This is not true. Although async/await doesn't execute requests in parallel, you can do this by using other features of the Task Parallel Library such as Task.WaitAll.

CHAPTER 5

Deploying web applications and services

Designing and building your application are often perceived as the most important aspects of software development. However, after you have built your application, you have to deploy it to a production environment in which it can actually be used by your users.

When deploying your application, you face a wide range of possibilities. One important decision is where to run your application. You can choose to deploy your application or service to a private environment, in which you have your own servers; or you can choose to deploy it to Windows Azure, in which the cloud infrastructure that Microsoft provides will host your application.

But just choosing where to run your application is not the only challenge. In more complex applications, you have to configure databases, Internet Information Services (IIS) settings, assemblies, certificates, and other configuration settings.

Postponing thinking about deployment to the last phase of your development process can lead to unforeseen problems. This is why techniques such as *continuous integration* (continuously merging the work that developers are doing throughout the day) and *continuous deployment* (continuously deploying new features in an automated way) are popular. Being able to automate your deployment process in a reliable and repeatable way helps you constantly deliver new value to your users.

This chapter focuses on the different possibilities for deploying your application or service to an on-premises or cloud environment by using tools such as Web Deploy. It shows how to automate the process by using Team Foundation Server (TFS) and Team Foundation Service, and it helps you move to a continuous deployment strategy in which you can quickly respond to changes and deliver a great application.

Deploying web applications and services makes up approximately 19 percent of the exam questions.

Objectives in this chapter:

- Objective 5.1: Design a deployment strategy
- Objective 5.2: Choose a deployment strategy for a Windows Azure web application
- Objective 5.3: Configure a web application for deployment
- Objective 5.4: Manage packages by using NuGet

- Objective 5.5: Create, configure, and publish a web package
- Objective 5.6: Share assemblies between multiple applications and servers

Objective 5.1: Design a deployment strategy

Planning your deployment is an important part of your application design. If you design a nice scalable architecture and build a great application without planning for a deployment environment, you will face issues later on.

Deploying a simple application can be as easy as copying the files from your development PC to a live web server. For more complex applications, it can also be as complicated as using automated Windows PowerShell scripts to configure and deploy your application to multiple environments without any human action. This objective outlines the different deployment options you have to make an informed decision.

You can expect questions on the exam that focus on the differences between the various deployment strategies. For example, you need to know what is important when changing a deployment from a single server to a web farm.

> **This objective covers how to:**
> - Deploy a web application by using XCopy
> - Create an IIS install package
> - Deploy to web farms
> - Automate a deployment from TFS or Build Server

Deploying a web application by using XCopy

When working on your application or service in Visual Studio, you work with a lot of files. Some of those files contain code; others contain markup or configuration settings. When deploying your ASP.NET application to a production environment, a couple of those files are required:

- Global.asax
- Web.config
- Content files (JavaScript, CSS, images)
- Views
- Compiled assemblies

The easiest way to deploy files to a production environment is to do it manually. By using a *File Transfer Protocol (FTP)* connection or a *Remote Desktop* session, you can connect to your target server and copy the files.

These types of deployment are referred to as *XCopy deployments*. XCopy is a DOS command that stands for extended copy. It enables you to copy multiple files at once to a target destination. Today, the name XCopy is often used to describe a manual deployment. As you can understand, these types of deployment are useful only when your application has no special installation requirements, such as modifications to the registry or other files that are located outside of your application folder.

The XCopy DOS command has the following syntax:

```
xcopy /I /S /E <source path> <destination path>
```

The /I option indicates that you are copying a folder. The /S option specifies that you want to copy all subdirectories (and /E indicates to copy subfolders even if they are empty). By issuing this command, the whole content of the folder will be copied from source to target.

The XCopy command has a lot of options that you can use to configure what should be copied. For example, the */d* option specifies that only files that are newer should be copied. When regularly updating your website, the /d option can save you time by updating only the files that you have changed.

> **MORE INFO   XCOPY SYNTAX**
>
> For an overview of all the XCopy options, see *http://www.microsoft.com/resources/*.

Configuring IIS

The first time you copy the files for your website to your server, you need to configure the website. This is done in *Internet Information Services (IIS)*. IIS is a web server that you can use to host a wide range of applications on Windows, such as ASP.NET projects and WCF Services. You need to tell IIS where the folder for your website is located and how it should be made available to users.

> **MORE INFO   INSTALLING IIS**
>
> By default, IIS is not installed. For the steps to configure IIS on Windows 8 or on Windows Server 2012, see *http://www.iis.net/learn/application-frameworks/scenario-build-an-aspnet-website-on-iis/configuring-step-1-install-iis-and-asp-net-modules*.

Assume that you have created an ASP.NET Model-View-Controller (MVC) application that's located at C:\Development\MyApp, and you want to copy it to C:\inetpub\wwwroot\MyApp. To do this, run the following XCopy command from a console:

```
xcopy /I /S C:\Development\MyApp C:\inetpub\wwwroot\MyApp
```

You open Internet Information Services (IIS) Manager (see Figure 5-1) to configure a new website that points to this directory.

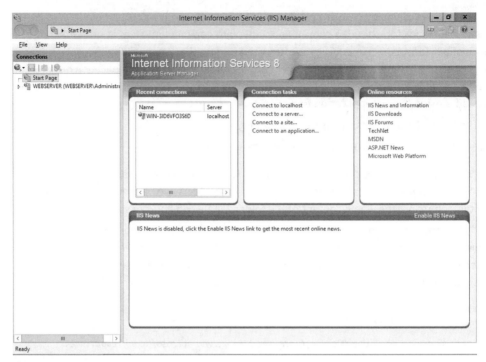

FIGURE 5-1 IIS Manager

For the exam, you need to know how to create and configure a website. You take the steps described here to create a website. Remember to give the site a name to distinguish it from other sites and point the website to the folder on your hard drive (for example, C:\inetpub\wwwroot\MyApp).

Normally, you assign a host name to your site that can then be used by IIS to map incoming requests on port 80 (the default port for HTTP traffic) to your website. You can also change the port number to something else, such as 81, and leave the host name empty so you can reach your site on the unique port number. Figure 5-2 shows the final configuration in IIS.

FIGURE 5-2 Configuration for adding a new website in IIS

After you configure your website, you can reach it by opening a browser and going to *http://localhost:81*. This sends a request to IIS that maps the port number to your configured website.

After you have configured your website, you can continue modifying and extending your code and then use the XCopy command to deploy a new version.

> **MORE INFO   CONFIGURING IIS**
>
> This is only a basic introduction to IIS, which is a complex product with a lot of options. On the exam, you aren't likely to be tested on specific IIS knowledge, but if you want to know more about how to configure IIS, see *http://www.iis.net/*.

Preparing a website for deployment

While the XCopy command is running, IIS notices the file changes and starts refreshing your website. This can lead to errors when your website will respond to requests while the deployment is only partially completed.

To avoid showing errors to your users, you can take your website temporarily offline while your deployment is running by placing a file called App_offline.htm in the root of your website. You can use this file to show a nice message to any user visiting your site. When the deployment is finished, remove this file so subsequent requests can be processed. Figure 5-3 shows an example of what this might look like.

FIGURE 5-3 An example App_offline.htm file

Your application domain can restart a couple of times while your website is being updated. Fortunately, ASP.NET offers a *web.config* setting that you can use to minimize the number of restarts. By adding the waitChangeNotification attribute to your web.config file, you can specify the number of seconds to wait before the application domain is allowed to restart:

```
<configuration>
  <system.web>
      <compilation debug="false" targetFramework="4.0" />
    <httpRuntime
      waitChangeNotification="5" />
  </system.web>
</configuration>
```

Tooling support for XCopy deployments

Using XCopy from the command line is probably not the preferred way of deploying your website. Besides not having a friendly user interface, another disadvantage of using XCopy is that all files in your project folder are copied to the destination folder. Fortunately, Visual Studio helps you with a couple of tools that can help you deploy your website in an easy way.

One such tool is the Copy Website Tool, which you can use when working with website projects. The Copy Website Tool enables you to copy files between a source and target website. The tool supports the following features:

- You can copy source files to the target site.

- You can copy files by using any connection protocol that is supported by Visual Studio, such as a local IIS, remote IIS, FTP, and HTTP (requires FrontPage Server Extensions).

- You can choose which files to synchronize from your source to the target server, or vice versa.

- You can automatically copy the App_offline.html file to the root of your website when it starts deploying and remove it when it finishes.

As you can see, deployment this way is easy, but when your application grows, these XCopy deployment styles have their limits. This is when you want to look at another tool: the Publish Website tool (for website projects) or the Publish option (for web application projects).

Creating an IIS install package

Released in 2009, Web Deploy enables you to create a Web Deploy package that contains not only the website that you want to publish but also other configuration options such as database settings, IIS settings, registry options, or assemblies that you want to put in the global assembly cache (GAC).

The Web Deployment Framework helps you by simplifying your deployment process. It enables you to deploy from Visual Studio 2012, IIS, the command prompt, and Windows PowerShell. It also helps you when you work with complex environments such as a web farm, where you can synchronize different web servers using Web Deploy.

The Web Deployment Framework has a set of built-in providers that enable you to configure the machine you want to deploy to.

When the deployment of your application becomes increasingly more complex, the Web Deployment Framework is the tool that you want to use.

> **MORE INFO**   **WEB DEPLOY PACKAGES**
>
> For more information on Web Deploy packages, see Objective 5.5, "Create, configure, and publish a web package."

Automating a deployment from TFS or Build Server

A couple of years ago, it was not unusual to ship a new version of a product only once every couple of years. At the start of a project, you would come up with a big list of features that the customer wanted, and you would start developing. The biggest problem with this approach is that it's hard for a customer to know upfront what he really wants, so a lot of projects didn't make their deadlines or didn't deliver a product that fully solved the needs of the customer.

Software development is slowly changing to resolve these types of issues. *Agile software development*, although sometimes used as a buzzword, is becoming the norm. Agile methods are based on an *iterative* and *incremental* process. Instead of doing a lot of design at the start of a project and delivering only when everything is ready, you start working in shorter periods. This enables you to evolve your requirements and the solution you are developing while the project is maturing.

Agile methodologies such as eXtreme Programming (XP) and SCRUM describe a process in which you engage the customer in your development process by showing them the progress you are making not just at the end of your development process but also continually during development. This requires a new way of deploying applications. If you want to show your application to your customer every two weeks, you can't spend days manually configuring and updating your servers. Instead, you want to automate the way your applications are deployed. Your software should be ready to be released at any time.

This idea is called *continuous delivery*. Of course, moving to such a process requires changes both in how you use your technology and in how you work. Because of this, a new culture, DevOps (Developer Operation), is emerging. In a DevOps culture, everyone works collaboratively on making sure that the application is always ready for deployment.

You can even go one step farther and move to *continuous deployment*, in which every change that is made by a developer on the team gets automatically deployed to the production environment. Of course, this is not something that every business wants, but having such a quick feedback loop can be useful. A continuous feedback loop exists between defining, developing, and operating your application.

EXAM TIP

The exam states that you should know how to automate a deployment from TFS or Build Server. Knowing the conceptual idea behind automatic deployments can help you if you get any scenarios about it on the exam.

To achieve continuous deployment, you need automation of all possible parts of your deployment process. Automating the deployment process begins with automating the integration of the work that the developers do. *Continuous integration* (CI) is all about making sure that your codebase stays healthy while developers make changes and check them in to source control.

You first want to make sure that the code compiles. You do this by using a Build Server that compiles the code whenever a developer checks in some new code. The Build Server of TFS supports this. You can create continuous integration builds that execute whenever a check-in finishes. If you have a lot of developers working on your project, you can switch your CI build to a rolling build. This will roll several check-ins into one build to improve performance.

After that, you want to verify the quality of the code. You do this by first executing *unit tests*, which are automated pieces of code that invoke some functionality in your system and verify the outcome. This can include the price calculation algorithm for your online web shop, the filter options for your search page, or another functionality that your application has. Unit tests don't have any external dependencies (such as a database or the file system). By using *dependency injection* and *mocking tools*, you replace the external dependencies by in-memory objects during your unit tests. This ensures that your unit tests execute quickly and that you can control the environment in which they run.

Unit tests can help you catch a lot of subtle bugs. However, they won't find any errors that occur only when working against real dependencies. This is where *integration tests* are used. In your web shop, for example, an integration test would create a new order and then check whether the data is correctly written to the database, the (test) payment provider is called, and an email is sent to the user. These tests are slower, and normally there aren't a lot of them. But they are an important piece of continuous integration.

Microsoft supports the whole continuous integration and continuous deployment process with its Application Lifecycle Management (ALM) solution in the form of TFS. TFS is a complete solution for managing your project, from code to bug tracking and change management. At BUILD 2011, Microsoft also announced a cloud-hosted version of TFS: Team Foundation Service. Both these ALM tools can help you set up continuous deployment.

EXAM TIP

For the exam, it's good to know that TFS is hosted on-premises on your own server. Team Foundation Service is hosted in the cloud and is updated every three weeks.

When using Team Foundation Service, you can set up a continuous deployment process when you host your website or services in Windows Azure. You can do this from a TFS or Git repository. You can also use other options, such as Github, Dropbox, or Bitbucket. If you look at Figure 5-4, you see a screen shot of the Windows Azure Management Portal. As you can see, you have an option available for setting up deployment from source control.

After selecting the location of your code, Windows Azure monitors your code repository for changes. When you do a new check-in, your code is automatically deployed to Windows Azure. Using the Management Portal, you can roll back deployments if something goes wrong. This is a nice integrated process. You don't have to make any manual changes to automatically deploy to Windows Azure.

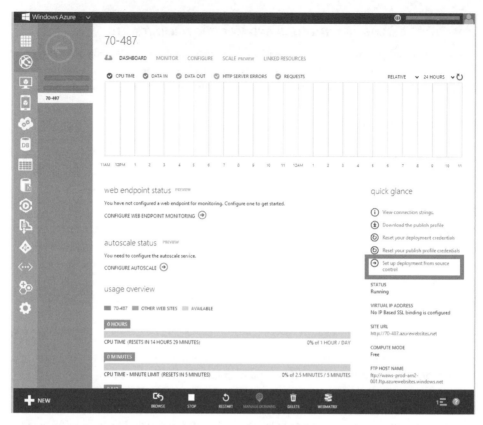

FIGURE 5-4 Configuring deployment from source control in Windows Azure

> **MORE INFO** **CONTINUOUS DELIVERY TO WINDOWS AZURE**
>
> For a walkthrough on how to set up continuous delivery to Windows Azure using Team Foundation Service, see *http://www.windowsazure.com/en-us/develop/net/common-tasks/publishing-with-tfs/.*

Achieving the same level of automation can also be done from an on-premises version of TFS. Your applications are built by the MSBuild command-line tool. This tool enables you to create a Windows Azure package from your code. If you create a new cloud project, you can run the following command from within your project folder to get a Windows Azure package:

```
MSBuild /target:Publish /p:PublishDir=\\myserver\drops\
```

After testing this command on your Build Server and making sure that everything works correctly, you can now use this command to further automate your build.

You do this by editing the Build Definition files that TFS uses. These files contain a workflow that describes all the steps you want TFS to take to build your project. If you add the Publish command to your workflow, your automatic build creates a Windows Azure package. You can use special Windows PowerShell commands to deploy the package to Windows Azure as a part of your build.

> **MORE INFO** **CONTINUOUS DELIVERY TO WINDOWS AZURE**
>
> For a walkthrough on how to set up continuous delivery to Windows Azure using an on-premises TFS, see *http://www.windowsazure.com/en-us/develop/net/common-tasks/ continuous-delivery/.*

Deploying to web farms

When you expect a high load on your application, you need some way to make sure that your application stays responsive. A simple way to achieve better performance is to buy better hardware and increase the capacity of the server you are running your application on. You can do this by adding more memory, a faster CPU, a solid-state drive (SSD), or other better-quality hardware. This is called *scale up*. Especially with a database server, adding more memory can give you a huge performance improvement. But scale up has its limitations. Specialized server hardware can be expensive, especially when you also need a backup server in case your main one fails.

Instead of scaling up, you can also *scale out*. This means that you use multiple servers that all work together to host your website or service. Those servers can all be composed of commodity hardware, and together they form what's called a *distributed environment* or *web farm*. Of course, there are other costs that come into play when scaling out. You will need more licenses for software and more space in your server racks, and you will probably have a higher power consumption.

EXAM TIP

It's important to know the difference between scaling up and scaling out for the exam. Make sure that you understand the advantages and disadvantages of both solutions.

This is why cloud solutions such as Windows Azure are so attractive. Instead of buying and maintaining all those servers yourself, you just pay for the capacity you need on a pay-as-you go basis. If your workload differs throughout the day, month, or even year, you can use the elastic capabilities of Windows Azure to add or remove servers from your web farm. Now that Windows Azure has shifted to a model in which you are billed for the minutes you use a service, this can save you a lot of money.

A web farm uses some kind of *load balancer*. It can be a software implementation, such as Windows Network Load Balancing, or some dedicated hardware. The load balancer is responsible for distributing the requests across all your servers and making sure that they are used in the most efficient way. By having multiple servers, you can increase the reliability of your application. When a server fails for any reason, the load balancer detects this and won't send any requests to this failed server anymore.

The exam objectives state that you should know how to design a deployment strategy for a web farm because deploying an application to a web farm does require extra work.

Normally, you need to configure only one server. Now you need to create the IIS applications and application pools on each server and make sure that they are configured exactly the same everywhere (this includes encryption certificates, optional components, and other extensions to IIS). When you use Windows Azure, a lot of those steps are automatically taken care of.

One other thing you need to take care of is the way you deal with *session state*. In ASP.NET and WCF, you can use a unique per-user session store to store data between requests. Normally, this data is stored in the memory of your server. When using a web farm, subsequent user requests can be handled by different servers; this leads to problems when the session data is stored in memory. To resolve this, you need to move the session state out of process to an external machine or even a database. That way, the session data of a user can be accessed by all servers in your web farm. For the exam, it's important to know the different session states:

- InProc is the default setting that stores the session data in memory on the server.
- StateServer stores the session data in a separate process called the ASP.NET state service.
- SQLServer mode stores session state in a SQL Server database.
- Off mode disables session state.

You can also choose to activate session affinity, meaning that the user requests will be handled by the same server during the user's session. However, not all load balancers support this.

Instead of using session state, you can also use other techniques, such as storing data in the query string or in the HTML that you send to the client. Of course, this can't be used when your data is sensitive, and it shouldn't be allowed to be seen or modified by the user.

> **MORE INFO**   **CONFIGURING SESSION-STATE MODES**
>
> For more information on how to configure the different session-state modes, see *http://msdn.microsoft.com/en-us/library/ms178586.aspx*.

Objective summary

- An XCopy deployment refers to a simple deployment in which you copy all the files necessary for your website or service to the server.
- When the deployment of your application becomes more complex, you can use the Web Deployment Framework for your deployment needs.
- Being able to continuously deploy your application is becoming more and more important. TFS, Team Foundation Service, and Windows Azure offer a nice end-to-end solution for automating your deployment.
- A web farm can be used when you want to increase the performance and reliability of your application. A web farm uses extra servers (scaling out) to serve requests. You need to prepare your application to be able to run it on a web farm.

Objective review

Answer the following questions to test your knowledge of the information in this objective. You can find the answers to these questions and explanations of why each answer choice is correct or incorrect in the "Answers" section at the end of this chapter.

1. You need to deploy an application that requires some changes to the registry. Which deployment strategy do you use?

    A. Copy the website.

    B. FTP client.

    C. Web Deploy.

    D. A web farm.

2. You are planning to deploy your application to an on-premises web farm. You use session state to store some user data. Which session state mode do you use? (Choose all that apply.)

   A. InProc

   B. StateServer

   C. Off

   D. SQL Server

3. You want to adopt a continuous deployment strategy. Which elements are important? (Choose all that apply.)

   A. Build server

   B. Unit tests

   C. Integration tests

   D. A web farm

Objective 5.2: Choose a deployment strategy for a Windows Azure web application

A lot of the concepts discussed in the previous objective apply to deploying a cloud service to Windows Azure. However, because of the unique features that Windows Azure offers, you have additional questions and options when deploying your application.

This objective focuses on deploying an application to Windows Azure with minimal downtime in an automated way. The exam requires you to know the advantages of the various strategies. You should also be able to understand the various configuration files.

This objective covers how to:

- Perform an in-place upgrade and Virtual IP (VIP) Swap
- Configure an upgrade domain
- Create and configure input and internal endpoints
- Specify operating system configuration

Performing an in-place upgrade and VIP Swap

When updating servers in an on-premises web farm environment, you normally stop each server one at a time, update it, and then bring it back online. This way, the other servers remain active while your upgrade is processing, and they can keep serving user requests.

Windows Azure offers you three ways to update your application:

- Delete and redeploy
- In-place update
- VIP Swap

Deleting your cloud service and redeploying it is easy, but it requires downtime for your service. You need to use the delete and redeploy option when you want to change the number of endpoints or the ports of endpoints. Any effective firewall changes require a delete and redeploy strategy. The same is true for updating certificates and migrations to another guest operating system. For other changes, you can use a VIP Swap or an in-place update, which doesn't require any downtime.

Configuring an upgrade domain

When you perform an in-place upgrade, Windows Azure stops the instances, updates them, and then brings them back online. Windows Azure doesn't stop all instances at once. Instead, it stops instances that are assigned to the same upgrade domain.

When Windows Azure creates new services in a cloud service deployment, they are automatically assigned to an upgrade domain. When updating your service, Windows Azure cycles through your update domains and takes them offline one by one. This way, you won't have any downtime on your service.

If you look at the instance tab in your Management Portal, you can see the instances and the update and fault domains they are assigned to (see Figure 5-5).

STATUS	ROLE	SIZE	UPDATE DOMAIN ↑	FAULT DOMAIN 🔎
✓ Running	XCopyDeployment	Small	0	0
✓ Running	XCopyDeployment	Small	1	1

FIGURE 5-5 Instance settings in Windows Azure Management Portal

A *fault domain* is automatically assigned by Windows Azure. You need at least two instances spread across two fault domains to have maximum availability guaranteed by Windows Azure.

By default, you have a maximum of five update domains. You can control how many upgrade domains you have by using the upgradeDomainCount attribute in your ServiceDefinition configuration file. You can have a maximum of 20 upgrade domains.

You can update your cloud service from the Windows Azure Management Portal or from Visual Studio. To update from Visual Studio, you have to upload a certificate to Windows Azure that associates your computer with your online subscription. Figure 5-6 shows the New Subscription dialog box for creating a new subscription in Visual Studio.

FIGURE 5-6 Creating a new Windows Azure subscription in Visual Studio

You can also log in to the Windows Azure Management Portal and upload a package directly to your cloud service.

While your in-place upgrade runs, your upgrade domains are updated one by one. This means that if you have more than two upgrade domains, different upgrade domains run a different version of your application at the same time. This is something you need to take into account. If, for example, your database schema also changed, you can get runtime errors when your old instances are trying to access the database. To overcome this problem, you can use a different technique called VIP Swap.

Upgrading through a VIP Swap

A Windows Azure cloud service has two environments: production and staging. Both environments offer the same hardware, but they have different virtual IP (VIP) and service URLs. Because the staging and production environment are identical, you can perform what's known as a *VIP Swap*.

When you execute a VIP Swap, the VIP and service URL of your staging and production environment are switched. This means that you can upload a new version of your app to the staging environment, test it, and then bring it into production by executing a VIP Swap. For uploading your new version to the staging environment, you still have to use the in-place upgrade or the delete and redeploy strategy.

After your VIP Swap is finished, you have both production and staging environments that use resources (and thus cost you money). To avoid extra costs, you can delete the staging environment (which is the old production environment) after your VIP Swap is finished.

A VIP Swap enables you to bring a complete set of instances into production at once, avoiding different versions in production. However, in the practice it could be that existing connections persist for some time. This connection still points to the old deployment. This is something you should keep in mind when doing a VIP swap.

You execute a VIP Swap by uploading your updated project to the staging environment. If you then navigate to the Windows Azure Management Portal, make certain that your staging instances are running. You can then click the Swap button on your staging cloud service deployment (see Figure 5-7).

FIGURE 5-7 Swap option in the Windows Azure Management Portal

If you need to make changes to the service definition (such as number of endpoints, endpoint ports, or certificates), you need to use a VIP Swap (or redeploy your service). If there are no changes to the service definition, you can use the in-place update to update your staging environment.

Creating and configuring input and internal endpoints

Your cloud services in Windows Azure communicate with the outside world and with each other. Windows Azure helps you secure your roles by using strict rules that are enforced by settings in the firewall and in the operating system that hosts your role.

You can use both *input endpoints* and *internal endpoints*. An input endpoint is used for external connections to your role. These connections can be made over HTTP, HTTPS, or TCP. Internal endpoints are used for communication between the roles in the datacenter in which they are located. These internal endpoints can use HTTP and TCP.

When using input endpoints, you declare a unique port on which you want your role to listen. This port is used by the load balancer of Windows Azure to connect your role to the Internet. Your service can have 25 input endpoints defined, which can be distributed across your different roles. You can also declare 25 internal endpoints.

You declare a new internal or external endpoint in the ServiceDefinition.csdef file in your cloud project. When you create a new cloud project with one web role and one worker role, the file looks like this:

```xml
<?xml version="1.0" encoding="utf-8"?>
<ServiceDefinition name="WindowsAzure1" xmlns="http://schemas.microsoft.com/
ServiceHosting/2008/10/ServiceDefinition" schemaVersion="2013-03.2.0">
  <WebRole name="MyWebApp" vmsize="Small">
    <Sites>
      <Site name="Web">
        <Bindings>
          <Binding name="Endpoint1" endpointName="Endpoint1" />
        </Bindings>
      </Site>
    </Sites>
    <Endpoints>
      <InputEndpoint name="Endpoint1" protocol="http" port="80" />
    </Endpoints>
    <Imports>
      <Import moduleName="Diagnostics" />
    </Imports>
  </WebRole>
  <WorkerRole name="MyWorkerRole" vmsize="Small">
    <Imports>
      <Import moduleName="Diagnostics" />
    </Imports>
  </WorkerRole>
</ServiceDefinition>
```

> **NOTE** **MULTIPLE ROLES IN ONE CLOUD PROJECT AID**
>
> When using a cloud project you can add multiple roles to one single project—for example, a web role that's public for your users and a worker role that's internal and does all the processing. Those projects can be deployed together and form one single cloud project.

> **MORE INFO** **SERVICEDEFINITION SCHEMA**
>
> For a complete description of the ServiceDefinition schema, see *http://msdn.microsoft.com/en-us/library/windowsazure/ee758711.aspx*.

The web role has one input endpoint defined. This is the default endpoint that listens to port 80, the default port for HTTP traffic.

The worker role has no endpoints declared. You can add an input endpoint by adding the following XML to the WorkerRole element:

```
<Endpoints>
    <InputEndpoint name="WorkerRoleInput" port="8080" protocol="http" localPort="8080"/>
</Endpoints>
```

Now the load balancer forwards any incoming requests to port 8080 to your role. One thing to note is that when working with the local Windows Azure emulator, ports are re-mapped to avoid conflicts. The emulator takes the first port that's available on your local PC. This means that port 80 will be remapped to 81 (if it's not in use) and 8080 to 8081.

Inside your worker role, you can now use an HTTPListener to listen for incoming requests:

```
public override void Run()
{
    HttpListener listener = new HttpListener();
    listener.Prefixes.Add("http://*:8081/");
    listener.Start();

    while (true)
    {
        HttpListenerContext context = listener.GetContext();
        HttpListenerRequest request = context.Request;
        HttpListenerResponse response = context.Response;

        string responseString = "<HTML><BODY> Hello world!</BODY></HTML>";
        byte[] buffer = System.Text.Encoding.UTF8.GetBytes(responseString);
        response.ContentLength64 = buffer.Length;
        System.IO.Stream output = response.OutputStream;
        output.Write(buffer, 0, buffer.Length);
        output.Close();
    }
}
```

This code creates an instance of the HttpListener class and starts it to listen to port 8081. You then use the GetContext method to wait for an incoming request. When a request arrives, a string with an HTML page containing the words Hello World! is written. If you run this code and navigate to *http://127.0.0.1:8081* in your browser, you will see the text Hello World! returned from your worker role.

You can also edit the endpoint configuration of your project by using the editor in Visual Studio. Open the editor by double-clicking the name of your role in your cloud services project. You can see what the endpoints look like in Figure 5-8.

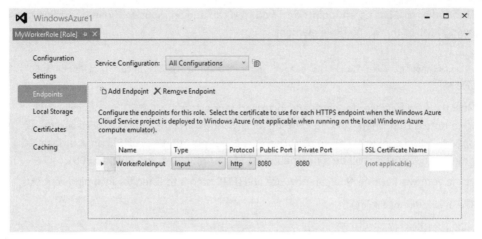

FIGURE 5-8 Editing endpoints in the Visual Studio editor

To select an input or internal endpoint, you can also choose the option of an InstanceInputEndpoint, also called *direct ports*. This way, you can use a range of ports on your public IP address that are then mapped to a port on your role instances. You define a direct port like this:

```
<InstanceInputEndpoint name="Endpoint2" localPort="1000" protocol="tcp">
    <AllocatePublicPortFrom>
        <FixedPortRange min="10016" max="10020"/>
    </AllocatePublicPortFrom>
</InstanceInputEndpoint>
```

The parent element specifies the local port you want to use on your roles and the protocol. The AllocatePublicPortFrom element then specifies a range of ports that you want to use publicly.

> **MORE INFO   CONFIGURING DIRECT PORTS**
>
> For more information on how to configure direct ports, see *http://msdn.microsoft.com/en-us/library/windowsazure/dn127053.aspx*.

Specifying operating system configuration

The ServiceDefinition.csdef file specifies settings that are used to configure a complete cloud service. You can also configure settings for your specific roles.

You do this by using the ServiceConfiguration.cscfg files. There are two versions of this file: one for your local development emulator and one when you deploy to the cloud. In this file, you can configure how many instances you want for each role, configuration settings for your diagnostics, and other things such as certificates.

You can also specify the version of your operating system that you want to use in Windows Azure. If you create a new cloud project with one web role and one worker role, you get the following ServiceConfiguration file for the cloud deployment:

```xml
<?xml version="1.0" encoding="utf-8"?>
<ServiceConfiguration serviceName="WindowsAzure1"
      xmlns="http://schemas.microsoft.com/ServiceHosting/2008/10/ServiceConfiguration"
      osFamily="3" osVersion="*" schemaVersion="2013-03.2.0">
  <Role name="MyWebApp">
    <Instances count="1" />
    <ConfigurationSettings>
      <Setting name="Microsoft.WindowsAzure.Plugins.Diagnostics.ConnectionString" value=
"UseDevelopmentStorage=true" />
    </ConfigurationSettings>
  </Role>
  <Role name="MyWorkerRole">
    <Instances count="1" />
    <ConfigurationSettings>
      <Setting name="Microsoft.WindowsAzure.Plugins.Diagnostics.ConnectionString" value=
"UseDevelopmentStorage=true" />
    </ConfigurationSettings>
  </Role>
</ServiceConfiguration>
```

At the top-level element, you see settings for osFamily and osVersion.

The osFamily attribute can be one of the following values:

- Specifies the OS family that is substantially compatible with Windows Server 2008 SP2. This Guest OS family retiring began on June 1, 2013, and will complete on June 1, 2014. You should not use this OS to create new installations.

- Specifies the OS family that is substantially compatible with Windows Server 2008 R2.

- Specifies the OS family that is substantially compatible with Windows Server 2012.

The osVersion attribute is used to specify the version of the guest OS that your role should run. You can set this value to * if you want to run on the newest version. This enables automatic upgrades and is a recommended best practice. You can also enter a specific version manually. You are then responsible for changing this value to update to later versions. Your version should follow the following format:

```
WA-GUEST-OS-M.m_YYYYMM-nn
```

Where:

- *WA-GUEST-OS* is a fixed string.

- *M.m* refers to the major and minor versions.

- *YYYY* refers to the year.

- *MM* refers to the month.

- *nn* serves as a sequence number to differentiate between releases, which typically supersede previous releases.

Thought experiment
Updating your cloud service

In this thought experiment, apply what you've learned about this objective. You can find answers to these questions in the "Answers" section at the end of this chapter.

Your company distributes a cloud service with multiple worker and web roles. A new update will soon be available, and you are considering the different options you have for updating the cloud service.

With this in mind, answer the following questions:

1. What is the difference between VIP Swap and in-place upgrade?

2. Which one do you prefer? Why?

Objective summary

- There are three different ways of updating your cloud service: delete and redeploy, in-place update, and VIP Swap.

- An in-place upgrade means that Windows Azure will update your instances according to the upgrade domain they belong to. This can lead to running multiple versions of your service at the same time.

- A cloud service can be deployed to both a staging and a production environment. A VIP Swap brings your staging environment into production and your production environment to staging.

- Your roles can have internal and external endpoints. You define these endpoints in your ServiceDefinition.csdef file.

- In the ServiceConfiguration.cscfg file, you can configure settings such as the number of instances you want for each role. You can also configure which operating system you want to run on.

Objective review

Answer the following questions to test your knowledge of the information in this objective. You can find the answers to these questions and explanations of why each answer choice is correct or incorrect in the "Answers" section at the end of this chapter.

1. You are deploying a new cloud service with only a web role, and you want to make sure that you get the maximum guaranteed uptime, even during upgrades. How many instances do you need?

   A. 1

   B. 2

   C. 3

   D. 4

2. You want to be able to communicate directly from your web role to your worker role, and you want to make sure that your worker role stays secure by disallowing public access. What do you do?

   A. Add an InputEndpoint to the web role in your ServiceConfiguration.cscfg file.

   B. Add an InputEndpoint to your worker role in your ServiceConfiguration.cscfg file.

   C. Add an InternalEndPoint to the web role in your ServiceConfiguration.cscfg file.

   D. Add an InternalEndPoint to your worker role in your ServiceConfiguration.cscfg file.

3. You want to follow the recommended best practices for configuring your Windows Azure Guest OS. Which values do you use? (Choose all that apply.)

   A. osFamily="3"

   B. osFamily="1"

   C. osVersion="*"

   D. osVersion="WA-GUEST-OS-2.12_201208-02"

Objective 5.3: Configure a web application for deployment

When deploying your application, there are a couple of things you can already configure in your development environment. You can make sure, for example, that the correct settings are used for things like your database connection or WCF configuration.

This objective covers several different ways to prepare your application for deployment, including an on-premises environment or on Windows Azure. You need to know both of these configurations for the exam.

Switching from production/release mode to debug

When building your projects, you use a *build configuration*. Two configurations are declared by default: *release* and *debug*. For the exam, you should know the differences between these configurations and the scenarios in which they should be used.

In release mode, your code is optimized for running as fast as possible. Of course, this is something that you want to use when your code is deployed to your production server.

However, release mode is not handy when you are debugging your applications. When you compile an application in debug mode, extra instructions are added to your compiled code. This ensures that debugging is supported, and that you can easily step through your code with a debugger.

In addition to your build configuration, there is also a debug switch in your web.config file:

```
<configuration>
  <system.web>
    <compilation debug="true" targetFramework="4.5" />
  </system.web>
</configuration>
```

By setting this value to false, you turn debug mode off.

In Visual Studio, you also have an option to select which debuggers you want to load when debugging your project, as you can see in Figure 5-9.

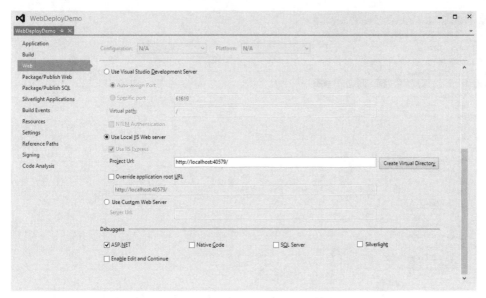

FIGURE 5-9 Selecting available debuggers for your ASP.NET application

The enabled debuggers work only when your code is compiled with debugging information.

Transforming web.config by XSLT

In your web.config file, you store all kinds of settings such as connection strings, WCF configurations, and custom appSettings. While they run on your development PC, you have set them to values that make sense for your local environment.

When you deploy your application, you have to change those values to configure your application correctly. Doing this manually takes time and can lead to errors. One way to deal with this problem is to use the *web.config transformation* syntax. When using this, you define an XML file that describes the changes that you want to apply to your web.config file. Web.config transformations are popular, and you can expect questions on how to use them on the exam.

When you create a new ASP.NET Model-View-Controller (MVC) application, transformation files for the debug and release configuration are created (see Figure 5-10).

FIGURE 5-10 The web.config file with two nested transformation files

Web.config transformations work with a special XML-Document-Transform syntax. Here is an example of a transformation file that changes your connection string and configures customErrors:

```xml
<?xml version="1.0"?>
<configuration xmlns:xdt="http://schemas.microsoft.com/XML-Document-Transform">
  <connectionStrings>
    <add name="MyDB"
      connectionString="value for the deployed Web.config file"
      xdt:Transform="SetAttributes" xdt:Locator="Match(name)"/>
  </connectionStrings>
  <system.web>
    <customErrors defaultRedirect="GenericError.htm"
      mode="RemoteOnly" xdt:Transform="Replace">
      <error statusCode="500" redirect="InternalError.htm"/>
    </customErrors>
  </system.web>
</configuration>
```

You start with specifying the correct namespace for your transformation file. After that, you can place the elements that you want to change. By using the xdt:Transform and xdt:Locator attributes, you configure how the element should be located and what should happen when it is found.

In the case of the customErrors element, you completely replace it with a new value on transformation. The connection string is used only to change the actual value of the connection string.

For your locator attribute, you can use the following values:

- Condition specifies an XPath expression that is appended to the current element's XPath expression.

- Match selects the element or elements that have a matching value for the specified attribute or attributes.

- XPath specifies an absolute XPath expression that is applied to the development web.config file.

For the transform attribute, you can use the following:

- Insert
- InsertBefore
- InsertAfter
- Remove
- RemoveAll
- RemoveAttributes
- SetAttributes

> **MORE INFO** **WEB.CONFIG TRANSFORMATION SYNTAX**
>
> For examples of how to use web.config transformation, see *http://msdn.microsoft.com/en-us/library/dd465326.aspx*.

Using SetParameters to set up an IIS app pool

Web.config transformation is being done at compile time. If you know beforehand to which environment you will publish, web.config transformation is a great tool. The transformation process, however, is not something that you can change at installation time.

When using Web Deploy packages, you have another option. If you want to create one Web Deploy package and then deploy it to multiple locations, you can use *parameterization*. When creating a Web Deploy package, a couple of files are created for you:

- [project name].zip is the Web Deployment package.

- [project name].deploy.cmd offers a convenient way of deploying your application from the command line.

- [project name].SetParameters.xml provides a set of values that MSDeploy.exe uses to deploy your package.

The SetParameters file is dynamically generated for you. It's based on the settings that you specified in your project settings and other configuration settings files in your project (such as web.config). For example, if you have a connection string in your web.config file, it will be picked up, and a parameter for your connection string will be added to the SetParameters.xml file.

You can configure extra values for parameterization by passing a Parameters.xml file to Web Deploy when creating the package. In this file, you indicate the file that you want to parameterize, what variable you want to change, and what the default value is. These values will later be used by Web Deploy to ask the user for input.

When you import a package through the IIS Manager, you get a dialog box that asks you for the values for all parameters you specified. When doing it from the command prompt, you use the SetParameters.xml file.

In most scenarios, you won't need any custom parameterization if you use Visual Studio. However, in a couple of scenarios, it can be useful to add custom parameters to your deployment package like custom appSettings, WCF service configuration at install time, or a web package that's going to be installed by end users in several different scenarios.

In Visual Studio, you can add the Parameters.xml file to the root of your web project. Here you see a typical example that enables the user to modify an appSetting:

```
<?xml version="1.0" encoding="utf-8" ?>
<parameters >
  <parameter name="Log Folder Location" description="Please provide a shared location
where the app can write log files to" defaultValue="\\Logs\MvcApp\Logs\" tags="">
    <parameterEntry kind="XmlFile" scope="\\web.config$" match="/configuration/
appSettings/add[@key='LogFolder']/@value" />
  </parameter>
 </parameters>
```

The parameter element has a few attributes:

- **name**   The name you specify is shown in IIS Manager when you import the package.
- **description**   The description you use is also shown in IIS Manager.
- **defaultValue**   This value is preloaded in the text box in IIS Manager so a user can just accept this value when importing your package.
- **scope**   A regular expression that shows the files to which the parameter applies.
- **match**   In the case of an XmlFile, an XPath expression that selects the XML node that you want to change.
- **kind**   Specifies the kind of resource the parameter will be applied to (such as XmlFile or TextFile).

Say you have the following endpoint configuration for WCF in the system.ServiceModel section of your web.config file:

```
<client>
  <endpoint address="http://localhost:8080/MyService.svc" binding="basicHttpBinding"
            bindingConfiguration="BasicHttpBinding_MyService"
            contract="ServiceReference.IMyService"
            name="BasicHttpBinding_MyService"/>
</client>
```

Of course, the localhost address is something you want to be able to change during an installation. To do this, you can add the following to your Parameters.xml file:

```
<parameter name="WCF My Endpoint Address"
          description="Please provide the Endpoint address for MyService that this
          application needs to call" defaultValue="http://localhost:8080/MyService.svc"
          tags="">
  <parameterEntry kind="XmlFile" scope="\\web.config$"
                  match="//system.serviceModel/client/endpoint/@address" />
</parameter>
```

If you now run the Publish process from Visual Studio, the SetParameters.xml file contains an extra entry for your WCF My Endpoint Address with a default value of *http://localhost:8080/MyService.svc*.

Of course, you can't use this to only change the address. You can also use it to configure your bindings and behaviors. Every XML element of your web.config file (or other files) can be parameterized.

> **MORE INFO** **USING PARAMETERS**
>
> For a complete description of how to use parameters in more complex scenarios, see *http://www.iis.net/learn/develop/windows-web-application-gallery/reference-for-the-web-application-package.*

If you're not using Visual Studio but instead the command prompt, you can use the declareParamFile and setParamFile options to specify a Parameters.xml and SetParameters. xml file:

```
msdeploy.exe -verb:sync -source:apphostconfig="default web site/application"
-dest:archivedir="C:\packages\application" -declareParamFile="C:\source\application\
deployment\declareParamsFile.xml"

msdeploy.exe -verb:sync -dest:apphostconfig="default web site/application"
-source:archivedir="C:\packages\application" -setParamFile="C:\source\application\
deployment\setParamsFile.xml"
```

Changing the SetParameters.xml file by hand each time is not what you want if you run in an automated environment. If you want to automate changing the values for setParameters in your build process, you can use something called XmlPoke. XmlPoke is an MSBuild task that you can run during your build process.

> **MORE INFO** **XMLPOKE**
>
> For an example of how to use XmlPoke, see *http://www.asp.net/web-forms/tutorials/deployment/web-deployment-in-the-enterprise/configuring-parameters-for-web-package-deployment.*

EXAM TIP

Make sure that you understand both web.config transformations and the use of parameters. Remember that transformations are done at compile time, and parameter values are set during deployment.

Configuring Windows Azure configuration settings

A Windows Azure cloud project has two configuration files:

- ServiceConfiguration.Cloud.cscfg
- ServiceConfiguration.Local.cscfg

By using these files, you can configure your cloud service. The local file contains values that will be used by your Windows Azure emulator. The cloud file will be used when deploying your application to Windows Azure.

Inside your configuration file, you can specify settings such as the number of role instances to deploy for each role, the values of any configuration settings, and the thumbprints for certificates associated with a role.

You can also specify the virtual hard disk when you are working with a virtual machine. If your service is part of a virtual network, you can configure your virtual network through this file.

> **MORE INFO** **CONFIGURING THE GUEST OS**
>
> Objective 5.2, "Choose a deployment strategy for Windows Azure web applications," shows you how to use the service configuration to configure the Windows Azure Guest OS you want your roles to run on.

If you create a new cloud project with a web and a worker role, you get the following configuration file:

```xml
<?xml version="1.0" encoding="utf-8"?>
<ServiceConfiguration serviceName="WindowsAzure1"
       xmlns="http://schemas.microsoft.com/ServiceHosting/2008/10/ServiceConfiguration"
       osFamily="3" osVersion="*" schemaVersion="2013-03.2.0">
  <Role name="MyWebApp">
    <Instances count="1" />
    <ConfigurationSettings>
      <Setting name="Microsoft.WindowsAzure.Plugins.Diagnostics.ConnectionString"
               value="UseDevelopmentStorage=true" />
    </ConfigurationSettings>
  </Role>
  <Role name="MyWorkerRole">
    <Instances count="1" />
    <ConfigurationSettings>
      <Setting name="Microsoft.WindowsAzure.Plugins.Diagnostics.ConnectionString"
               value="UseDevelopmentStorage=true" />
```

```
    </ConfigurationSettings>
  </Role>
</ServiceConfiguration>
```

The role element specifies the name of your role. It can also specify a vmName that it uses as the Domain Name System (DNS) name of your Virtual Machine (VM).

Nested in your role element, you can configure the number of instances that your role should be deployed to. Your ConfigurationSettings is a collection of name value pairs. In the configuration generated by Visual Studio, you see one entry that describes where the diagnostic data should be stored. This is a value you should change when doing an actual deployment.

Another element you can add is the Certificate element:

```
<Certificates>
    <Certificate name="<certificate-name>" thumbprint="<certificate-thumbprint>"
                 thumbprintAlgorithm="<algorithm>" />
</Certificates>
```

Your Certificate elements describe the thumbprint and the algorithm associated with a certificate.

You can have one other element: OsImage:

```
<OsImage href="<vhd_image_name>" />
```

This specifies the name of a Virtual Hard Disk (VHD) image for a VM role.

Next to the roles configuration, you can also have NetworkConfiguration. This section specifies Virtual Network and DNS values. This element is optional. An example of the schema of the NetworkConfiguration might be the following:

```
<NetworkConfiguration>
    <Dns>
      <DnsServers>
        <DnsServer name="name1" IPAddress="IPAddress1" />
      </DnsServers>
    </Dns>
    <VirtualNetworkSite name="name1"/>
    <AddressAssignments>
      <InstanceAddress roleName="roleName1">
        <Subnets>
          <Subnet name="name1" />
        </Subnets>
      </InstanceAddress>
    </AddressAssignments>
  </NetworkConfiguration>
</ServiceConfiguration>
```

This element describes the network configuration into which your service will be deployed.

MORE INFO **CONFIGURING A VIRTUAL NETWORK**

For more information on using the NetworkConfiguration element to configure a virtual network, see *http://msdn.microsoft.com/en-us/library/windowsazure/jj156091.aspx*.

Thought experiment
Preparing for deployment

In this thought experiment, apply what you've learned about this objective. You can find answers to these questions in the "Answers" section at the end of this chapter.

You are creating a complex web application that will be deployed to multiple, on-premises servers. You are working with development, testing, acceptance, and production environments; and you want to automate your deployment as much as possible.

With this in mind, answer the following questions:

1. Which configuration do you want to release to each of your different environments?

2. Do you want to use Web.config transformations or parameters with Web Deploy for your deployment pipeline?

Objective summary

- A projects is built with a configuration. You can use a debug and release configuration or create custom configurations.

- Web.config transformations are a way of transforming your web.config file by using a special syntax. This way, you can easily change values for things such as connection strings or WCF settings.

- Web Deploy can use parameters to specify which values in your configuration can be changed during installation. By using a SetParameters.xml file, you can define the values you want to use.

- Windows Azure is configured by using a ServiceConfiguration.cscfg file. There are two files: one for your local environment and one for the cloud. Using these files, you can configure your roles and network configuration.

Objective review

Answer the following questions to test your knowledge of the information in this objective. You can find the answers to these questions and explanations of why each answer choice is correct or incorrect in the "Answers" section at the end of this chapter.

1. You want to deploy your ASP.NET MVC application to your own web server for produc-
    tion. Which steps do you take? (Choose all that apply.)

    A. Change the debug attribute of the web.config to false.

    B. Build a release configuration.

    C. Disable the ASP.NET debugger in the Debuggers section of your project
        properties.

    D. Build a debug configuration.

2. You want to remove your debug element from the web.config file by using web.config
    transformations. Which syntax do you use?

    A. <compilation xdt:Transform="Replace" />

    B. <compilation xdt:Transform="RemoveAttributes(debug)" xdt:Locator="Condition(@
        debug='true')" />

    C. <compilation xdt:Transform="RemoveAttributes(debug)"
        xdt:Locator="Match(name)" />

    D. <compilation xdt:Transform="RemoveAttributes(debug)" />

3. You are using parameters for your Web Deploy. You want to automate the creation of
    the SetParameters file and make sure that it has the correct values. What do you use?

    A. XmlPoke with MSDeploy.

    B. MSDeploy with the setParamFile attribute.

    C. XmlPoke with MSBuild.

    D. This is not possible. You need to edit the SetParameters file manually.

Objective 5.4: Manage packages by using NuGet

Today, there are a lot of libraries. Some help you build web applications: jQuery, Modernizr,
and Knockout. Others focus on architectural issues: dependency injection tools such as Ninject or StructureMap.

   When building your applications, it pays to know which libraries are out there so you can
save time by reusing code that's already developed and well tested. But searching the web for
available libraries, looking for a download location, and adding them to your project can be
time-consuming, especially when the library gets regular updates and you have to repeat the
whole process.

   The same is true for internal libraries. Maybe you have some code that you want to use
in several of your projects. Keeping the libraries up to date and making sure that everyone
knows they exist and knows how to use them can be difficult tasks.

You are expected to know how to manage packages with NuGet for the exam. You should also be able to define the necessary steps for creating your own NuGet feed. This section explains how NuGet as a package manager manages libraries internally and externally, and ensures that you can consume them with minimal effort.

> **This objective covers how to:**
> - Install and update an existing NuGet package
> - Create and configure a NuGet package
> - Connect to a local repository cache
> - Set up your own package repository

Installing and updating an existing NuGet package

At *http://nuget.org*, you can find the NuGet gallery. This gallery contains all packages that are currently available. At the time of writing, there are tens of thousands of packages that are downloaded millions of times.

As you can see, this offers you a wealth of potentially useful packages that you can use in your own projects. Almost all popular frameworks, such as jQuery, Json.NET, or the Entity Framework, are available from NuGet. If the exam asks you to reference a popular library, you should immediately think of NuGet.

Starting with Visual Studio 2012, the project templates are based on NuGet packages. Instead of distributing one fixed version of a library with Visual Studio, Microsoft chose to use the packages available from NuGet in its templates.

If you create a new ASP.NET MVC project based on the Internet template in Visual Studio 2012, you get a file called packages.config in the root of your project. You can see the contents of this file in Listing 5-1.

LISTING 5-1 packages.config

```xml
<?xml version="1.0" encoding="utf-8"?>
<packages>
  <package id="DotNetOpenAuth.AspNet" version="4.1.4.12333" targetFramework="net45" />
  <package id="DotNetOpenAuth.Core" version="4.1.4.12333" targetFramework="net45" />
  <package id="DotNetOpenAuth.OAuth.Consumer" version="4.1.4.12333"
targetFramework="net45" />
  <package id="DotNetOpenAuth.OAuth.Core" version="4.1.4.12333" targetFramework="net45"
/>
  <package id="DotNetOpenAuth.OpenId.Core" version="4.1.4.12333" targetFramework="net45"
/>
  <package id="DotNetOpenAuth.OpenId.RelyingParty" version="4.1.4.12333"
targetFramework="net45" />
  <package id="EntityFramework" version="5.0.0" targetFramework="net45" />
  <package id="jQuery" version="1.8.2" targetFramework="net45" />
  <package id="jQuery.UI.Combined" version="1.8.24" targetFramework="net45" />
```

```
  <package id="jQuery.Validation" version="1.10.0" targetFramework="net45" />
  <package id="knockoutjs" version="2.2.0" targetFramework="net45" />
  <package id="Microsoft.AspNet.Mvc" version="4.0.20710.0" targetFramework="net45" />
  <package id="Microsoft.AspNet.Mvc.FixedDisplayModes" version="1.0.0"
targetFramework="net45" />
  <package id="Microsoft.AspNet.Razor" version="2.0.20715.0" targetFramework="net45" />
  <package id="Microsoft.AspNet.Web.Optimization" version="1.0.0"
targetFramework="net45" />
  <package id="Microsoft.AspNet.WebApi" version="4.0.20710.0" targetFramework="net45" />
  <package id="Microsoft.AspNet.WebApi.Client" version="4.0.20710.0"
targetFramework="net45" />
  <package id="Microsoft.AspNet.WebApi.Core" version="4.0.20710.0"
targetFramework="net45" />
  <package id="Microsoft.AspNet.WebApi.OData" version="4.0.0" targetFramework="net45" />
  <package id="Microsoft.AspNet.WebApi.WebHost" version="4.0.20710.0"
targetFramework="net45" />
  <package id="Microsoft.AspNet.WebPages" version="2.0.20710.0" targetFramework="net45"
/>
  <package id="Microsoft.AspNet.WebPages.Data" version="2.0.20710.0"
targetFramework="net45" />
  <package id="Microsoft.AspNet.WebPages.OAuth" version="2.0.20710.0"
targetFramework="net45" />
  <package id="Microsoft.AspNet.WebPages.WebData" version="2.0.20710.0"
targetFramework="net45" />
  <package id="Microsoft.Data.Edm" version="5.2.0" targetFramework="net45" />
  <package id="Microsoft.Data.OData" version="5.2.0" targetFramework="net45" />
  <package id="Microsoft.jQuery.Unobtrusive.Ajax" version="2.0.30116.0"
targetFramework="net45" />
  <package id="Microsoft.jQuery.Unobtrusive.Validation" version="2.0.30116.0"
targetFramework="net45" />
  <package id="Microsoft.Net.Http" version="2.0.20710.0" targetFramework="net45" />
  <package id="Microsoft.Web.Infrastructure" version="1.0.0.0" targetFramework="net45"
/>
  <package id="Modernizr" version="2.6.2" targetFramework="net45" />
  <package id="Newtonsoft.Json" version="4.5.11" targetFramework="net45" />
  <package id="System.Spatial" version="5.2.0" targetFramework="net45" />
  <package id="WebGrease" version="1.3.0" targetFramework="net45" />
</packages>
```

As you can see, a typical ASP.NET MVC project uses quite a lot of packages. Packages can contain all types of content. Some packages consist of a set of assemblies that are automatically referenced when you add them to your project. Others contain JavaScript and CSS files that are added to the correct folders in your project. Other packages modify your web.config file or add code to your project.

EXAM TIP

Remember that a NuGet package is not only about adding references to your project. A NuGet package can contain all kinds of data, such as code or script files and even configuration changes that can be added to your project.

This also makes it clear why NuGet is so popular. Instead of having to manually download assemblies, reference them in your project, change some configuration settings, and write some code, this can all be done in an automated way using NuGet.

Using the Manage NuGet Packages window

You can use Visual Studio to get a more graphical view of the packages you have installed in a project or in your solution by opening the Manage NuGet Packages window. To view all the packages in your solution, open it from Tools → Library Package Manager → Manage NuGet Packages for solutions. As you can see in Figure 5-11, this window shows the packages you have installed in your solution.

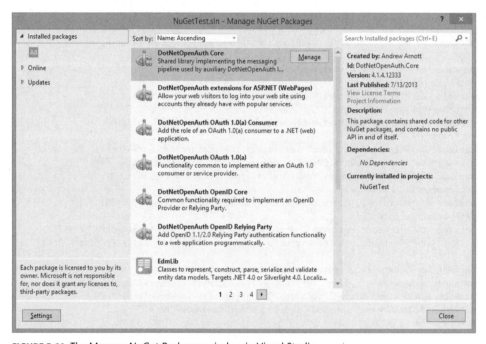

FIGURE 5-11 The Manage NuGet Packages window in Visual Studio

To view the installed packages for only one project, you can right-click the References folder in Solution Explorer and choose Manage NuGet Packages. Both windows look identical. The only difference is that the solution-wide option lets you select which projects you want to apply changes to.

You can use the NuGet package window to install new packages. By selecting the Online option, you can search the NuGet gallery directly from Visual Studio and select the packages you want to install.

You also see an Update tab in the window. When you select this tab, Visual Studio will determine whether there are updates for any of the packages you have installed in your project. You can then easily update your packages to the newest version.

One big advantage of using NuGet to install a package is that it automatically detects any required dependencies and installs them together with your package. This way, you never have to manually search for any dependencies or other prerequisites. This is all taken care of for you by NuGet.

Package Manager Console

The Manage NuGet Packages window is one option to install packages into your solution. You can also use the Package Manager Console. This console is a Windows PowerShell window that's integrated into Visual Studio. By opening this console, you can execute commands to install, update, and remove packages. Figure 5-12 shows how this console looks when you open it for the first time.

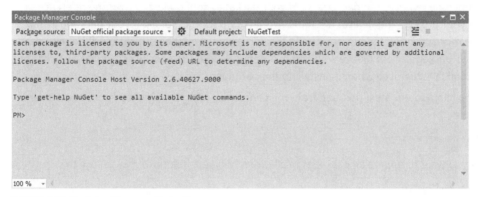

FIGURE 5-12 Package Manager Console

Let's say you want to add a new package to your project. You can do this from the console by using the install-package command. For example, the following line adds Ninject (a dependency injection library) to your project:

```
Install-package Ninject
```

After executing this command (by hitting Enter), you get the following result:

```
You are downloading Ninject from Ninject Project Contributors, the license
agreement to which is available at https://github.com/ninject/ninject/raw/master/
LICENSE.txt. Check the package for additional dependencies, which may come
with their own license agreement(s). Your use of the package and dependencies
constitutes your acceptance of their license agreements. If you do not accept the
license agreement(s), then delete the relevant components from your device.
Successfully installed 'Ninject 3.0.1.10'.
Successfully added 'Ninject 3.0.1.10' to NuGetTest.
```

If you now look in your References folder, you see a new reference to a Ninject assembly. This assembly is located in your solution folder in a folder called packages. Each package is downloaded to a folder and referenced from your project.

When you type in the Package Manager Console, it's sometimes hard to remember the exact name of a command or the name of a package. You can use the Tab key to show a drop-down list with possible options. If you type **i** and then press Tab, you get a drop-down list for all commands starting with the letter "i". You can then scroll through this list and pick the command you want. If there is only one option left pressing Tab automatically selects that option. So if you type **install-p** and then press Tab, it automatically expands to Install-Package.

The same trick works when selecting a package name. Pressing Tab displays a list of packages that you can use to find the package you are looking for.

You can remove a package from your project by using the uninstall-package command. If you want to remove Ninject, use the following line:

```
Uninstall-Package Ninject
```

This code removes the package from your packages.config file, removes the reference from your project, and deletes the folder from your packages folder. If your package install made more changes, to your app.config file, for example, all those changes will be removed so your package doesn't leave any clutter. If dependencies were installed for you, they are not automatically removed when uninstalling the package.

You can also update a package from the console by using the Update-Package command like this:

```
Update-Package Ninject
```

If you want to update all packages in all projects in your solution, you can use this:

```
Update-Package
```

If you want to update only the packages in a specific project, you can use the –Project parameter to specify the project name:

```
Update-Package -Project NuGetTest
```

By default, all the commands you run will execute against the first project in your solution. This is the project name displayed in the Default Project drop-down list in the console window. By changing this drop-down list, you can target another project with your commands or use the –Project parameter to select a different project.

Some packages also offer extra commands that are integrated into the console. For example, after you install the Entity Framework (EF) package, you can use commands such as Enable-Migrations, Add-Migration, and Update-Database to use Code First Migrations.

> ***MORE INFO*** **NUGET WINDOWS POWERSHELL REFERENCE**
>
> For a list of the available Windows PowerShell commands and their parameters in NuGet, see *http://docs.nuget.org/docs/Reference/Package-Manager-Console-PowerShell-Reference.*

Sharing packages with your team

Including all the packages that you install into your project in your source control is not a best practice. All this package data needs to be stored on your source control server and has to be downloaded to each user who accesses your project. If you forget to add a package to source control, other users will get compile errors because of missing packages.

When you right-click your solution file in Visual Studio, you can Enable Package Restore On Build. A solution folder called .nuget is added that contains the NuGet.exe file. If you now build your project, NuGet will see whether all packages are correctly downloaded. If a package is missing, it will download it from NuGet and add it to the packages folder. This way you can be sure that everyone has all the required packages installed without having to share the packages through source control.

If you want to change the default location of where packages are installed, you can do this through a configuration file. You do this by adding a nuget.config file to your solution with the following content:

```
<configuration>
  <config>
    <add key=" repositoryPath" value=" C:\myteam\teampackages" />
  </config>
</configuration>
```

Creating and configuring a NuGet package

NuGet is based on the idea that everyone can add new packages to the NuGet gallery. This means that if you have a project of your own that you want to share with others, you can easily add it to the official NuGet gallery so everyone can access it.

Understanding the content of a package

A NuGet package is described by a package manifest, the nuspec file. This file uses XML to describe your package. It contains information such as the version, title, author(s), description, release notes, and dependencies of your package. A nuspec file looks something like this:

```
<?xml version="1.0" encoding="utf-8"?>
<package xmlns="http://schemas.microsoft.com/packaging/2010/07/nuspec.xsd">
  <metadata>
    <id>sample</id>
    <version>1.0.0</version>
    <authors>Microsoft</authors>
    <dependencies>
      <dependency id="another-package" version="3.0.0" />
      <dependency id="yet-another-package"/>
    </dependencies>
  </metadata>
</package>
```

MORE INFO **NUSPEC REFERENCE**

For a list of all the elements that you can use in a nuspec file, see *http://docs.nuget.org/ docs/reference/nuspec-reference*.

In addition to this manifest file, the package contains your assemblies, content files, and other tools that you want to distribute. NuGet follows a convention over configuration approach, meaning that you don't need to configure a lot of settings if you just follow some simple rules. One of those rules is the way in which you structure your package. You can use the following three folders:

- \lib
- \content
- \tools

The lib folder is used for your assemblies. If you target different platforms (for example, Windows Phone, Windows Store, and the full .NET Framework) you can use subfolders to separate those versions of your project, following the NuGet naming convention.

The *content* folder can contain files such as configuration files, images, JavaScript files, Cascading Style Sheets (CSS), or other files that you want to distribute with your package. All files contained in your content folder will be included in your project. This means that if you have an image file in \content\images\myimg.png, this file will end up as \images\myimg.png in the target project.

The files you put in the content folder can also be used to apply transformations to your configuration files. If you create a file called app.config.transformation or web.config. transformation, NuGet will use those files during installation to apply changes to the configuration files. It does so by adding the XML elements from your transformation files that are missing in the target files.

Transformations can also be used on code files. You create a file with a .cs.pp extension such as MyUtil.cs.pp, and add it to the content folder in your package. Maybe you want to add code to the Global.asax file or add some classes to the project. Transformations are most often used to insert the correct namespace when adding code.

The following file uses the $rootnamespace$ token to make sure that the correct namespace is used:

```
namespace $rootnamespace$.Models
{
    public class Person
    {
        public string FirstName;
        public string LastName;
    }
}
```

Next to the lib and content folders, you can also use a tools folder. In this folder, you can put Windows PowerShell scripts that run when your package is loaded, installed, and uninstalled:

- Init.ps1 runs every time a solution that contains your package is loaded.
- Install.ps1 runs when your package is installed into a solution.
- Uninstall.ps1 runs when your package is uninstalled.

If your package doesn't have anything in the content and lib folders, it is considered as a solution level package. You can use it if all you want to do is add commands to the Package Manager Console.

For example, if you install the EF package in your project, you get the following content for the tools folder:

- EntityFramework.PowerShell.dll
- EntityFramework.PowerShell.Utility.dll
- EntityFramework.PS3.psd1
- EntityFramework.psd1
- EntityFramework.psm1
- init.ps1
- install.ps1
- migrate.exe
- Redirect.config
- Redirect.VS11.config

The EF team created init.ps1 and install.ps1 files that are called by NuGet. The install file is run only once and initializes a ConnectionFactoryConfigurator. The init file is called every time the EF package is loaded in a solution. This file makes sure that all EF–specific Windows PowerShell commands are added to the NuGet Package Manager Console window. As you can see, there is even an .exe file that is a part of the package.

Creating your own NuGet package

You can create your own NuGet packages by using the command line or by using a visual designer. If you want to use the command line, you need to make sure that you have the NuGet.exe file (which can be downloaded from *http://nuget.codeplex.com/releases/view/58939*). Make sure that you add the location of your NuGet.exe file to your path environment variable so you can use it from a command prompt.

The first command you have to run is this:

```
NuGet Update -self
```

This will update your version of NuGet to the latest version. Now you can start creating your package. If you just want to create a package from an assembly, you can run the following command:

```
nuget spec MyAssembly.dll
```

This code creates a MyAssembly.nuspec file for you that contains your manifest. You can now edit this file to make sure that things such as the title and description and the dependencies are correct. After that, you can create your package:

```
nuget pack MyAssembly.nuspec
```

This code results in a MyAssembly.dll.1.0.0.nupkg package file. You can now test your package from Visual Studio by opening a project and executing the following command from the Package Manager Console:

```
install-package MyAssembly.dll -Source "C:\<location_of_your_package>"
```

If you now look at the references of your project, you will see that there is a new reference to MyAssembly. You can also create a NuGet package from a Visual Studio project. You do this by first creating a nuspec file by running the following command from the folder in which your csproj file is located:

```
nuget spec
```

This will create a nuspec file with some special tokens such as id, version, author, and description. The data for these tokens is loaded from your AssemblyInfo.cs file. By default, the AssemblyInfo.cs file does not contain those tokens. You need to edit this file and add additional data or remove tokens if you want static data.

After you finish with your nuspec file, you need to create your package:

```
nuget pack MyProject.csproj
```

This code creates a package of your project file with the data that you put in your nuspec file.

If you want to create a more complex package that uses the tools, content, and lib folders, you need to create your package manually. You start with a default spec file created from scratch by running this:

```
nuget spec
```

Then you need to edit the nuspec file that's created and fill in all the values you want. After that, create your three folders (lib, content, and tools) and copy all the necessary files to the correct folder. Now you can run one final NuGet command to create your package:

```
nuget pack YourPackage.nuspec
```

Now that your package is ready, you can publish it to NuGet. You need an application programming interface (API) key that you get when you register for an account on NuGet. You can copy this API key and then configure NuGet with it:

```
NuGet SetApiKey Your-API-Key
```

Now you can run the following to publish your package to NuGet:

```
NuGet Push YourPackage.nupkg
```

If you don't like the command line, you can also use a Windows GUI application to create a package. You can download the package from *http://nuget.codeplex.com/releases/59864/clickOnce/NuGetPackageExplorer.application*. This tool enables you to create your manifest with a nice graphical editor. You can then add files to the tools, lib, and content folders and press the Publish button to publish your package to NuGet.

You can also use the NuGet Package Explorer to open packages both from your local PC and directly from the package feed. You can then read the manifest and check the content of the package.

Setting up your own package repository

NuGet displays packages from the package sources that you have configured. When installing Visual Studio, you get a default package reference to the official package source of NuGet.

You can add additional package sources that NuGet can use to install packages from. Maybe you have some packages that you want to share with your development team, or you want to have a local backup of the packages that you will install for a presentation or something.

A local feed can easily be created by going to the Tools menu, selecting Library Package Manager and then clicking Package Manager Settings. If you look at the Package Source tab, you can see the window shown in Figure 5-13.

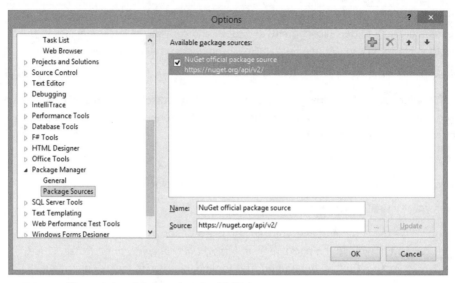

FIGURE 5-13 The package sources options for NuGet

To add a local folder as a package source, you can click the Add button, enter a name, and point to a folder on your computer. You then need to add your .nupkg package files to this folder. After that, you can select your local package source from the package source drop-down list in the Package Manager Console. The feed also shows up in the Online tab of the Manage NuGet Packages window.

You can also create a remote feed that needs to run on IIS. Of course, you can choose to make it publicly available or only internal. You create a remote feed by starting with an empty web application in Visual Studio. In your project, install the NuGet.Server package, which will add all the code necessary to expose your packages as an Atom Syndication Format (ATOM) feed.

A Packages folder is now inside your project. You can add your package files to this folder, or you can use the appSettings element of the web.config file to configure a different path (virtual or absolute).

If you want, you can also enable publishing to your custom remote feed, just as you can publish packages to the official NuGet gallery. To do this, you need to add an API key to the appSettings element. If you leave the API key empty, publishing is disabled.

That's all that's required. You can now deploy your application to IIS and access the feed of available packages by navigating to *http://<locationofyoursite>/nuget/*. If you add this URL as a package source to the Packet Manager, you can now install packages from this server into your projects.

This gives you a wealth of possibilities. You can, for example, now create custom Visual Studio templates that use the best practices of your development team and reference your company's packages that are hosted on your own feed, so everyone starts with the correct baseline.

Thought experiment
Should you use NuGet?

In this thought experiment, apply what you've learned about this objective. You can find answers to these questions in the "Answers" section at the end of this chapter.

You are working in a small company that runs a lot of web development projects each year. Each time you start a new project, you evaluate the current state of technologies and you try to use the newest technologies available. However, your colleagues feel that they want control over what gets used in all the projects. You are thinking of introducing NuGet to them and you are trying to prepare a good argument.

With this in mind, answer the following questions:

1. Are you still in control over what gets added to your project when using NuGet? Is that an advantage or a disadvantage?

2. How can NuGet help you stay on the cutting edge of new releases?

3. Would it be useful to create your own package repository?

Objective summary

- NuGet, which is a package manager that's part of Visual Studio, is the preferred way to add external libraries to your projects.

- You can use the Package Manager Console or the visual NuGet Package Manager to install, update, and remove packages from your projects.

- You can create custom packages by using the Nuget.exe file or the NuGet Package Explorer.

- A custom package is described by a manifest file and can contain other assemblies, content files, and additional Windows PowerShell scripts.

- You can create custom package sources locally on your PC or remotely by installing the NuGet.Server package in an empty ASP.NET Web Application.

Objective review

Answer the following questions to test your knowledge of the information in this objective. You can find the answers to these questions and explanations of why each answer choice is correct or incorrect in the "Answers" section at the end of this chapter.

1. You want to update jQuery package in your ASP.NET MVC 4 application in the easiest way possible. What do you do? (Choose all that apply.)

   A. Download the newest version from *http://jquery.com*.

   B. Run the command Update-Package jQuery from the Developer command prompt.

   C. Run the command Update-Package jQuery from the Package Manager Console.

   D. Click the update button in the Package Manager window for the jQuery package.

2. You want to package a custom package that uses the lib, content, and tool folders. Which command do you use?

   A. nuget pack MyProject.csproj

   B. nuget spec MyAssembly.dll

   C. nuget pack package.nuspec

   D. nuget push package.nupkg

3. You want to expose a read-only feed of custom packages on your internal web server to your colleagues. Which steps do you take? (Choose all that apply.)

   A. Set the API key in your appSettings.

   B. Install the NuGet.Server package.

   C. Deploy your application to IIS.

   D. Create a new Empty ASP.NET Web Application.

Objective 5.5: Create, configure, and publish a web package

As you saw in the first objective of this chapter, deploying an application can be a complex task. One of the best ways to deploy your website or service is by using the Web Deployment Framework or Web Deploy.

In this objective, you will look at how to create Web Deployment packages and how to deploy them to your servers. Web Deploy is an important aspect of deploying applications nowadays, and you will be tested on it for the exam.

Creating an IIS InstallPackage

There are several ways to create a Web Deployment package. You can use Visual Studio, IIS, the command prompt, or Windows PowerShell to create and deploy your packages. Visual Studio is the easiest way to deploy; Windows PowerShell and the command prompt give you a lot of power but are more difficult to use.

Visual Studio

In Visual Studio, you can use the Publish tool to create a Web Deploy package. When doing this you can add database script files, change the database connections in your web.config and execute EF Code First Migrations on destination.

Visual Studio does not offer you all the features that you can configure when creating a package, but it's one of the easiest ways to create a package.

You start the publish process by choosing Publish *<YourProjectName>* from the Build menu. Figure 5-14 shows the start page of your wizard. The first time, you need to create a publish profile. This profile is stored as a part of your solution. This way, you can add your profile to source control and reuse it each time you publish your app. This is called one-click publishing. Next time, you only need to click Publish, and a Web Deploy will be automatically executed. You can create multiple profiles for different scenarios. Maybe you are running in a DTAP (development, test, acceptance, production) environment and you want a publish profile for each of these locations. By creating multiple profiles, you can easily store your deployment settings.

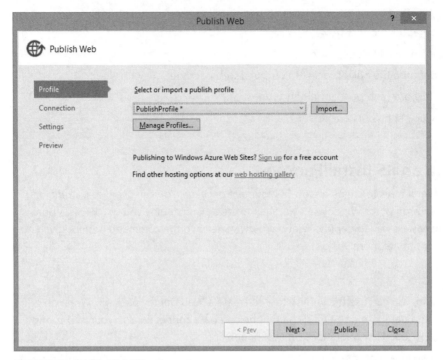

FIGURE 5-14 Publish Web Wizard

When deploying to Windows Azure Websites, you don't have to create the publish profile manually. When you log in to your Windows Azure Management Portal, you can download a publish profile for your website. If you import this file into Visual Studio, your project is automatically configured for deployment to your Windows Azure Websites.

If you want to create your own profile, you can create a new one, give it a name, and then navigate to the second page of the wizard. Here you can select your publish method. If you want to use Web Deploy, you need to choose Web Deploy or Web Deploy Package.

Web Deploy directly deploys your application to a remote server that has the Web Deploy service installed. For this to work, you need to enter the address of the server and the credentials for connecting to the server.

> **MORE INFO   CONFIGURING YOUR SERVER FOR WEB DEPLOY**
>
> For instructions on how to configure your web server for Web Deploy, see *http://www.iis. net/learn/install/installing-publishing-technologies/installing-and-configuring-web-deploy.*

If you want to create a package, select the Web Deploy Package option (see Figure 5-15). Now you can enter a location where you want to store the package and the name of the site you want to deploy to (this can be changed later when deploying the package).

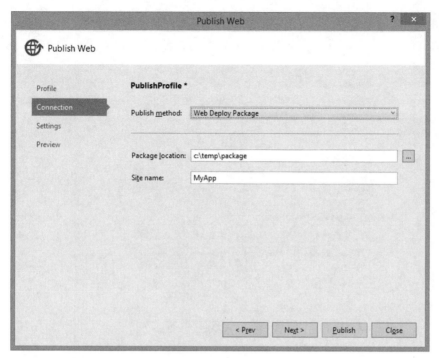

FIGURE 5-15 Selecting a publish method

The third page of your wizard enables you to configure additional settings (see Figure 5-16). On this page, you can select your deployment configuration (Release by default), precompile your site, exclude files from App_Data, and configure your database.

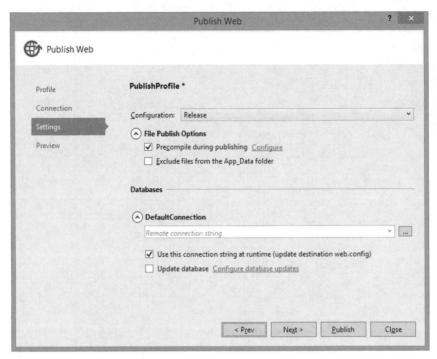

FIGURE 5-16 Configuring additional publish settings

After you click Publish, Visual Studio will build a Web Deploy package for you. You can then use this package and deploy it to IIS, both by manually importing it from IIS Manager or from the command line.

There are some extra options that you can configure through the properties page of your project. If you open the project properties, you will see a page for Package/Publish Web and Package/Publish SQL.

On the Package/Publish Web page, you can select the files you want to deploy. This way, you can choose the assets that you want to deploy with your project. You can select to only deploy the required files, all files in your project, or all files stored in your project folder. You can also select an option to include your IIS Express settings and deploy them to the target server. This way, you can be sure that every deployment server is correctly configured.

The Package/Publish SQL page is disabled by default, showing a message that you can now control these settings through the Publish Wizard. If you want, you can enable the settings page and configure settings for database deployment.

If you use the Entity Framework, you can use Code First Migrations to update the target database on deployment. You can also use more complex features such as the dbDacFx or dbFullSql Provider.

> **MORE INFO**   **CONFIGURING DATABASE DEPLOYMENT FOR WEB DEPLOY**
>
> For more information on how to deploy your database, see *http://msdn.microsoft.com/ en-us/library/dd394698.aspx*.

IIS

The IIS Manager supports both creating and importing Web Deployment packages. You can create a package for an application, site, or even a complete server. IIS provides you with more control over the creation of your package than Visual Studio does.

To integrate Web Deploy with IIS, you need to run the installer that you can find at *http:// www.iis.net/downloads/microsoft/web-deploy*. It will add extra options to your IIS Manager for importing and exporting applications.

> **MORE INFO**   **CONFIGURING A SERVER FOR WEB DEPLOY**
>
> When installing Web Deploy on a server, you need to configure the server to enable re-mote publishing. This way, you can use Web Deploy to remotely install a Web Deployment package on your server.
>
> You can find detailed instructions on how to configure your server at the ASP.NET website: *http://www.asp.net/web-forms/tutorials/deployment/configuring-server-environments-for-web-deployment/configuring-a-web-server-for-web-deploy-publishing-(remote-agent)*.

When exporting a complete server package, you create a Web Deploy that contains the configuration for your web server. This includes configuration from applicationHost.config, IIS registry settings, SSL certificates, and the content of all web applications hosted on your server.

You export a package by opening the IIS Manager and then selecting the application, site, or server that you want to export. By clicking Export Application in the right action pane, you start a wizard that will help you configure your package. You can see the wizard in Figure 5-17.

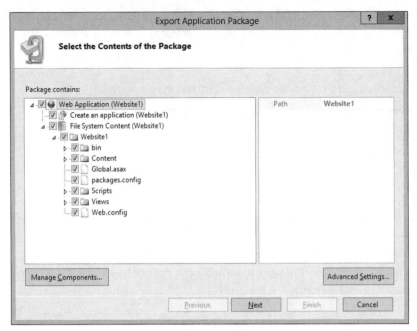

FIGURE 5-17 Configuring additional publish settings

If you select the Manage Components option, you can configure additional providers for things like setting registry keys or deploying assemblies to the GAC. You can also select a provider to deploy a database with your package.

The next step in the wizard enables you to configure parameters for the providers you have configured. The parameters are used on deployment, so you can configure the providers you have selected. You can use a parameter for the name of your website or the location of the database, for example.

This is useful when you want to deploy your package to a testing and production environment. You probably want to use the same database schema, but vary the location of your database servers. By using a parameter, you can change this value when executing your deployment.

> **MORE INFO**   **EXPORTING A PACKAGE FROM IIS**
>
> For a complete example of exporting a package from IIS, see *http://www.iis.net/learn/ publish/using-web-deploy/export-a-package-through-iis-manager.*

After creating your package, you can now import it in IIS. You do this by selecting your server or site and selecting the Import Package options in the right action pane. Packages that you import this way can be created by Visual Studio, by IIS, or from the command prompt. After selecting the location of your package, you go through a wizard in which you can select the content you want to deploy. You also specify the values for the parameters that you created when exporting your package.

When importing a package, you have the option of setting the whatif flag, which shows you the list of actions that will be performed during deployment without actually performing the deployment. This way, you can see whether everything is configured correctly.

Command-line tools

In addition to using tools such as Visual Studio and IIS, you can also use command-line tools. Although they are harder to work with, they offer you a lot of flexibility. Especially when you want to set up a continuous deployment process, you will want to look at the command-line tools because they can be integrated with your build process.

> **NOTE LOCATION OF MSDEPLOY**
>
> Normally, MSDeploy is added to your environment variables so you can access it from a command prompt. If you experience problems running MSDeploy, make sure that you have installed Visual Studio 2012 Service Pack 1.

One such command-line tool is MSDeploy. You can use MSDeploy for the following:

- Live server-to-server synchronization
- Package creation
- Package deployment

When working with MSDeploy, make sure that you are an administrator. The following command, for example, executes a synchronization between two servers with the whatif flag:

```
msdeploy -whatif -verb:sync -source:iisApp="Default Web Site/MyApp"
         -dest:iisApp="Default Web Site/MyApp", computerName=Server2
```

This command has a couple of important segments:

- **verb**   Specifies the required operation (delete, dump, getDependencies, getSystemInfo, or sync).
- **source**   Specifies the source of the data for the verb argument.
- **dest**   Specifies the destination of a synchronization operation.
- **whatif**   Specifies that the command should run without making any actual changes.

As you can see, the whole syntax for using MSDeploy can become quite difficult. When you create a Web Deployment package through Visual Studio, it also generates a .cmd file that you can use to install the package from the command line. You can edit the SetParameters.xml file to change parameter values for your deployment.

The following command deploys your package to a remote server running the Web Management Service:

```
ProjectName.deploy.cmd /y /m:https://DestinationServerName:8172/MSDeploy.axd
```

For the exam, it's not reasonable that you memorize all options of Web Deploy. However, knowing the basic syntax, for example, the whatif flag, is important. Try to experiment with MSDeploy, and use the commands to prepare for the exam.

Next to using MSDeploy from a regular command prompt, you can also use the Web Deployment Framework from Windows PowerShell. Windows PowerShell is a very powerful tool. It looks like a command line, but with extra capabilities. It's built in .NET and it gives you full access to the Component Object Model (COM) and Windows Management Instrumentation (WMI).

If you want to use Web Deploy from within Windows PowerShell, you need to install the WDeploySnapin3.0 snap-in. Just as with the regular MSDeploy command-line tool, you can use Windows PowerShell to synchronize servers and create packages.

If you open a new Windows PowerShell window, you can execute the following commands to get a list of available Windows PowerShell commands for Web Deploy:

```
Add-PSSnapin WDeploySnapin3.0
Get-Command -module WDeploySnapin3.0
```

Figure 5-18 shows the result of executing these commands.

FIGURE 5-18 The commands for the WDeploySnapin3.0 Windows PowerShell snap-in

When you want to execute a remote deployment with Windows PowerShell, you first create a publish settings file. You can do this by using the New-WDPublishSettings command in Windows PowerShell:

```
$cred = Get-Credential
New-WDPublishSettings -ComputerName WebServer -Site WebSite1 -Credentials $cred
-AllowUntrusted -SiteUrl "http://www.mywebsite.com" -FileName C:\temp\mywebsite.
publishsettings -AgentType wmsvc
```

The first line shows you a dialog box in which you can enter the credentials you want to use for the deployment. However, you need to be careful because the credentials are stored as plain text in the resulting file. The second line creates a new publish profile. It is stored in the file C:\temp\mywebsite.publishsettings. After running this command, you have an XML file with the following content:

```
<?xml version="1.0" encoding="utf-8"?>
<publishData>
  <publishProfile
    publishMethod="MSDeploy"
    publishUrl="WebServer"
    msdeploySite="WebSite1"
    userName="Administrator"
    userPWD="p@ssw0rd"
    destinationAppUrl="http://www.mywebsite.com"
    SQLServerDBConnectionString=""
    mySQLDBConnectionString=""
    msdeployAllowUntrustedCertificate="True"
    agentType="WMSvc"
    useNTLM="False" />
</publishData>
```

After creating the publish settings file, you can use the Sync-WDApp command to deploy your application:

```
Sync-WDApp "MyApp" " MyAppDeployedWithPowerShell" -DestinationPublishSettings "C:\
temp\mywebsite.publishsettings"
```

> **MORE INFO**   **USING WINDOWS POWERSHELL TO DEPLOY TO WINDOWS AZURE**
>
> For information on how to use Windows PowerShell to deploy to Windows Azure, see
> *http://msdn.microsoft.com/en-us/library/windowsazure/jj554332.aspx*.

Configuring the build process to output a web package

To automate the deployment of your web application, you need to integrate with your build process. Normally, you do this by using TFS to run your builds. By modifying the build template, you can create a package and deploy it to a testing or production environment.

You use MSBuild to create a package like this:

```
MSBuild "MyProjectName.csproj" /T:Package
```

The /T option specifies the MSBuild Target that you want to use. If you remove the Package option, MSBuild just compiles your project.

By default, MSBuild uses the Debug configuration for your project. This is probably not what you want. To specify a different configuration, such as Release, use the /P parameter:

```
MSBuild "MyProjectName.csproj" /T:Package /P:Configuration=Release
```

Now to integrate this with TFS, you need to edit your Build Definition. You can find the Build Definitions in the Build tab of the Team Explorer in Visual Studio. A Build Definition contains all the settings that TFS uses to run your build.

Inside your Build Definition, you can specify additional parameters that should be passed to MSBuild. By specifying the /T:Package and /P:Configuration=Release parameters, you will generate a package each time a build runs on TFS.

Instead of only creating the package, you can also start an automatic deployment by specifying /p:DeployOnBuild=True. By using a correctly configured publish setting file, you can now deploy your application automatically on each build.

> **MORE INFO** **CONFIGURING TFS FOR CONTINUOUS DEPLOYMENT**
>
> For a walkthrough on how to configure TFS for continuous deployment, see *http://vishaljoshi.blogspot.nl/2010/11/team-build-web-deployment-web-deploy-vs.html*.

Applying pre- and post-condition actions

Web Deploy also enables you to execute custom actions before or after running the deployment of your application.

You can execute a command to run on the destination computer by using the runCommand option:

```
msdeploy -verb:sync -source:runcommand=d:\test.bat -dest:auto,computername=Server1
```

By using the preSync and postSync options, you can run a command before or after your deployment:

```
msdeploy -verb:sync -source:contentPath="C:\Test1" -dest:contentPath="C:\Test2"
-preSync:runcommand="c:\MyBatchFile.bat"
```

> ### *Thought experiment*
> ### Moving to continuous deployment
>
> In this thought experiment, apply what you've learned about this objective. You can find answers to these questions in the "Answers" section at the end of this chapter.
>
> You are planning an internal presentation for your colleagues to show them the benefits of automating your deployment. Currently, you are doing manual deployments in which you just copy the required files through FTP to the target servers. Database updates are always done manually.
>
> With this in mind, answer the following questions:
>
> **1.** What are the advantages that continuous deployment can give you? Make a list.
>
> **2.** Which techniques do you need for this?

Objective summary

- Web Deploy is the recommended way to deploy web applications.
- You can create and deploy a Web Deploy package through Visual Studio, the IIS, command line, and Windows PowerShell.
- You can configure different providers for deploying extra content such as database, registry settings, or assemblies.
- You can configure your build process to automatically create and deploy your application.
- By using the runCommand, preSync, and postSync options, you can execute additional tasks when executing a deployment.

Objective review

Answer the following questions to test your knowledge of the information in this objective. You can find the answers to these questions and explanations of why each answer choice is correct or incorrect in the "Answers" section at the end of this chapter.

1. You want to deploy your website to Windows Azure Websites. What can you do? (Choose all that apply.)

   A. Create a new publish profile and choose the Web Deploy option. Enter the credentials of your server and publish your website.

   B. Download the publish profile from the Management Portal and import it in Visual Studio.

   C. Use FTP publishing to copy your files directly to Windows Azure.

   D. Create a Web Deploy package and upload it to the Management Portal.

2. You are using the command line, and you want to see whether your deployment is configured correctly. What do you use?

   A. postSync

   B. preSync

   C. verb

   D. whatif

3. You want to create and deploy a package from the command line. Which command do you use?

   A. MSBuild "MyProjectName.csproj" /T:Package /P:Configuration=Release

   B. MSBuild "MyProjectName.csproj" /T:Package

   C. MSBuild "MyProjectName.csproj" /T:Package /P:Configuration=Release;DeployOn Build=True

   D. MSBuild "MyProjectName.csproj" /P:Configuration=Release;DeployOnBuild=True

Objective 5.6: Share assemblies between multiple applications and servers

Your web applications and services consist of assembly files. Those assemblies contain all the code that you have written and metadata that describes your code. The code that you use from the .NET Framework is also contained in assembly files.

A large part of the deployment of a web application or service consists of the assembly files. You can choose to deploy your assemblies locally with your application, or you can deploy them to a centralized location (the GAC) on a server in which the assemblies are then shared by every application that needs them.

To be able to deploy an assembly to the GAC, you need to sign it with a strong name. This also means that you version your assemblies so you can deploy multiple versions of the same assembly to a server. This objective covers how to sign assemblies, deploy them to the GAC, and configure the specific version that is used by applications. You will also look at how to optimize assemblies for loading in a shared environment. For the exam, it's important to understand what the GAC is and how the versioning with assemblies works. When deploying an application, you need to know how to optimize your server for hosting multiple websites.

Preparing the environment for use of assemblies across multiple servers

If you create a new MVC project in Visual Studio 2012, you get references to libraries such as Entity Framework and Json.NET, and system dynamic-link libraries (DLLs) such as System.Web.Mvc.

When you create multiple applications and deploy them to the same server, all websites will have their own copies of those assemblies. This means that all those assemblies have to be read from disk and loaded into memory. This leads to many redundant loads that increase the startup time and memory usage of your websites.

ASP.NET has a feature called shadow copying that enables assemblies that are used in an application domain to be updated without unloading the AppDomain. Normally, this is required because the Common Language Runtime (CLR) will lock the assemblies so you can't just copy a new assembly over it. Shadow copying means that the original assembly is copied to a temporary location. The copied assembly is locked, and the original assembly can be updated with a new version.

Shadow copying moves your file to the Temporary ASP.NET Files folder. This folder can be found at C:\Windows\Microsoft.NET\Framework64\v4.0.30319 or C:\Windows\Microsoft.NET\Framework\v4.0.30319, depending on your server configuration. Shadow copying is on by default for the Bin DLLs folder.

ASP.NET 4.5 adds a new feature called assembly interning. Because all DLLs are already located in one location (the Temporary ASP.NET Files folder), interning analyzes this folder for duplicate assemblies. Those assemblies are then moved to a special location, and all the original references are replaced with what's called a symbolic link.

When a web application requests a shared DLL, the symbolic link points the application to the shared location. This way, all shared assemblies are loaded only once in memory. This decreases both memory usage and startup time of your websites.

You can use assembly interning by using the command-line tool aspnet_intern.exe. This file is a part of the VS11 SDK and can be found at C:\Program Files (x86)\Microsoft SDKs\Windows\v8.0A\bin\NETFX 4.0 Tools.

If you run the following command from a command line on your server, the aspnet_intern tool will analyze which assemblies are shared and move them to the specified location:

```
aspnet_intern -mode exec -sourcedir "C:\Windows\Microsoft.NET\Framework64\v4.0.30319\
Temporary ASP.NET Files" -interndir C:\CommonAssemblies
```

An assembly will be marked as shared when it's used three times or more, which means that you can easily test interning by deploying a default ASP.NET Web Application to your server in three different web applications. If you then run the aspnet_intern command, you see that it finds 17 shared assemblies.

The aspnet_intern tool also has an analyze mode that shows you which assemblies it can intern for you. You can run the analyze command with a verbose flag like this:

```
aspnet_intern -mode analyze -sourcedir "C:\Windows\Microsoft.NET\Framework64\v4.0.30319\
Temporary ASP.NET Files" -v
```

The exam won't require that you know all details about how to call the aspnet_intern tool. Understanding the concept behind it is the most important thing, but also try to experiment with the tool so you know the basic syntax.

Signing assemblies by using a strong name

The CLR supports two different types of assemblies: *strong-named assemblies* and *regular assemblies*.

A regular assembly is what Visual Studio generates for you by default. It's structurally identical to a strong-named assembly. They both contain metadata, a header, manifest, and all the types that are defined in your assembly.

When you take a regular assembly, you can sign it with a public/private key pair that uniquely identifies the publisher of the assembly and the content of the assembly. A strong name consists of the simple text name of the assembly, its version number, and culture information. It also contains a public key and a digital signature. Strongly naming an assembly has several benefits:

- **Strong names guarantee uniqueness**. Your unique private key is used to generate the name for your assembly. No other assembly can have the exact same strong name.

- **Strong names protect your versioning lineage**. Because you control the private key, you are the only one who can distribute updates to your assemblies. Users can be sure that the new version originates from the same publisher.

- **Strong names provide a strong integrity check**. The .NET Framework sees whether a strong-named assembly has changed since the moment it was signed.

Overall, you can see that a strong-named assembly ensures users that they can trust the origin and content of an assembly. You generate a strong-named assembly by using your own private key to sign the assembly. Other users can verify the assembly by using the public key that is distributed with the assembly.

Signing an assembly can be done both at the command line and by using Visual Studio. The first step you have to take is to generate a key pair. A key pair is usually a file with an .snk extension that contains your public/private key information. When using the developer command prompt, you can run the following command to generate a new key pair file:

```
sn -k myKey.snk
```

An easier way is to use Visual Studio to generate the key pair file for you. You can open the property page of the project you want to sign and then navigate to the Signing tab, as shown in Figure 5-19.

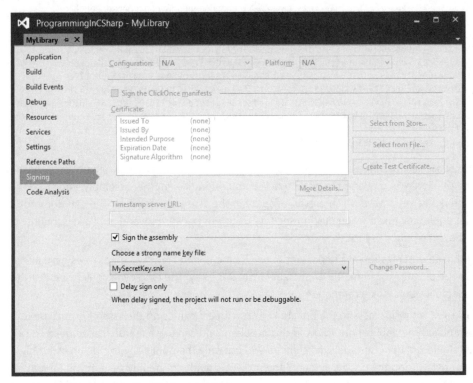

FIGURE 5-19 The Signing page in Visual Studio

By enabling the signing of the assembly, you can let Visual Studio generate a new key file, which is then added to your project and is used in the compilation step to strongly sign your assembly.

A strong-named assembly can reference only other assemblies that are also strongly named. This is to avoid security flaws where a depending assembly could be changed to influence the behavior of a strong-named assembly. When you add a reference to a regular assembly and try to invoke code from that assembly, the compiler issues an error:

```
Assembly generation failed -- Referenced assembly 'MyLib' does not have a strong name
```

After signing an assembly, you can view the public key by using the Strong Name tool (Sn.exe) that's installed with Visual Studio.

One of the strongly named assemblies that is installed with the .NET Framework is System. Data. You can execute the following command to get the public key of the System.Data.dll:

```
sn -Tp C:\Windows\Microsoft.NET\Framework\v4.0.30319\System.Data.dll
```

It displays the following:

```
Microsoft (R) .NET Framework Strong Name Utility Version 4.0.30319.17929 Copyright (c)
Microsoft Corporation.  All rights reserved.
Identity public key (hash algorithm: Unknown): 00000000000000000400000000000000
Signature public key (hash algorithm: sha256): 002400000c800000
14010000060200000024000052534131300080000010001006133399aff18ef1
a2c2514a273a42d9042b72321f1757102df9ebada69923e2738406c21e5b801552ab8d200a65a2
35e001ac9adc25f2d811eb09496a4c6a59d4619589c69f5baf0c4179a47311d92555cd006acc8b
5959f2bd6e10e360c34537a1d266da8085856583c85d81da7f3ec01ed9564c58d93d713cd0172c
8e23a10f0239b80c96b07736f5d8b022542a4e74251a5f432824318b3539a5a087f8e53d2f135f
9ca47f3bb2e10aff0af0849504fb7cea3ff192dc8de0edad64c68efde34c56d302ad55fd6e80f3
02d5efcdeae953658d3452561b5f36c542efdbdd9f888538d374cef106acf7d93a4445c3c73cd9
11f0571aaf3d54da12b11ddec375b3
Public key token is b77a5c561934e089
```

The *public key token* is a small string that represents the public key. It is generated by hashing the public key and taking the last 8 bytes. If you reference another assembly, you store only the public key token, which preserves space in the assembly manifest. The CLR does not use the public key token when making security decisions because several public keys might have the same public key token.

Within an organization, it's important to secure the private key. If all employees have access to the private key, someone might leak or steal the key. The employee could then distribute assemblies that look legitimate.

However, without access to the private key, developers can't sign the assembly and use it while building the application. To avoid this problem, you can use a feature called delayed or partial signing. When using delayed signing, you use only the public key to sign an assembly, and you delay using the private key until the project is ready for deployment. If you look at Figure 5-19, you can see that there is an option to activate delayed signing in Visual Studio.

EXAM TIP

Make sure that you understand the benefits of signing an assembly. Also make sure that you know when to use delayed signing.

Deploying assemblies to the global assembly cache

Assemblies that are local to an application are called private assemblies. You can easily deploy an application that only depends on private assemblies by copying it to a new location. Those assemblies are then contained in the bin folder of your application.

Another way to deploy an assembly is to deploy it to the GAC, which is a specialized library for storing assemblies. It is machine-wide and one of the locations the CLR checks when looking for an assembly. There is a big chance there will be questions on the exam regarding the GAC, so make sure that you know what it is and how to use it.

Normally, you want to avoid installing assemblies in the GAC. One reason to deploy to the GAC is when an assembly is shared by multiple applications. Other reasons for installing an assembly into the GAC can be the enhanced security (normally only users with administrator rights can alter the GAC) or if you want to deploy multiple versions of the same assembly.

Deploying an assembly in the GAC can be done in two ways:

- **For production scenarios**, use a specific installation program that has access to the GAC such as Windows Installer 2.0. For web scenarios, you can use the Web Deployment Framework with a provider for installing files into the GAC.

- **In development scenarios**, use a tool called the global assembly cache tool (Gacutil.exe).

You can view the content of your GAC by running the following command from a developer command prompt:

```
gacutil -l
```

This code returns a list of all the assemblies that are installed in the GAC. Installing an assembly in the GAC can be done with the following command:

```
gacutil -i [assembly name]
```

You can also remove an assembly from the GAC:

```
gacutil -u [assembly name]
```

When referencing a shared assembly from your project, you can add a reference to the file located in the GAC or to a local copy of it. When Visual Studio detects that there is a GAC version of the DLL you are referencing, it adds a reference to the GAC, not to the local version.

Implementing assembly versioning

In stark contrast with how DLLs worked before the .NET Framework, an assembly has a version number. Inside the assembly manifest, the assembly records its own version number and the version numbers of all the assemblies that it references.

Each assembly has a version number that has the following format:

```
{Major Version}.{Minor Version}.{Build Number}.{Revision}
```

- The Major Version is manually incremented for each major release. A major release should contain many new features or breaking changes.

- The Minor Version is incremented for minor releases that introduce only some small changes to existing features.

- The Build Number is automatically incremented for each build by the Build Server. This way, each build has a unique identification number that can be used to track it.

- The Revision is used for patches to the production environment.

When building an assembly, there are two version numbers that you need to take into account: the file version number and the .NET assembly version number.

If you create a new project in Visual Studio, it automatically adds an AssemblyInfo.cs file to the properties of your project. This file contains the following two lines:

```
[assembly: AssemblyVersion("1.0.0.0")]
[assembly: AssemblyFileVersion("1.0.0.0")]
```

AssemblyFileVersionAttribute is the one that should be incremented with each build. This is not something you want to do on the client, where it would get incremented with every developer build. Instead, you should integrate this into your build process on your Build Server.

AssemblyVersionAttribute should be incremented manually. This should be done when you plan to deploy a specific version to production.

Because the version of an assembly is important when the runtime tries to locate an assembly, you can deploy multiple versions of the same assembly to the GAC and avoid the DLL problem that happened with regular DLL files. This is called side-by-side hosting, in which multiple versions of an assembly are hosted together on one computer.

The process of finding the correct assembly starts with the version number that is mentioned in the manifest file of the original assembly to determine which assembly to load. These bindings can be influenced with specific configuration files, however.

Three configuration files are used:

- Application configuration files
- Publisher policy files
- Machine configuration files

Those configuration files can be used to influence the binding of referenced assemblies. Suppose, for example, that you have deployed an assembly to the GAC, and a couple of applications depend on it. Suddenly a bug is discovered, and you create a fix for it. The new assembly has a new version number, and you want to make sure that all applications use the new assembly.

You can do this by using a publisher policy file. In such a configuration file, you specify that if the CLR looks for a specific assembly, it should bind to the new version. This is an example of how such a file would look:

```
<configuration>
  <runtime>
    <assemblyBinding xmlns="urn:schemas-microsoft-com:asm.v1">
      <dependentAssembly>
        <assemblyIdentity name="myAssembly"
                          publicKeyToken="32ab4ba45e0a69a1"
                          culture="en-us" />
        <!-- Redirecting to version 2.0.0.0 of the assembly. -->
```

```
        <bindingRedirect oldVersion="1.0.0.0"
                         newVersion="2.0.0.0"/>
      </dependentAssembly>
    </assemblyBinding>
  </runtime>
</configuration>
```

This file instructs the CLR to bind to version 2 of the assembly instead of version 1. You need to deploy such a publisher policy to the GAC so that the CLR can use it when binding assemblies.

MORE INFO **PUBLISHER POLICY FILES**

For more information on how to create and deploy a publisher profile file, see *http://msdn. microsoft.com/en-us/library/8f6988ab.aspx*.

If you have an assembly deployed privately with your application, the CLR starts looking for it in the current application directory. If it can't find the assembly, it throws a w.

You can specify extra locations in which the CLR should look in the configuration file of the application. You use the probing section for this:

```
<configuration>
  <runtime>
    <assemblyBinding xmlns="urn:schemas-microsoft-com:asm.v1">
      <probing privatePath="MyLibraries;MyOtherLibraries\AFolder"/>
    </assemblyBinding>
  </runtime>
</configuration>
```

Another option is using the codebase element. A codebase element can specify a location for an assembly that is outside of the application's directory. This way, you can locate an assembly that's on another computer on the network or somewhere on the Internet. These assemblies have to be strongly named if they are not in the current application's folder. When the assembly is located on another computer, it is downloaded to a special folder in the GAC. Here is an example of using the codebase element to specify the location of an assembly somewhere on the web:

```
<configuration>
  <runtime>
    <assemblyBinding xmlns="urn:schemas-microsoft-com:asm.v1">
      <dependentAssembly>
        <assemblyIdentity name="myAssembly"
                          publicKeyToken="32ab4ba45e0a69a1"
                          culture="en-us" />
        <codeBase version="1.0.0.0"
                  href="http://www.mydomain.com/ReferencedAssembly.dll"/>
      </dependentAssembly>
    </assemblyBinding>
  </runtime>
</configuration>
```

EXAM TIP

The probing option can be used only to point to locations that are relative to the application path. If you want to locate assemblies somewhere else, you have to use the codebase element.

Creating an assembly manifest

Assemblies in the .NET Framework are completely self-describing. An assembly not only contains the code that you want to deploy but also metadata about that code and other assemblies it depends on.

The assembly manifest is the part that contains this data. If you look at Figure 5-20 you see a screen shot of the tool ILDasm. This tool can be used to analyze the content of a compiled assembly. This assembly named MyWebApplication contains a manifest and the code for your Controllers, Models, and other types.

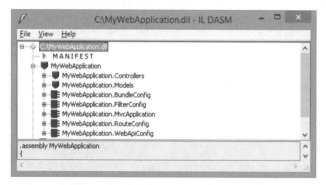

FIGURE 5-20 ILDasm showing the content of an assembly

The assembly manifest has a couple of functions:

- Enumerates the files that make up the assembly
- Governs how references to the assembly's types and resources map to the files that contain their declarations and implementations
- Enumerates other assemblies on which the assembly depends
- Provides a level of indirection between consumers of the assembly and the assembly's implementation details
- Renders the assembly self-describing

In addition to a list of all the files in the assembly, the type reference information (used for types exported from the assembly), and information on the referenced assembly, the manifest also describes the identity of the assembly.

This is done by the assembly name, version number, culture, and strong name information. Those four attributes are also stored in the manifest.

You can change the values that are used by using certain assembly-wide attributes such as AssemblyCultureAttribute, AssemblyTitleAttribute, and AssemblyDescriptionAttribute. You add those attributes to the AssemblyInfo.cs file located in the Properties folder of your project.

Normally, a manifest is contained in a Portable Executable (PE) file such as a DLL or .exe file, together with the Intermediate Language (IL) code that describes the assembly. You can also create a multifile assembly with a stand-alone manifest file or with the manifest incorporated into one of the PE files in the assembly.

Thought experiment
Choosing your technologies

In this thought experiment, apply what you've learned about this objective. You can find answers to these questions in the "Answers" section at the end of this chapter.

You are building a library that will contain some utility code. The idea is that the library can be shared by multiple web applications that you are developing.

With this in mind, answer the following questions:

1. Why should you sign your assembly?

2. What is the advantage of interning your assembly?

3. How you can you do this?

Objective summary

- You can intern an assembly by using the aspnet_intern tool to share an assembly that's used by multiple web applications. This process increases performance and uses less memory.

- An assembly can be strongly signed to make sure that no one can tamper with the content.

- Signed assemblies can be put in the GAC.

- An assembly will be versioned, and applications will use the assembly version they were developed with. It is possible to use configuration files to change these bindings.

- An assembly manifest contains metadata about the assembly. You can set the content of the manifest by using attributes.

Objective review

Answer the following questions to test your knowledge of the information in this objective. You can find the answers to these questions and explanations of why each answer choice is correct or incorrect in the "Answers" section at the end of this chapter.

1. You are building a strong-named assembly and you want to reference a regular assembly to reuse some code you built. What should you do?

    A. You first need to put the assembly in the GAC.

    B. Nothing. Referencing another assembly is always possible.

    C. You need to sign the other assembly before using it.

    D. You need to use the public key token of the other assembly to reference it.

2. You are building an assembly that will be used by a couple of server applications. You want to make the update process of this assembly as smooth as possible. Which steps should you take? (Choose all that apply.)

    A. Run aspnet_intern.

    B. Deploy the assembly to the GAC.

    C. Add an assemblyBinding section to each client application that points to the location of the assembly.

    D. Strongly name the assembly.

3. You want to deploy an assembly to a shared location on the intranet. Which steps should you take? (Choose all that apply.)

    A. Strongly name the assembly.

    B. Use the codebase configuration element in the applications that use the assembly.

    C. Deploy the assembly to the GAC.

    D. Use the assemblyBinding configuration element with the probing option.

Chapter summary

- Web Deploy is the most feature-rich deployment option that you have for your web applications. Web Deployment packages can contain your web application and other configuration data such as registry settings or assemblies that should be deployed to the GAC.

- When deploying to Windows Azure, you need to take into account that Windows Azure is a web farm. You should think about your session data, but also about your update mechanism. When updating your application, you can use an in-place upgrade, or delete and redeploy in combination with a VIP Swap.

- For configuration changes during deployment (such as connection strings or WCF configuration settings), you can use web.config transformations or parameterization.

- Using NuGet, which is a package manager tool integrated with Visual Studio, is the recommended way of installing and managing packages. You can create your own packages and distribute them in your own environment or globally.

- You can sign an assembly with a strong name. This enables you to deploy it to the global assembly cache and to apply interning.

Answers

This section contains the solutions to the thought experiments and answers to the lesson review questions in this chapter.

Objective 5.1: Thought experiment

1. A WCF Service can easily be deployed to Windows Azure. Because of the expected increase in users, Windows Azure is a good choice. Instead of buying big servers up-front to host the potential user load that you will get, you can start small and pay only for the resources you need. As your application starts growing, you can increase the capacity you have inside Windows Azure. This is a cost-effective way of hosting your application.

2. Because you are planning to expand the functionality of your application, it is wise to have a deployment process in place in which you can quickly update your application. Setting up a continuous deployment environment takes some time, but will make life easier when you start releasing updates for your application.

Objective 5.1: Review

1. **Correct answer:** C

   A. **Incorrect:** The Copy Website option can be used only to deploy the files of an ap-plication. You can't make any modifications to the registry.

   B. **Incorrect:** With an FTP client, you can copy your files to the server. However, you can't make any changes to the registry.

   C. **Correct:** Web Deploy enables you to use a provider that can make changes to the registry while deploying your application.

   D. **Incorrect:** A web farm is a description of how you will host your application. It's not a deployment technique.

2. **Correct answers:** B, D

   A. **Incorrect:** The InProc mode does not work in a web farm. Servers store the session data in memory, which makes it unavailable for other servers.

   B. **Correct:** Storing your data in a separate StateServer makes it available to all serv-ers in the web farm.

   C. **Incorrect:** Turning session state off is only an option when your application doesn't use any session state at all.

   D. **Correct:** Storing your data in a separate SQL Server makes it available to all servers in the web farm.

3. **Correct answers:** A, B, C

    A. **Correct:** Having a Build Server that tests your code and then executes a deployment is required.

    B. **Correct:** Unit tests are a part of continuous integration. They test your code in an automatic way so you can find bugs before deploying your code.

    C. **Correct:** Integration tests test your application in a more elaborate way than unit tests. Together with unit tests, they are important for automatic testing of your application.

    D. **Incorrect:** A web farm is not required to have a continuous deployment strategy. Even if you have a single server or are using the cloud, you can automatically deploy.

Objective 5.2: Thought experiment

1. With an in-place upgrade, you update your instances according to update domains. This will give you zero downtime.

2. With a VIP Swap, you promote your staging environment to production (and change your production environment to staging). A VIP Swap has the advantage of mitigating the risk of bringing multiple versions of your application into production at the same time.

Objective 5.2: Review

1. **Correct answer:** B

    A. **Incorrect:** The Windows Azure Service Level Agreement says that you must have two or more role instances in different fault and upgrade domains, so one instance is not enough.

    B. **Correct:** The Windows Azure Service Level Agreement says that you must have two or more role instances in different fault and upgrade domains.

    C. **Incorrect:** The Windows Azure Service Level Agreement says that you must have two or more role instances in different fault and upgrade domains. If you don't need three instances for performance, it is not necessary to deploy more than two instances.

    D. **Incorrect:** The Windows Azure Service Level Agreement says that you must have two or more role instances in different fault and upgrade domains. If you don't need four instances for performance, it is not necessary to deploy more than two instances.

2. **Correct answer:** D

   A. **Incorrect:** You should add an InternalEndPoint to your worker role. By adding extra endpoints to your web role, you don't enable communication to your worker role.

   B. **Incorrect:** You shouldn't add a public InputEndpoint to your worker. This will make your worker accessible from outside your cloud service. Instead, you should add an InternalEndPoint.

   C. **Incorrect:** You should add an InternalEndPoint to your worker role. By adding extra endpoints to your web role, you don't enable communication to your worker role.

   D. **Correct:** An InternalEndPoint to your worker role enables communication from the web role to the worker role.

3. **Correct answer:** C

   A. **Incorrect:** This specifies a fixed version of your OS. You should use an asterisk (*) to make sure you always get all updates.

   B. **Incorrect:** A value of 1 specifies one of the older Guest OSs.

   C. **Correct:** By using *, you don't depend on a specific version. You get automatic updates to your Guest OS.

   D. **Incorrect:** You shouldn't depend on a specific version. This disables automatic updates.

Objective 5.3: Thought experiment

1. On your development and test environments, you can use a debug configuration. This way, you can more easily debug your code and find errors. Acceptance and production want to use the release configuration. If you want more granular control, you can also add extra configurations for your environments.

2. Because you know beforehand to which environments you are going to deploy, it is easier to use Web.config transformations. Depending on the environment you work in, you might need to deploy the same DLL that passed quality control to production. This would require you to use parameterization to account for the differences between the environments.

Objective 5.3: Review

1. **Correct answers:** A, B

   A. **Correct:** By setting the debug attribute to false (or removing it), you enable certain optimizations that you want to use on your production environment.

   B. **Correct:** A release configuration has better performance and should be used in a production environment.

   C. **Incorrect:** The selected debuggers don't affect performance when there is no debug information in the assemblies. You don't have to explicitly turn them off.

   D. **Incorrect:** A debug configuration has a slower performance than a release configuration and should not be used for a production environment.

2. **Correct answer:** D

   A. **Incorrect:** You don't want to completely replace the compilation element. If this element contains other values, you want to remove only the debug attribute.

   B. **Incorrect:** You don't need the locator attribute. Without a locator attribute, Web Deploy matches your element to the existing element in web.config.

   C. **Incorrect:** You don't need the locator attribute. Without a locator attribute, Web Deploy matches your element to the existing element in web.config. Matching on name makes no sense because the compilation element doesn't have a name.

   D. **Correct:** You remove the debug attribute from the compilation element.

3. **Correct answer:** C

   A. **Incorrect:** XmlPoke is an MSBuild Task, not an MSDeploy parameter.

   B. **Incorrect:** The setParamFile is used to supply a Parameters.xml file that's used for parameterization. You will still have to edit the SetParameters.xml file.

   C. **Correct:** XmlPoke is an MSBuild task that you can use to edit XML files in an automated way.

   D. **Incorrect:** By using MSBuild with the XmlPoke task, you can edit your SetParameters automatically.

Objective 5.4: Thought experiment

1. You can see all the changes that NuGet made, but you are not totally in control anymore. NuGet downloads any dependencies for your package automatically. NuGet can also make changes to your configuration files and add code and other files to your project. However, this is not a disadvantage because NuGet makes only the changes that you had to make manually.

2. NuGet offers a simple way to update your packages to new releases. You can even use NuGet to download prerelease packages.

3. If you don't want to create custom packages or keep a local cache of packages, this is not necessary.

Objective 5.4: Review

1. **Correct answers:** C, D

   A. **Incorrect:** ASP.NET MVC 4 templates come with package references for all installed libraries. You can use NuGet to update the package.

   B. **Incorrect:** You should run this command from within Visual Studio in the Package Manager Console.

   C. **Correct:** This updates your jQuery from the Windows PowerShell command line.

   D. **Correct:** You can update the package in through a GUI.

2. **Correct answer:** C

   A. **Incorrect:** The pack command on a project file converts that project in a package.

   B. **Incorrect:** This creates a nuspec file, not a package.

   C. **Correct:** This creates your package with your lib, content, and tools folder.

   D. **Incorrect:** The push command is used to publish your package on NuGet.

3. **Correct answers:** B, C, D

   A. **Incorrect:** You can leave the API key empty to make sure that your feed is read-only.

   B. **Correct:** The NuGet.Server package contains all code for exposing your custom feed in a web project.

   C. **Correct:** Your custom feed needs to be hosted in IIS.

   D. **Correct:** A new empty ASP.NET Web Application is the basis of your custom feed.

Objective 5.5: Thought experiment

1. Because continuous deployment decreases your feedback cycle, you get much quicker feedback on your application. You can respond to customer demand more quickly. In the current world in which agile is the norm, this is definitely a requirement for most, if not all, applications.

2. Because you are using multiple servers and databases, Web Deploy is the best choice. By using the command line or Windows PowerShell tools, you can integrate with your build process and automatically update your servers. If you are using the Entity Framework, you can use automatic migrations. Otherwise, you can use one of the other techniques such as dbDacFx or dbFullSql.

Objective 5.5: Review

1. **Correct answers:** B, C

   A. **Incorrect:** You can download a publish profile from Windows Azure.

   B. **Correct:** This enables you to update your website directly from Visual Studio.

   C. **Correct:** You can use FTP publishing directly to Windows Azure Websites from Visual Studio.

   D. **Incorrect:** You can't upload a Web Deploy package for a website in the Management Portal.

2. **Correct answer:** D

   A. **Incorrect:** postSync executes a command after your synchronization has already run.

   B. **Incorrect:** preSync executes a command before your synchronization runs.

   C. **Incorrect:** verb is used to specify your required operation.

   D. **Correct:** Specifies that the command should run without making any changes. It displays an overview of what your deployment will execute, so you can inspect it.

3. **Correct answer:** C

   A. **Incorrect:** The package switch only creates a package. It doesn't deploy it.

   B. **Incorrect:** The package switch only creates a package. It doesn't deploy it. By default, this also generates a debug configuration.

   C. **Correct:** This packages and deploys the project with the correct configuration.

   D. **Incorrect:** You are missing the /T:package switch.

Objective 5.6: Thought experiment

1. Signing the assembly protects the assembly against tampering. The .NET Framework will check that the assembly hasn't been altered between signing and running. Signing is also a requirement to be able to use a digital certificate, so users of your application will know that you are the publisher of the application. A disadvantage could be that you can no longer reference other unsigned assemblies. If you own these assemblies, you can sign them yourself. If not, you have to ask their publisher to sign them.

2. The advantage of interning your assemblies is that your assembly won't be loaded multiple times into memory. Instead, one copy will be loaded that gets used by all web applications that reference it.

3. You can intern your assemblies by running the aspnet_intern tool regularly on your server.

Objective 5.6: Review

1. **Correct answer:** C

   A. **Incorrect:** An assembly in the GAC needs to be strongly named. Your assembly still won't be able to reference the unsigned assembly.

   B. **Incorrect:** A strong-named assembly cannot reference a non-strong-named assembly.

   C. **Correct:** You need to strongly name the other assembly before you can reference it.

   D. **Incorrect:** The public key token is a part of the manifest of a strong-named assembly. The non-strong-named assembly doesn't have this key information. It needs to be strongly named first.

2. **Correct answer:** B

   A. **Incorrect:** aspnet_intern is used to intern assemblies, meaning that only one copy of an assembly will be loaded in memory when it's referenced by multiple web applications. This is only for performance reasons. It doesn't mean you can update the assembly in one location.

   B. **Correct:** A shared assembly can be deployed in the GAC. Other applications can reference it there. When you want to update it, you can do so by deploying the new version to the GAC. By using configuration files, you can then let other applications reference your new assembly.

   C. **Incorrect:** You can use the assemblyBinding configuration element to add extra search locations for an assembly. It asks for changes to each client application, however. The GAC is the location in which a shared assembly needs to be deployed.

   D. **Incorrect:** Strongly naming an assembly doesn't make it a shared assembly. Each application still requires its own copy.

3. **Correct answers:** A, B

   A. **Correct:** Strongly naming the assembly is required to be able to reference it on the intranet.

   B. **Correct:** The codebase configuration element can be used to have local client applications know they can find an assembly on another location such as the intranet.

   C. **Incorrect:** Deploying it to the GAC doesn't put the assembly on the intranet.

   D. **Incorrect:** The probing option can be used only to give additional locations relative to the application path. It can't be used to point to the intranet.

Index

A

F

448

T

About the authors

BILL RYAN is a Software Architect at Dynamics Four, a Microsoft Gold Partner and one of the nation's most innovative Dynamics CRM consultancies. He lives in Greenville, SC, with his wife and daughter. Bill has won Microsoft's Most Valuable Professional award 9 years in a row in several different product groups and was one of 20 people invited into Microsoft's Data Access Insiders program. Bill has been actively involved in Microsoft's exam development for the last seven years, serving as a subject matter expert in various technologies including SQL Server Administration, Business Intelligence, .NET, Windows Communication Foundation, Workflow Foundation, and Windows Phone. Outside of technology, he spends his time listening to the Phil Hendrie show and wrangling the many rescue pups he and his wife have fostered.

WOUTER DE KORT is an independent technical coach, trainer, and developer at Seize IT. He is MCSD certified. As a software architect, he has directed the development of complex web applications. He has also worked as a technical evangelist, helping organizations stay on the cutting edge of web development. Wouter has worked with C# and .NET since their inception; his expertise also includes Visual Studio, Team Foundation Server, Entity Framework, Unit Testing, design patterns, ASP.NET, and JavaScript.

SHANE MILTON is a Senior Architect creating enterprise systems running in Windows Azure and is currently designing cloud-based Smart Grid solutions to manage energy for millions of homes and businesses throughout the US. As an active leader in training and educating teams in cloud technologies and various Agile techniques, he takes particular interest in offering his expertise to community user groups and regional conferences in and around Indianapolis.

Now that you've read the book...

Tell us what you think!

Was it useful?
Did it teach you what you wanted to learn?
Was there room for improvement?

Let us know at http://aka.ms/tellpress

Your feedback goes directly to the staff at Microsoft Press,
and we read every one of your responses. Thanks in advance!

 Microsoft